LAND OF THE LUSTROUS

9

HARUKO ICHIKAWA

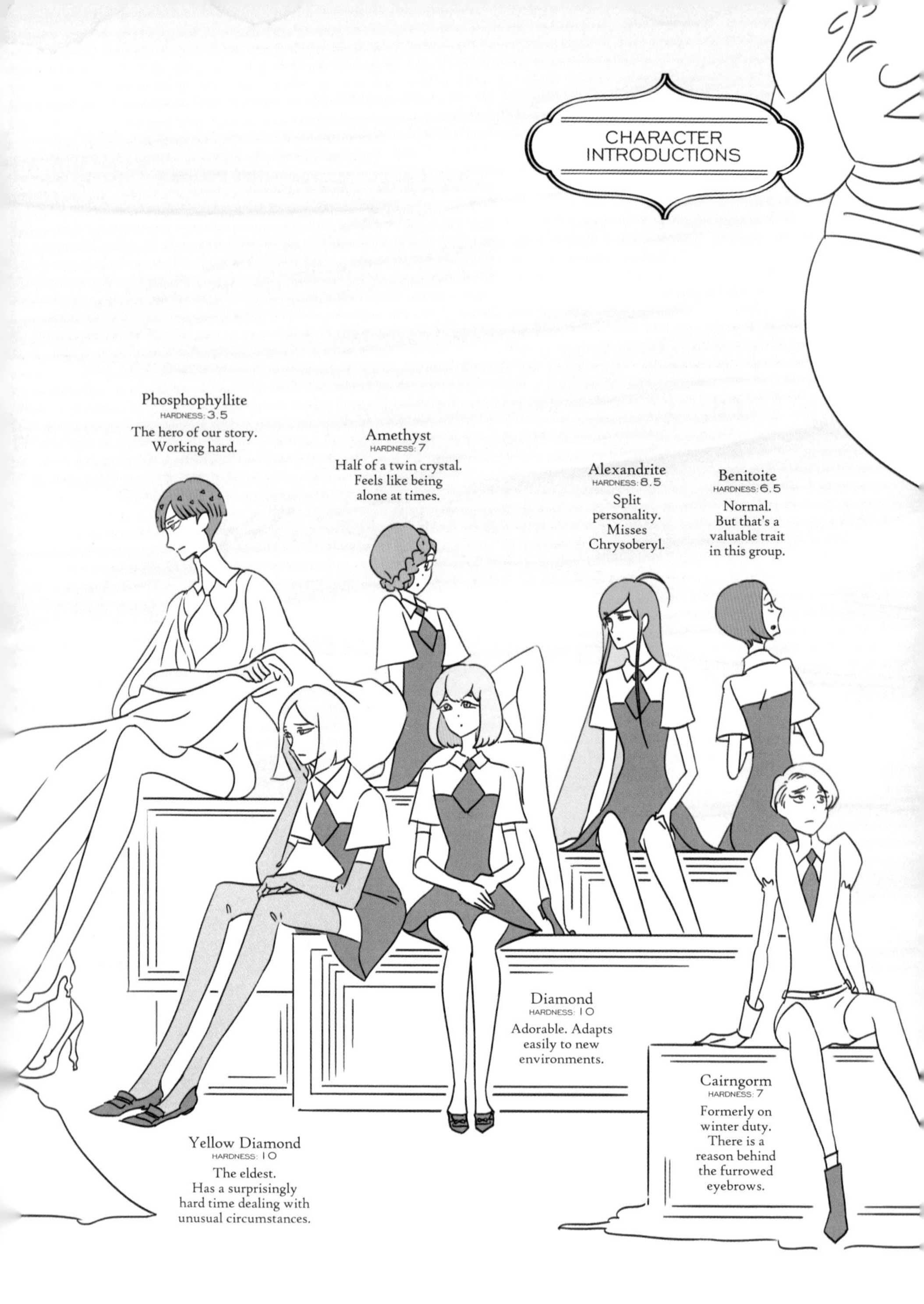
CHARACTER INTRODUCTIONS
Phosphophyllite
HARDNESS: 3.5
The hero of our story. Working hard.
Amethyst
HARDNESS: 7
Half of a twin crystal. Feels like being alone at times.
Alexandrite
HARDNESS: 8.5
Split personality. Misses Chrysoberyl.
Benitoite
HARDNESS: 6.5
Normal. But that's a valuable trait in this group.
Diamond
HARDNESS: 10
Adorable. Adapts easily to new environments.
Cairngorm
HARDNESS: 7
Formerly on winter duty. There is a reason behind the furrowed eyebrows.
Yellow Diamond
HARDNESS: 10
The eldest. Has a surprisingly hard time dealing with unusual circumstances.

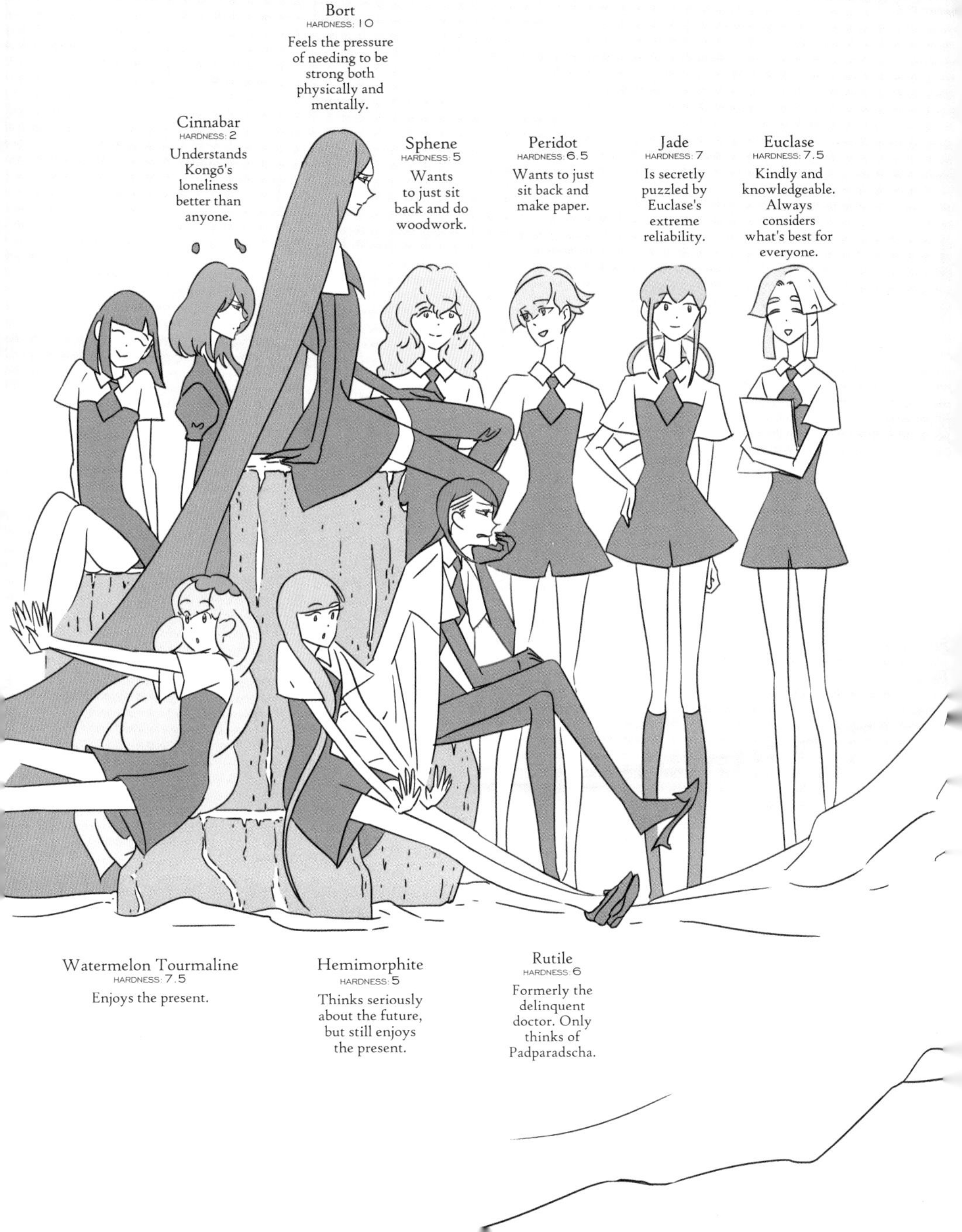
Bort
HARDNESS: 10
Feels the pressure of needing to be strong both physically and mentally.
Cinnabar
HARDNESS: 2
Understands Kongō's loneliness better than anyone.
Sphene
HARDNESS: 5
Wants to just sit back and do woodwork.
Peridot
HARDNESS: 6.5
Wants to just sit back and make paper.
Jade
HARDNESS: 7
Is secretly puzzled by Euclase's extreme reliability.
Euclase
HARDNESS: 7.5
Kindly and knowledgeable. Always considers what's best for everyone.
Watermelon Tourmaline
HARDNESS: 7.5
Enjoys the present.
Hemimorphite
HARDNESS: 5
Thinks seriously about the future, but still enjoys the present.
Rutile
HARDNESS: 6
Formerly the delinquent doctor. Only thinks of Padparadscha.

CONTENTS

CHAPTER 62:

Distant View

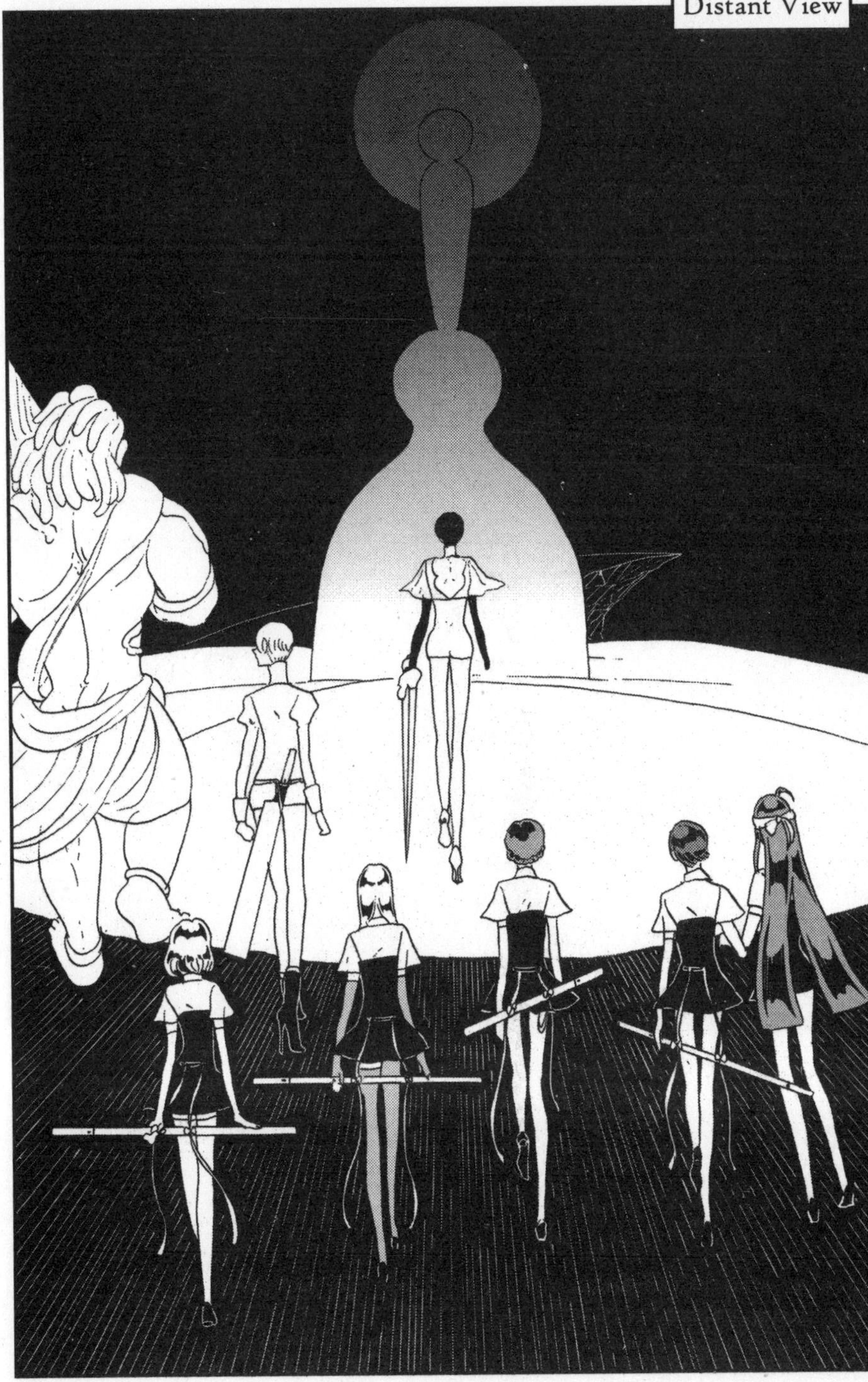

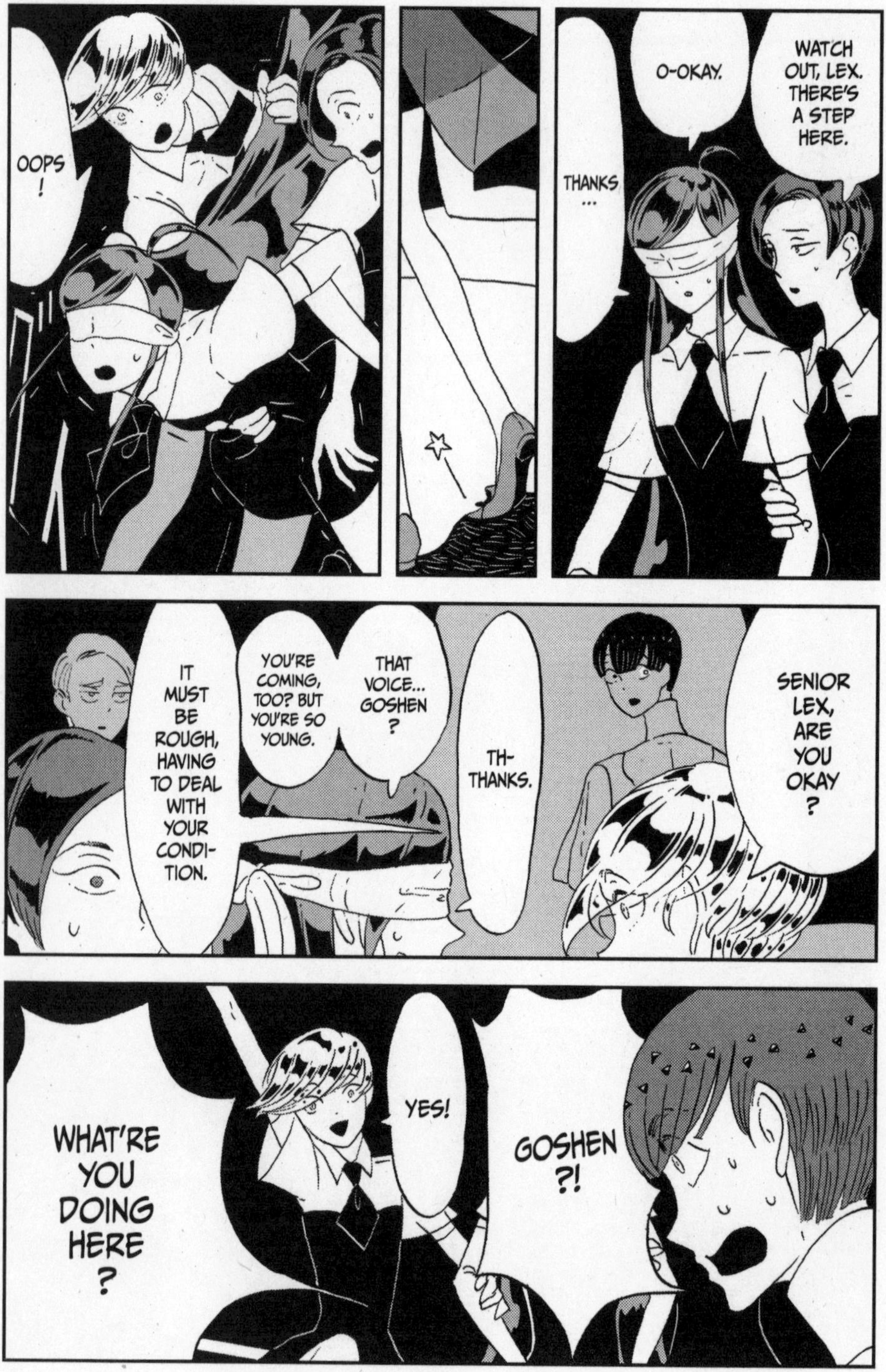
WATCH OUT, LEX. THERE'S A STEP HERE.
O-OKAY.
THANKS...
OOPS!
SENIOR LEX, ARE YOU OKAY?
TH-THANKS.
THAT VOICE... GOSHEN?
YOU'RE COMING, TOO? BUT YOU'RE SO YOUNG.
IT MUST BE ROUGH, HAVING TO DEAL WITH YOUR CONDITION.
GOSHEN?!
YES!
WHAT'RE YOU DOING HERE?

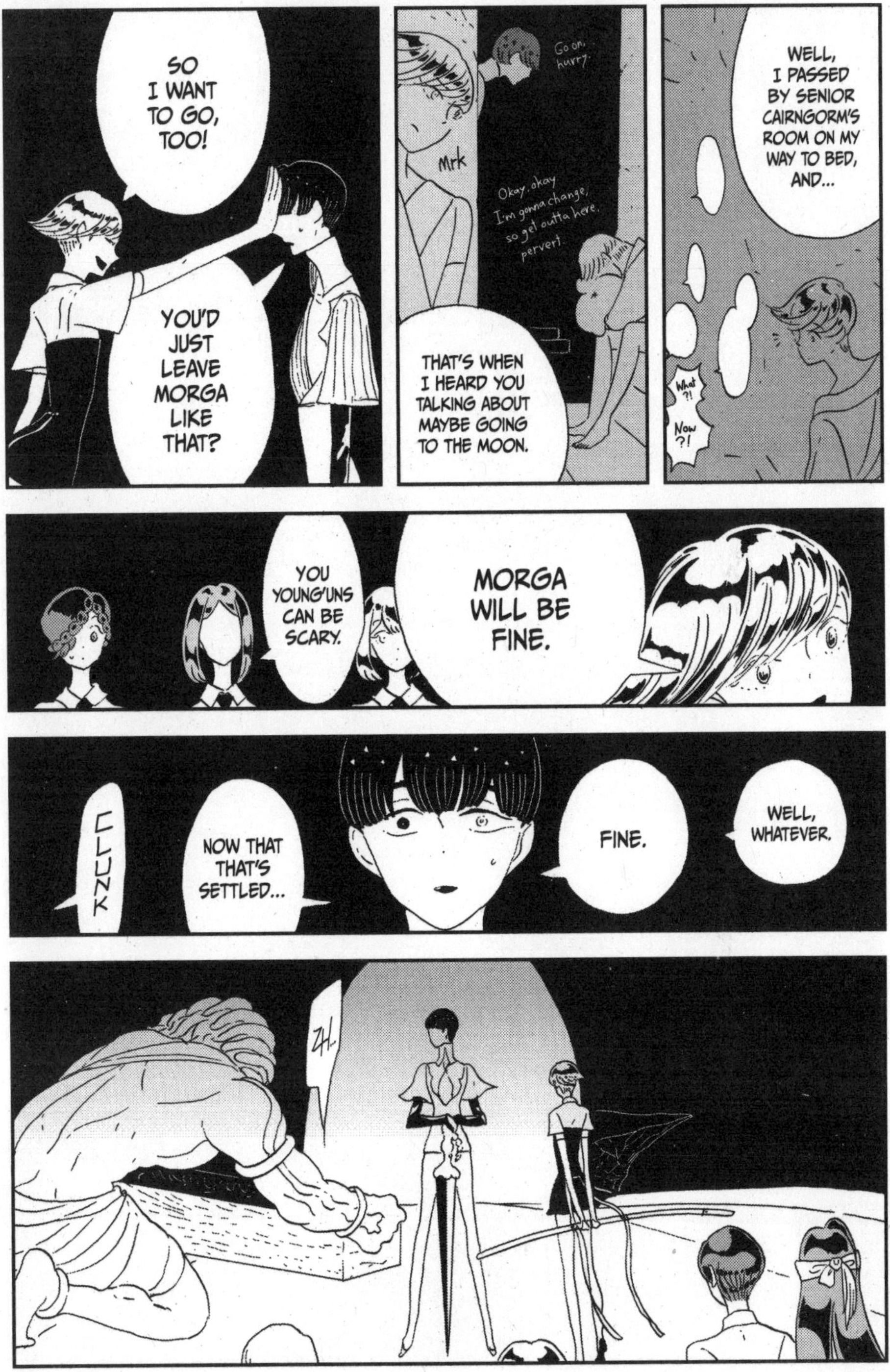
WELL, I PASSED BY SENIOR CAIRNGORM'S ROOM ON MY WAY TO BED, AND...
What?!
Now?!
Go on, hurry.
Mrk
Okay, okay. I'm gonna change, so get outta here, pervert.
THAT'S WHEN I HEARD YOU TALKING ABOUT MAYBE GOING TO THE MOON.
SO I WANT TO GO, TOO!
YOU'D JUST LEAVE MORGA LIKE THAT?
MORGA WILL BE FINE.
YOU YOUNG'UNS CAN BE SCARY.
WELL, WHATEVER.
FINE.
NOW THAT THAT'S SETTLED...
CLUNK
ZH...

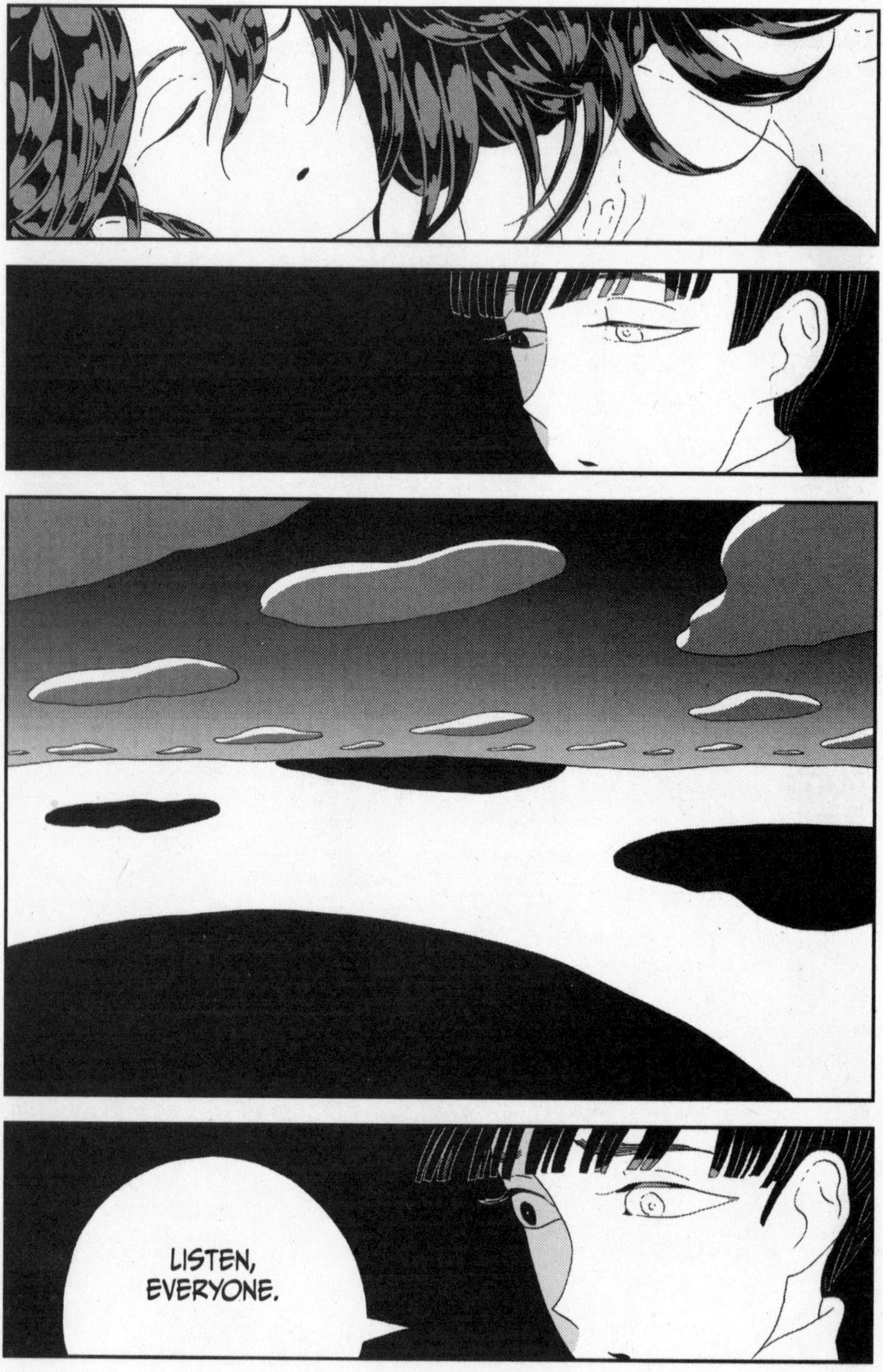
LISTEN, EVERYONE.

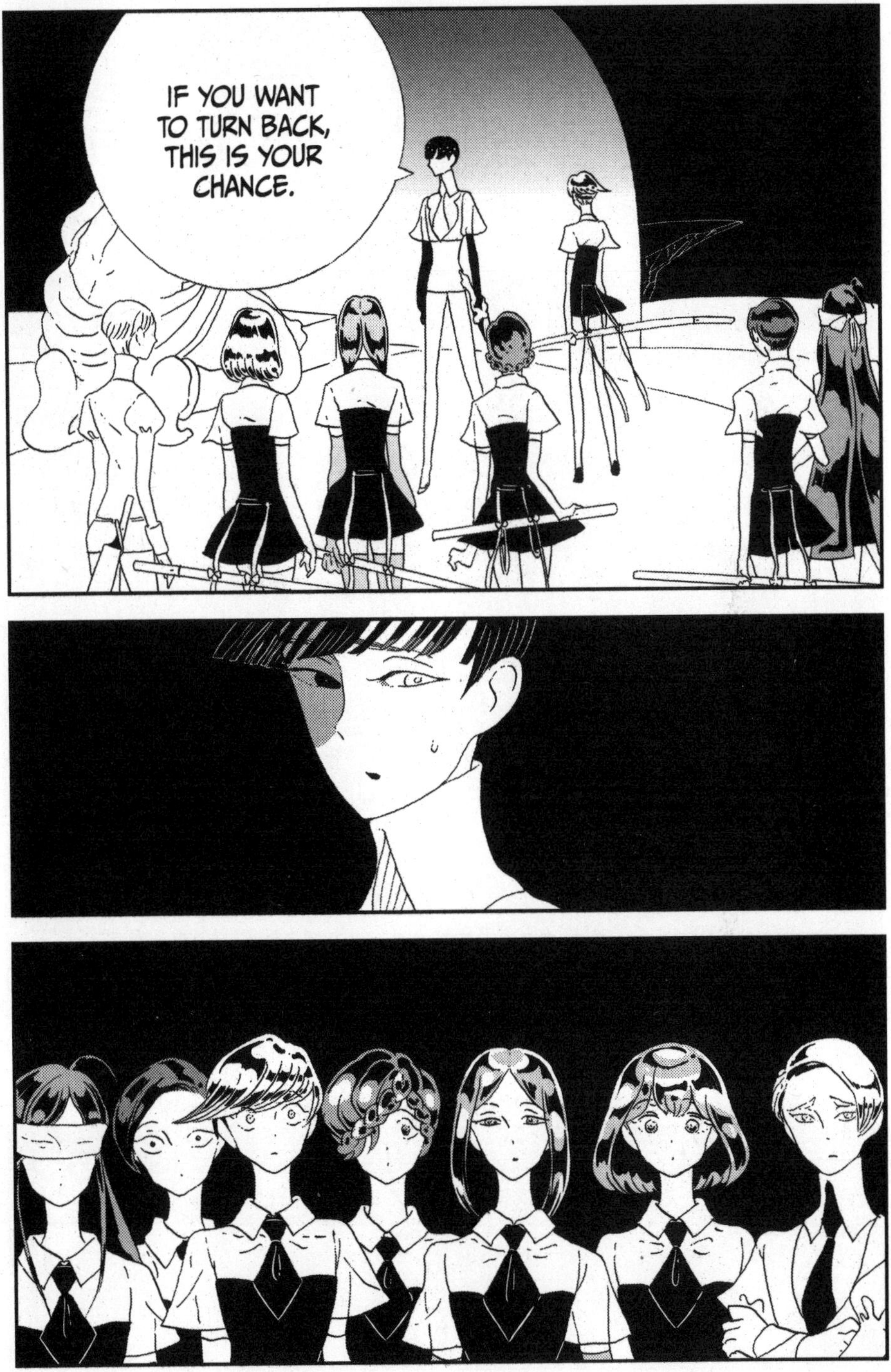
IF YOU WANT TO TURN BACK, THIS IS YOUR CHANCE.

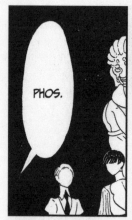

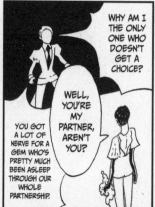

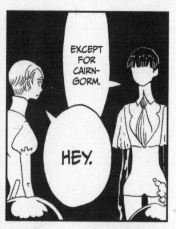

EXCEPT FOR CAIRN-GORM.
HEY.
WHY AM I THE ONLY ONE WHO DOESN'T GET A CHOICE?
WELL, YOU'RE MY PARTNER, AREN'T YOU?
YOU GOT A LOT OF NERVE FOR A GEM WHO'S PRETTY MUCH BEEN ASLEEP THROUGH OUR WHOLE PARTNERSHIP.
PHOS.
DON'T WORRY.
YOU'RE NOT THE ONLY ONE TO BLAME HERE.
WE EACH MADE OUR OWN DECISION.
YEAH.
AGREED.

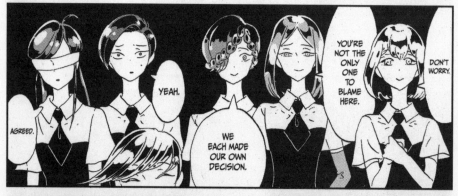

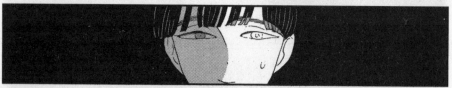

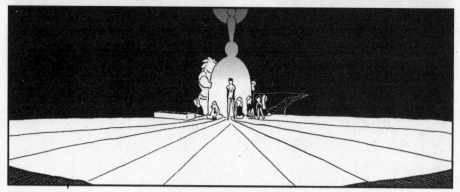

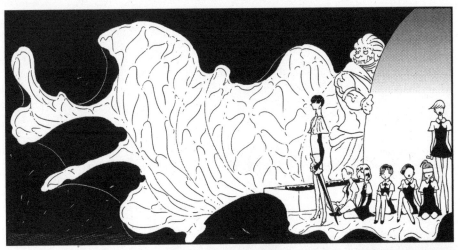

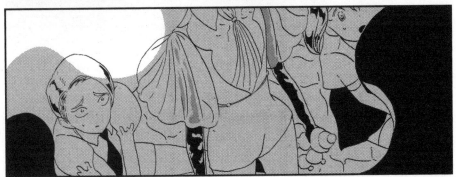

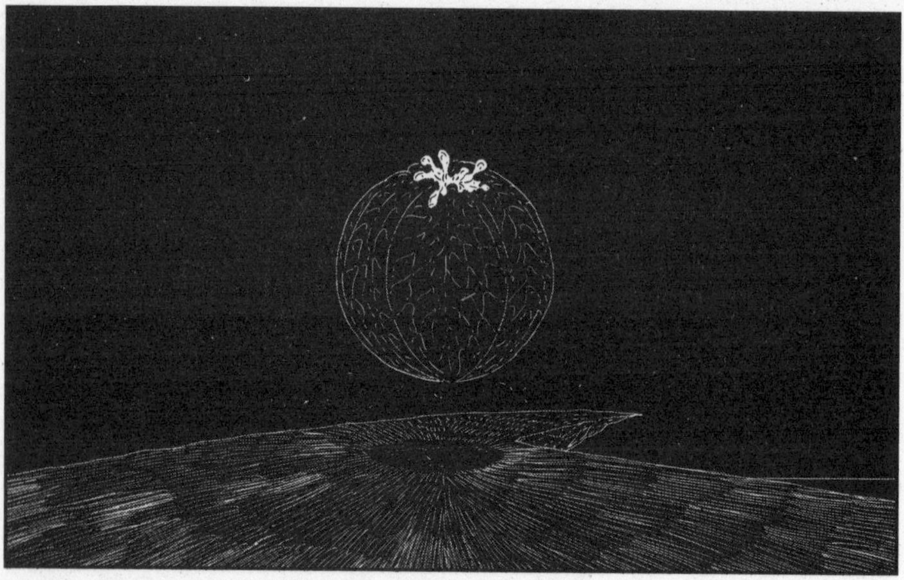

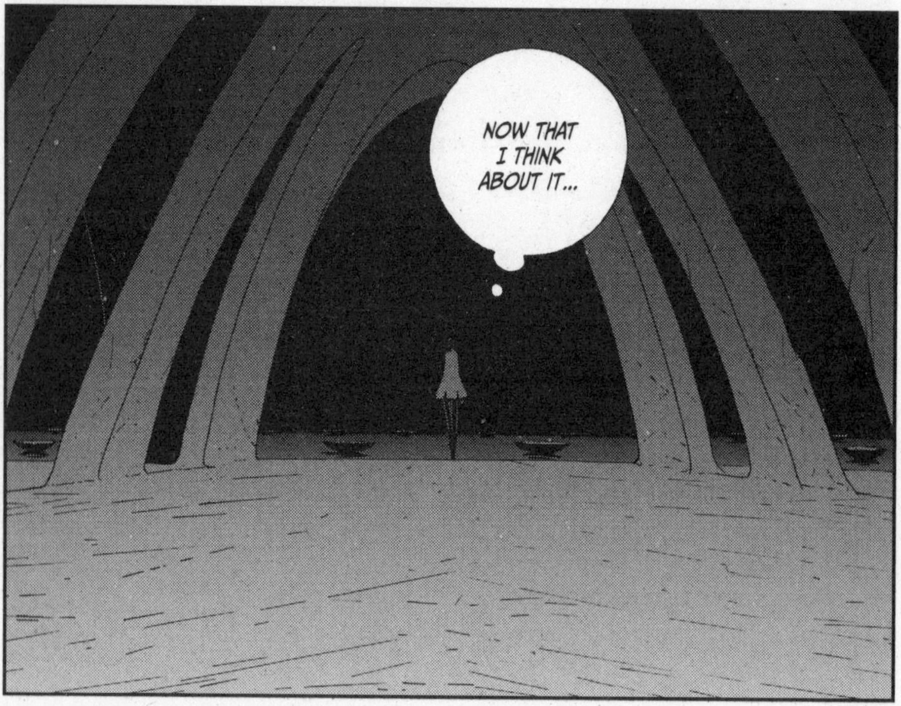
NOW THAT I THINK ABOUT IT...

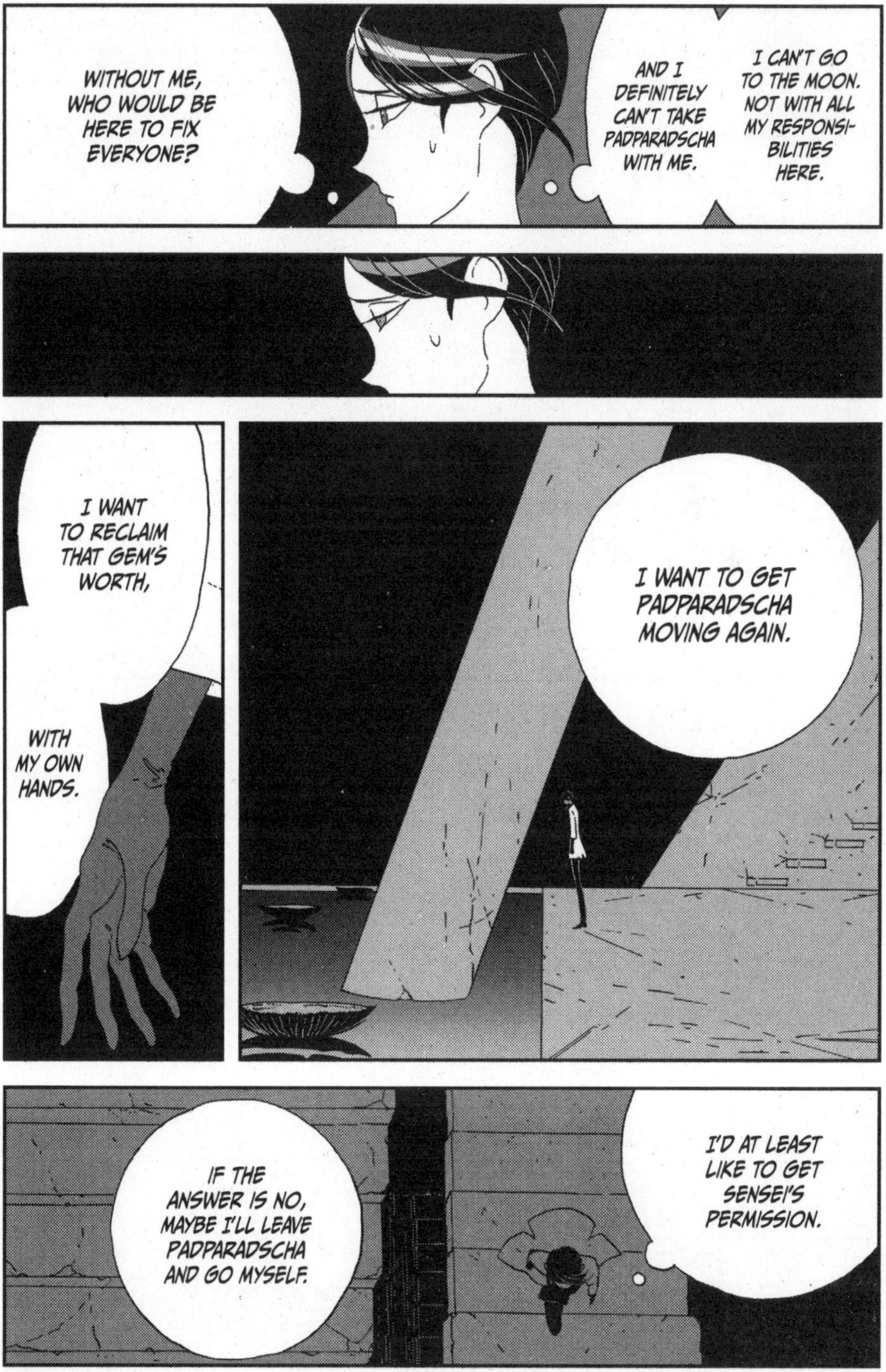
I CAN'T GO TO THE MOON. NOT WITH ALL MY RESPONSI-BILITIES HERE.
AND I DEFINITELY CAN'T TAKE PADPARADSCHA WITH ME.
WITHOUT ME, WHO WOULD BE HERE TO FIX EVERYONE?
I WANT TO GET PADPARADSCHA MOVING AGAIN.
I WANT TO RECLAIM THAT GEM'S WORTH,
WITH MY OWN HANDS.
I'D AT LEAST LIKE TO GET SENSEI'S PERMISSION.
IF THE ANSWER IS NO, MAYBE I'LL LEAVE PADPARADSCHA AND GO MYSELF.

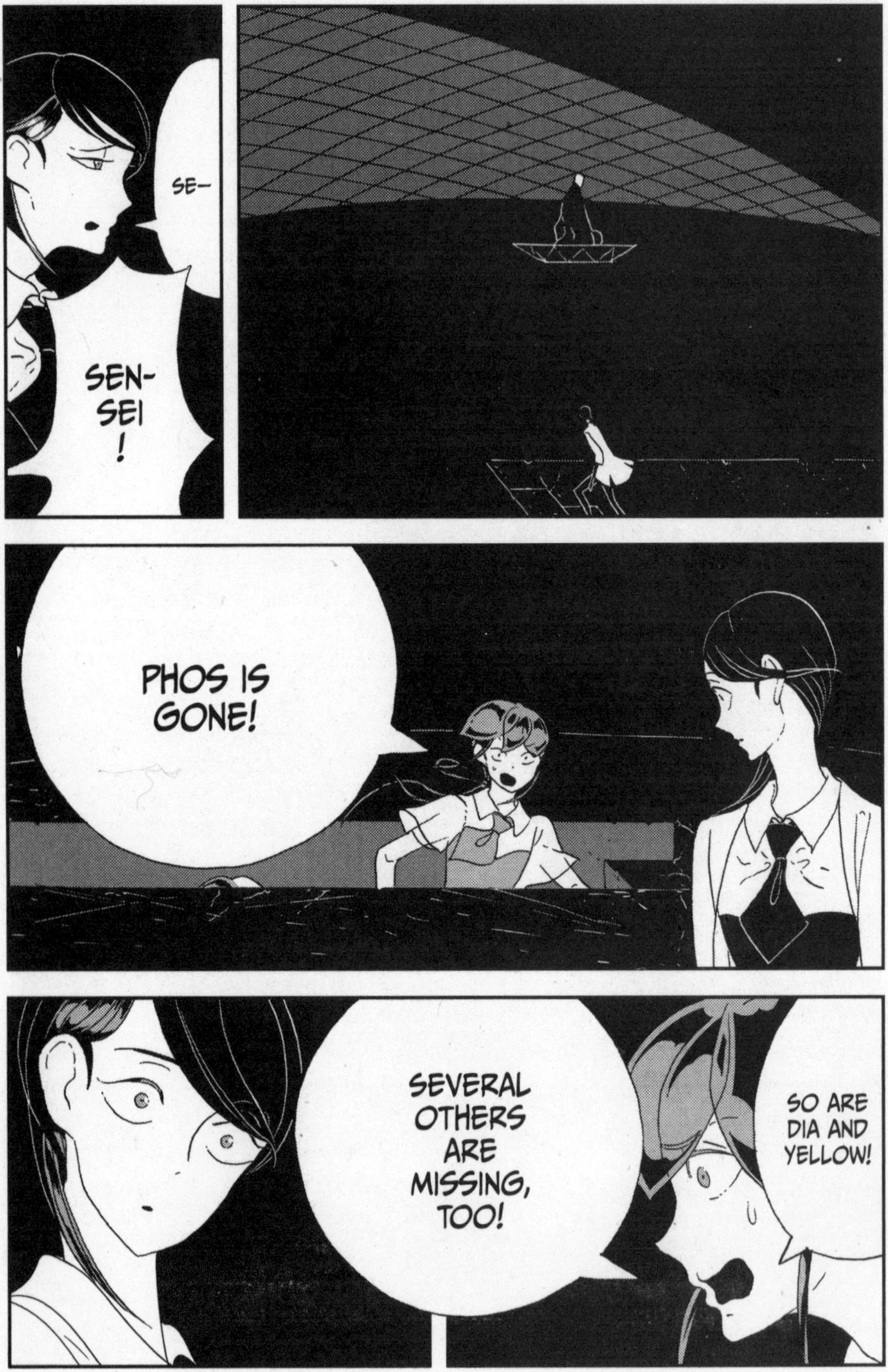
SE—
SEN-SEI!
PHOS IS GONE!
SO ARE DIA AND YELLOW!
SEVERAL OTHERS ARE MISSING, TOO!

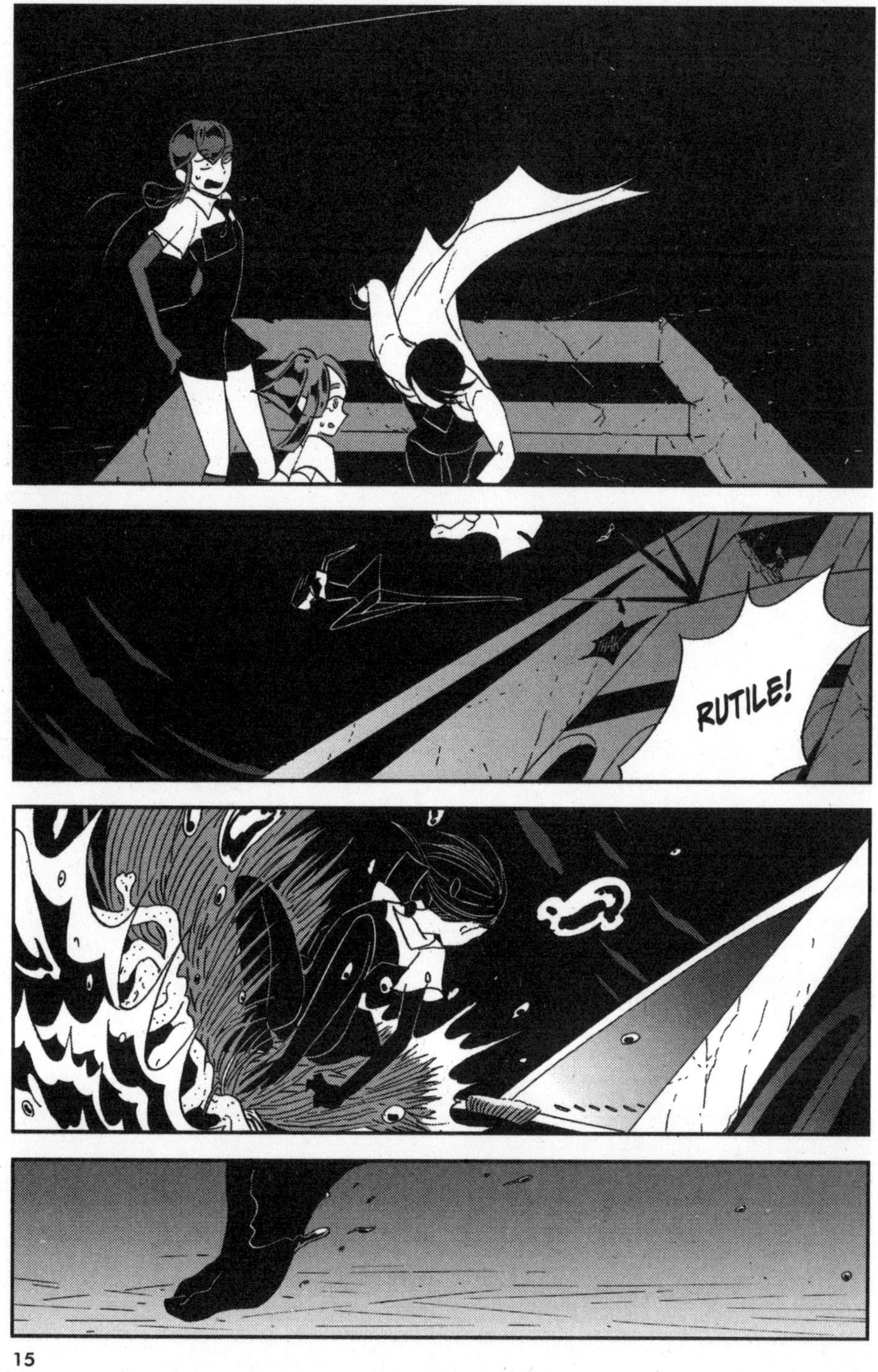
RUTILE!
THAK

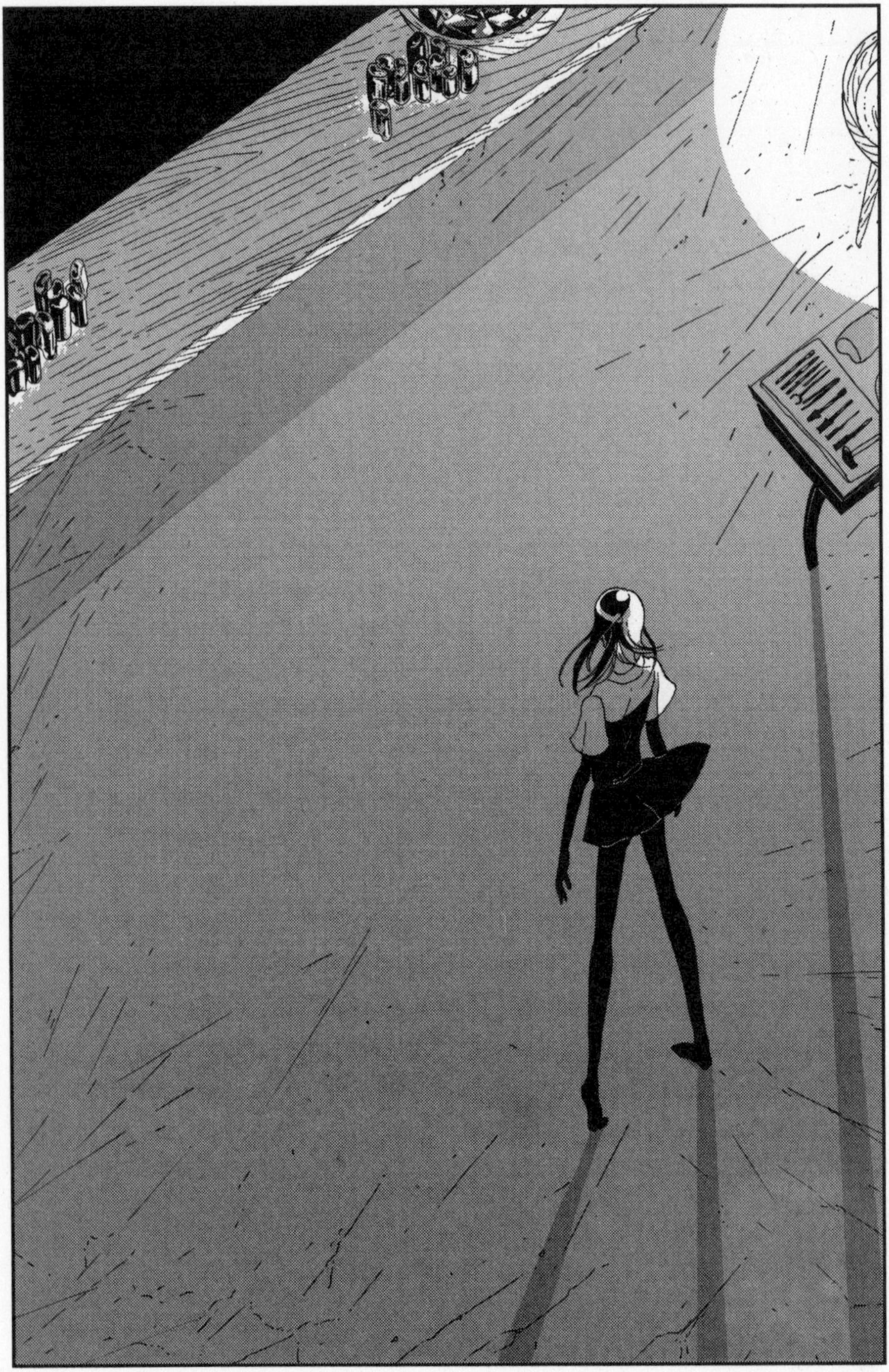

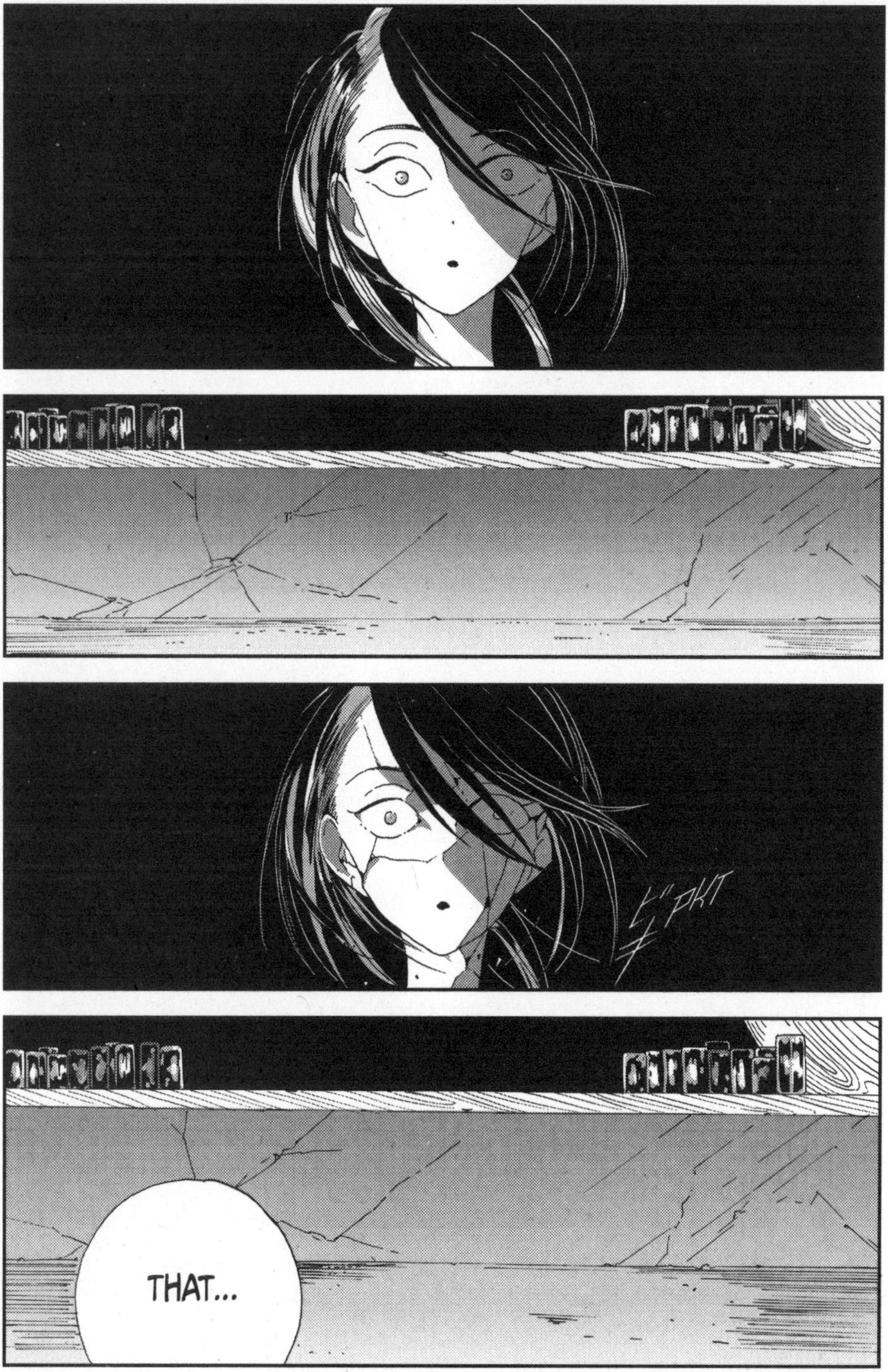
PKT
THAT...

THAT PIECE OF SLAG ...!

THE CAPE OF EMPTI- NESS.

EUC!

RUTILE!

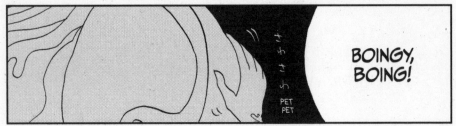

BOINGY, BOING!

PET PET

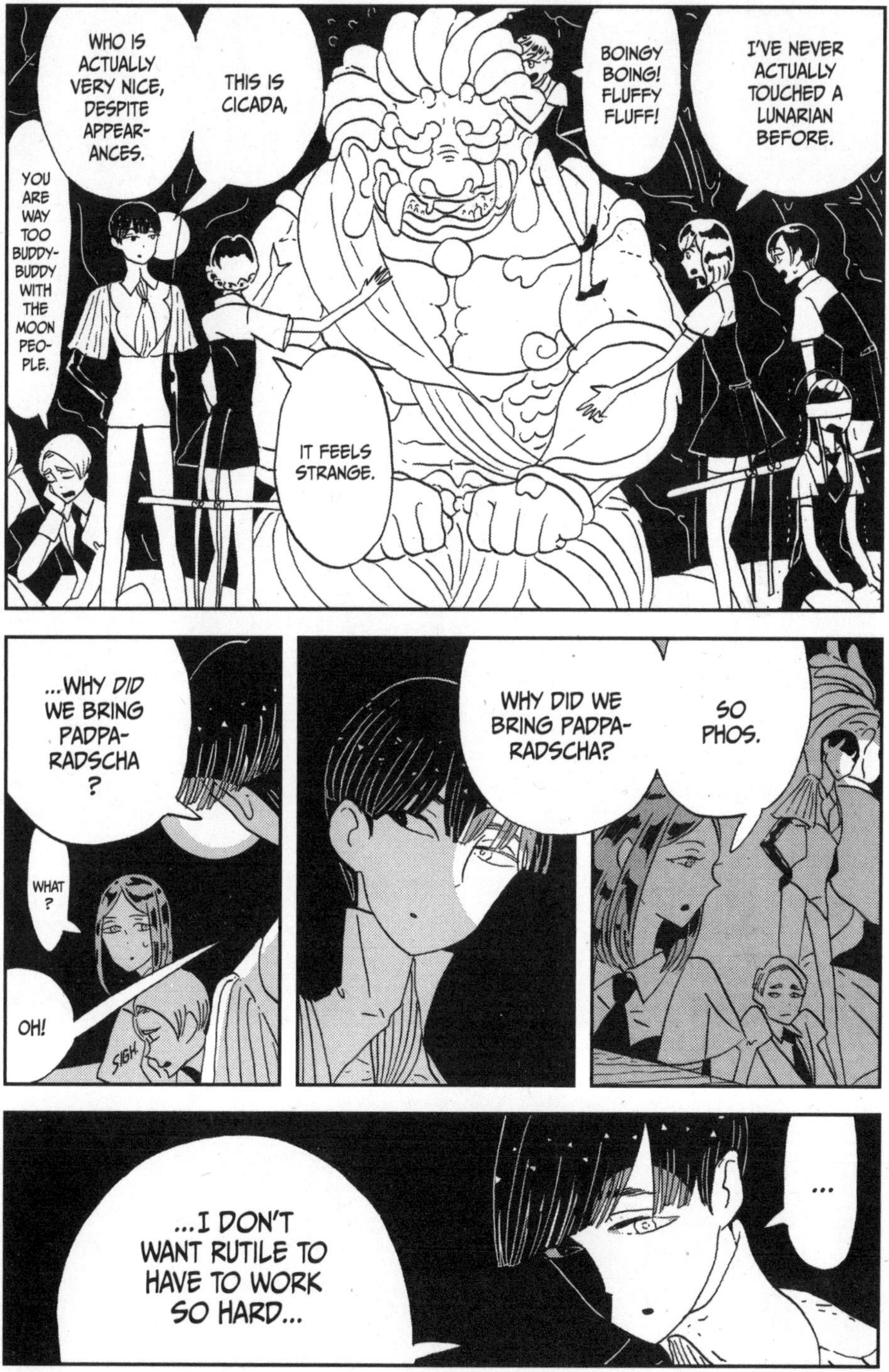
I'VE NEVER ACTUALLY TOUCHED A LUNARIAN BEFORE.
BOINGY BOING! FLUFFY FLUFF!
THIS IS CICADA,
WHO IS ACTUALLY VERY NICE, DESPITE APPEARANCES.
YOU ARE WAY TOO BUDDY-BUDDY WITH THE MOON PEOPLE.
IT FEELS STRANGE.
SO PHOS.
WHY DID WE BRING PADPARADSCHA?
...WHY *DID* WE BRING PADPARADSCHA?
WHAT?
OH!
SIGH
...
...I DON'T WANT RUTILE TO HAVE TO WORK SO HARD...

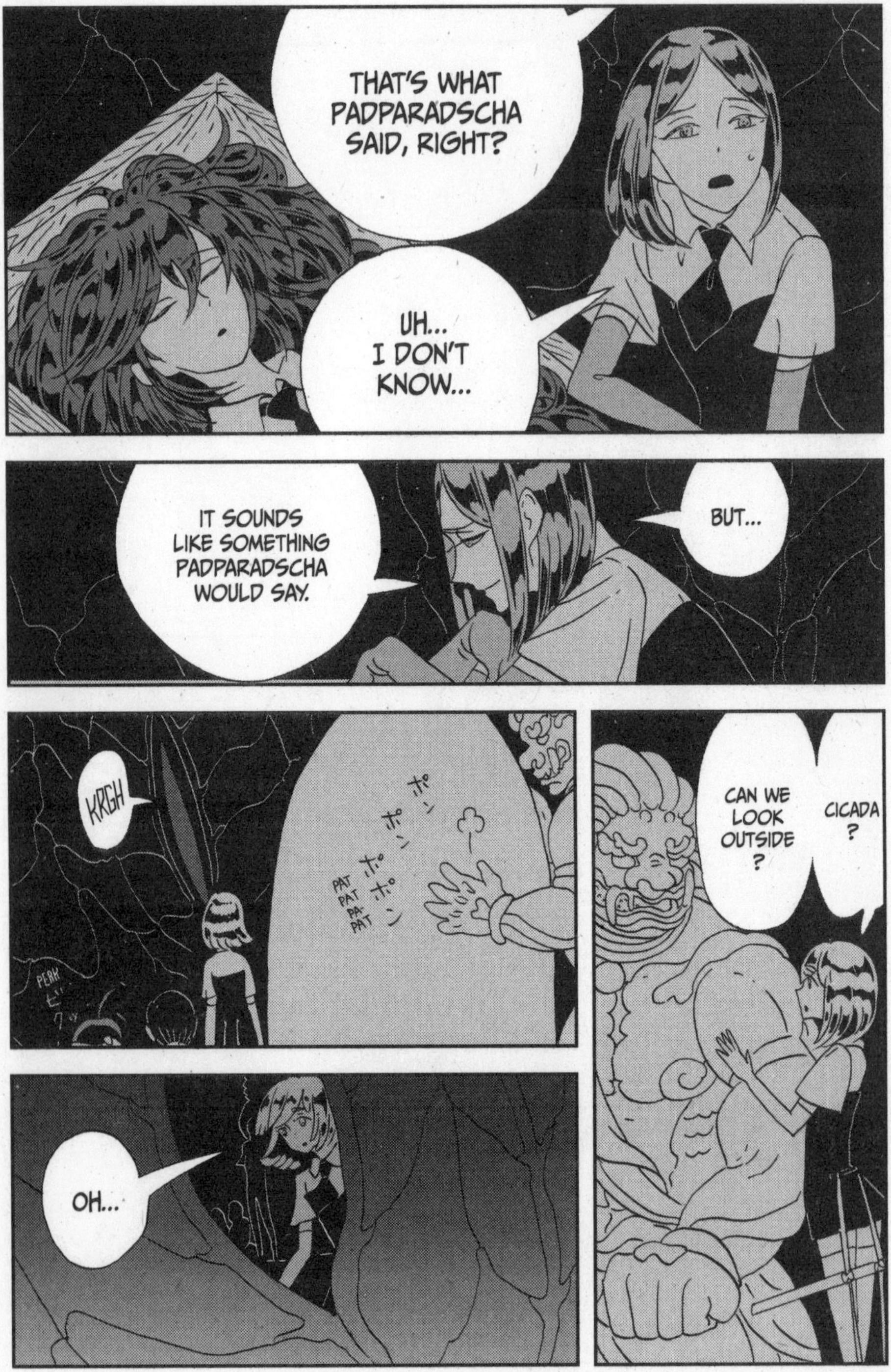
THAT'S WHAT PADPARADSCHA SAID, RIGHT?
UH... I DON'T KNOW...
IT SOUNDS LIKE SOMETHING PADPARADSCHA WOULD SAY.
BUT...
CICADA?
CAN WE LOOK OUTSIDE?
ポン ポン ポポン
PAT PAT PA-PAT
KRGH
PERK
ビクッ
OH...

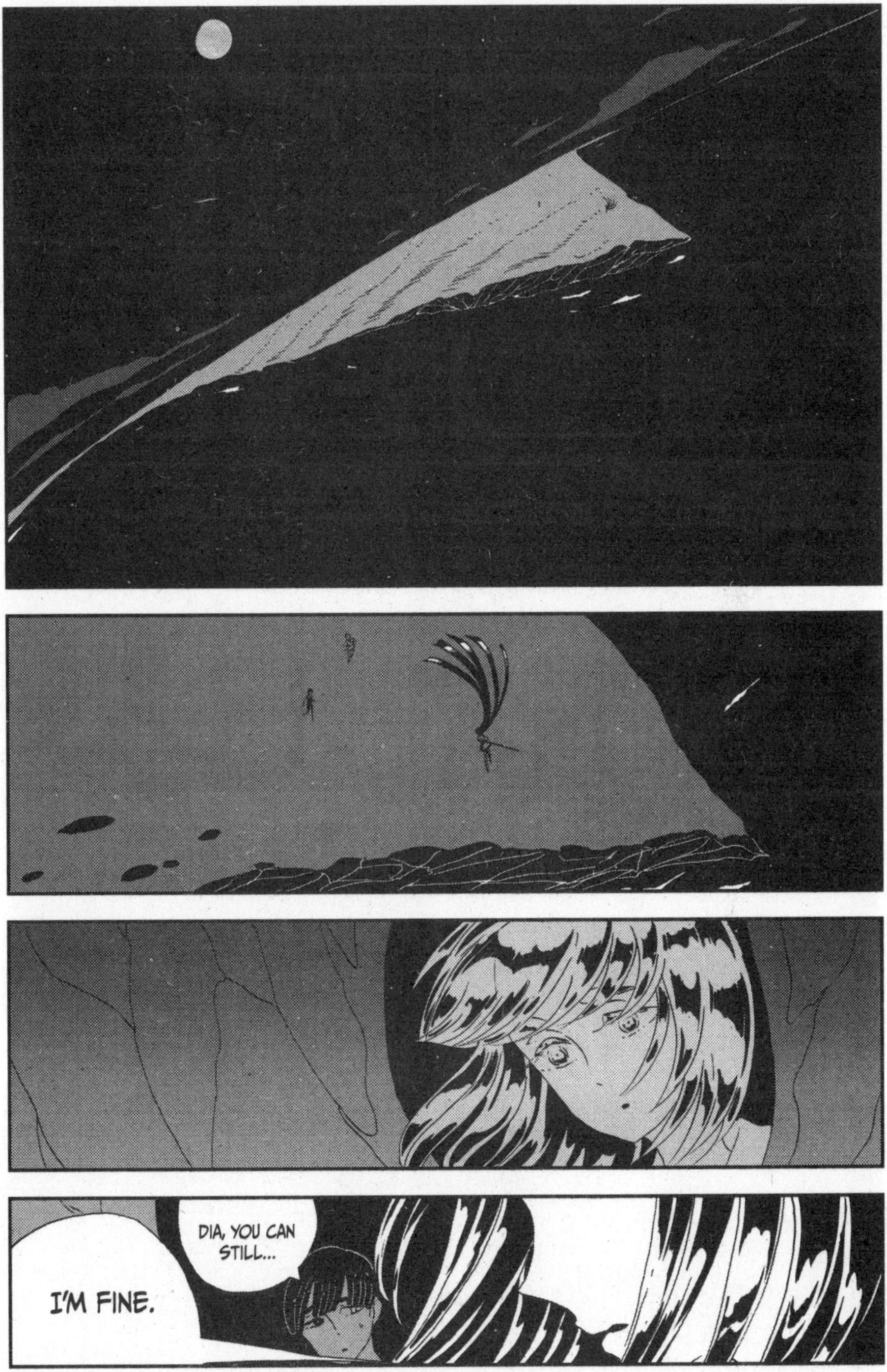
DIA, YOU CAN STILL...
I'M FINE.

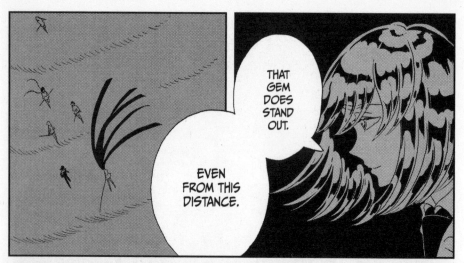

THAT GEM DOES STAND OUT.

EVEN FROM THIS DISTANCE.

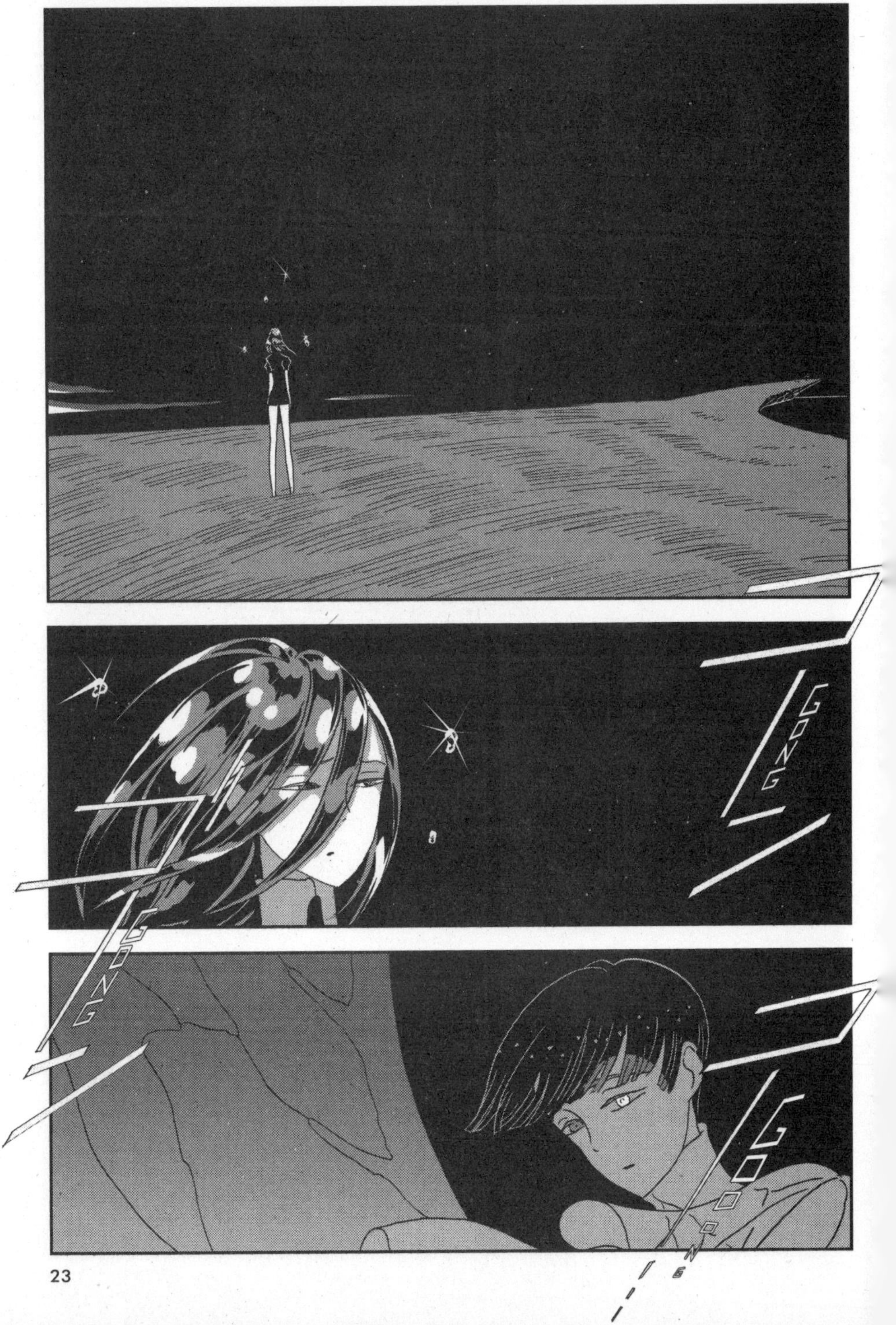
GONG
GONG
GOOONG

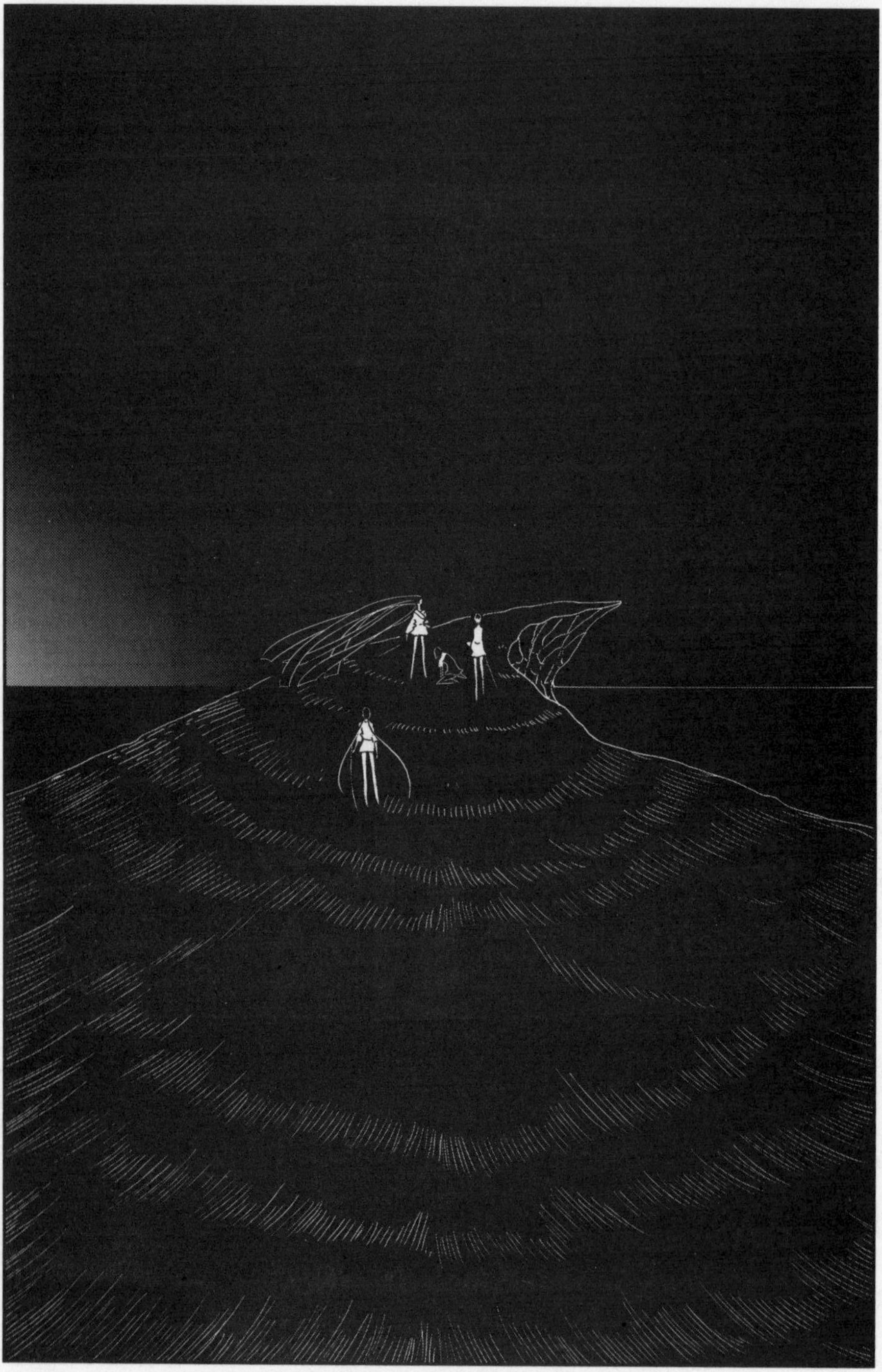

CHAPTER 62: Distant View END

CHAPTER 63:

High Hopes

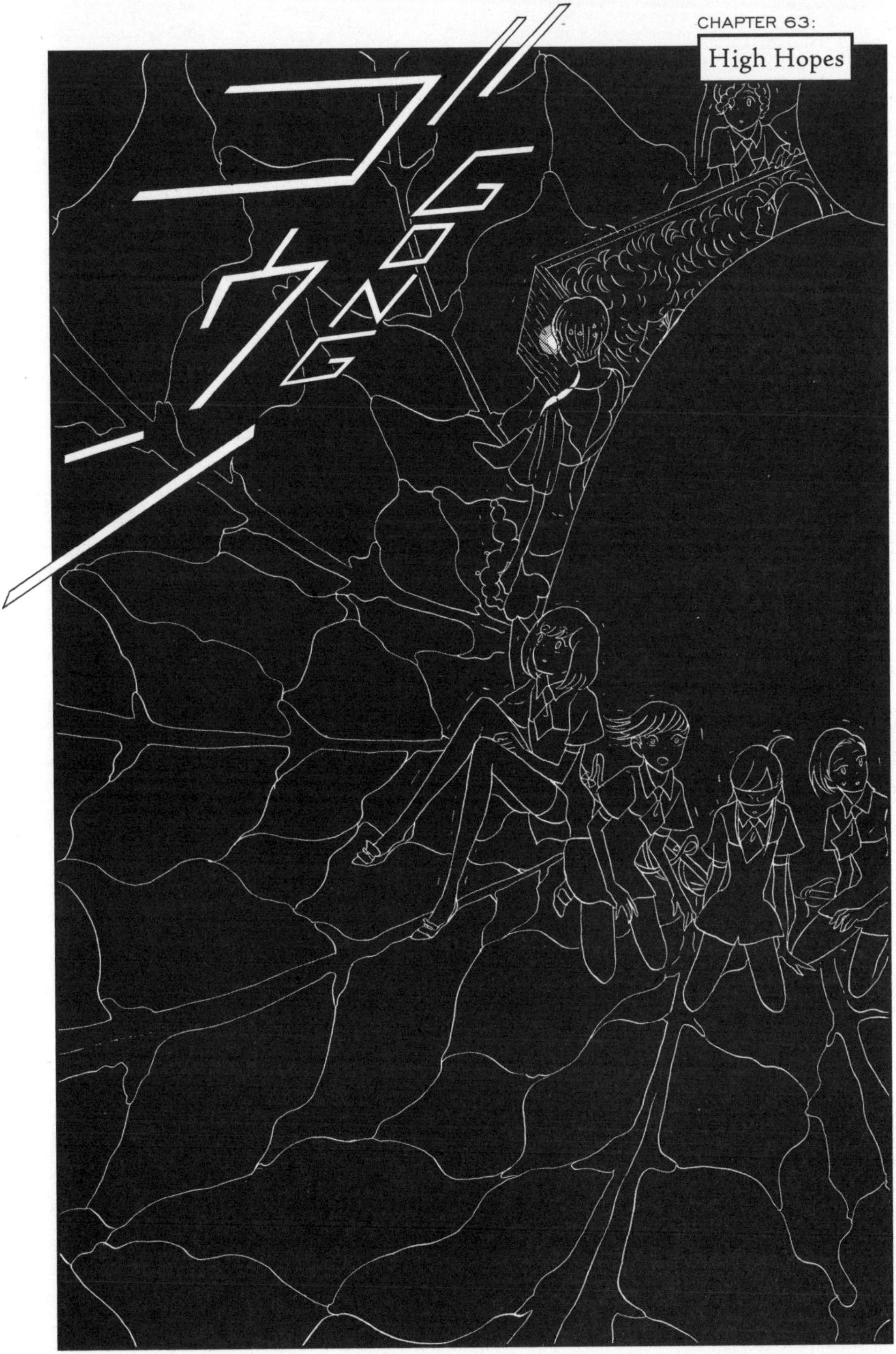
GONG

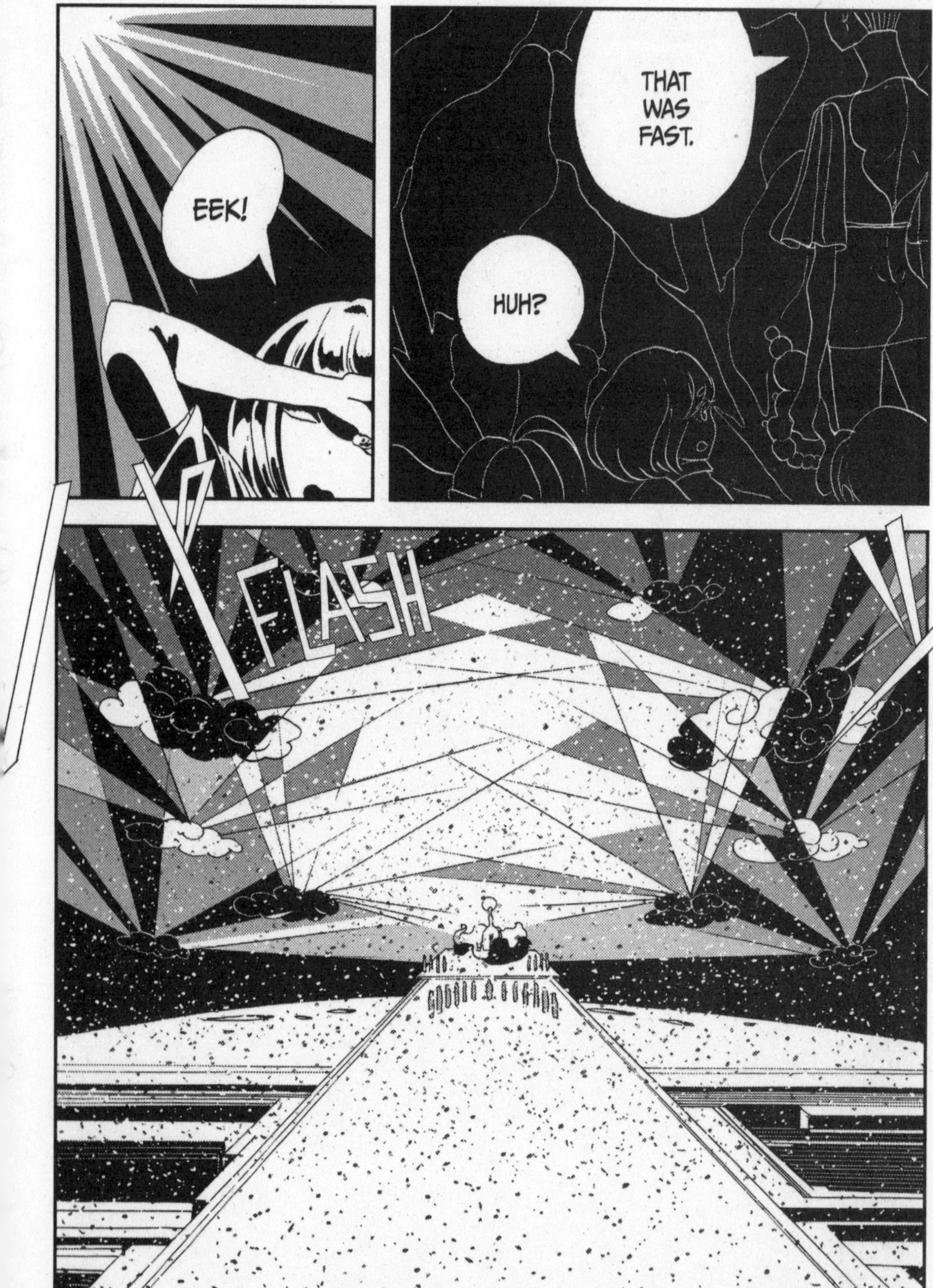
THAT WAS FAST.
HUH?
EEK!
FLASH

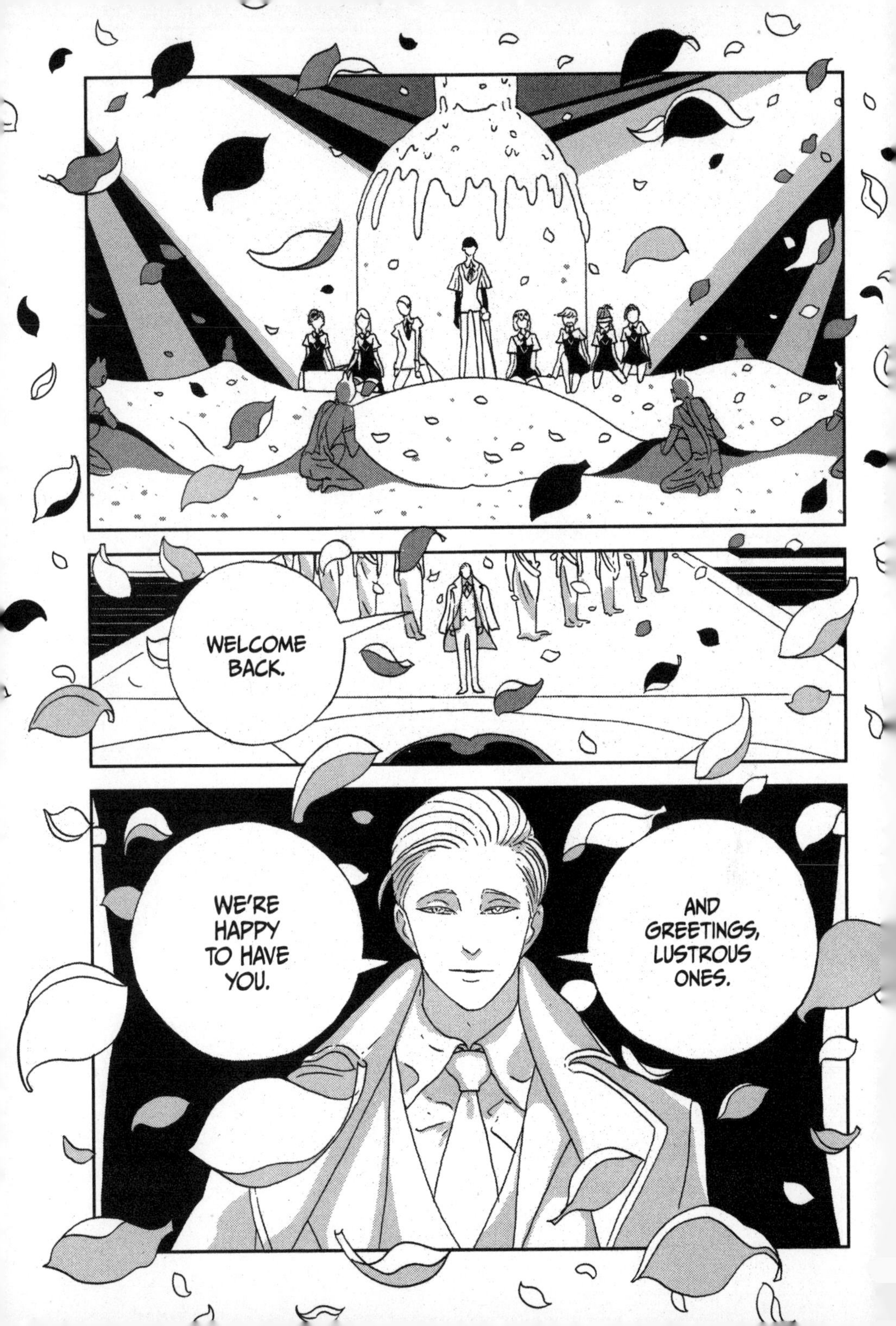
WELCOME BACK.
AND GREETINGS, LUSTROUS ONES.
WE'RE HAPPY TO HAVE YOU.

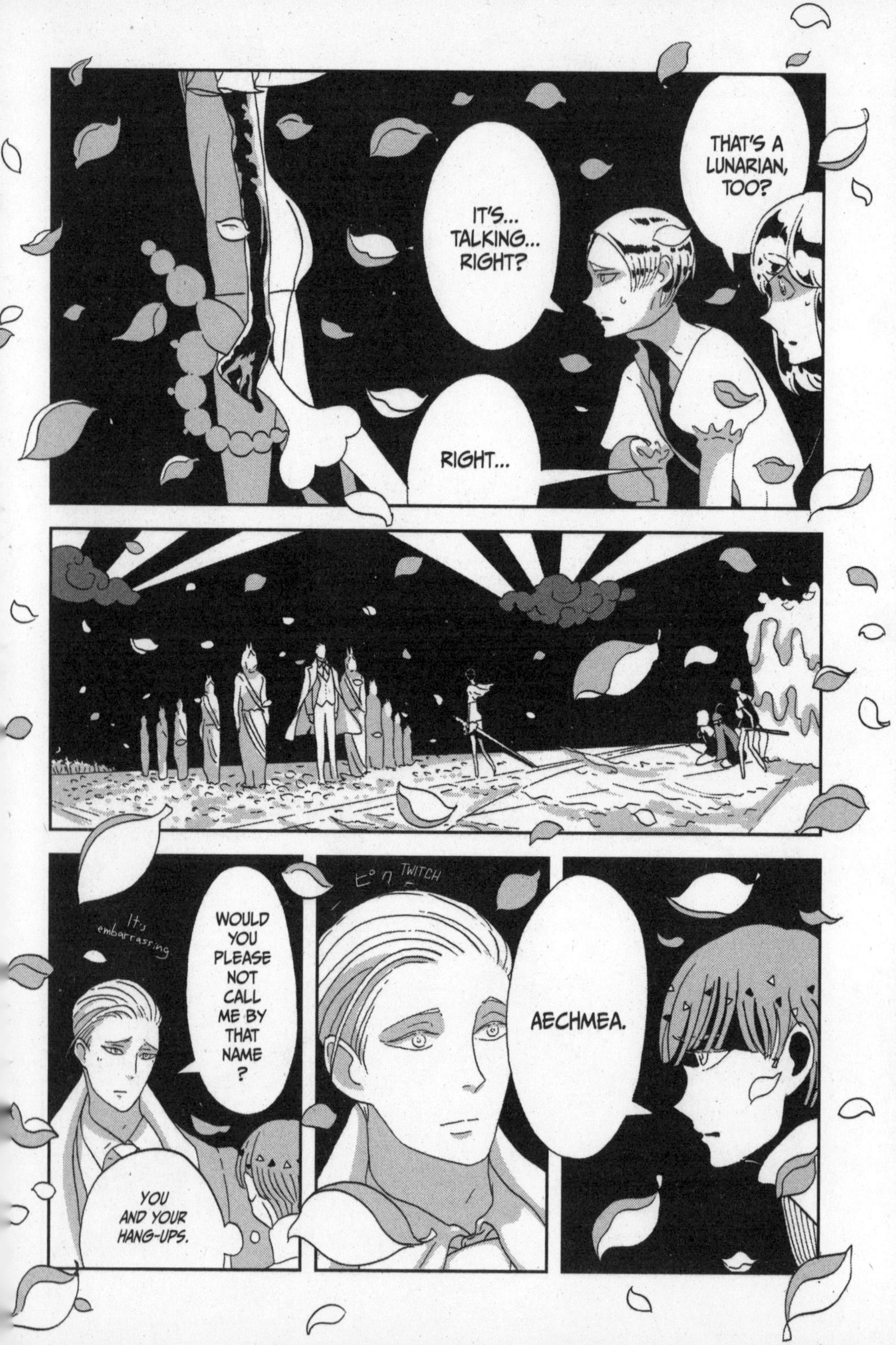
THAT'S A LUNARIAN, TOO?
IT'S... TALKING... RIGHT?
RIGHT...
AECHMEA.
ピク TWITCH
WOULD YOU PLEASE NOT CALL ME BY THAT NAME?
It's embarrassing
YOU AND YOUR HANG-UPS.

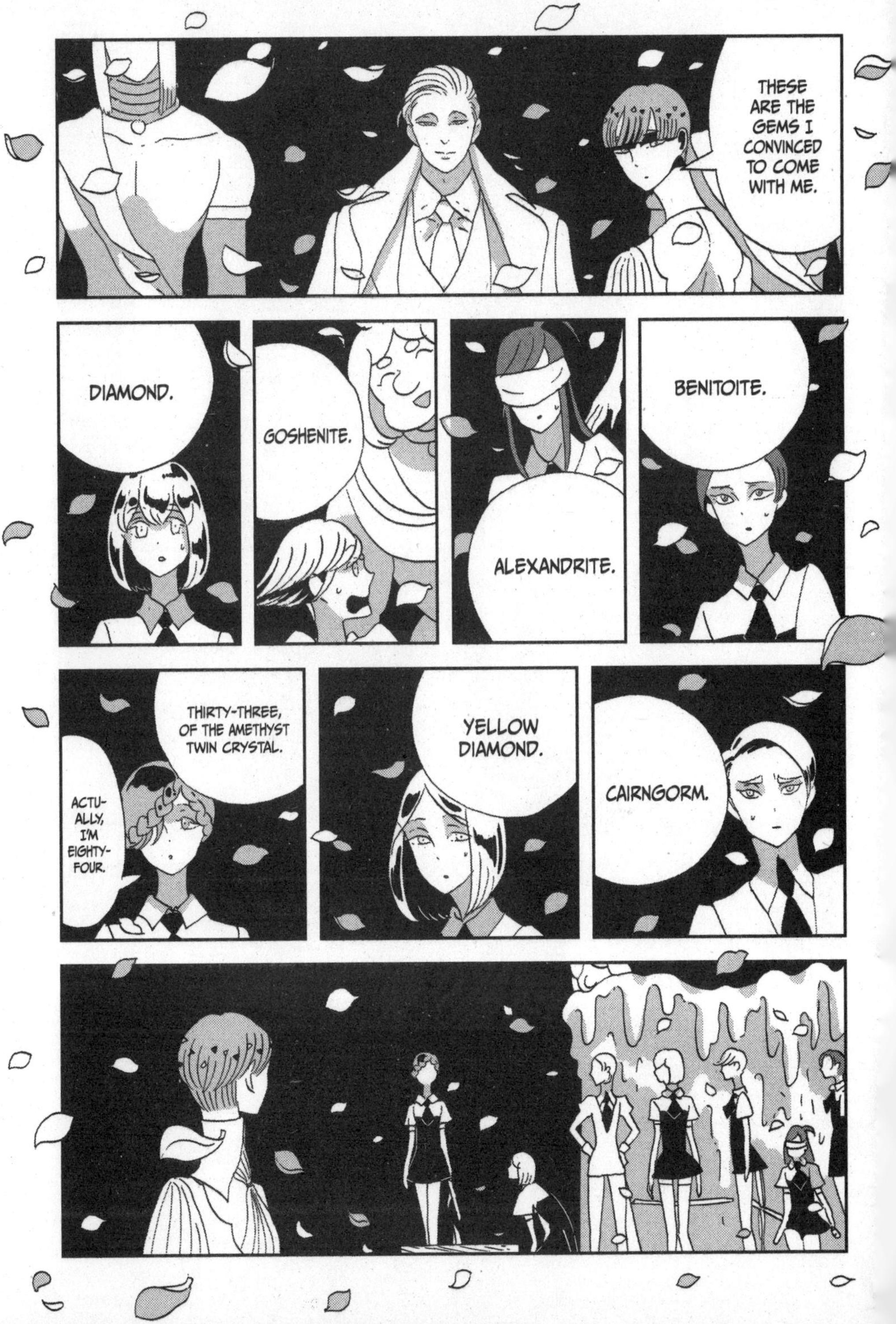
THESE ARE THE GEMS I CONVINCED TO COME WITH ME.
BENITOITE.
ALEXANDRITE.
GOSHENITE.
DIAMOND.
CAIRNGORM.
YELLOW DIAMOND.
THIRTY-THREE, OF THE AMETHYST TWIN CRYSTAL.
ACTU-ALLY, I'M EIGHTY-FOUR.

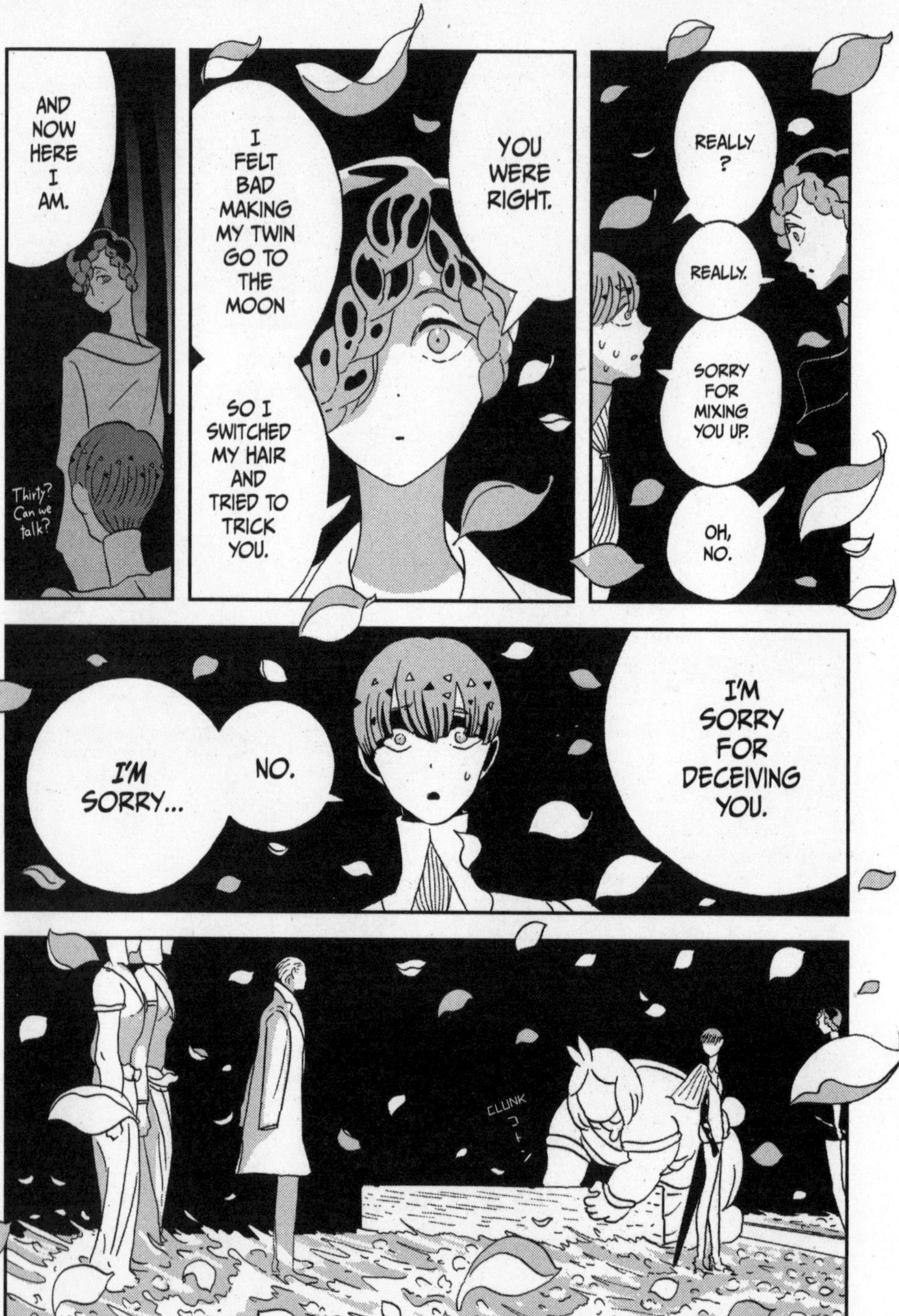
REALLY ?
REALLY.
SORRY FOR MIXING YOU UP.
OH, NO.
YOU WERE RIGHT.
I FELT BAD MAKING MY TWIN GO TO THE MOON
SO I SWITCHED MY HAIR AND TRIED TO TRICK YOU.
AND NOW HERE I AM.
Thirty? Can we talk?
I'M SORRY FOR DECEIVING YOU.
NO.
I'M SORRY...
CLUNK

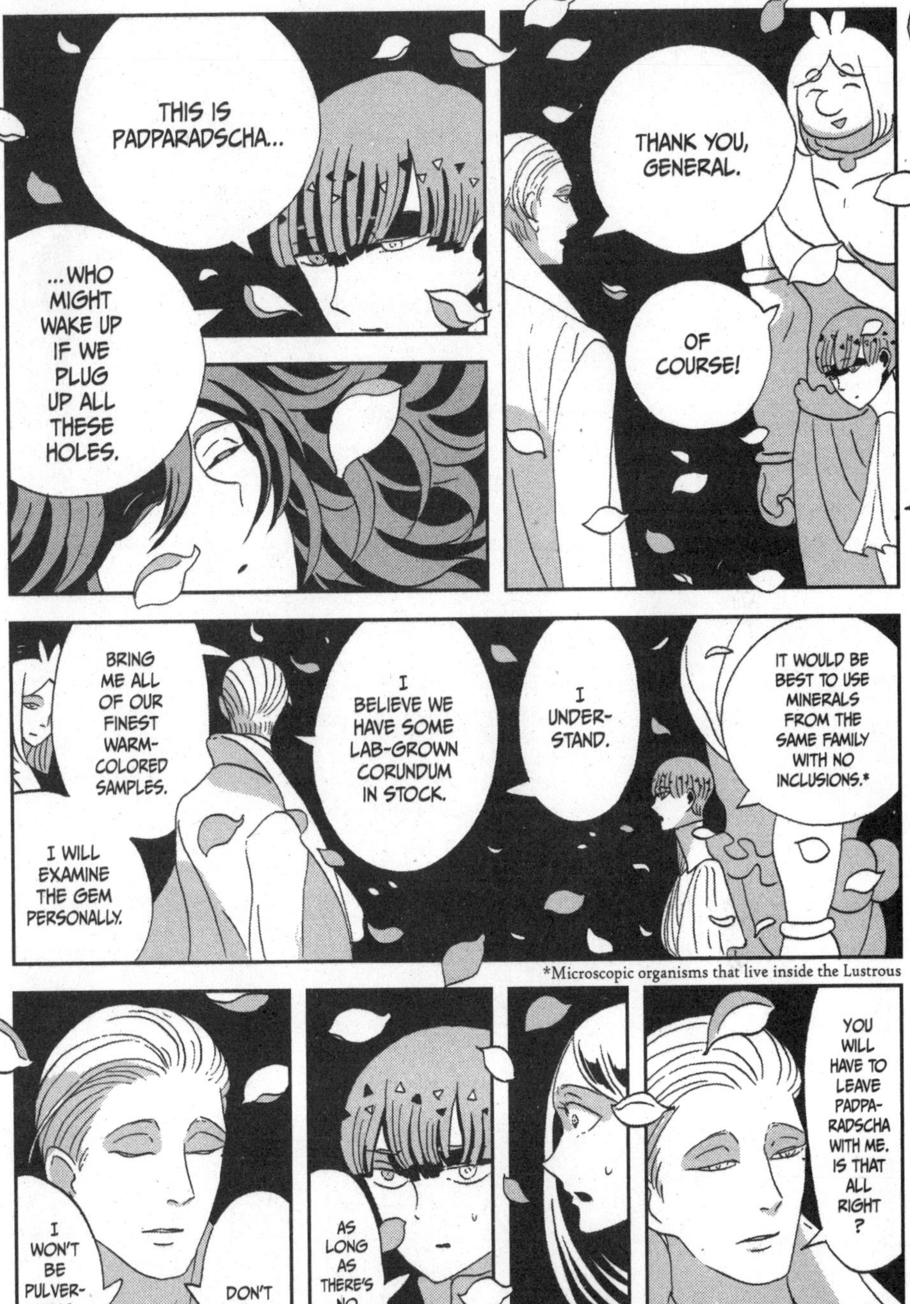
THANK YOU, GENERAL.
OF COURSE!
THIS IS PADPARADSCHA...
...WHO MIGHT WAKE UP IF WE PLUG UP ALL THESE HOLES.
IT WOULD BE BEST TO USE MINERALS FROM THE SAME FAMILY WITH NO INCLUSIONS.*
I UNDER-STAND.
I BELIEVE WE HAVE SOME LAB-GROWN CORUNDUM IN STOCK.
BRING ME ALL OF OUR FINEST WARM-COLORED SAMPLES.
I WILL EXAMINE THE GEM PERSONALLY.
YOU WILL HAVE TO LEAVE PADPARADSCHA WITH ME. IS THAT ALL RIGHT?
AS LONG AS THERE'S NO SMASH-ING.
DON'T WORRY.
I WON'T BE PULVER-IZING THIS ONE.

*Microscopic organisms that live inside the Lustrous

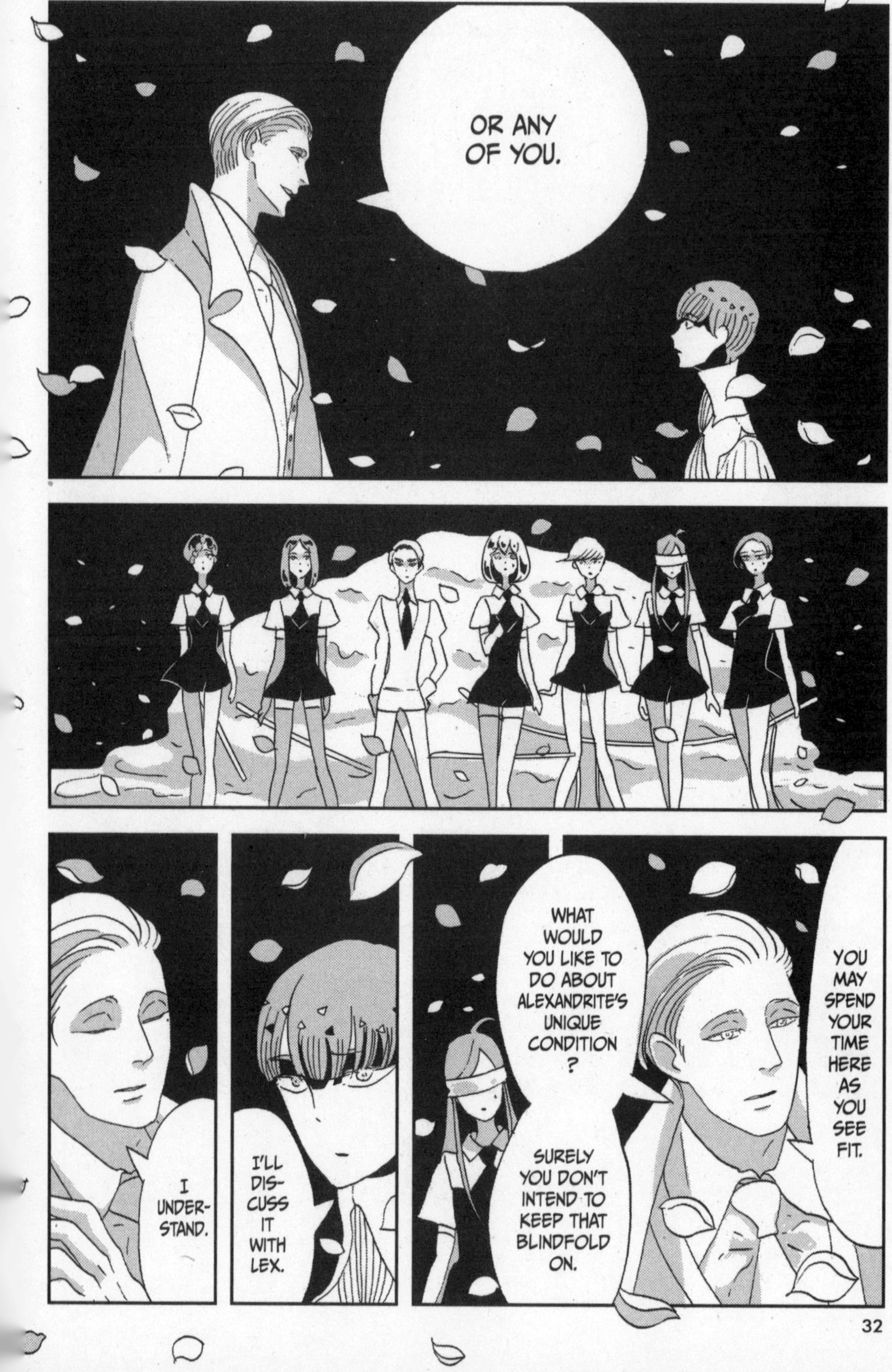
OR ANY OF YOU.
YOU MAY SPEND YOUR TIME HERE AS YOU SEE FIT.
WHAT WOULD YOU LIKE TO DO ABOUT ALEXANDRITE'S UNIQUE CONDITION ?
SURELY YOU DON'T INTEND TO KEEP THAT BLINDFOLD ON.
I'LL DIS-CUSS IT WITH LEX.
I UNDER-STAND.

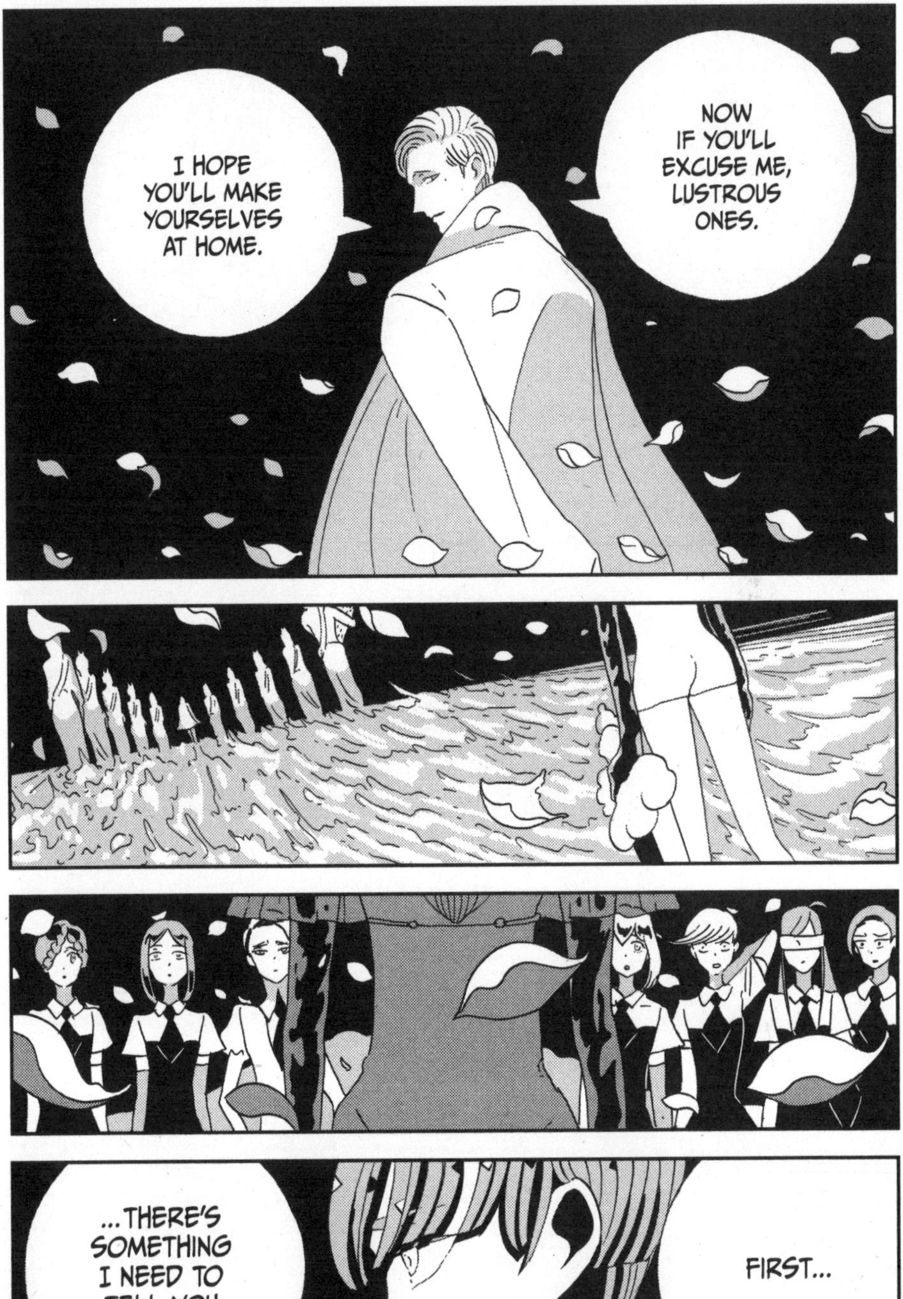
NOW IF YOU'LL EXCUSE ME, LUSTROUS ONES.
I HOPE YOU'LL MAKE YOURSELVES AT HOME.
FIRST...
...THERE'S SOMETHING I NEED TO TELL YOU ALL.

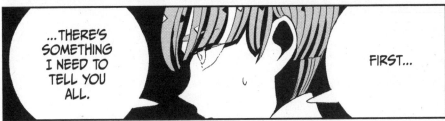

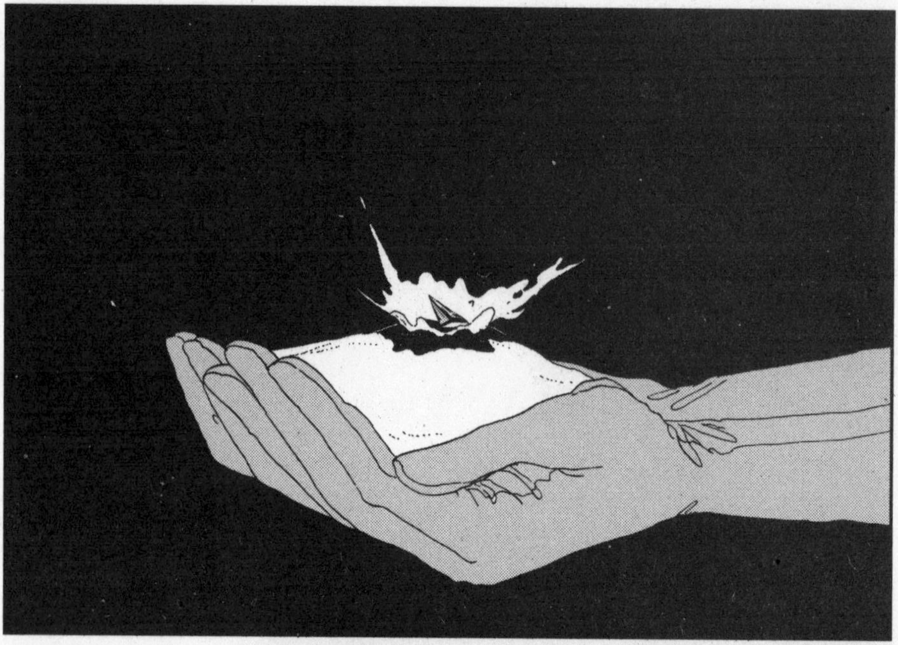

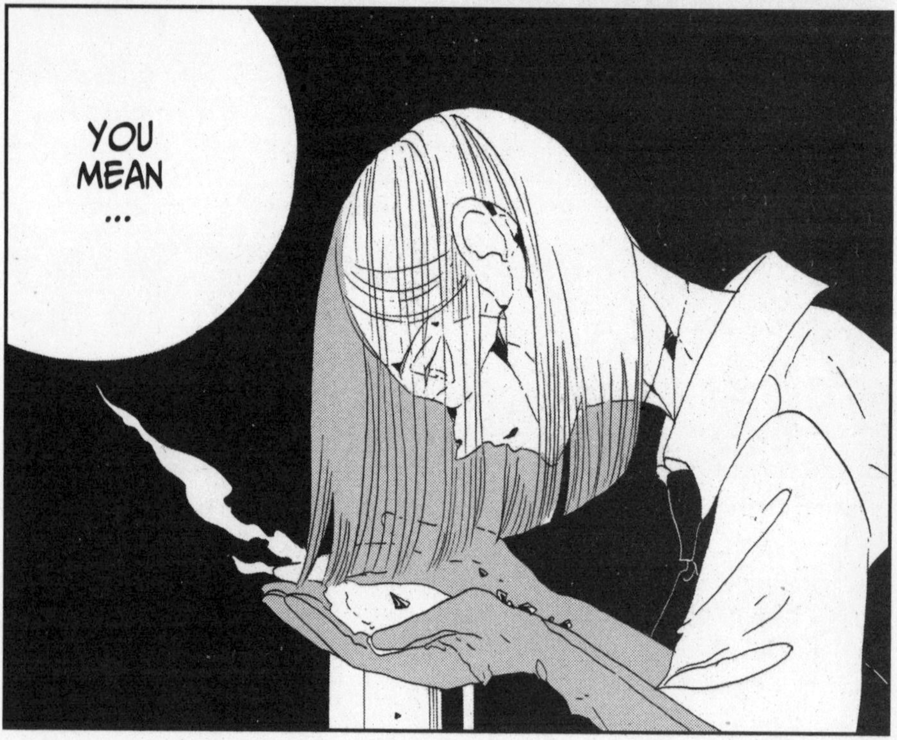
YOU MEAN ...

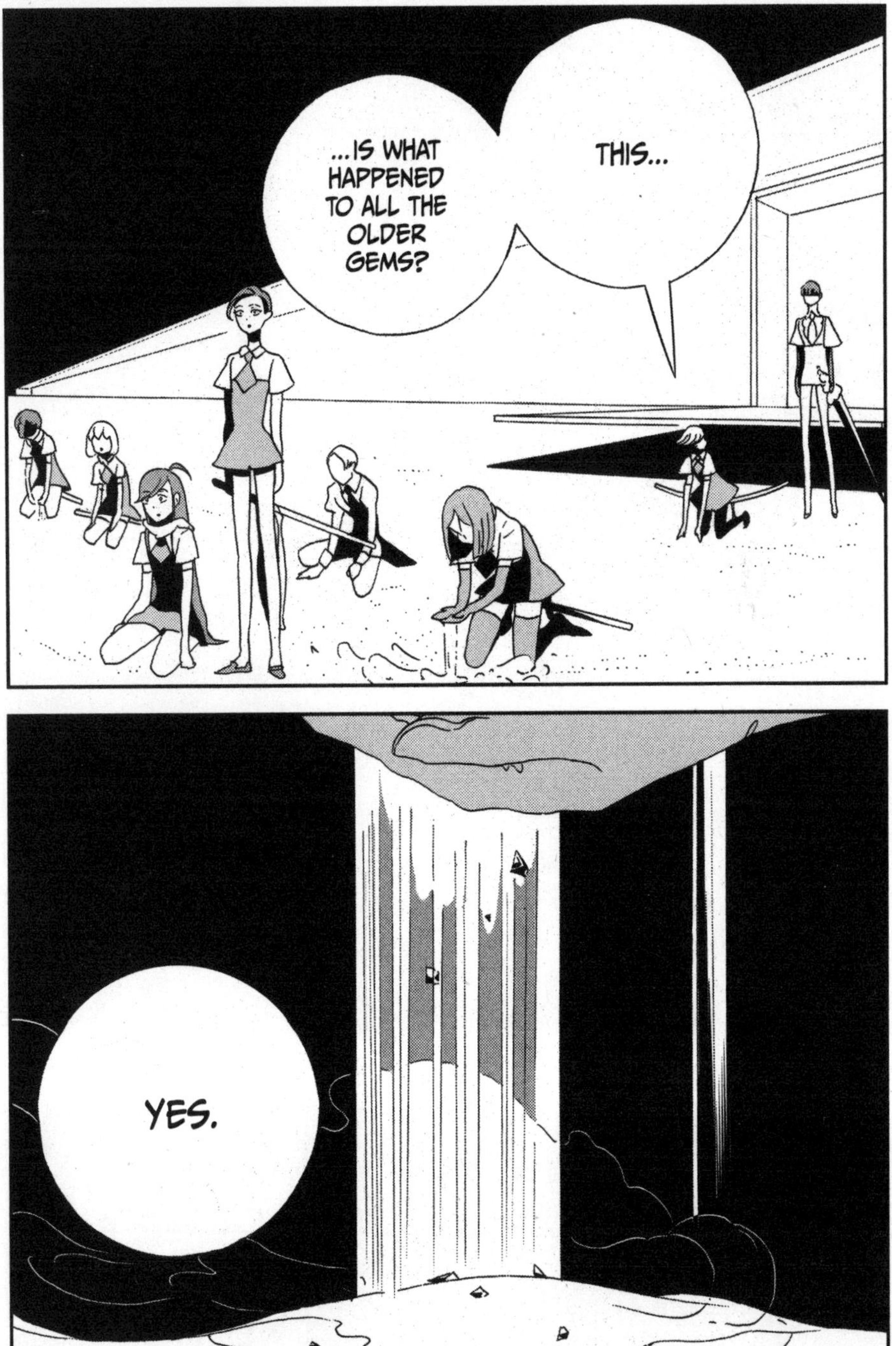
THIS...
...IS WHAT HAPPENED TO ALL THE OLDER GEMS?
YES.

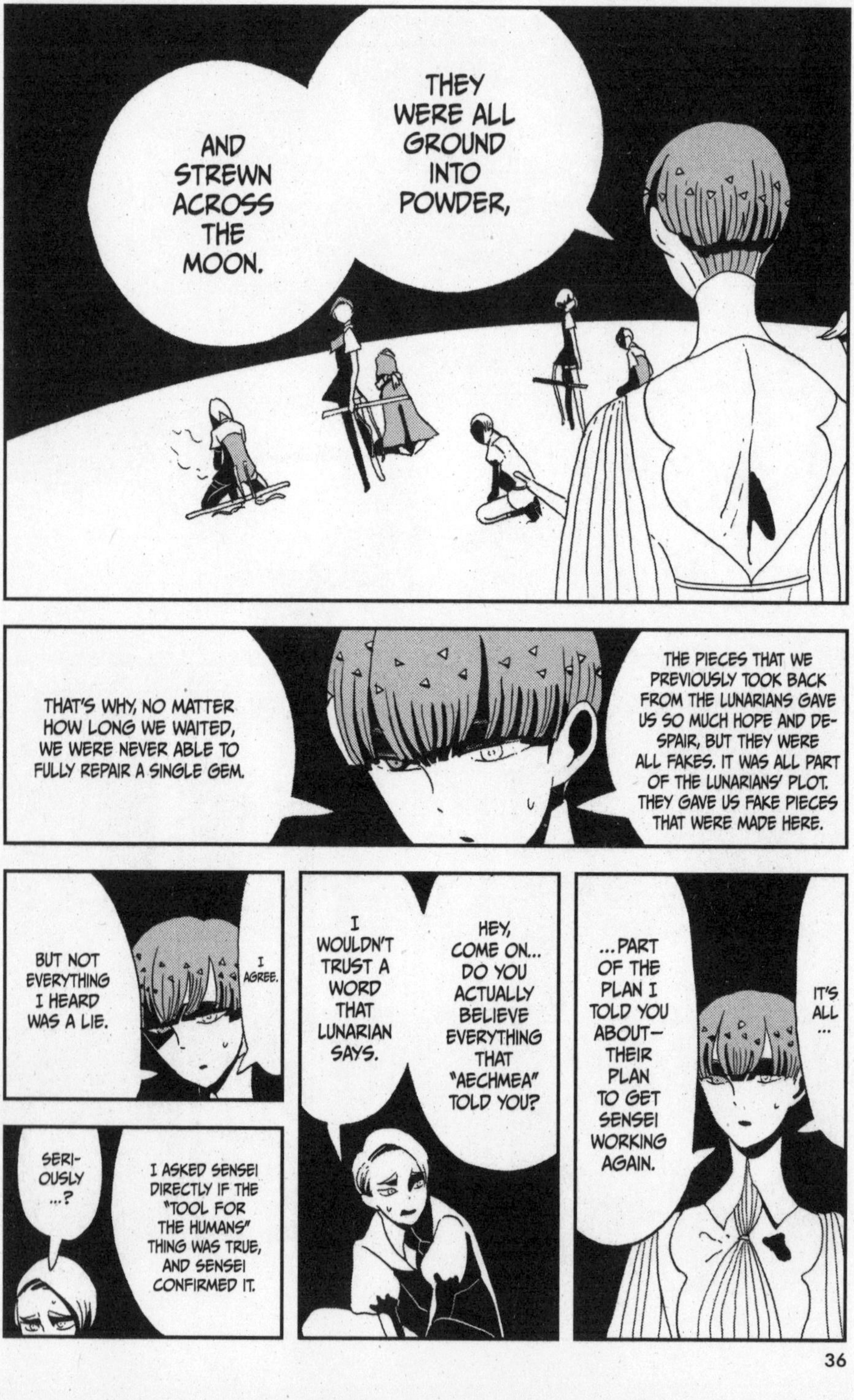
THEY WERE ALL GROUND INTO POWDER,
AND STREWN ACROSS THE MOON.
THE PIECES THAT WE PREVIOUSLY TOOK BACK FROM THE LUNARIANS GAVE US SO MUCH HOPE AND DE-SPAIR, BUT THEY WERE ALL FAKES. IT WAS ALL PART OF THE LUNARIANS' PLOT. THEY GAVE US FAKE PIECES THAT WERE MADE HERE.
THAT'S WHY, NO MATTER HOW LONG WE WAITED, WE WERE NEVER ABLE TO FULLY REPAIR A SINGLE GEM.
IT'S ALL...
...PART OF THE PLAN I TOLD YOU ABOUT—THEIR PLAN TO GET SENSEI WORKING AGAIN.
HEY, COME ON... DO YOU ACTUALLY BELIEVE EVERYTHING THAT "AECHMEA" TOLD YOU?
I WOULDN'T TRUST A WORD THAT LUNARIAN SAYS.
I AGREE.
BUT NOT EVERYTHING I HEARD WAS A LIE.
I ASKED SENSEI DIRECTLY IF THE "TOOL FOR THE HUMANS" THING WAS TRUE, AND SENSEI CONFIRMED IT.
SERI-OUSLY ...?

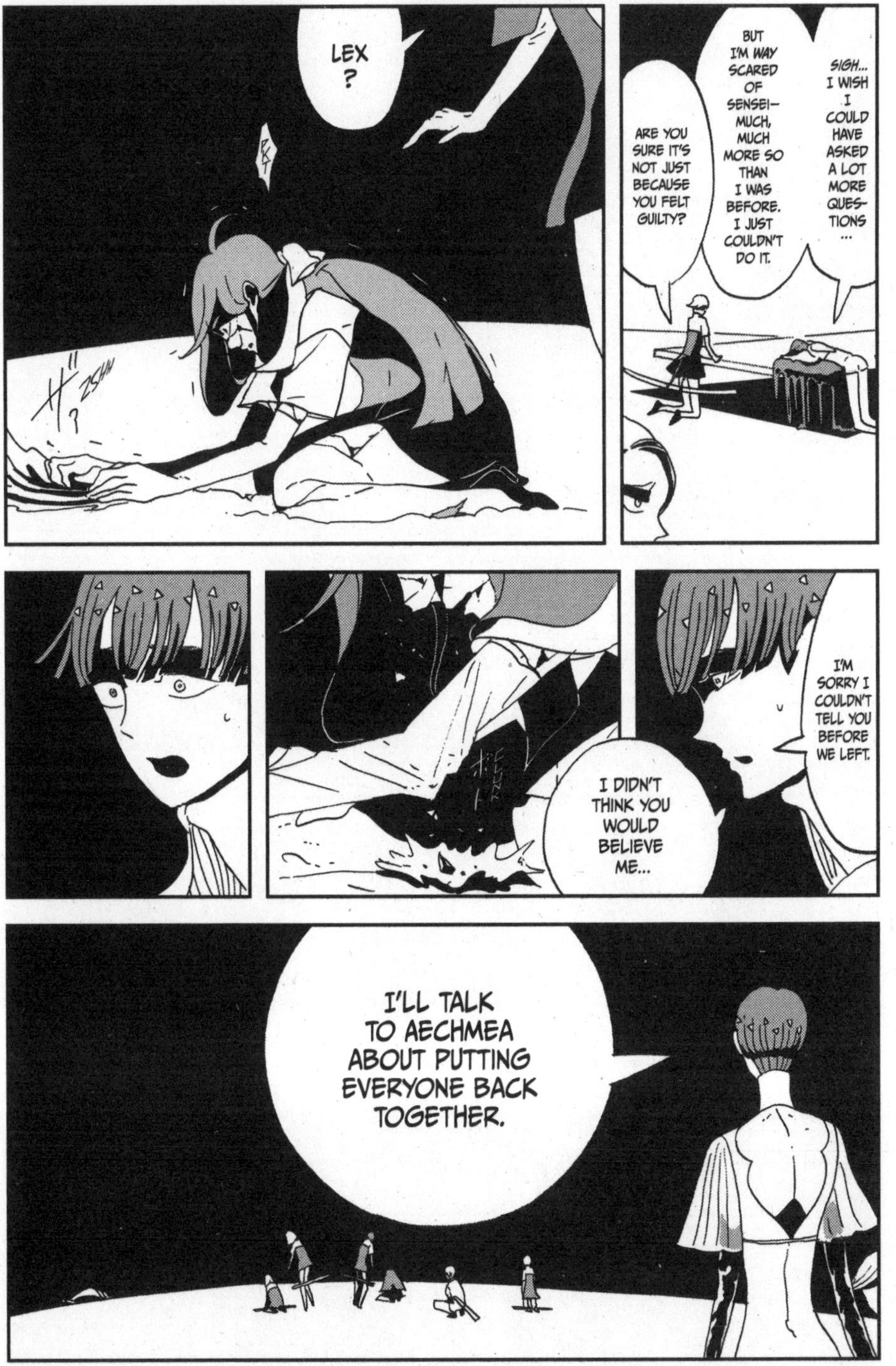
SIGH... I WISH I COULD HAVE ASKED A LOT MORE QUESTIONS...
BUT I'M WAY SCARED OF SENSEI—MUCH, MUCH MORE SO THAN I WAS BEFORE. I JUST COULDN'T DO IT.
ARE YOU SURE IT'S NOT JUST BECAUSE YOU FELT GUILTY?
LEX?
PKT
ZSHH
I'M SORRY I COULDN'T TELL YOU BEFORE WE LEFT.
I DIDN'T THINK YOU WOULD BELIEVE ME...
CLUNK
I'LL TALK TO AECHMEA ABOUT PUTTING EVERYONE BACK TOGETHER.

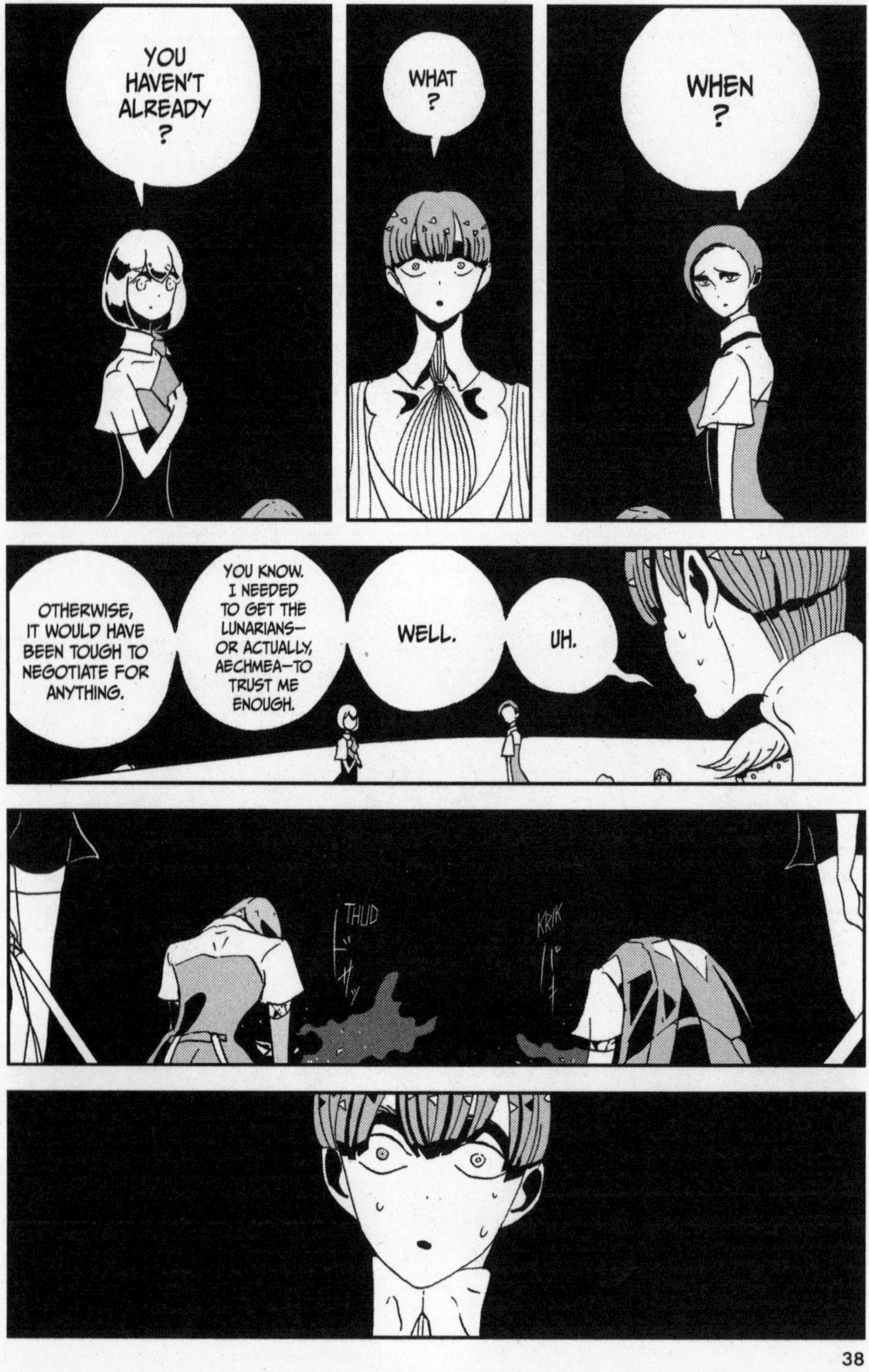
WHEN ?
WHAT ?
YOU HAVEN'T ALREADY ?
UH.
WELL.
YOU KNOW. I NEEDED TO GET THE LUNARIANS— OR ACTUALLY, AECHMEA—TO TRUST ME ENOUGH.
OTHERWISE, IT WOULD HAVE BEEN TOUGH TO NEGOTIATE FOR ANYTHING.
KRIK
THUD

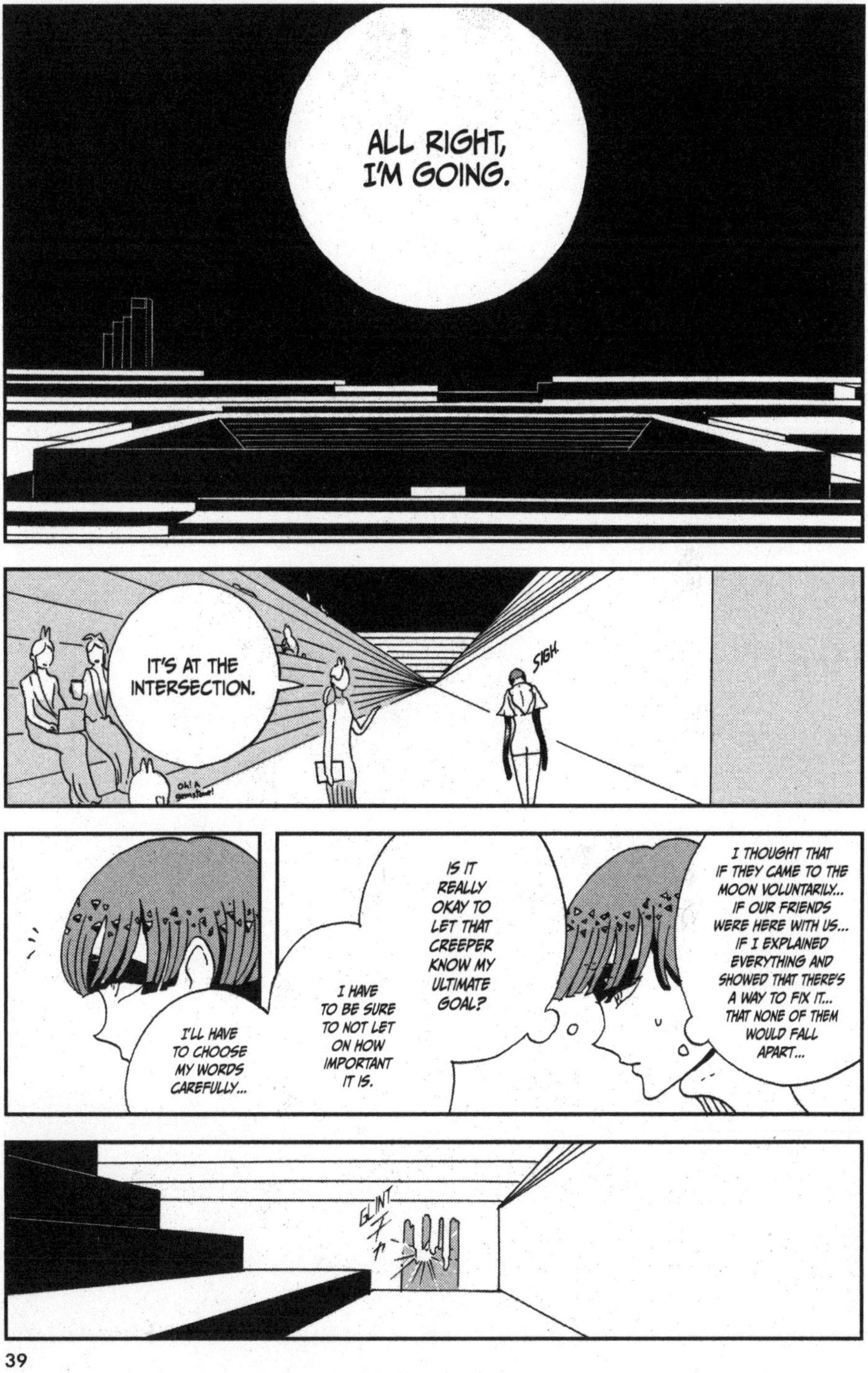
ALL RIGHT, I'M GOING.
SIGH.
IT'S AT THE INTERSECTION.
Oh! A gemstone!
I THOUGHT THAT IF THEY CAME TO THE MOON VOLUNTARILY... IF OUR FRIENDS WERE HERE WITH US... IF I EXPLAINED EVERYTHING AND SHOWED THAT THERE'S A WAY TO FIX IT... THAT NONE OF THEM WOULD FALL APART...
IS IT REALLY OKAY TO LET THAT CREEPER KNOW MY ULTIMATE GOAL?
I HAVE TO BE SURE TO NOT LET ON HOW IMPORTANT IT IS.
I'LL HAVE TO CHOOSE MY WORDS CAREFULLY...
GLINT

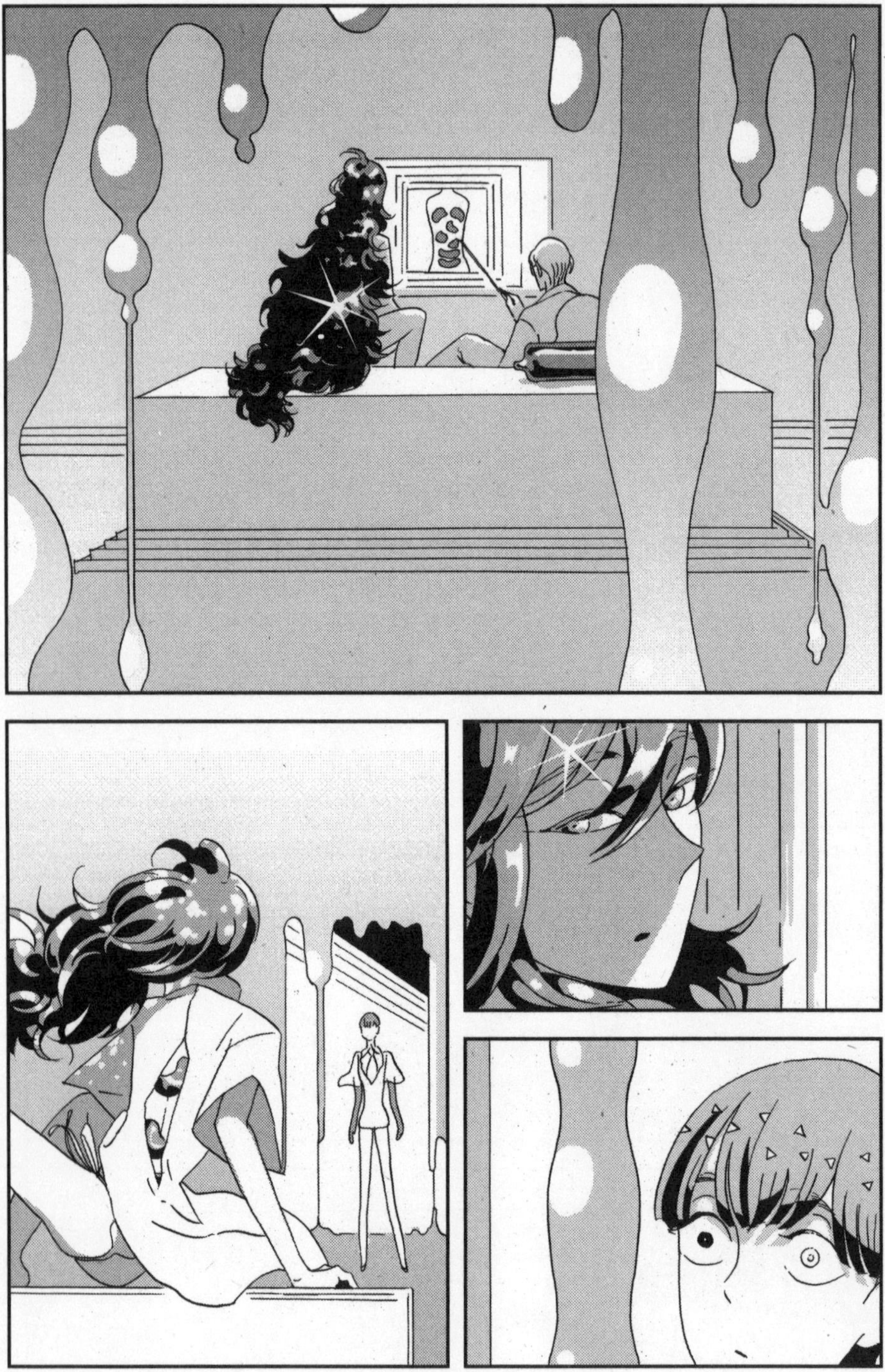

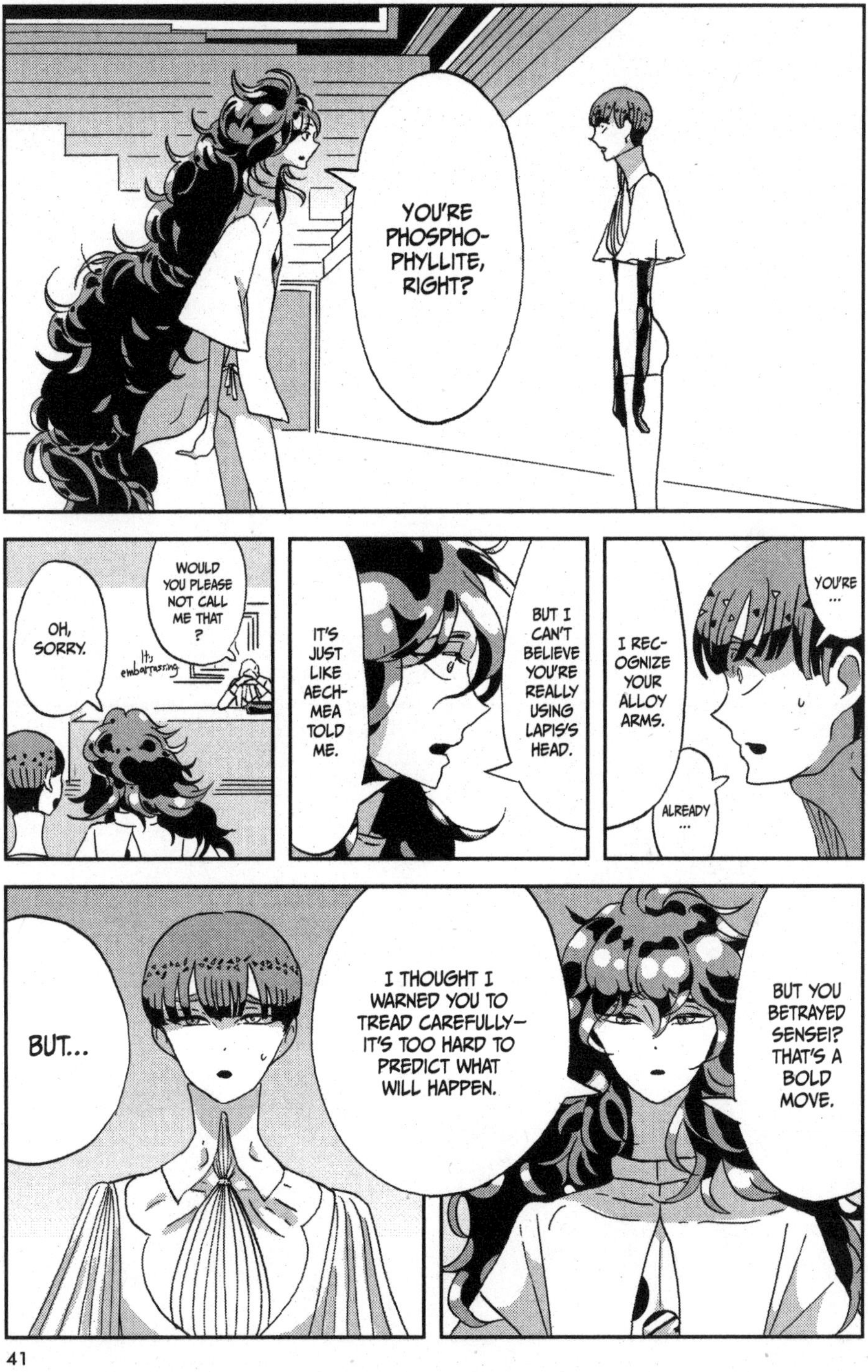
YOU'RE PHOSPHOPHYLLITE, RIGHT?
YOU'RE ...
I RECOGNIZE YOUR ALLOY ARMS.
ALREADY ...
BUT I CAN'T BELIEVE YOU'RE REALLY USING LAPIS'S HEAD.
IT'S JUST LIKE AECHMEA TOLD ME.
WOULD YOU PLEASE NOT CALL ME THAT?
It's embarrassing.
OH, SORRY.
BUT YOU BETRAYED SENSEI? THAT'S A BOLD MOVE.
I THOUGHT I WARNED YOU TO TREAD CAREFULLY— IT'S TOO HARD TO PREDICT WHAT WILL HAPPEN.
BUT...

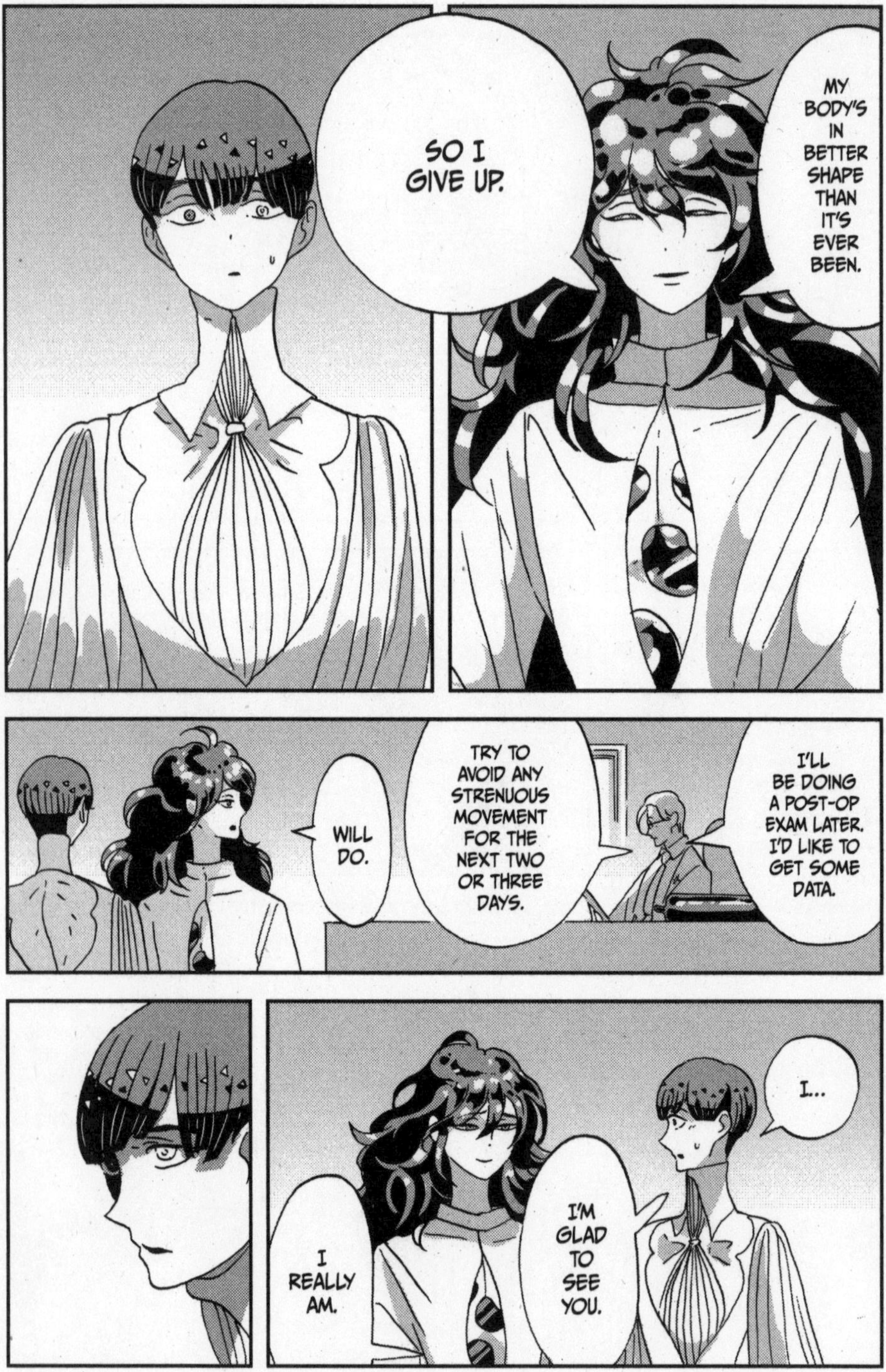
MY BODY'S IN BETTER SHAPE THAN IT'S EVER BEEN.
SO I GIVE UP.
I'LL BE DOING A POST-OP EXAM LATER. I'D LIKE TO GET SOME DATA.
TRY TO AVOID ANY STRENUOUS MOVEMENT FOR THE NEXT TWO OR THREE DAYS.
WILL DO.
I...
I'M GLAD TO SEE YOU.
I REALLY AM.

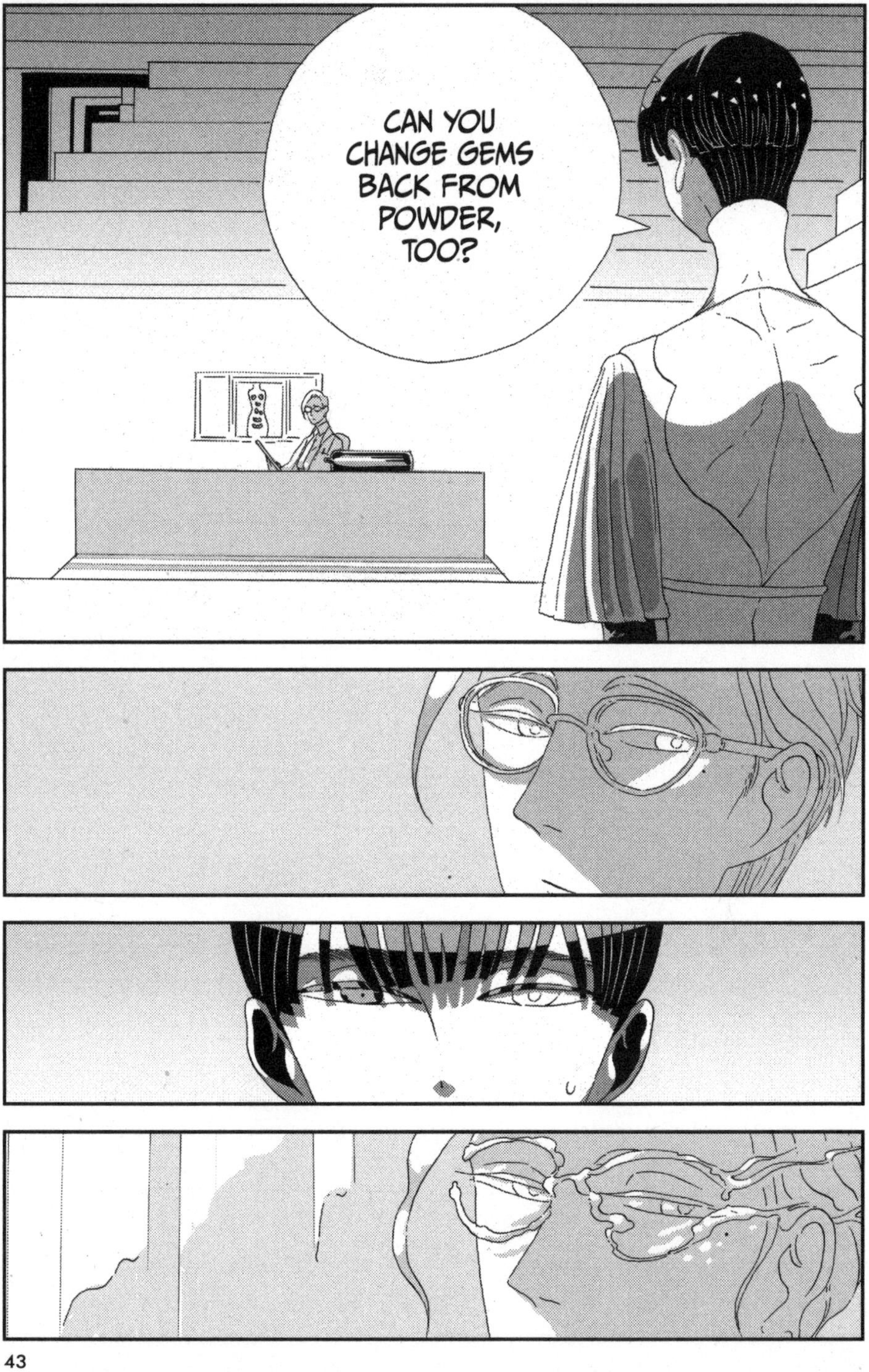
CAN YOU CHANGE GEMS BACK FROM POWDER, TOO?

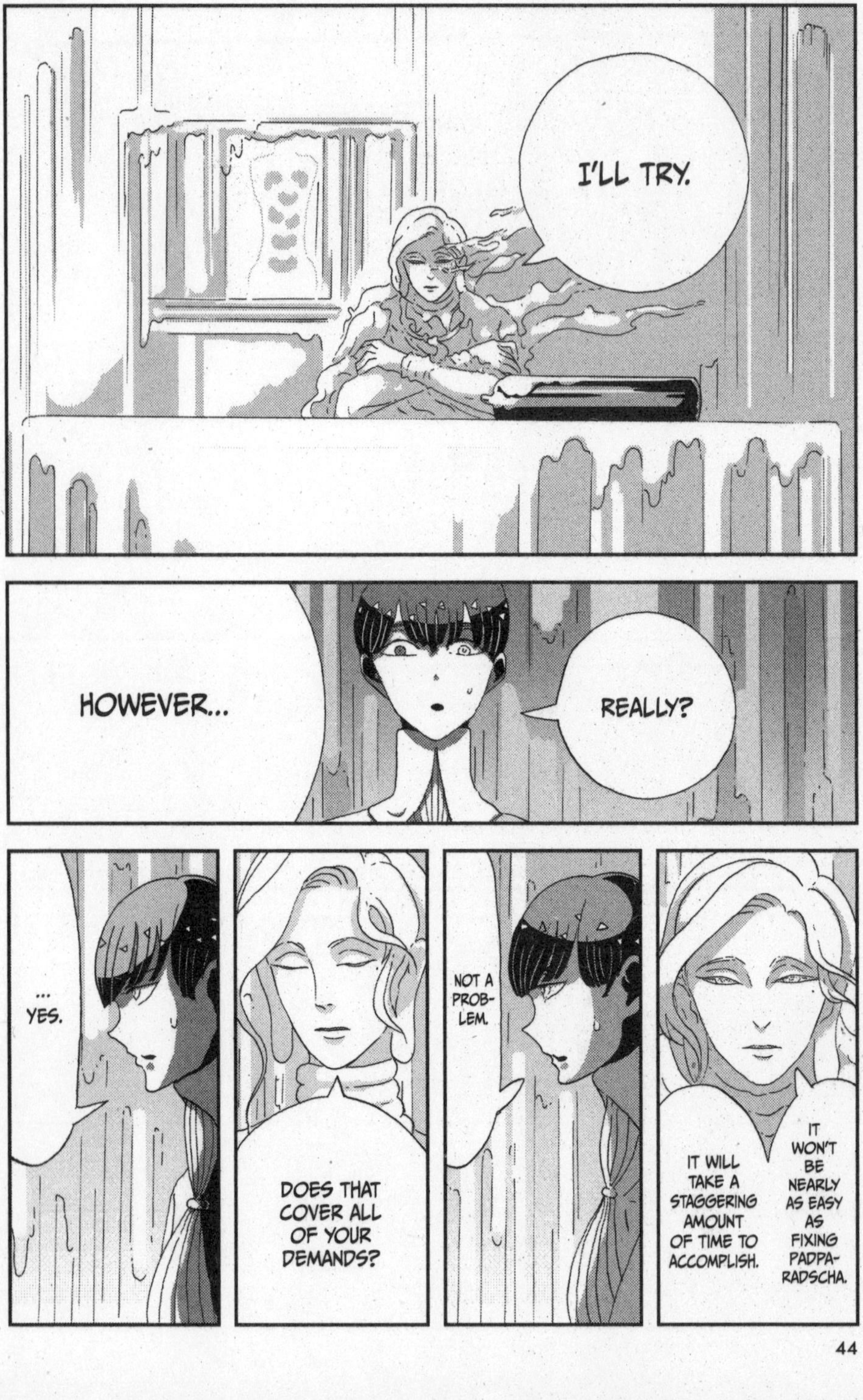
I'LL TRY.
REALLY?
HOWEVER...
IT WON'T BE NEARLY AS EASY AS FIXING PADPA-RADSCHA.
IT WILL TAKE A STAGGERING AMOUNT OF TIME TO ACCOMPLISH.
NOT A PROB-LEM.
DOES THAT COVER ALL OF YOUR DEMANDS?
... YES.

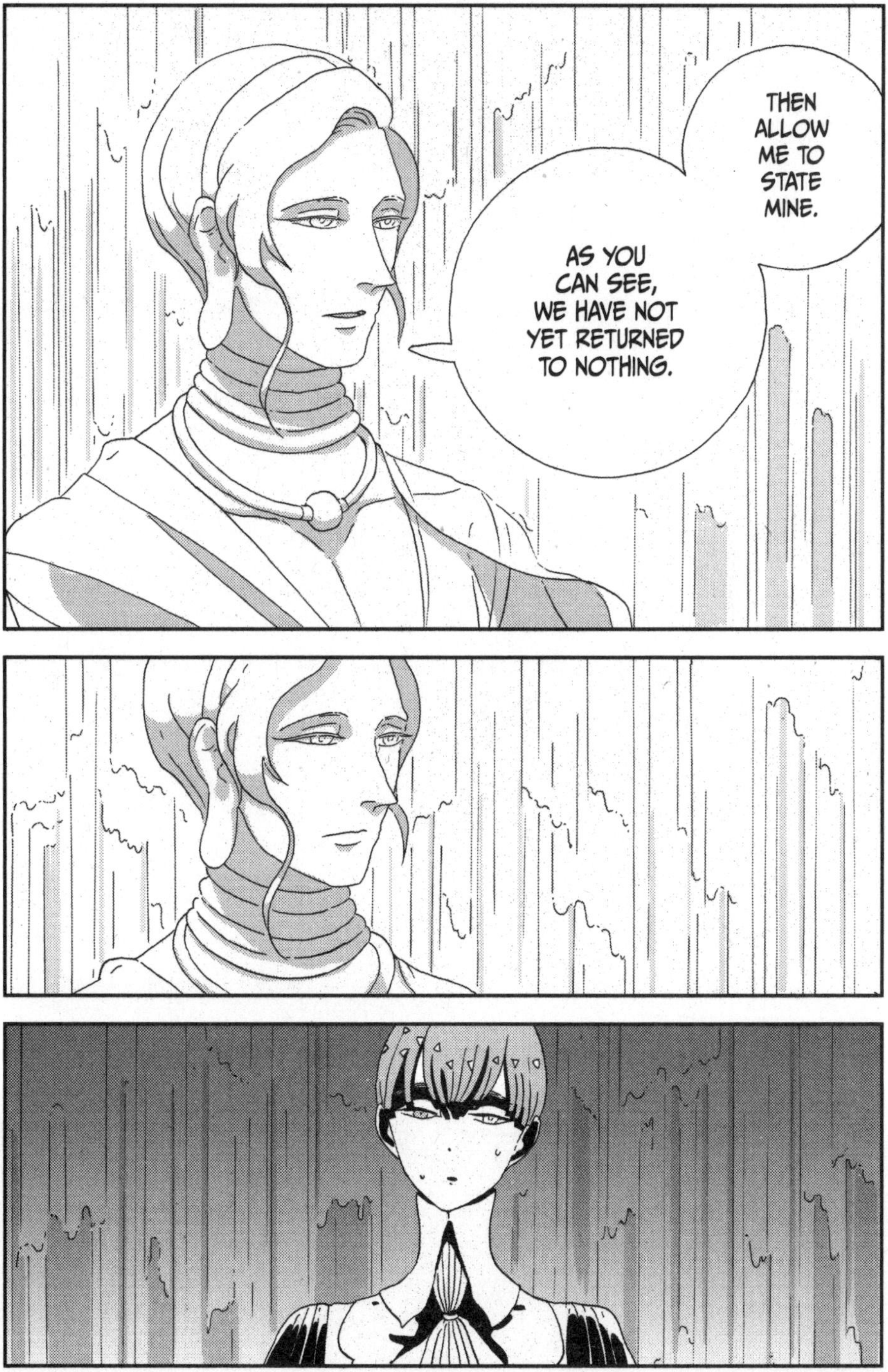
THEN ALLOW ME TO STATE MINE.
AS YOU CAN SEE, WE HAVE NOT YET RETURNED TO NOTHING.

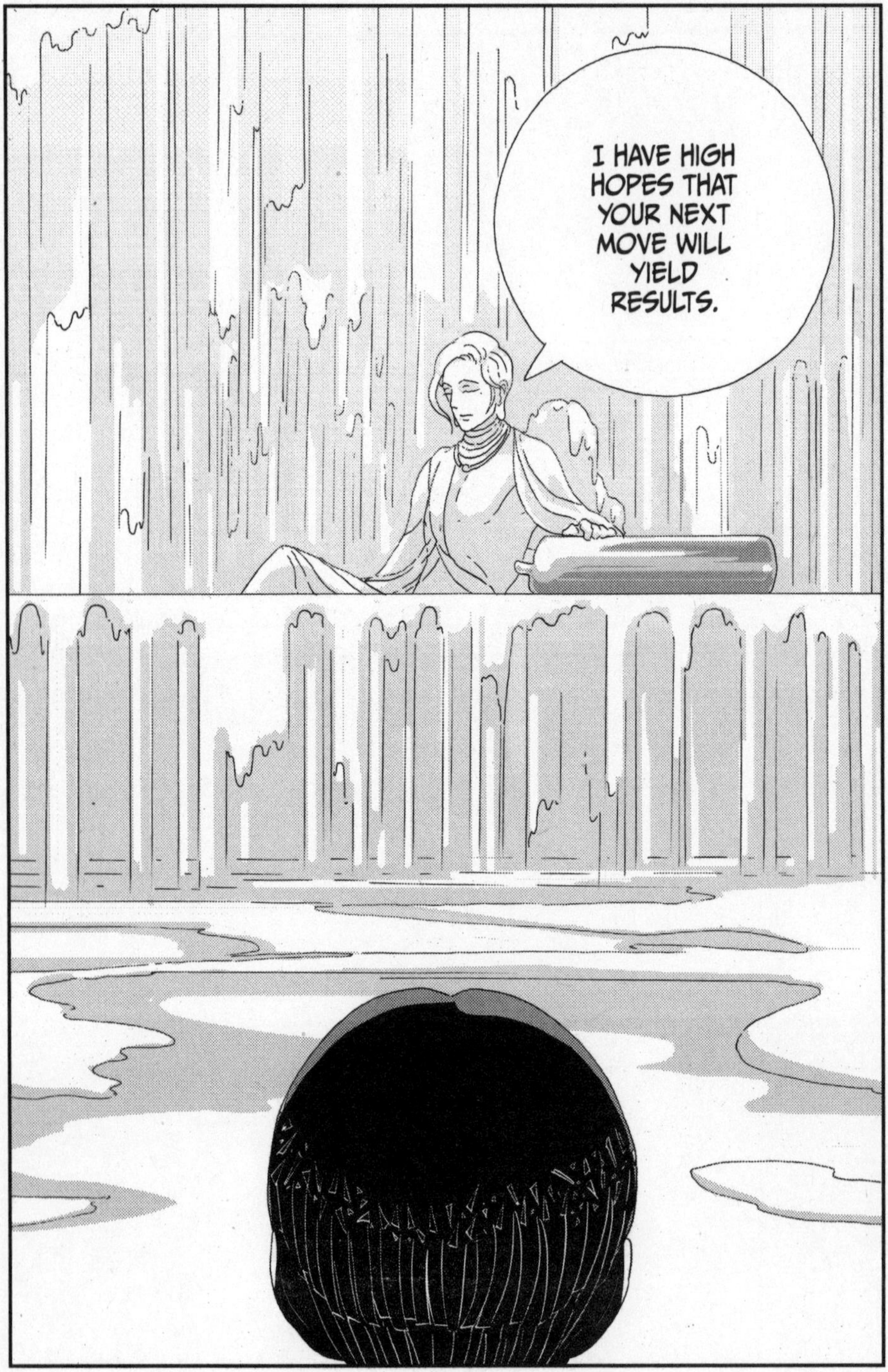
I HAVE HIGH HOPES THAT YOUR NEXT MOVE WILL YIELD RESULTS.

CHAPTER 63: High Hopes END

CHAPTER 64:

One Day

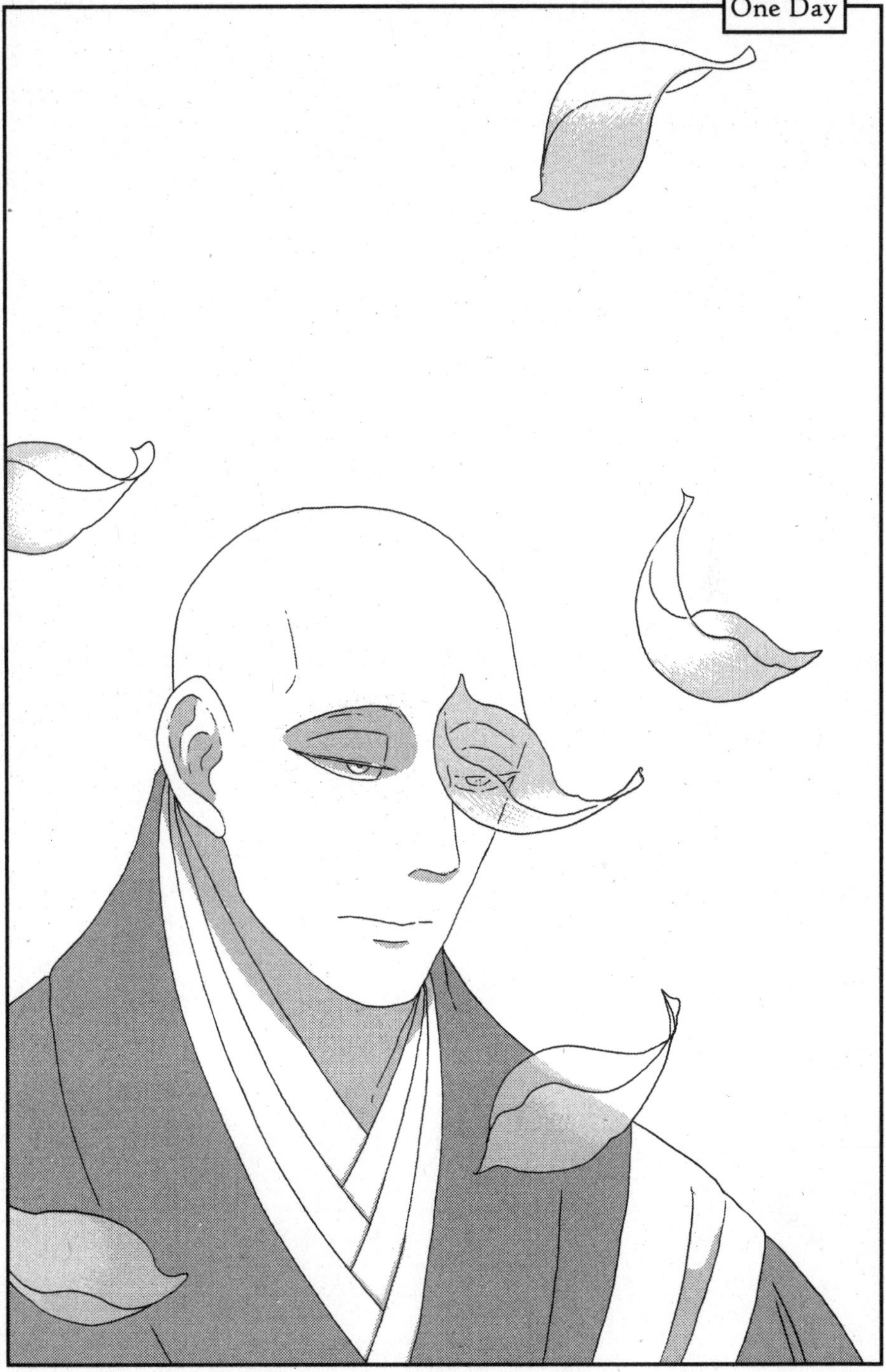

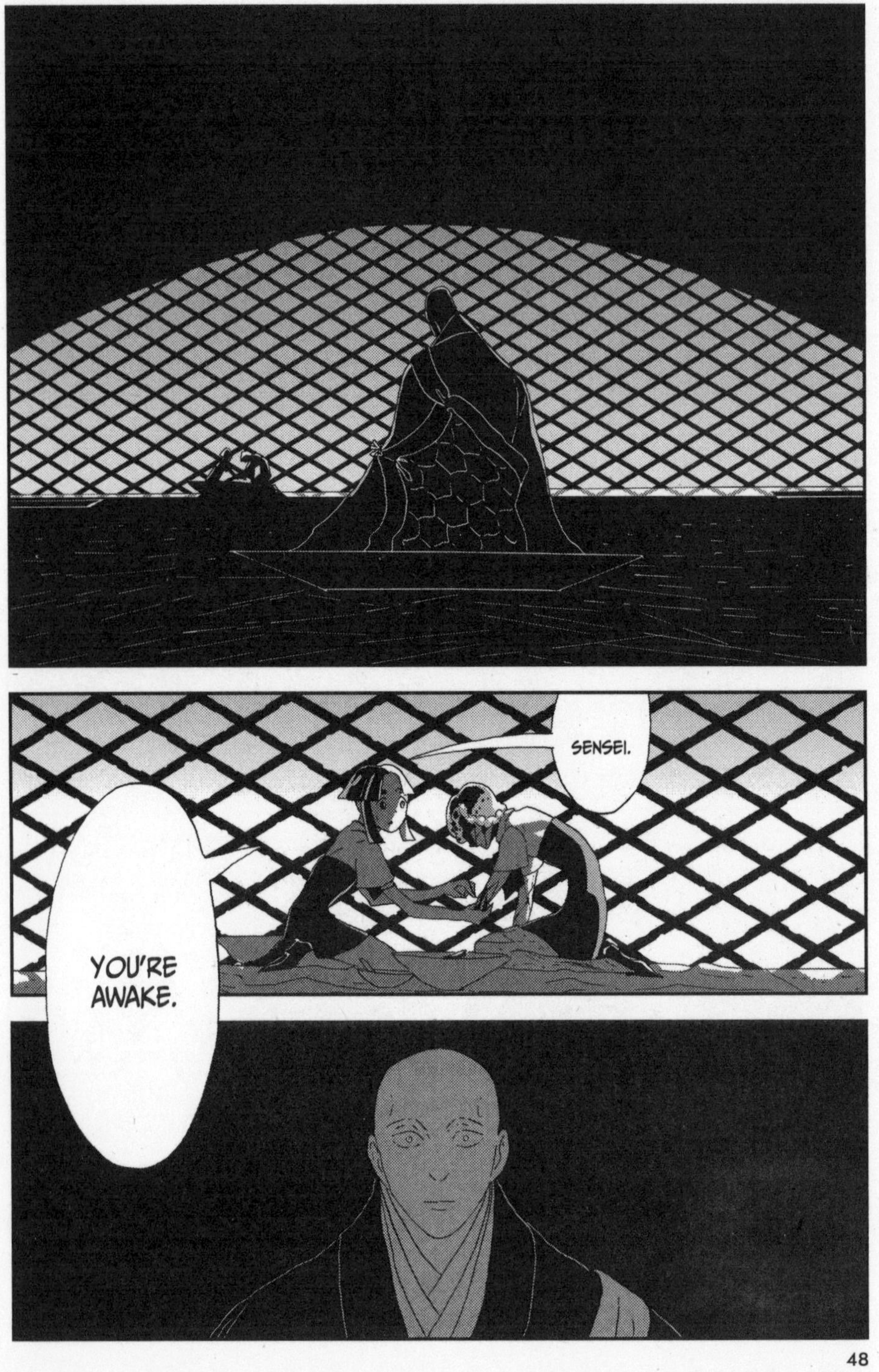
SENSEI.
YOU'RE AWAKE.

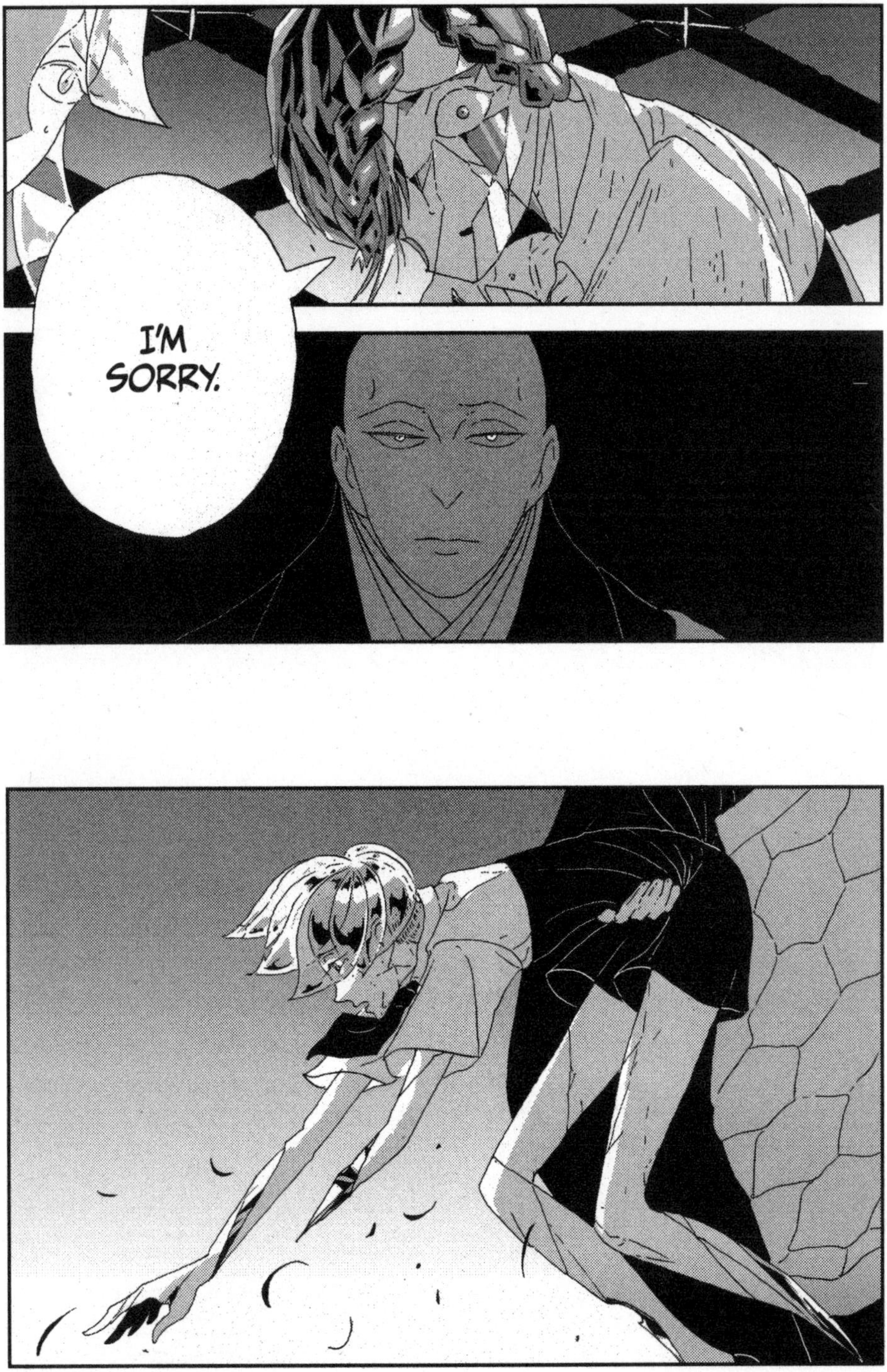
I'M SORRY.

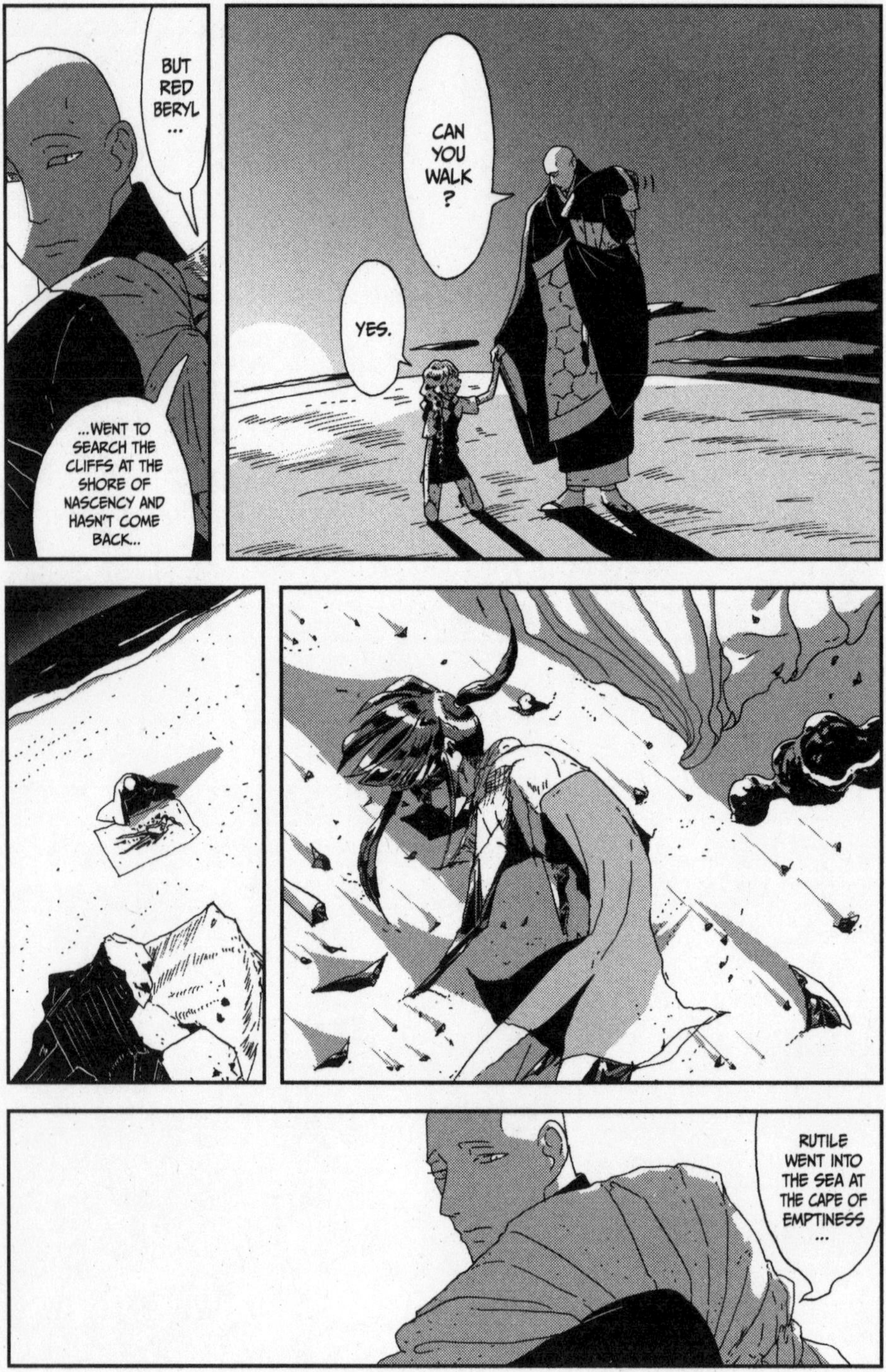
CAN YOU WALK?
YES.
BUT RED BERYL...
...WENT TO SEARCH THE CLIFFS AT THE SHORE OF NASCENCY AND HASN'T COME BACK...
RUTILE WENT INTO THE SEA AT THE CAPE OF EMPTINESS...

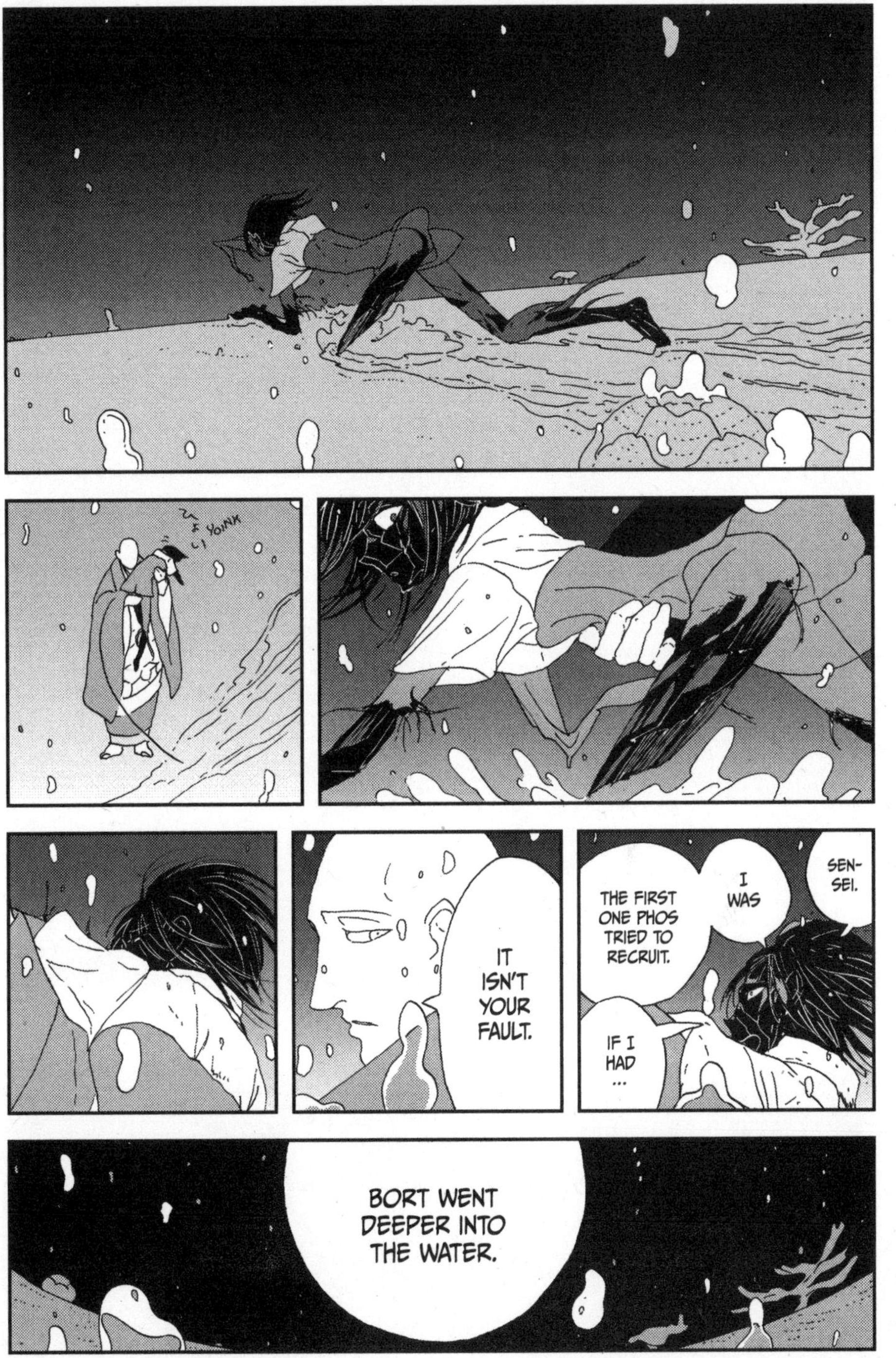
YOINK
SEN-SEI.
I WAS THE FIRST ONE PHOS TRIED TO RECRUIT.
IF I HAD ...
IT ISN'T YOUR FAULT.
BORT WENT DEEPER INTO THE WATER.

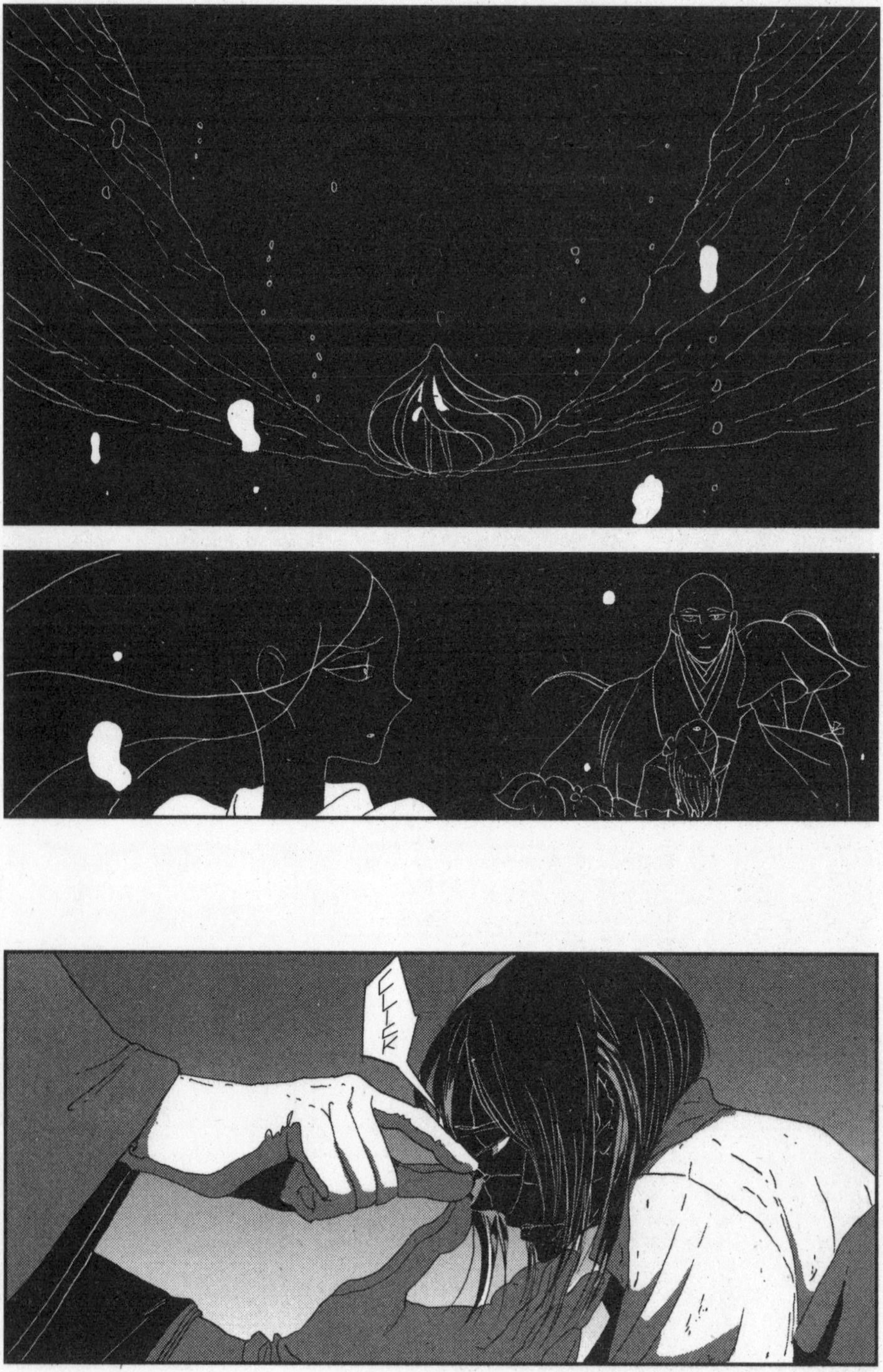
CLICK

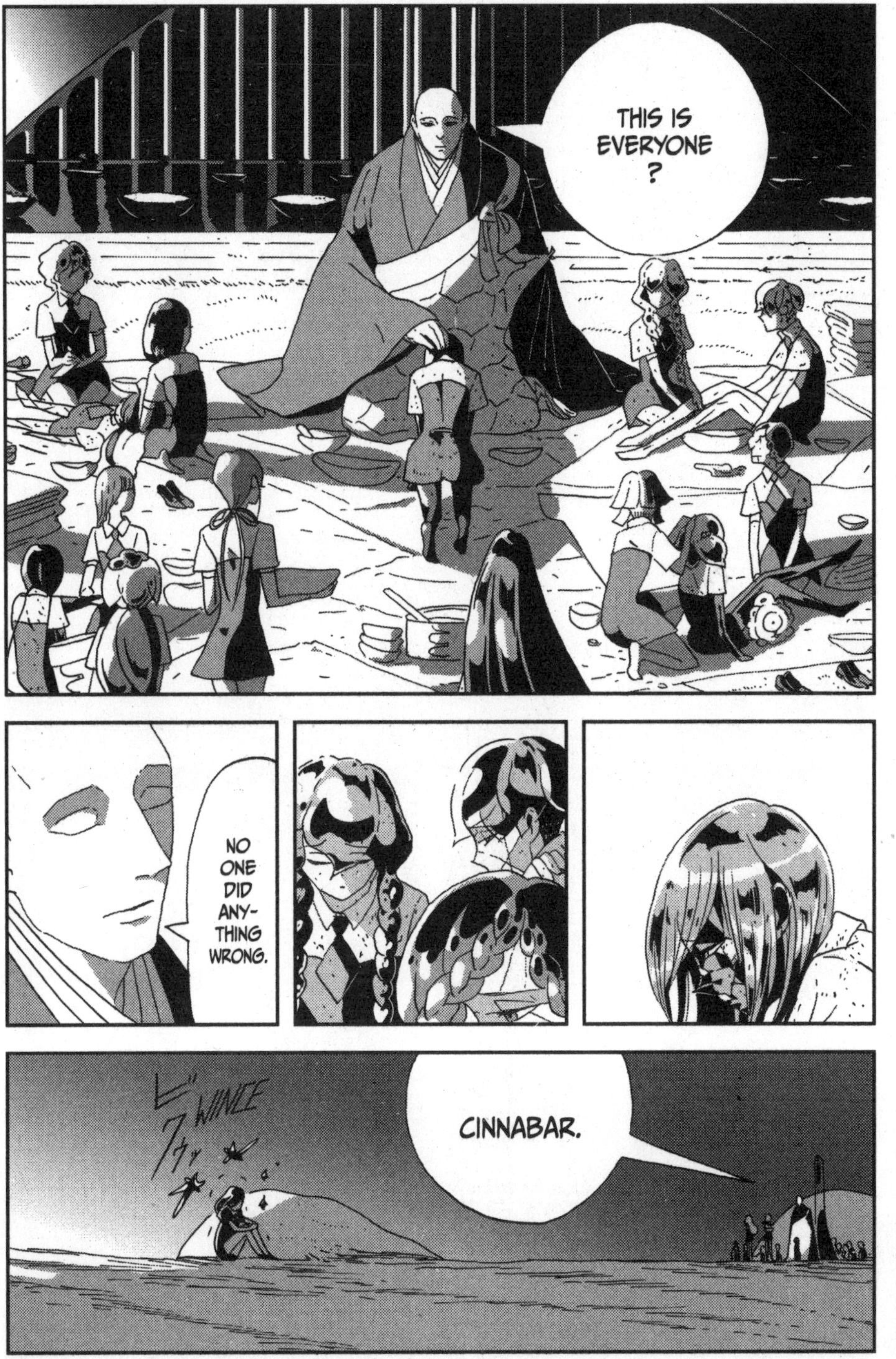
THIS IS EVERYONE ?
NO ONE DID ANY-THING WRONG.
CINNABAR.
WINCE

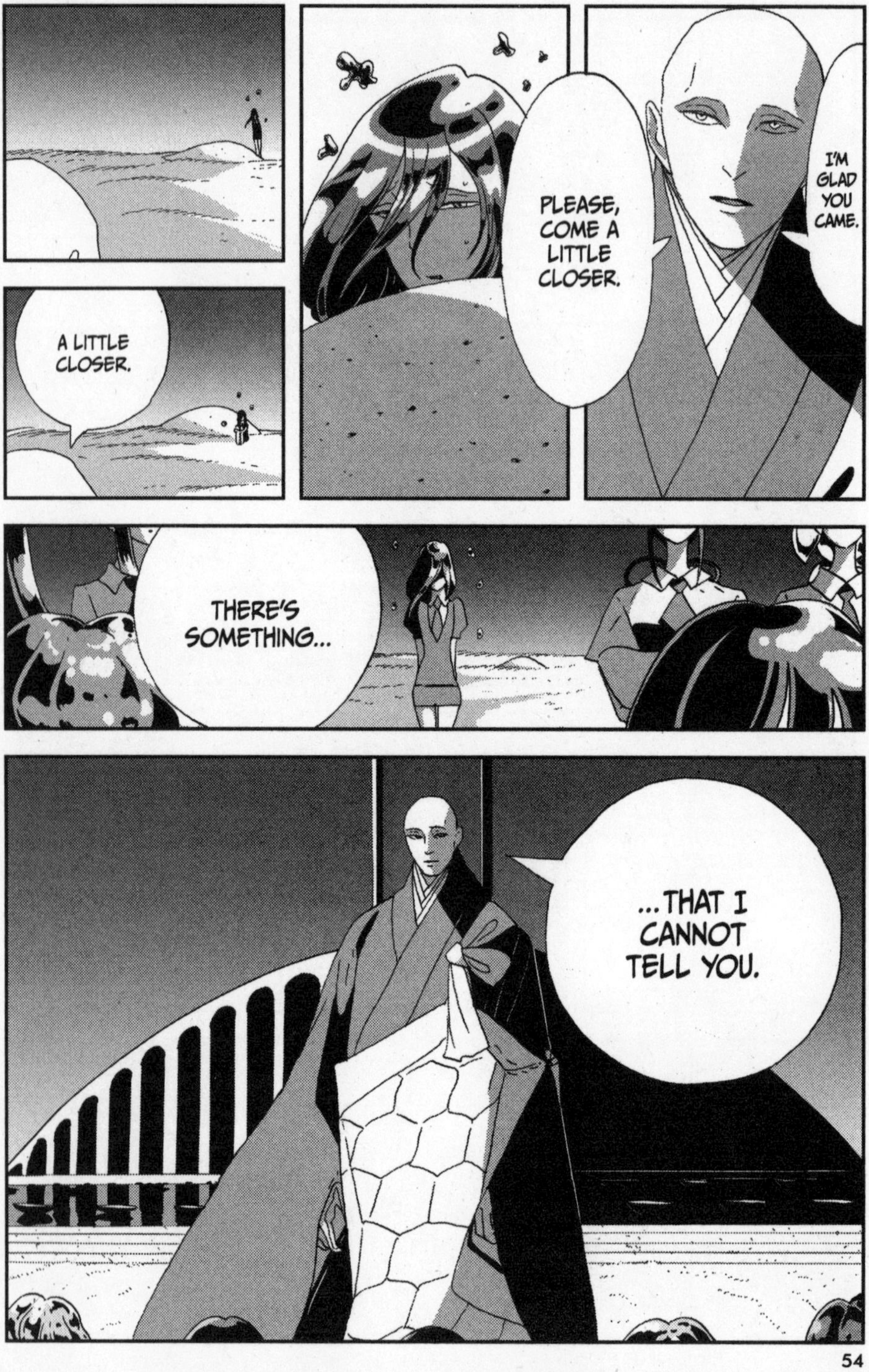
I'M GLAD YOU CAME.
PLEASE, COME A LITTLE CLOSER.
A LITTLE CLOSER.
THERE'S SOMETHING...
...THAT I CANNOT TELL YOU.

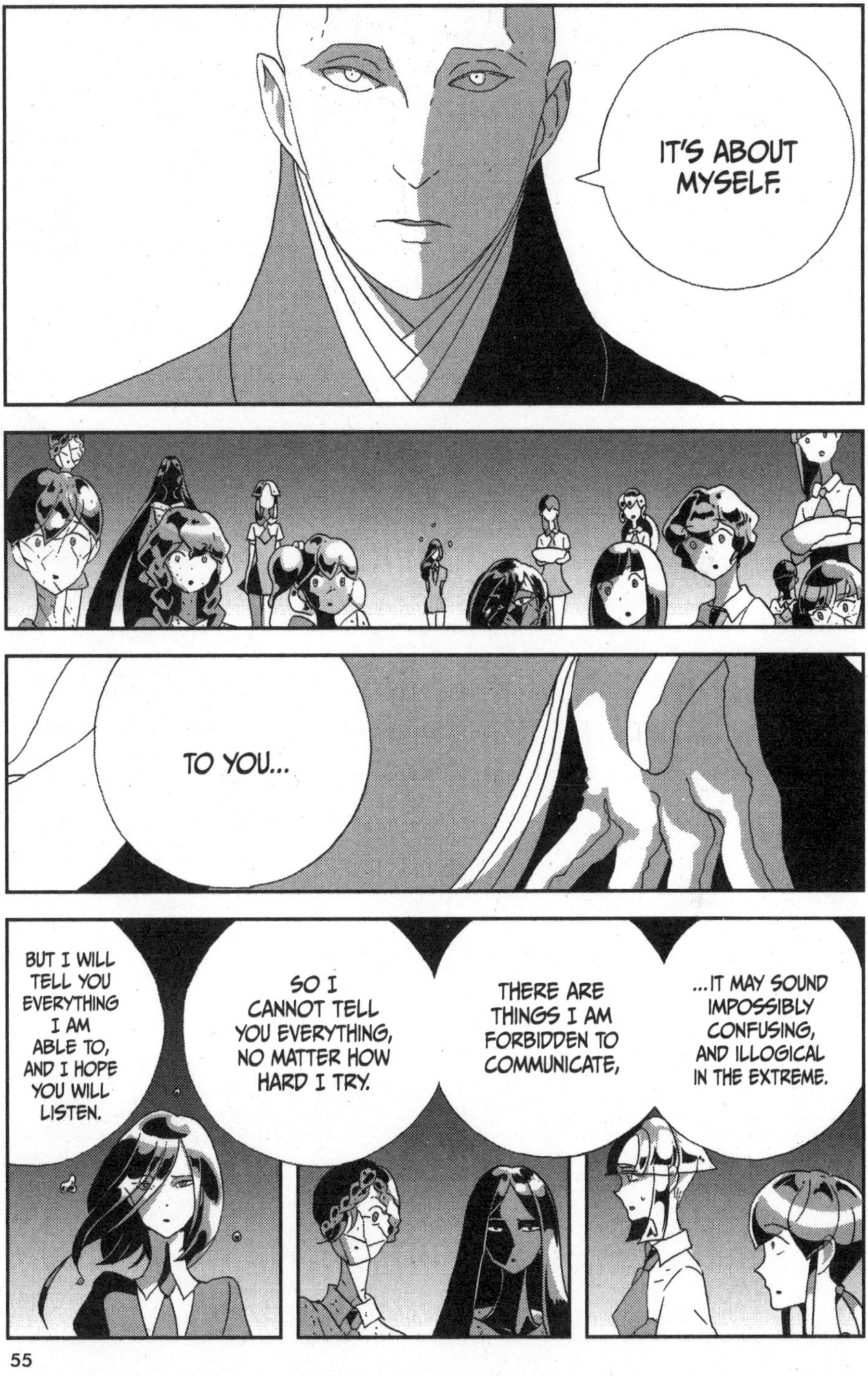
IT'S ABOUT MYSELF.
TO YOU...
...IT MAY SOUND IMPOSSIBLY CONFUSING, AND ILLOGICAL IN THE EXTREME.
THERE ARE THINGS I AM FORBIDDEN TO COMMUNICATE,
SO I CANNOT TELL YOU EVERYTHING, NO MATTER HOW HARD I TRY.
BUT I WILL TELL YOU EVERYTHING I AM ABLE TO, AND I HOPE YOU WILL LISTEN.

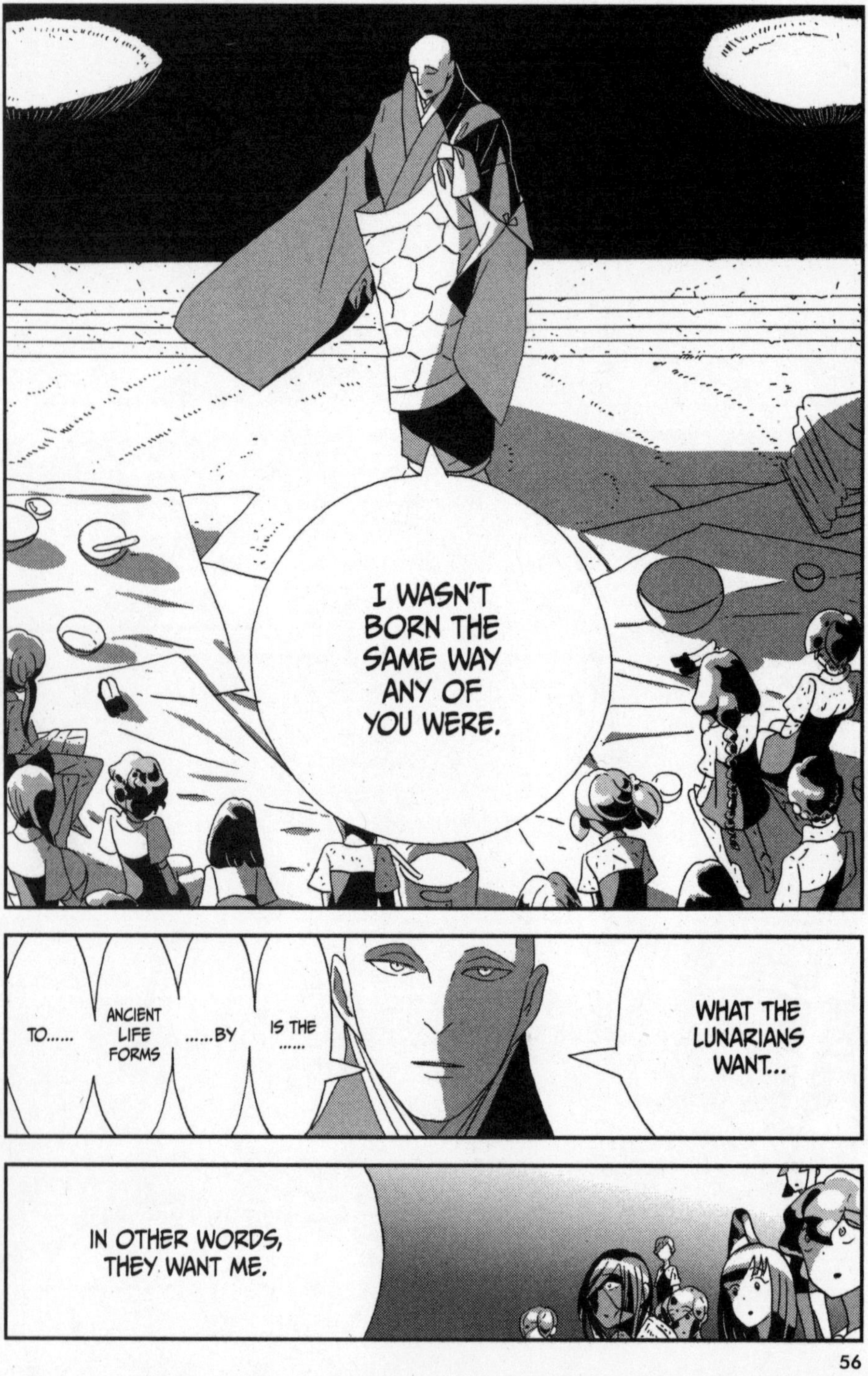
I WASN'T BORN THE SAME WAY ANY OF YOU WERE.
WHAT THE LUNARIANS WANT...
IS THE ......
......BY
ANCIENT LIFE FORMS
TO......
IN OTHER WORDS, THEY WANT ME.

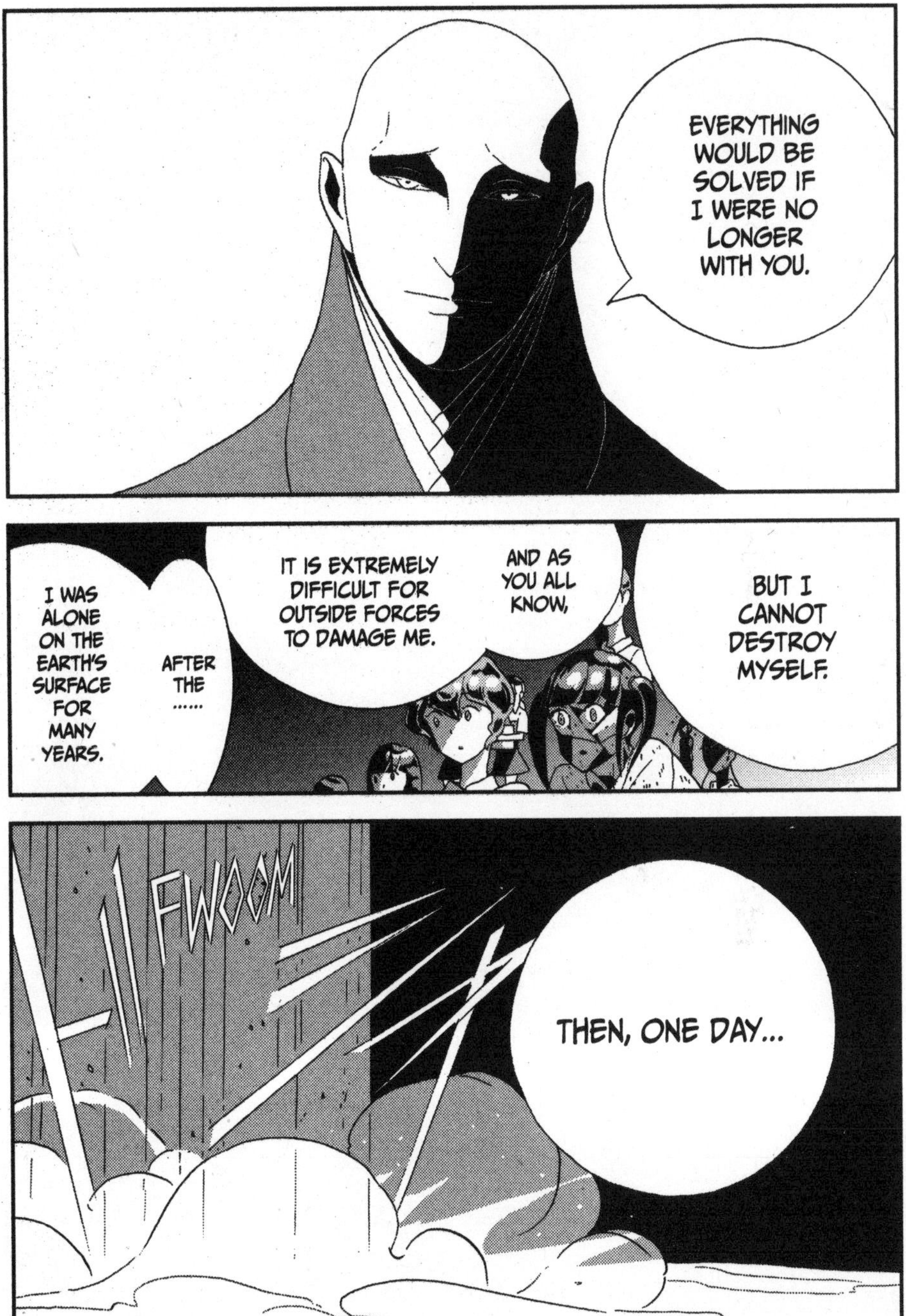
EVERYTHING WOULD BE SOLVED IF I WERE NO LONGER WITH YOU.
BUT I CANNOT DESTROY MYSELF.
AND AS YOU ALL KNOW,
IT IS EXTREMELY DIFFICULT FOR OUTSIDE FORCES TO DAMAGE ME.
AFTER THE ......
I WAS ALONE ON THE EARTH'S SURFACE FOR MANY YEARS.
THEN, ONE DAY...
FWOOM

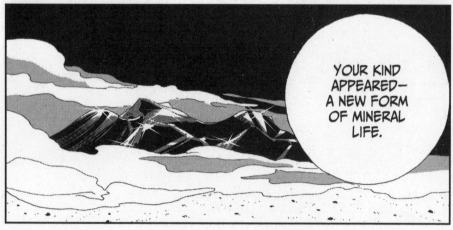

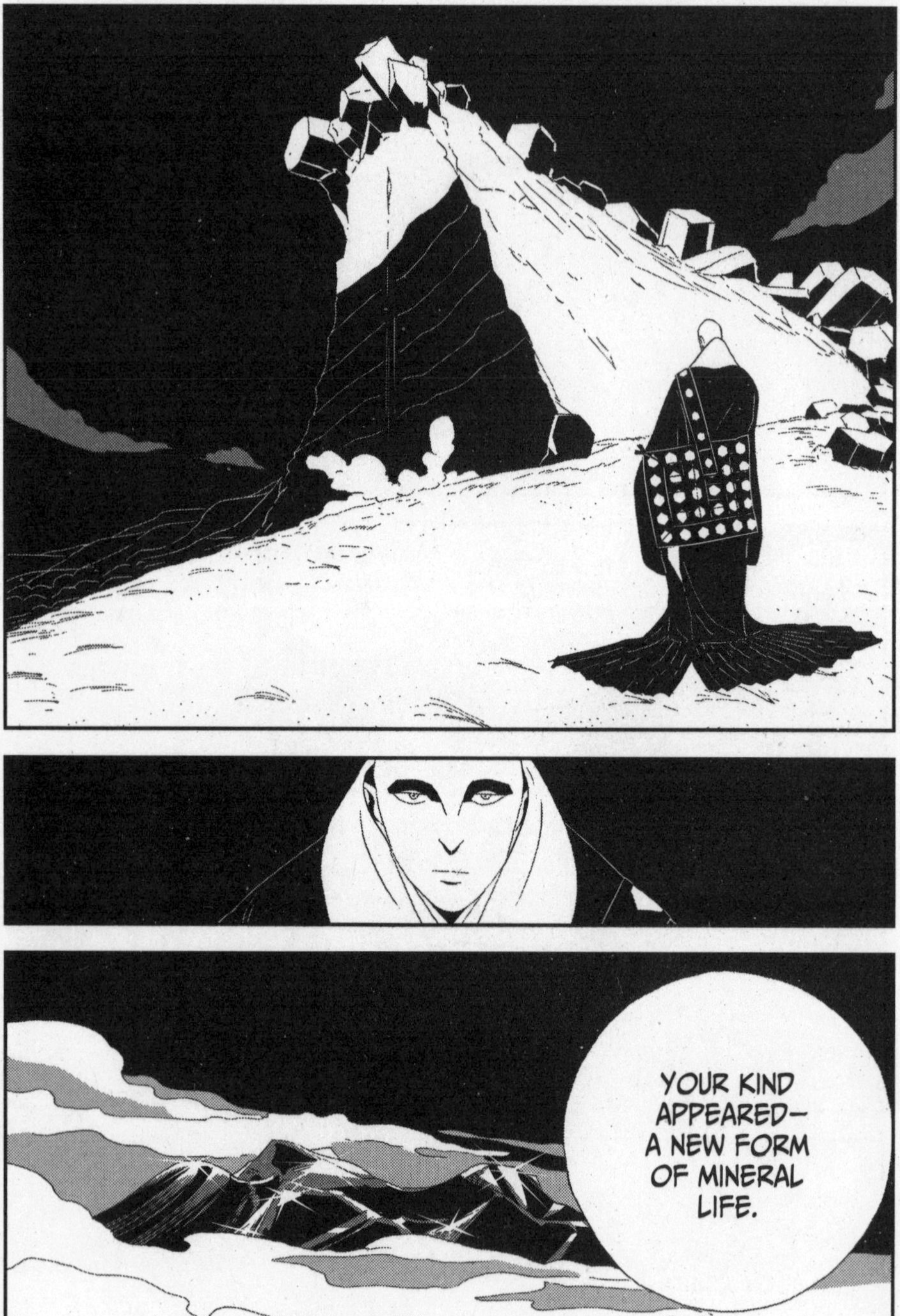
YOUR KIND APPEARED— A NEW FORM OF MINERAL LIFE.

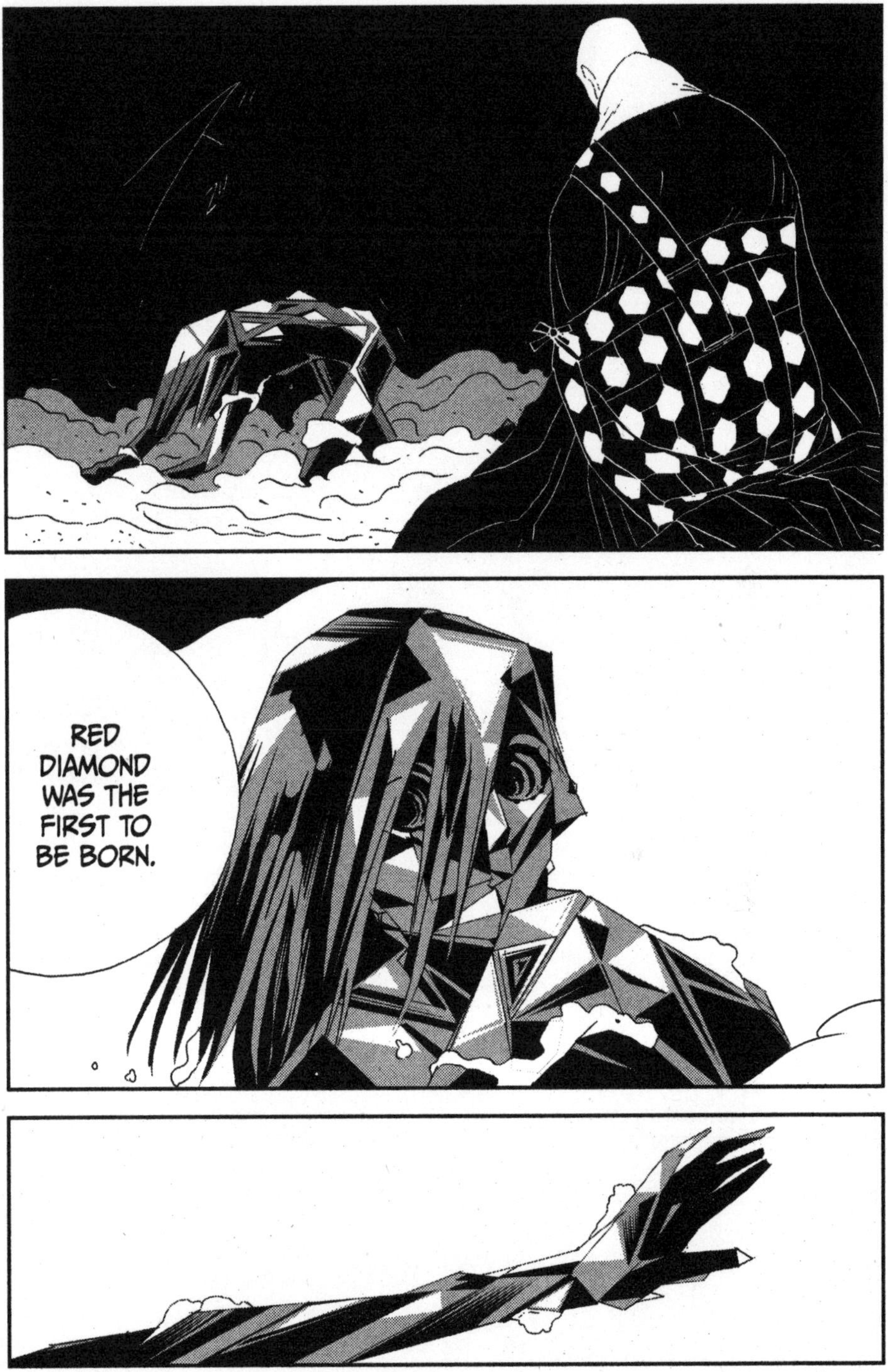
RED DIAMOND WAS THE FIRST TO BE BORN.

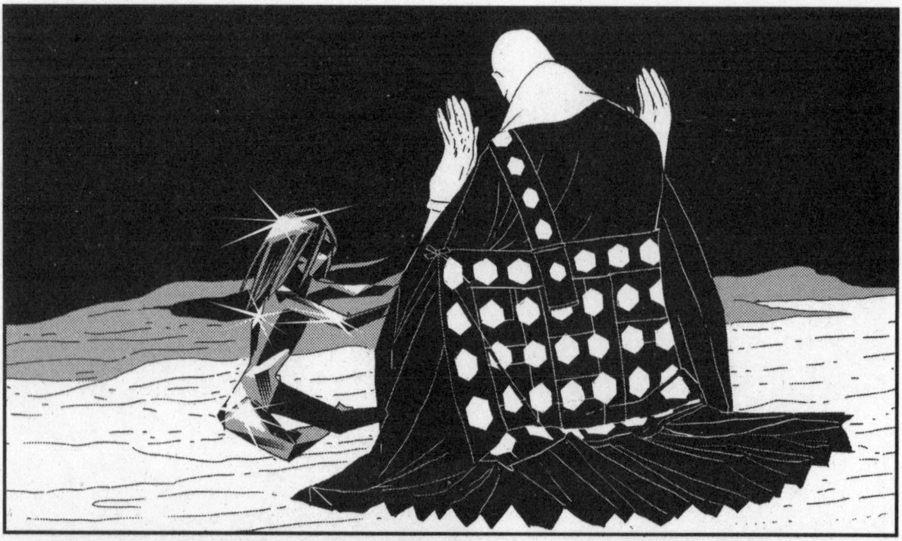

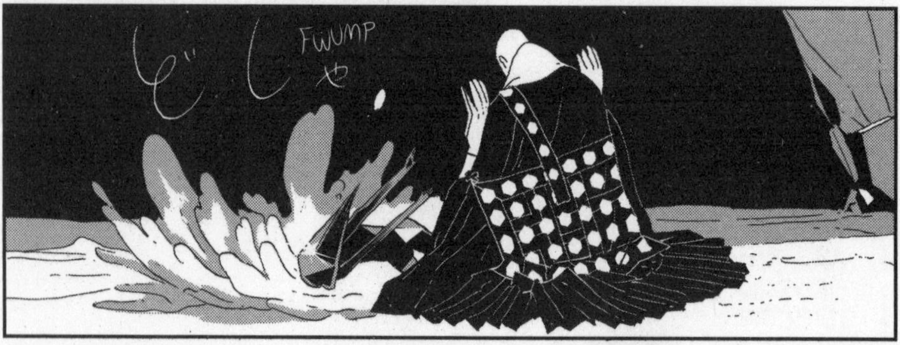
FWUMP

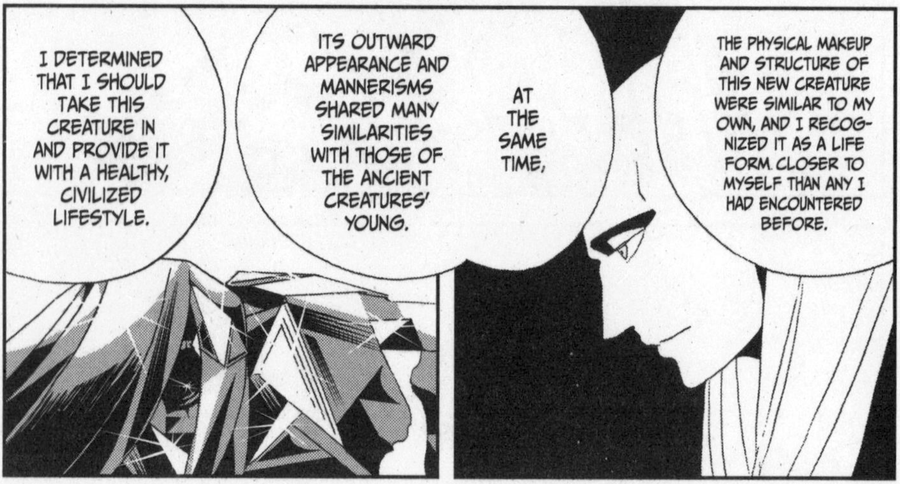
THE PHYSICAL MAKEUP AND STRUCTURE OF THIS NEW CREATURE WERE SIMILAR TO MY OWN, AND I RECOGNIZED IT AS A LIFE FORM CLOSER TO MYSELF THAN ANY I HAD ENCOUNTERED BEFORE.
AT THE SAME TIME,
ITS OUTWARD APPEARANCE AND MANNERISMS SHARED MANY SIMILARITIES WITH THOSE OF THE ANCIENT CREATURES' YOUNG.
I DETERMINED THAT I SHOULD TAKE THIS CREATURE IN AND PROVIDE IT WITH A HEALTHY, CIVILIZED LIFESTYLE.

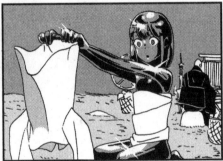

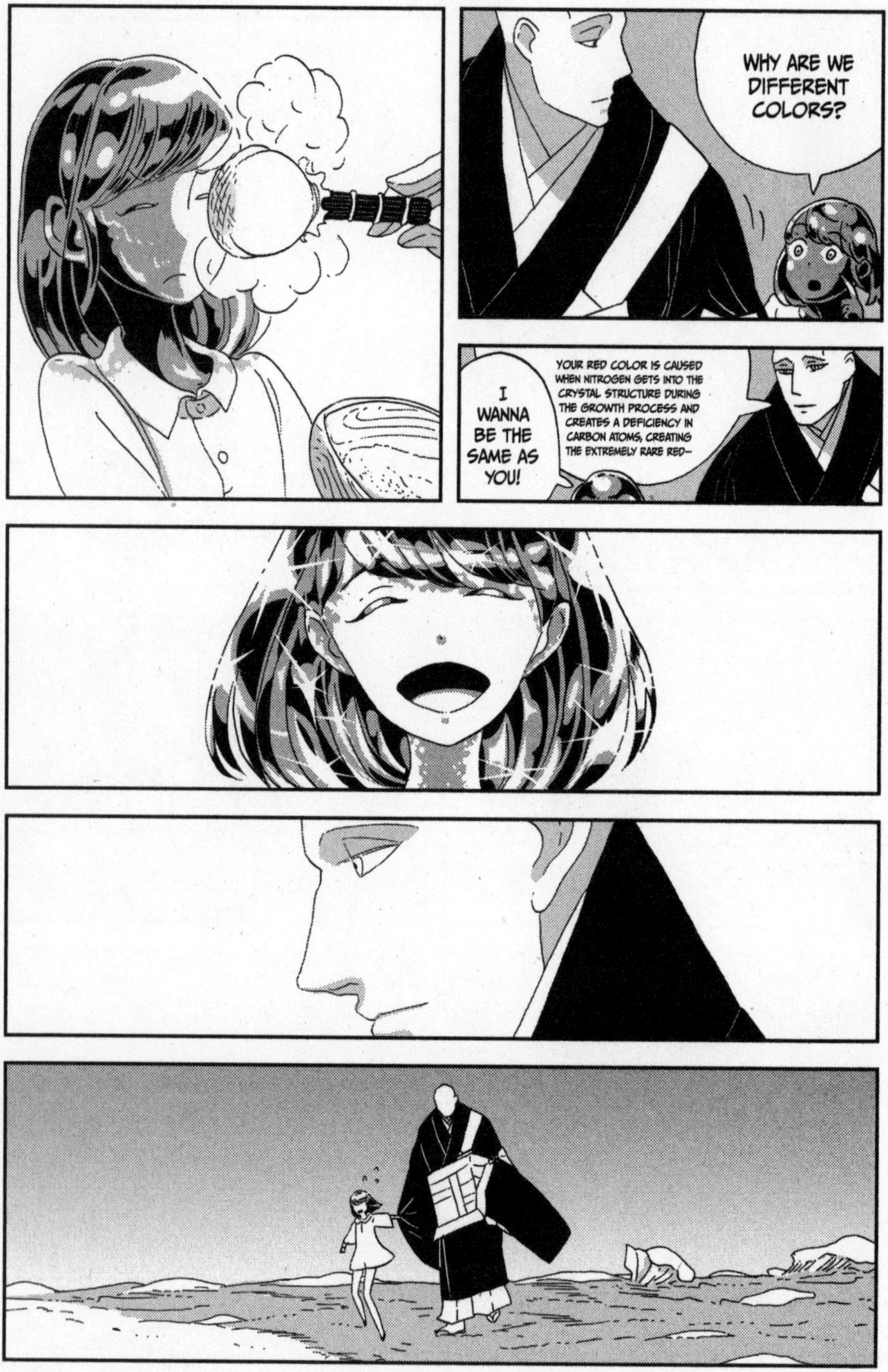
WHY ARE WE DIFFERENT COLORS?
YOUR RED COLOR IS CAUSED WHEN NITROGEN GETS INTO THE CRYSTAL STRUCTURE DURING THE GROWTH PROCESS AND CREATES A DEFICIENCY IN CARBON ATOMS, CREATING THE EXTREMELY RARE RED—
I WANNA BE THE SAME AS YOU!

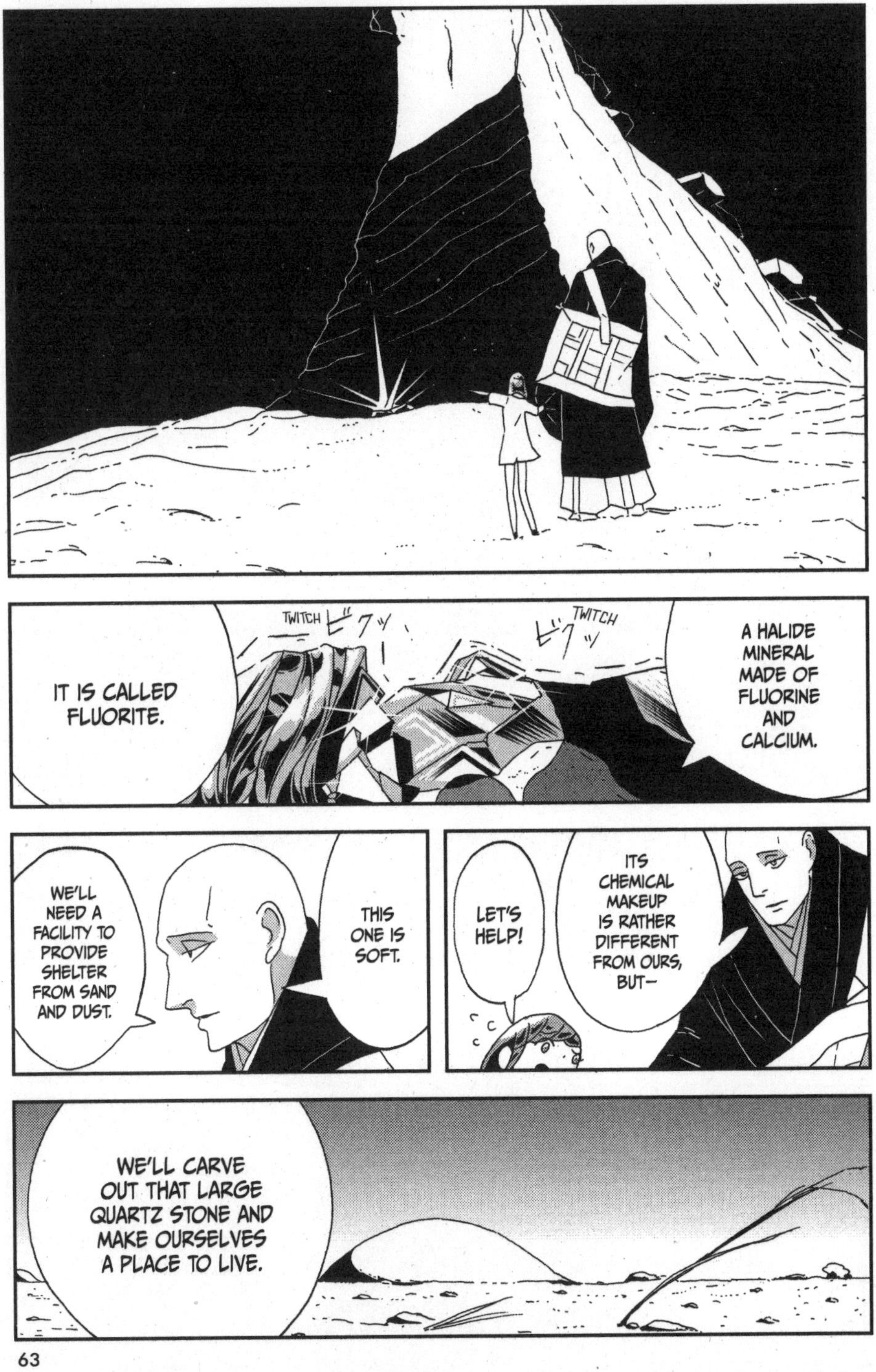
A HALIDE MINERAL MADE OF FLUORINE AND CALCIUM.
TWITCH ビクッ
TWITCH ビクッ
IT IS CALLED FLUORITE.
ITS CHEMICAL MAKEUP IS RATHER DIFFERENT FROM OURS, BUT—
LET'S HELP!
THIS ONE IS SOFT.
WE'LL NEED A FACILITY TO PROVIDE SHELTER FROM SAND AND DUST.
WE'LL CARVE OUT THAT LARGE QUARTZ STONE AND MAKE OURSELVES A PLACE TO LIVE.

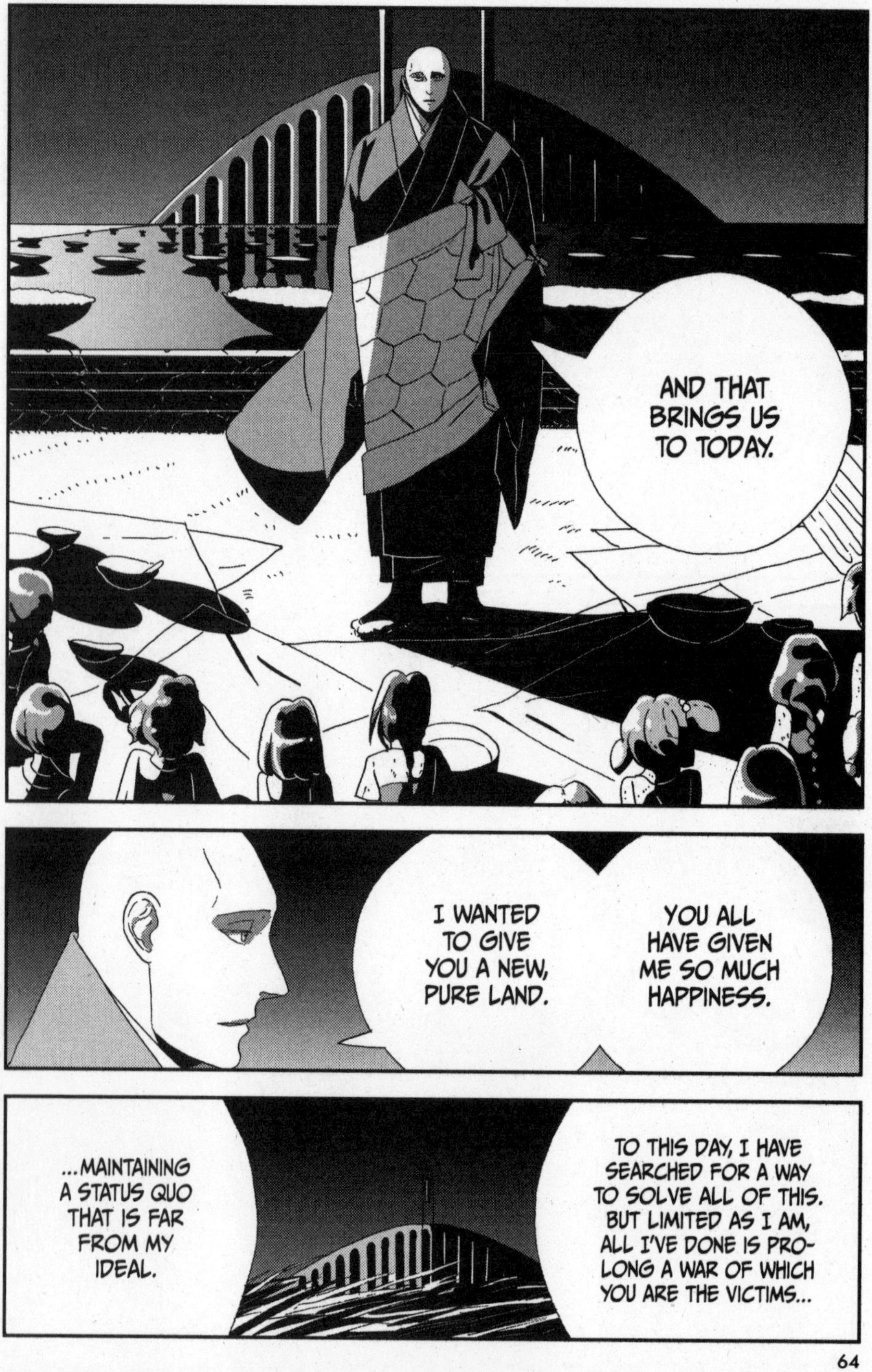
AND THAT BRINGS US TO TODAY.
YOU ALL HAVE GIVEN ME SO MUCH HAPPINESS.
I WANTED TO GIVE YOU A NEW, PURE LAND.
TO THIS DAY, I HAVE SEARCHED FOR A WAY TO SOLVE ALL OF THIS. BUT LIMITED AS I AM, ALL I'VE DONE IS PRO-LONG A WAR OF WHICH YOU ARE THE VICTIMS...
...MAINTAINING A STATUS QUO THAT IS FAR FROM MY IDEAL.

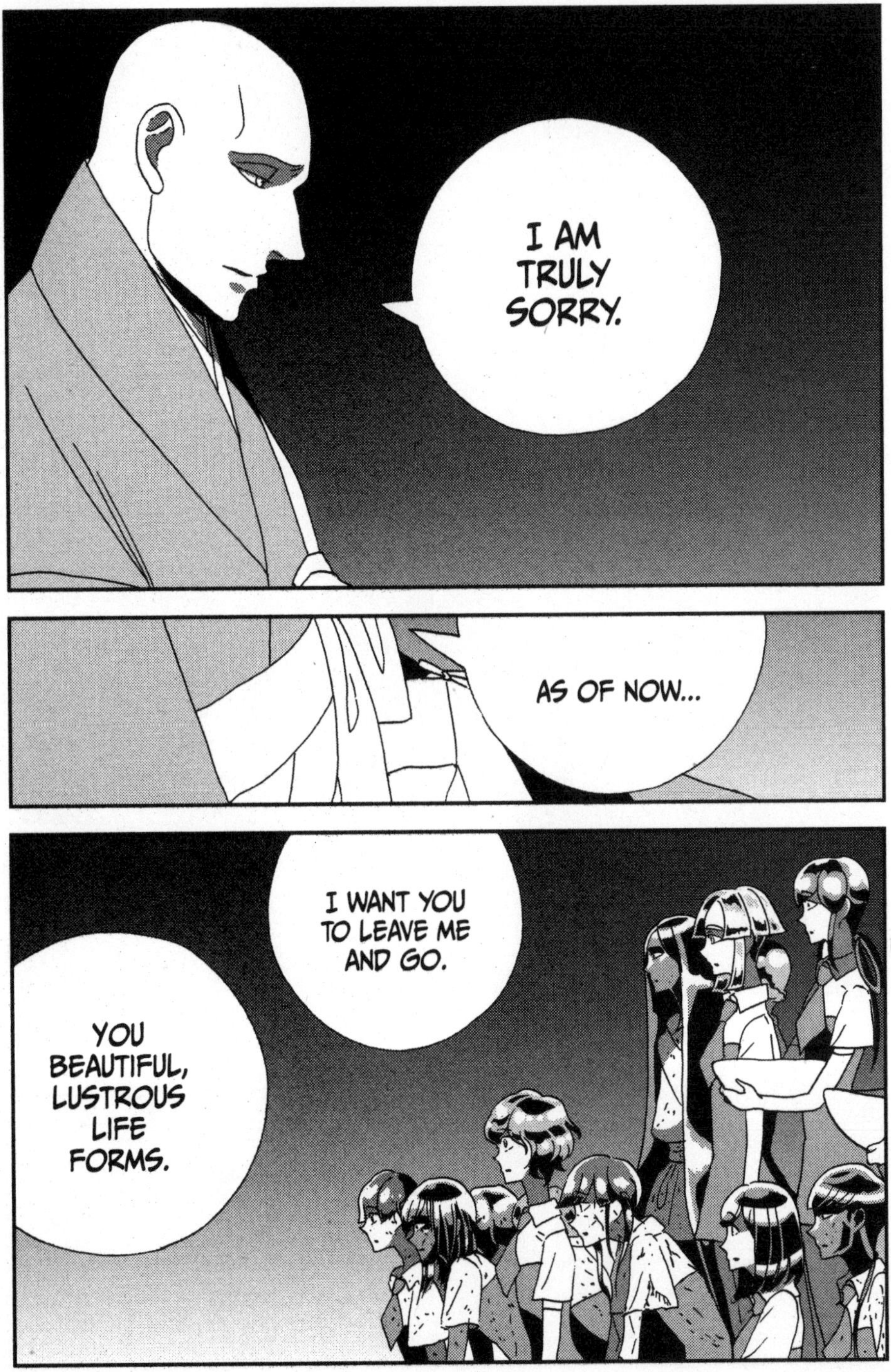
I AM TRULY SORRY.
AS OF NOW...
I WANT YOU TO LEAVE ME AND GO.
YOU BEAUTIFUL, LUSTROUS LIFE FORMS.

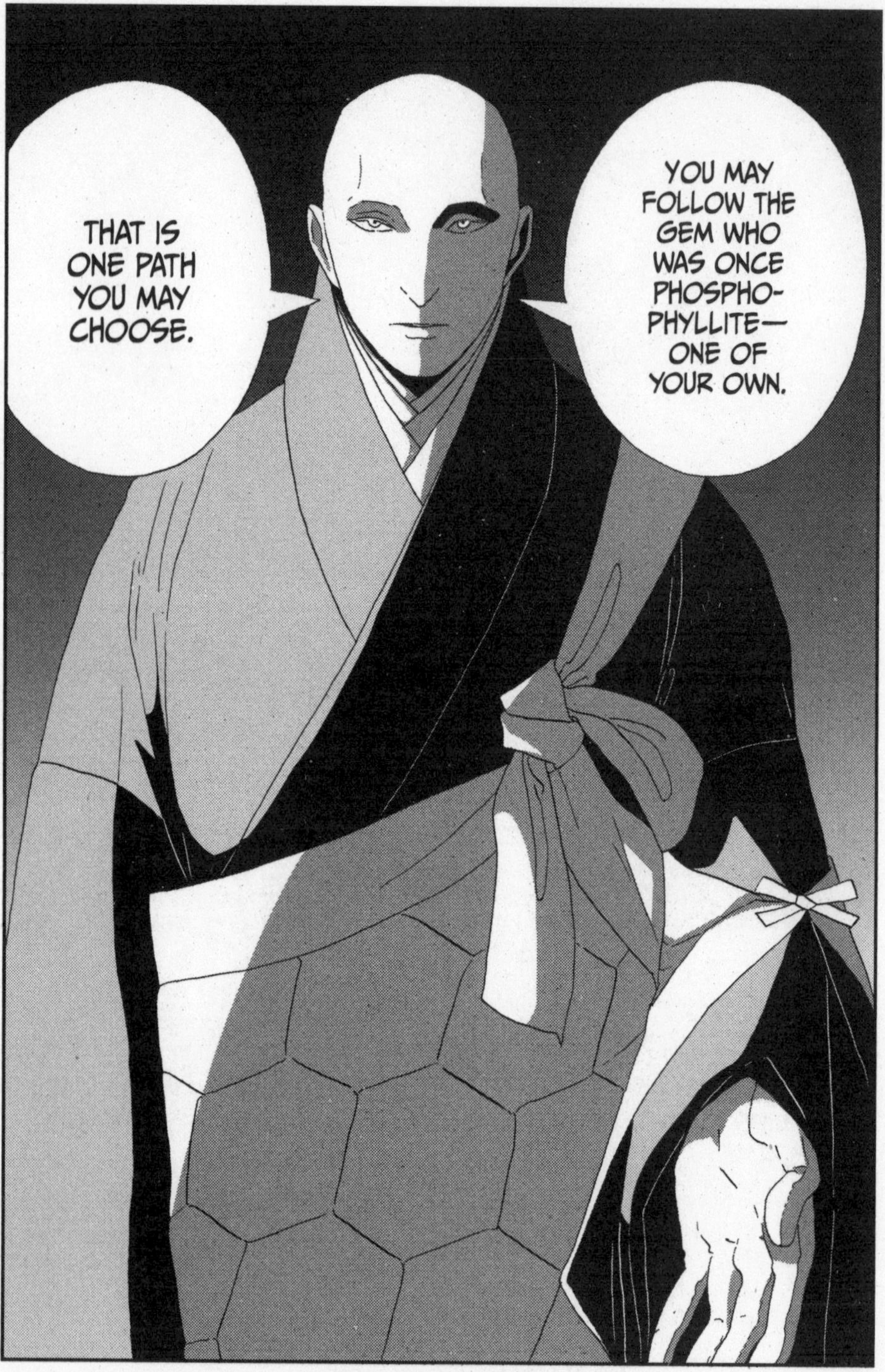
YOU MAY FOLLOW THE GEM WHO WAS ONCE PHOSPHO-PHYLLITE—ONE OF YOUR OWN.
THAT IS ONE PATH YOU MAY CHOOSE.

CHAPTER 64: One Day END

CHAPTER 65:

Today

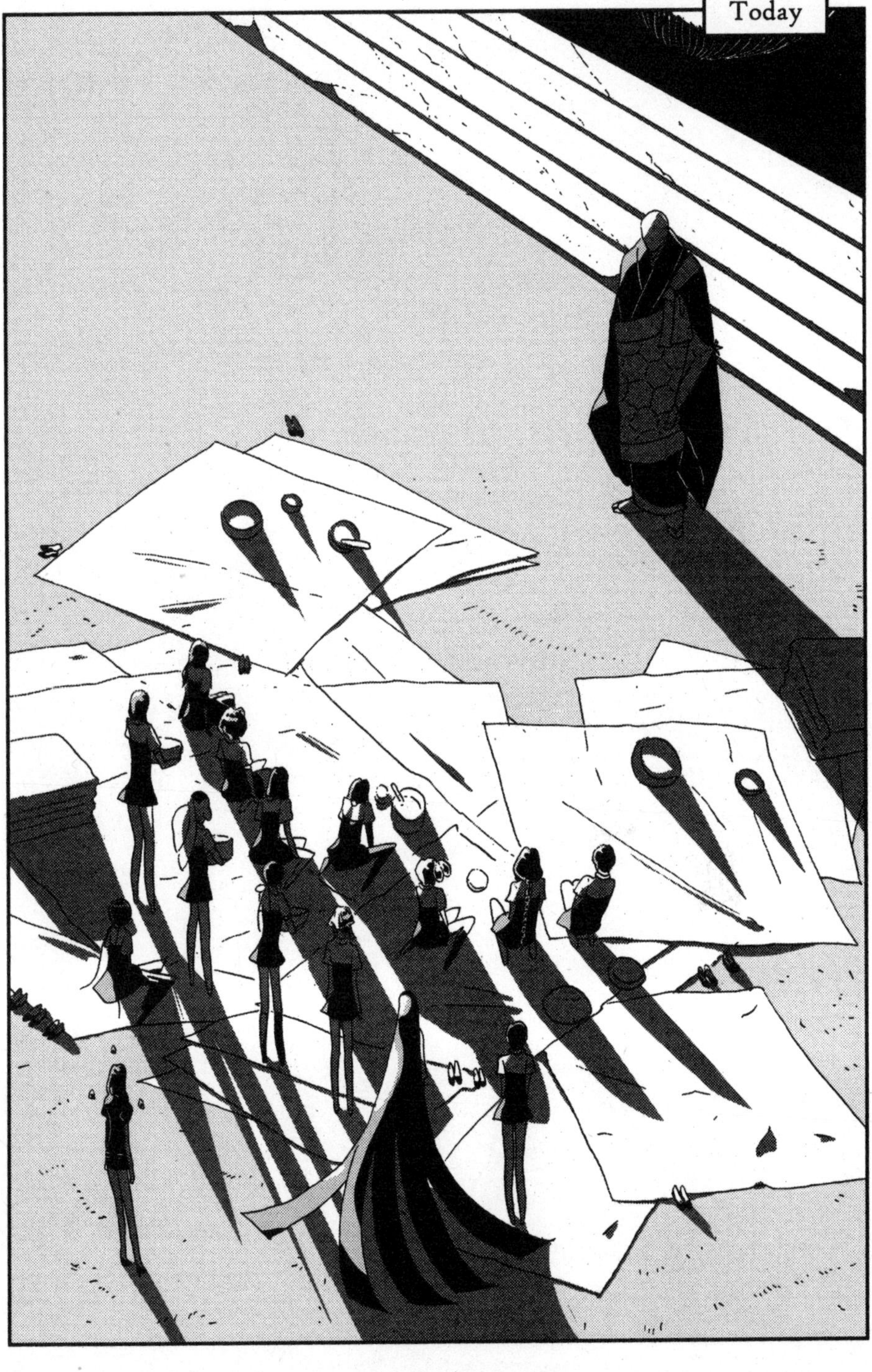

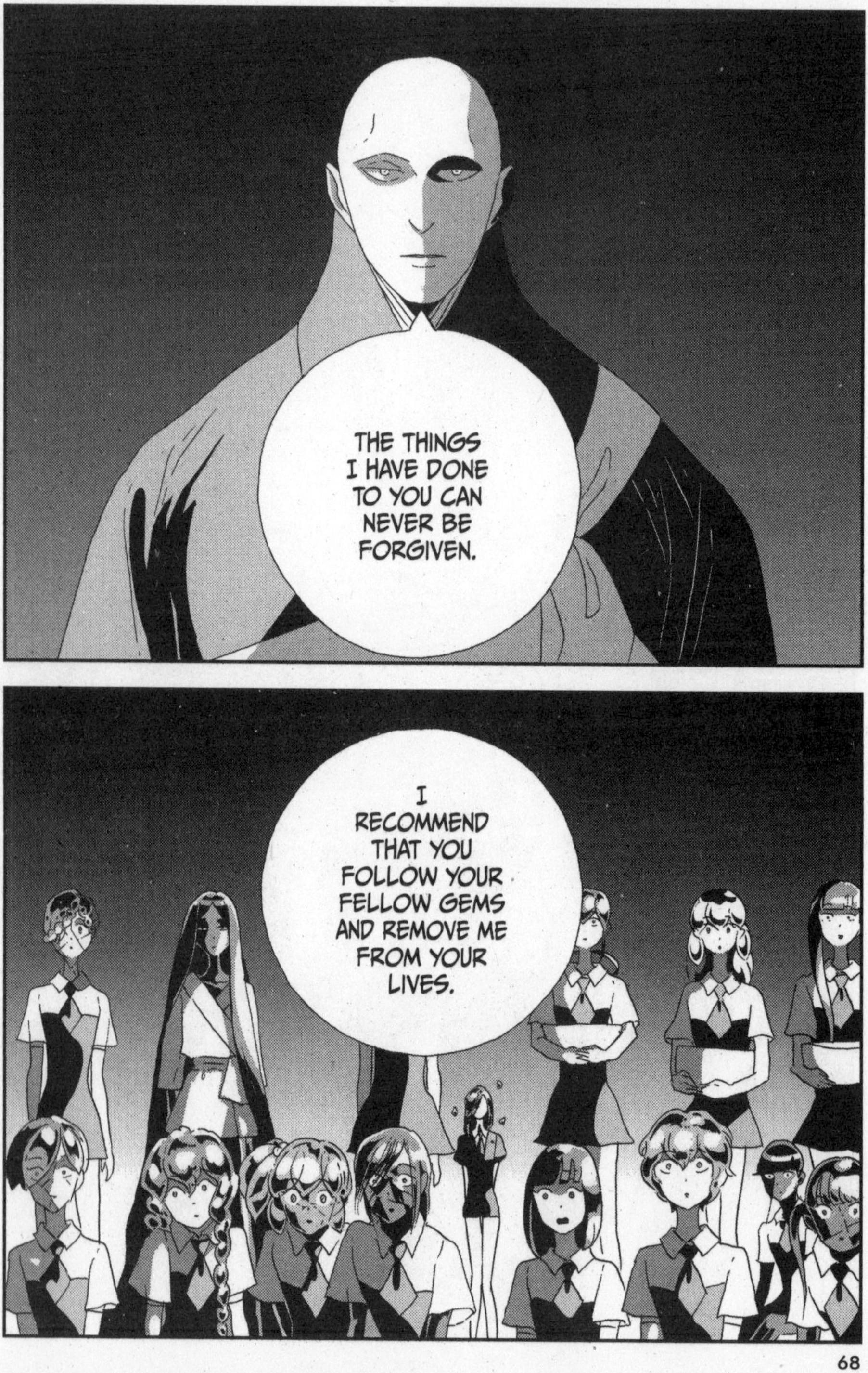
THE THINGS I HAVE DONE TO YOU CAN NEVER BE FORGIVEN.
I RECOMMEND THAT YOU FOLLOW YOUR FELLOW GEMS AND REMOVE ME FROM YOUR LIVES.

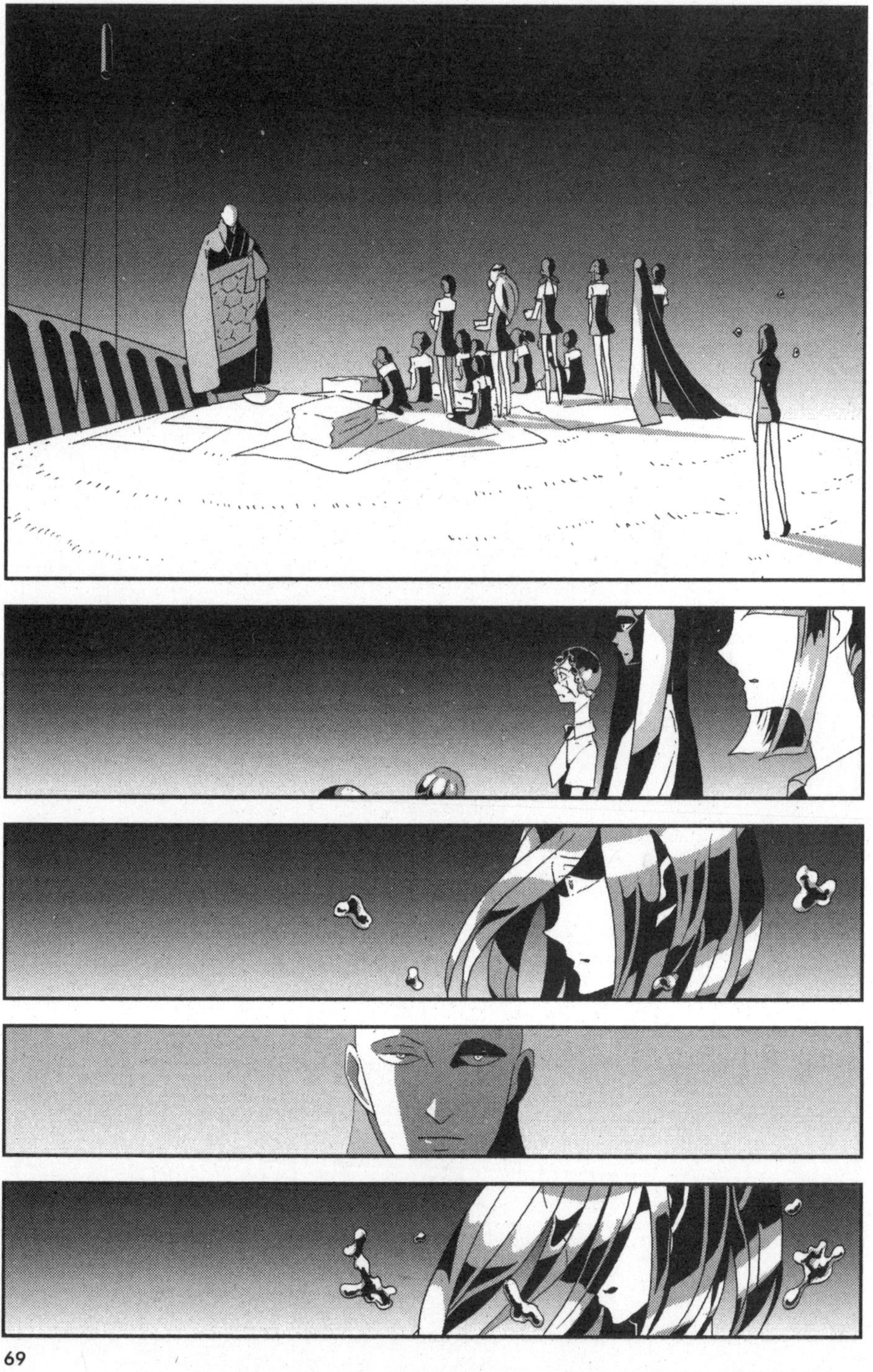

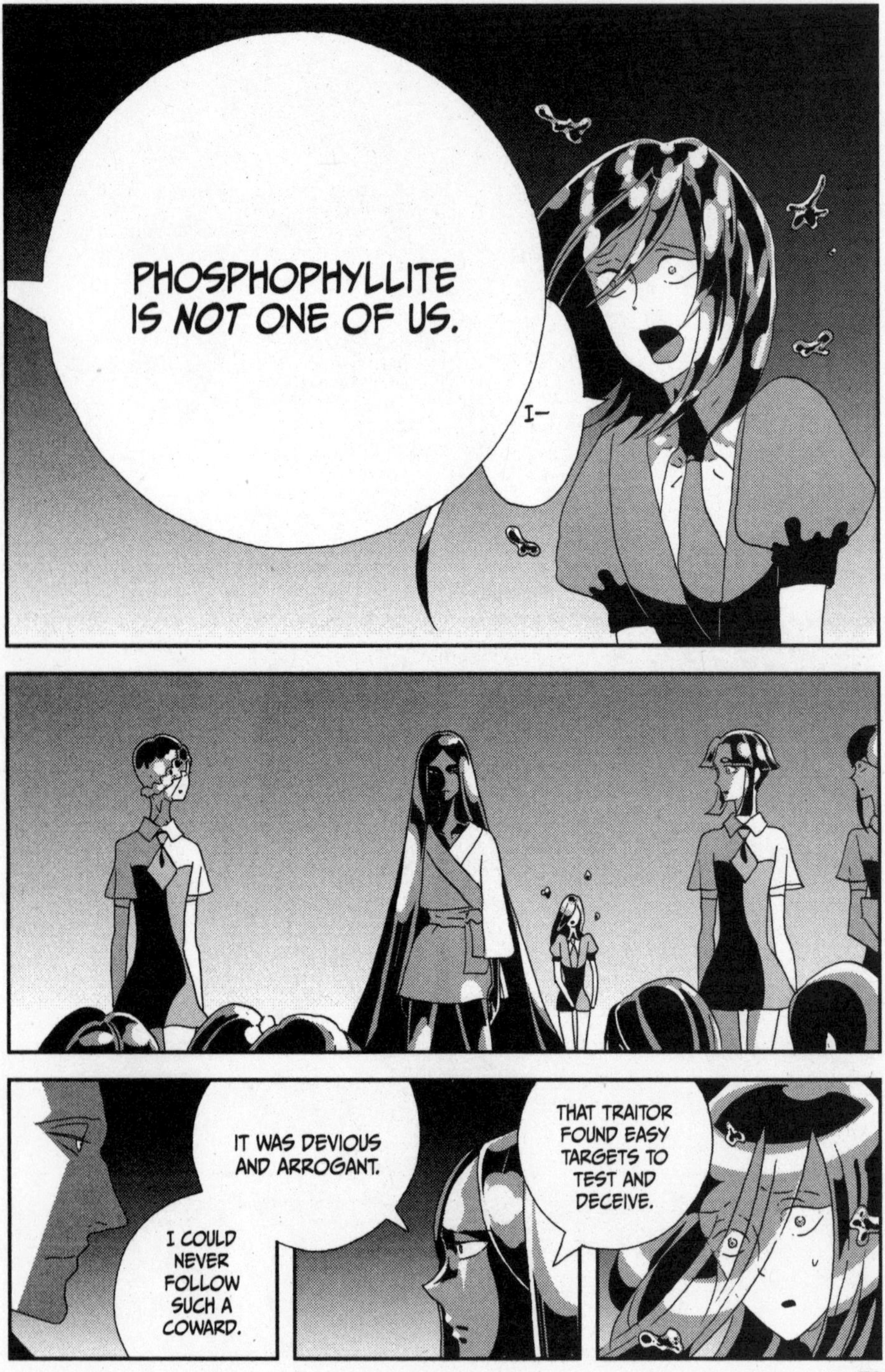
I—
PHOSPHOPHYLLITE IS NOT ONE OF US.
THAT TRAITOR FOUND EASY TARGETS TO TEST AND DECEIVE.
IT WAS DEVIOUS AND ARROGANT.
I COULD NEVER FOLLOW SUCH A COWARD.

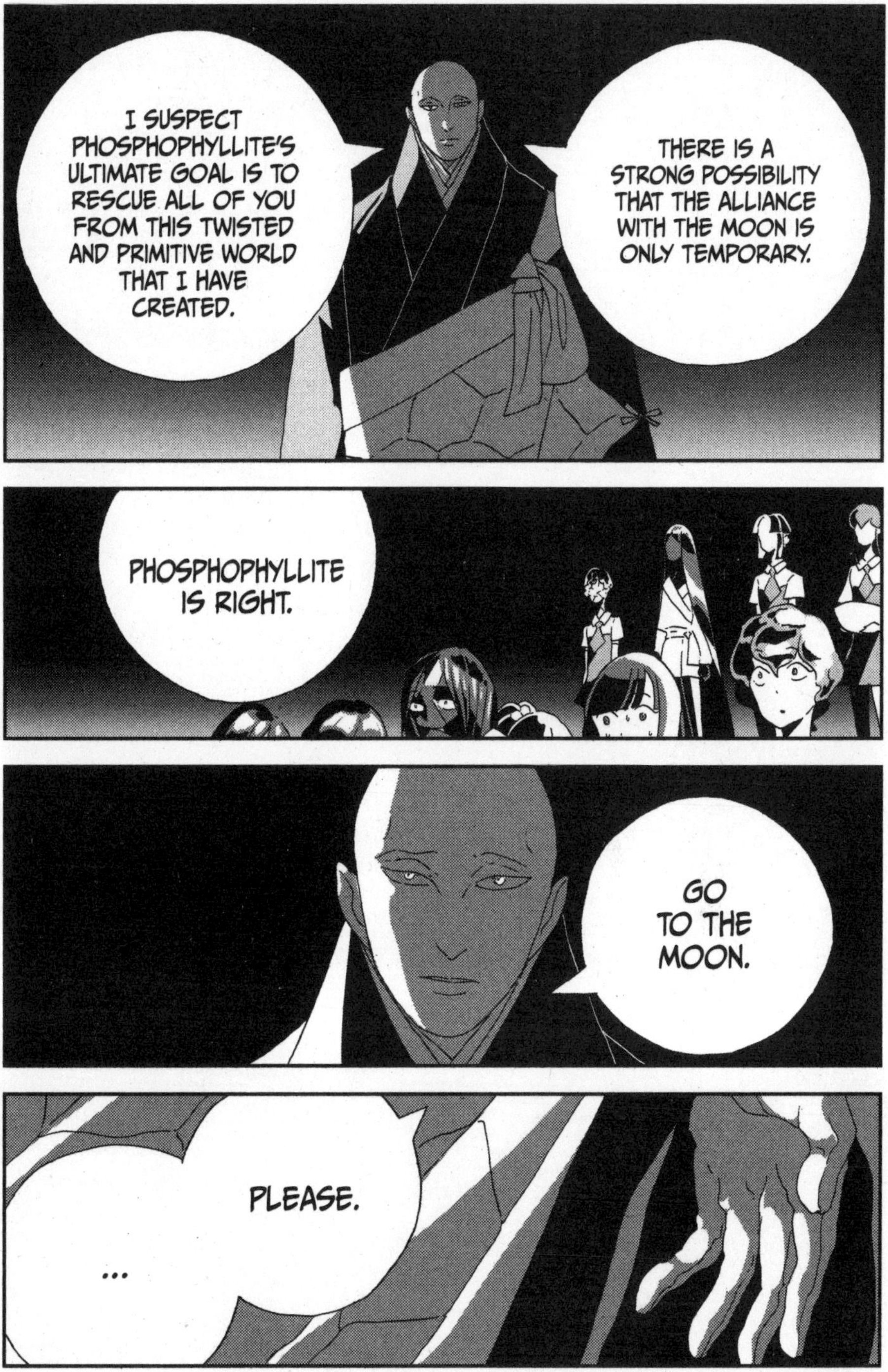
THERE IS A STRONG POSSIBILITY THAT THE ALLIANCE WITH THE MOON IS ONLY TEMPORARY.
I SUSPECT PHOSPHOPHYLLITE'S ULTIMATE GOAL IS TO RESCUE ALL OF YOU FROM THIS TWISTED AND PRIMITIVE WORLD THAT I HAVE CREATED.
PHOSPHOPHYLLITE IS RIGHT.
GO TO THE MOON.
PLEASE.
...

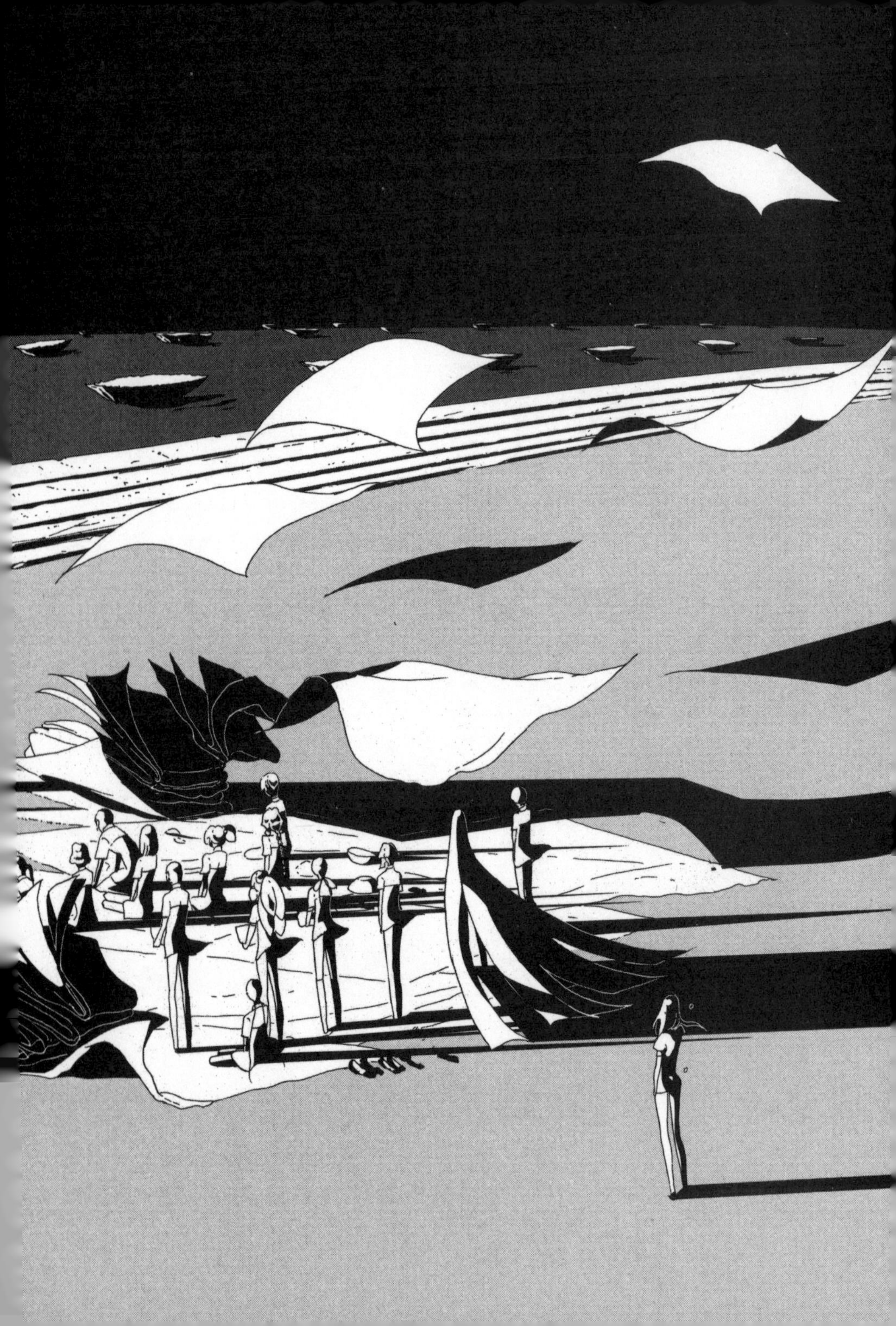

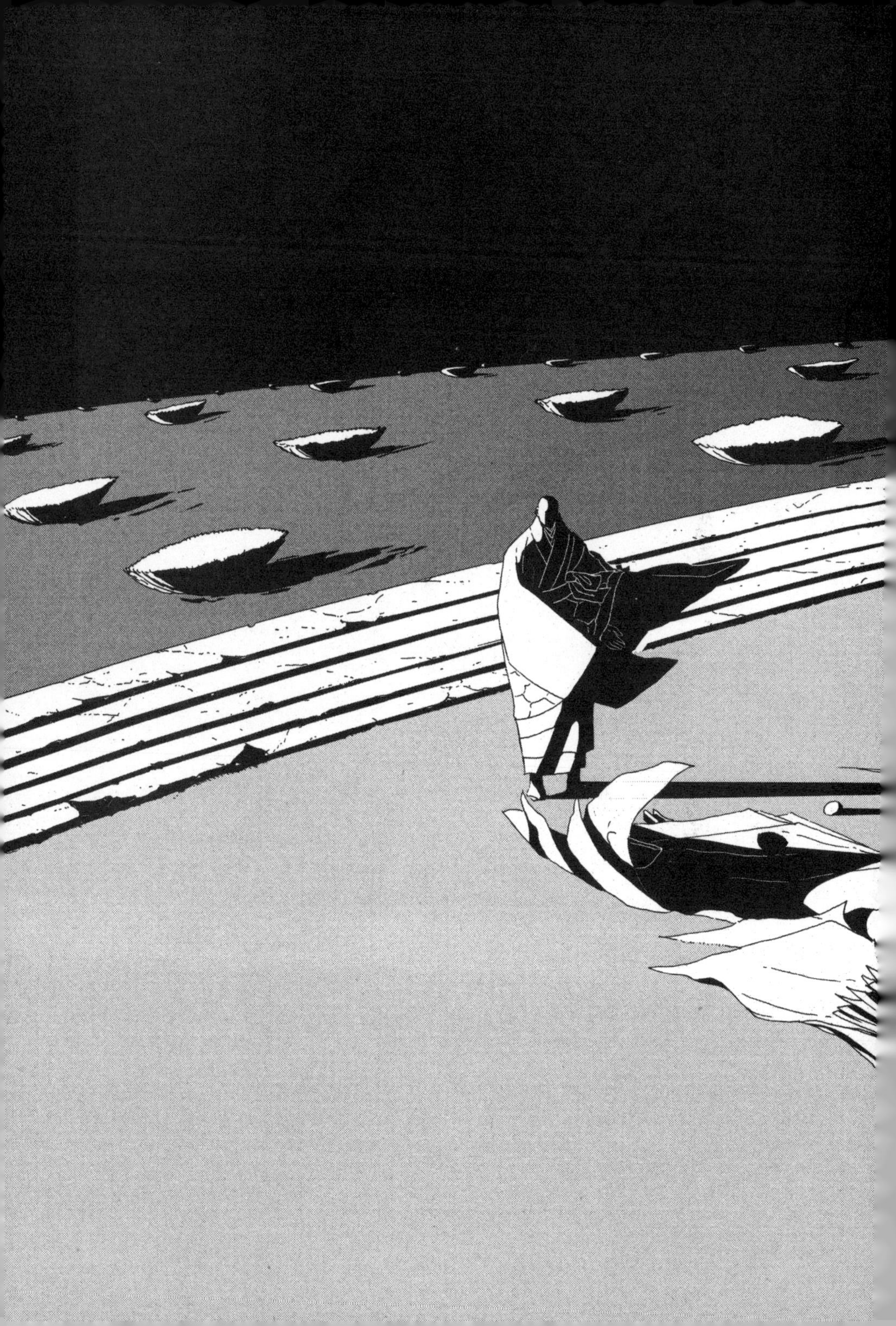

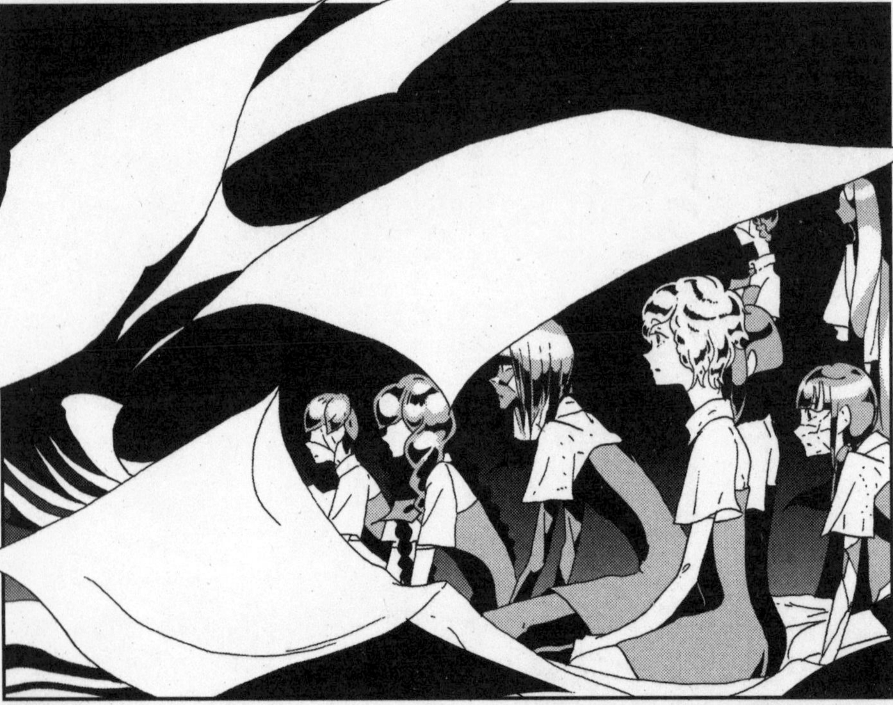
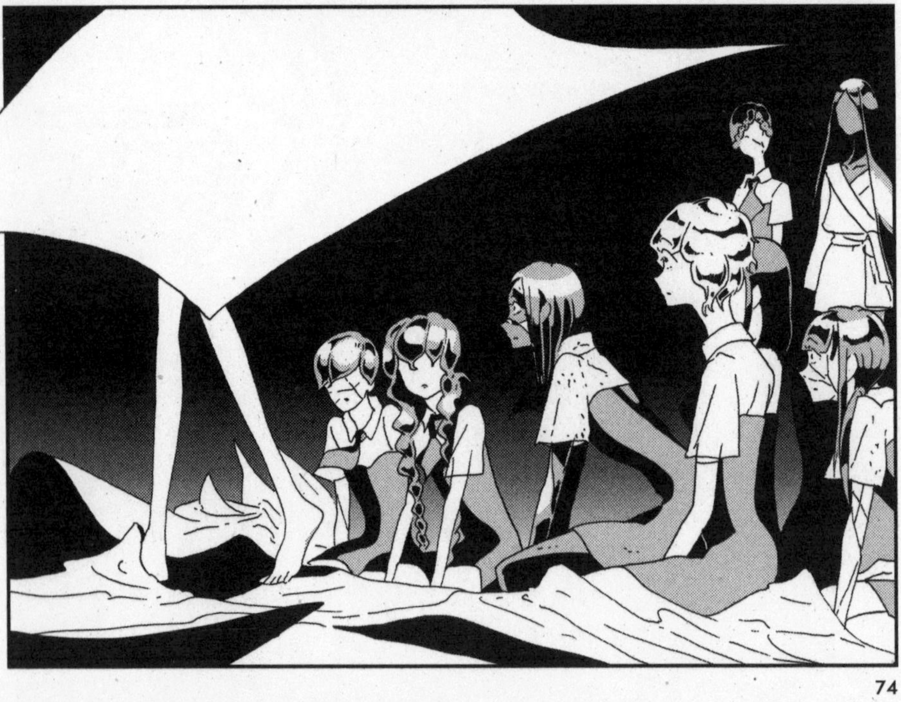

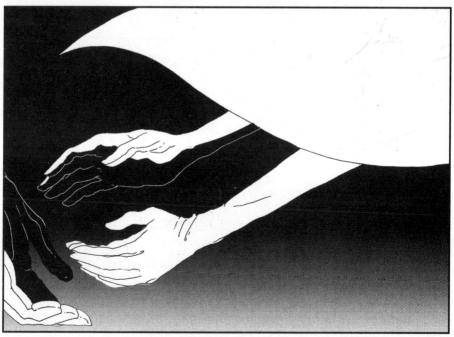

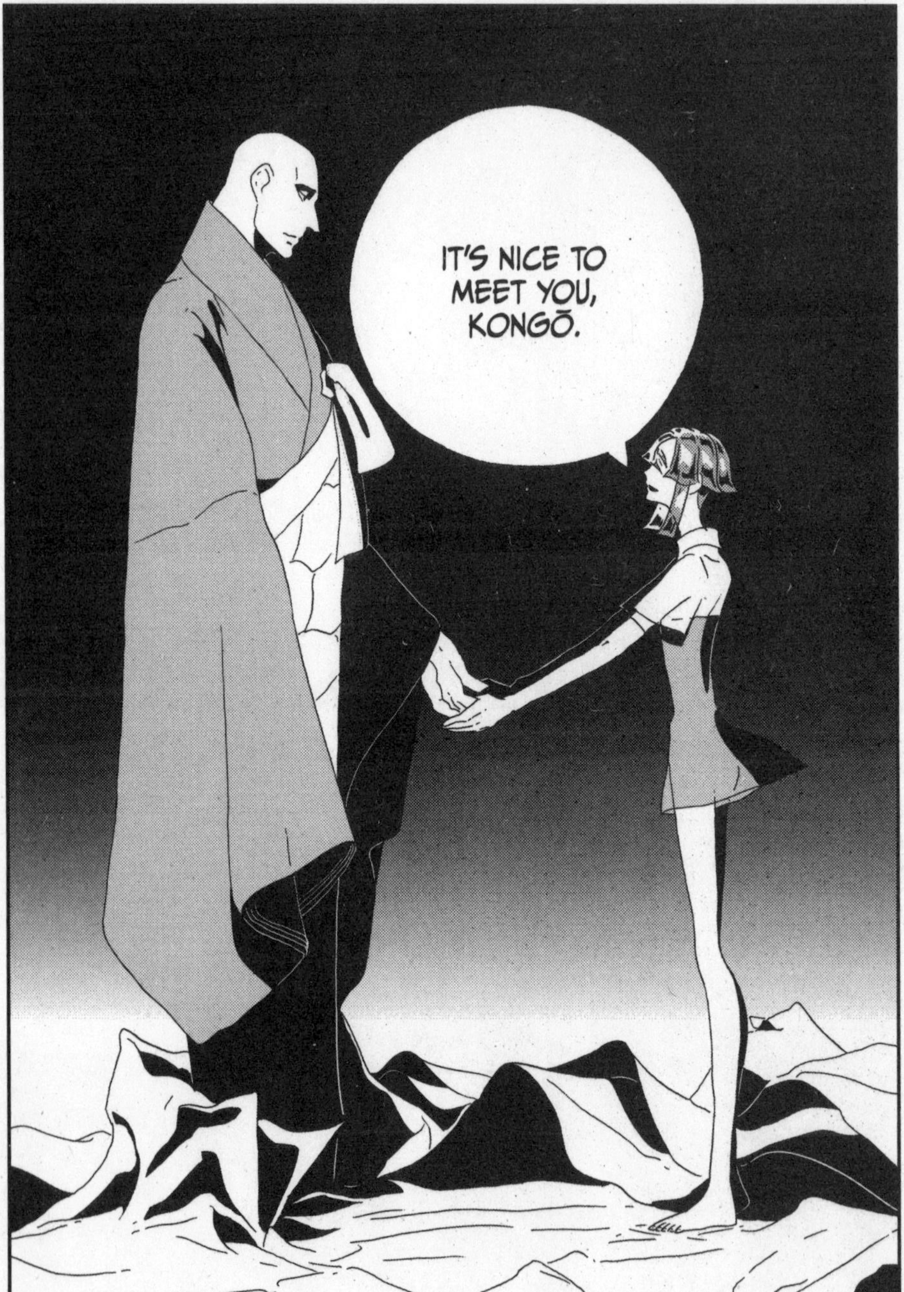
IT'S NICE TO MEET YOU, KONGŌ.

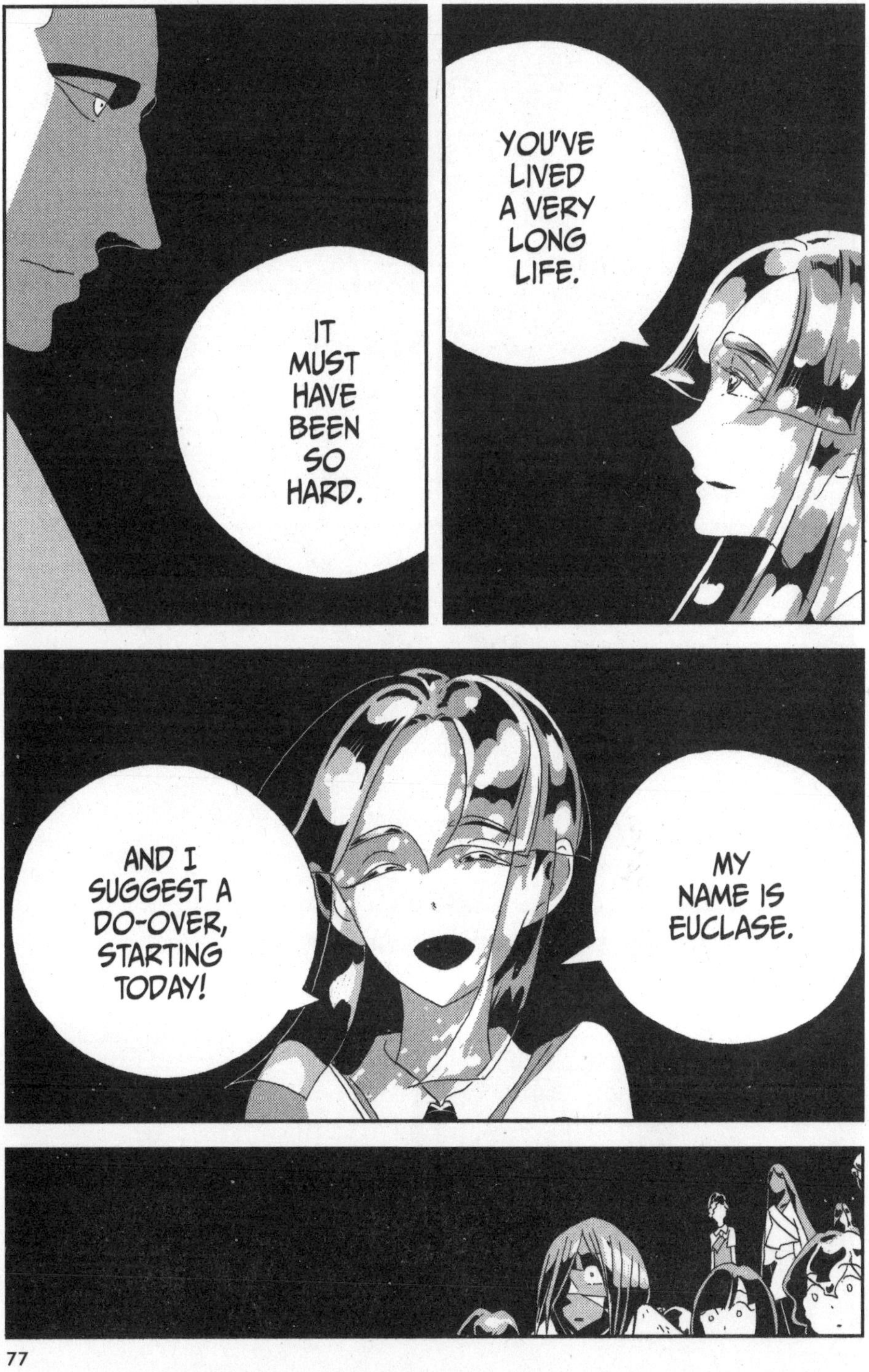
YOU'VE LIVED A VERY LONG LIFE.
IT MUST HAVE BEEN SO HARD.
MY NAME IS EUCLASE.
AND I SUGGEST A DO-OVER, STARTING TODAY!

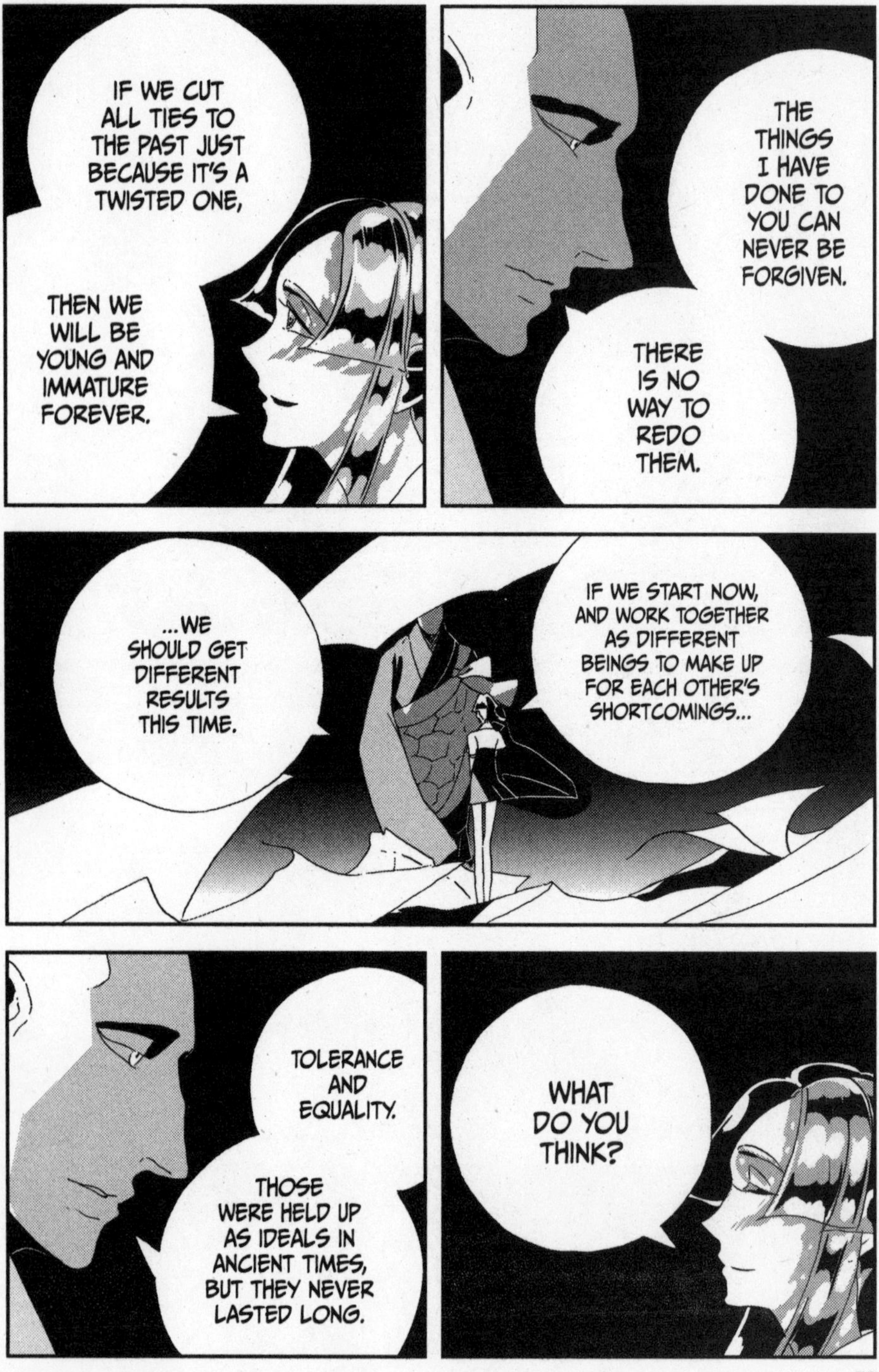
THE THINGS I HAVE DONE TO YOU CAN NEVER BE FORGIVEN.
THERE IS NO WAY TO REDO THEM.
IF WE CUT ALL TIES TO THE PAST JUST BECAUSE IT'S A TWISTED ONE,
THEN WE WILL BE YOUNG AND IMMATURE FOREVER.
IF WE START NOW, AND WORK TOGETHER AS DIFFERENT BEINGS TO MAKE UP FOR EACH OTHER'S SHORTCOMINGS...
...WE SHOULD GET DIFFERENT RESULTS THIS TIME.
WHAT DO YOU THINK?
TOLERANCE AND EQUALITY.
THOSE WERE HELD UP AS IDEALS IN ANCIENT TIMES, BUT THEY NEVER LASTED LONG.

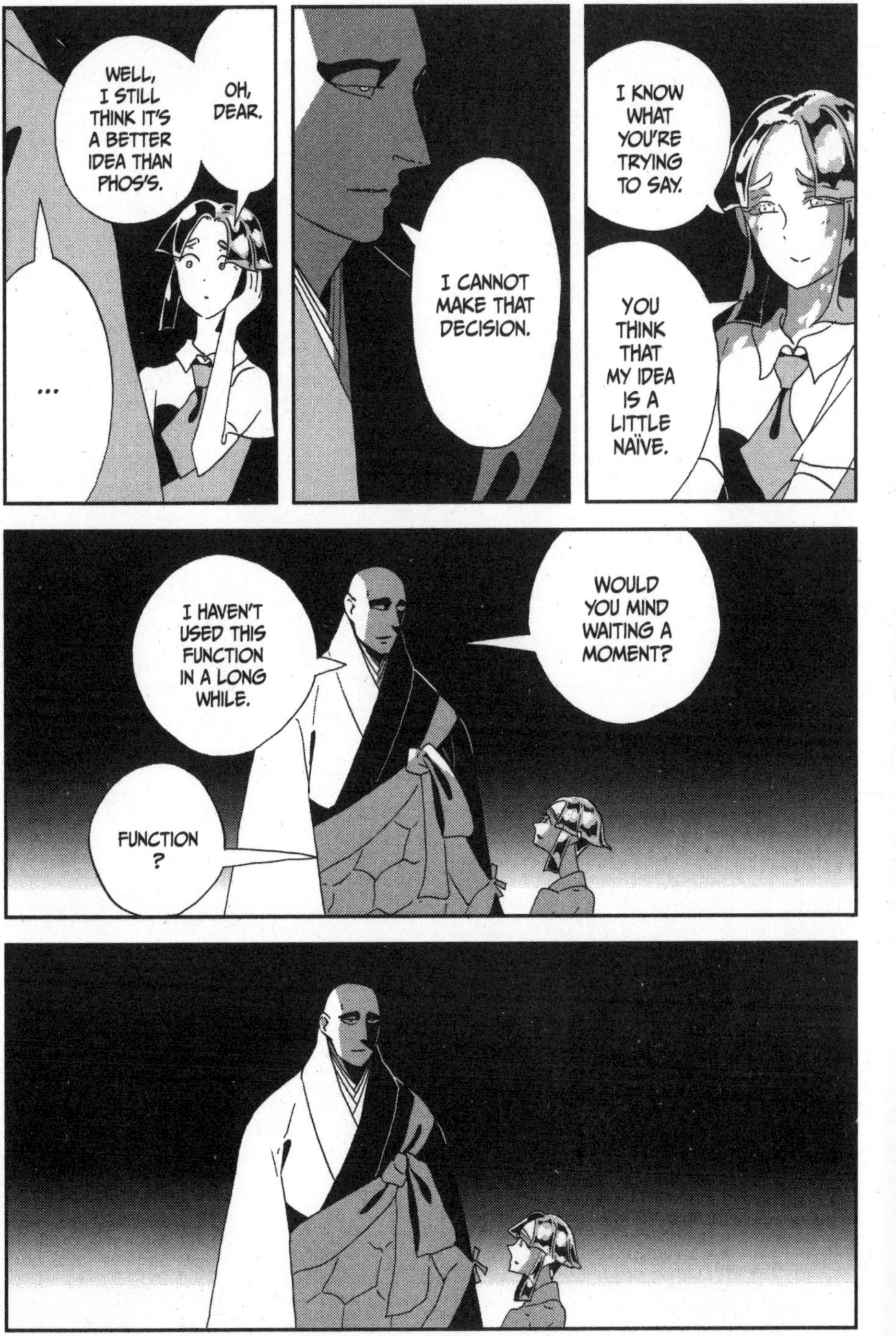
I KNOW WHAT YOU'RE TRYING TO SAY.
YOU THINK THAT MY IDEA IS A LITTLE NAÏVE.
I CANNOT MAKE THAT DECISION.
OH, DEAR.
WELL, I STILL THINK IT'S A BETTER IDEA THAN PHOS'S.
...
WOULD YOU MIND WAITING A MOMENT?
I HAVEN'T USED THIS FUNCTION IN A LONG WHILE.
FUNCTION?

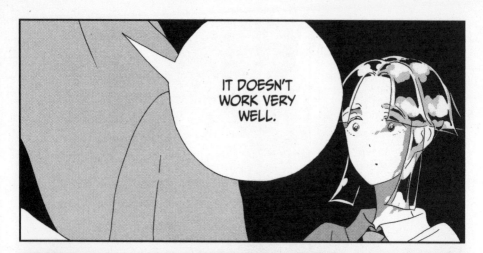

IT DOESN'T WORK VERY WELL.
ASSUMING THAT THE CORRECTNESS OF PHOSPHOPHYLLITE'S ACTIONS IS OUTSIDE OUR PREDICTIVE CAPABILITIES...
...AND CONSIDERING THAT YOUR PROPOSAL IS AN UNPRECEDENTED ONE, BEFITTING FUTURE LIFE FORMS,
THEN, FOR THE TIME BEING...
I'LL ALLOW IT.

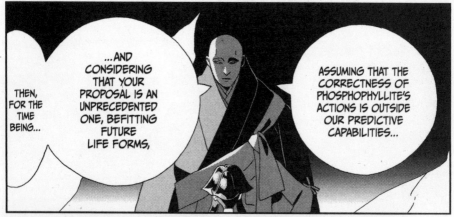

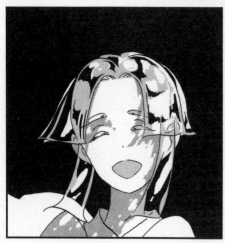

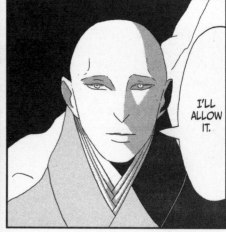

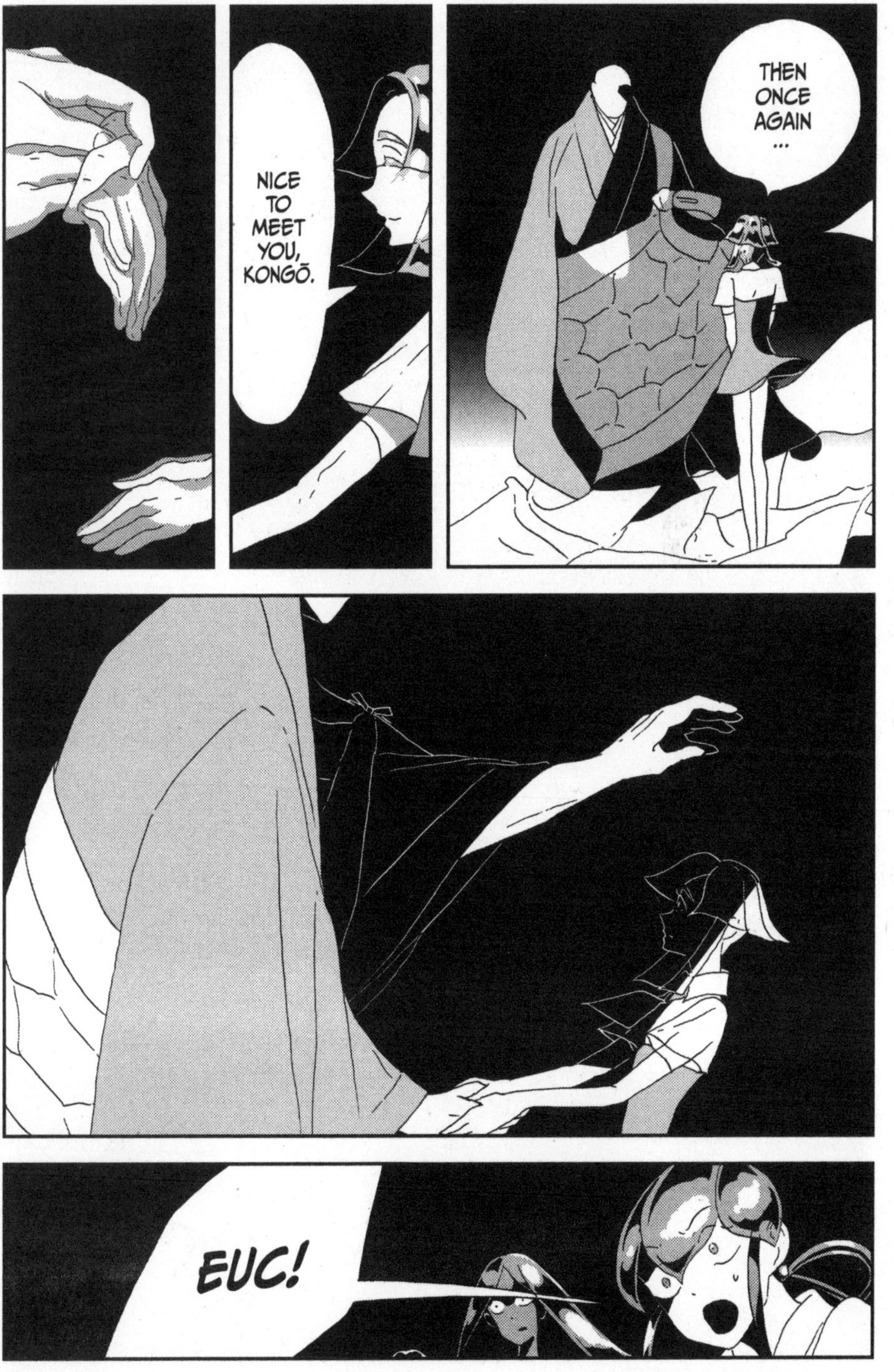
THEN ONCE AGAIN ...
NICE TO MEET YOU, KONGŌ.
EUC!

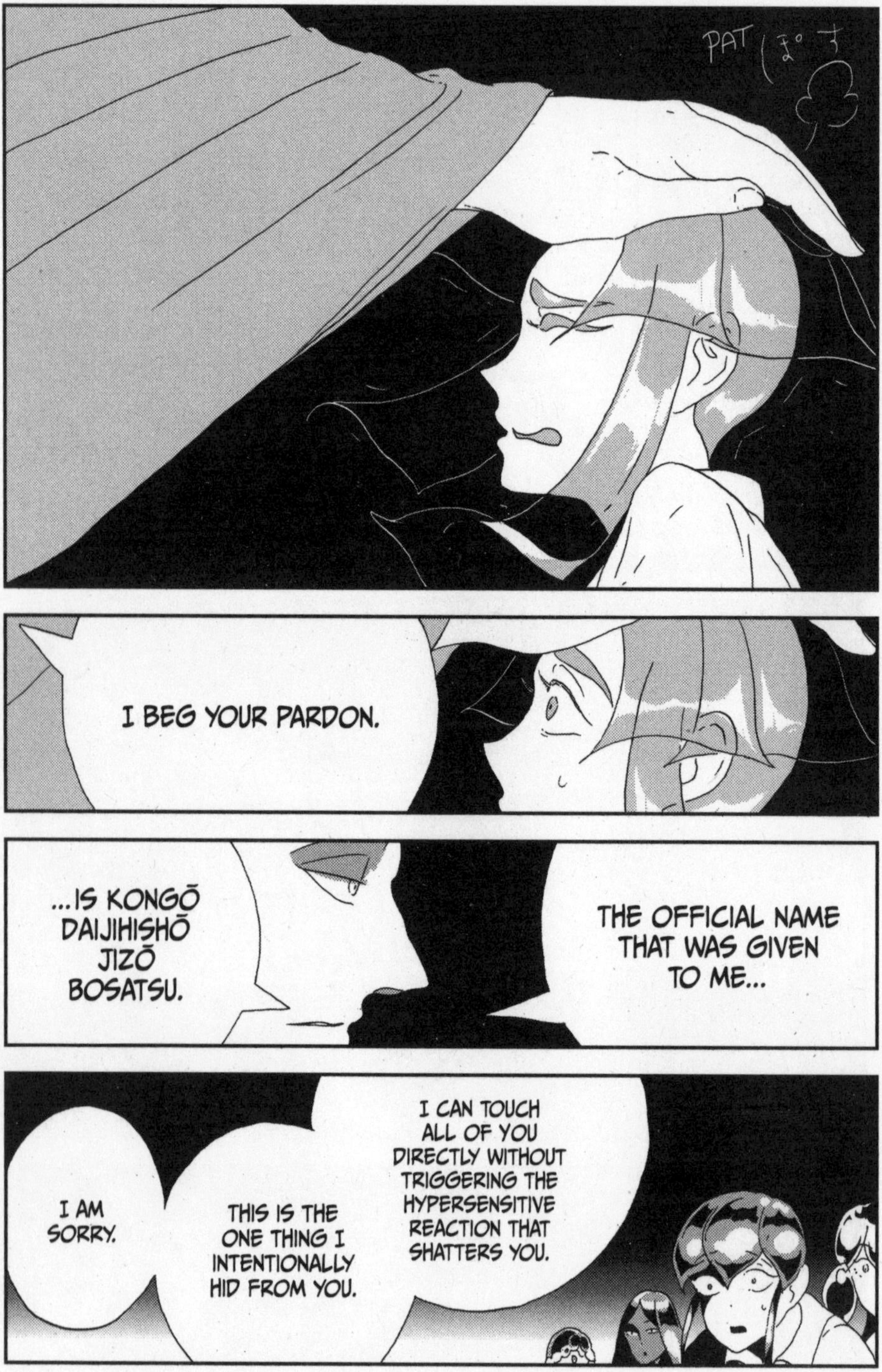
PAT ぽす
I BEG YOUR PARDON.
THE OFFICIAL NAME THAT WAS GIVEN TO ME...
...IS KONGŌ DAIJIHISHŌ JIZŌ BOSATSU.
I CAN TOUCH ALL OF YOU DIRECTLY WITHOUT TRIGGERING THE HYPERSENSITIVE REACTION THAT SHATTERS YOU.
THIS IS THE ONE THING I INTENTIONALLY HID FROM YOU.
I AM SORRY.

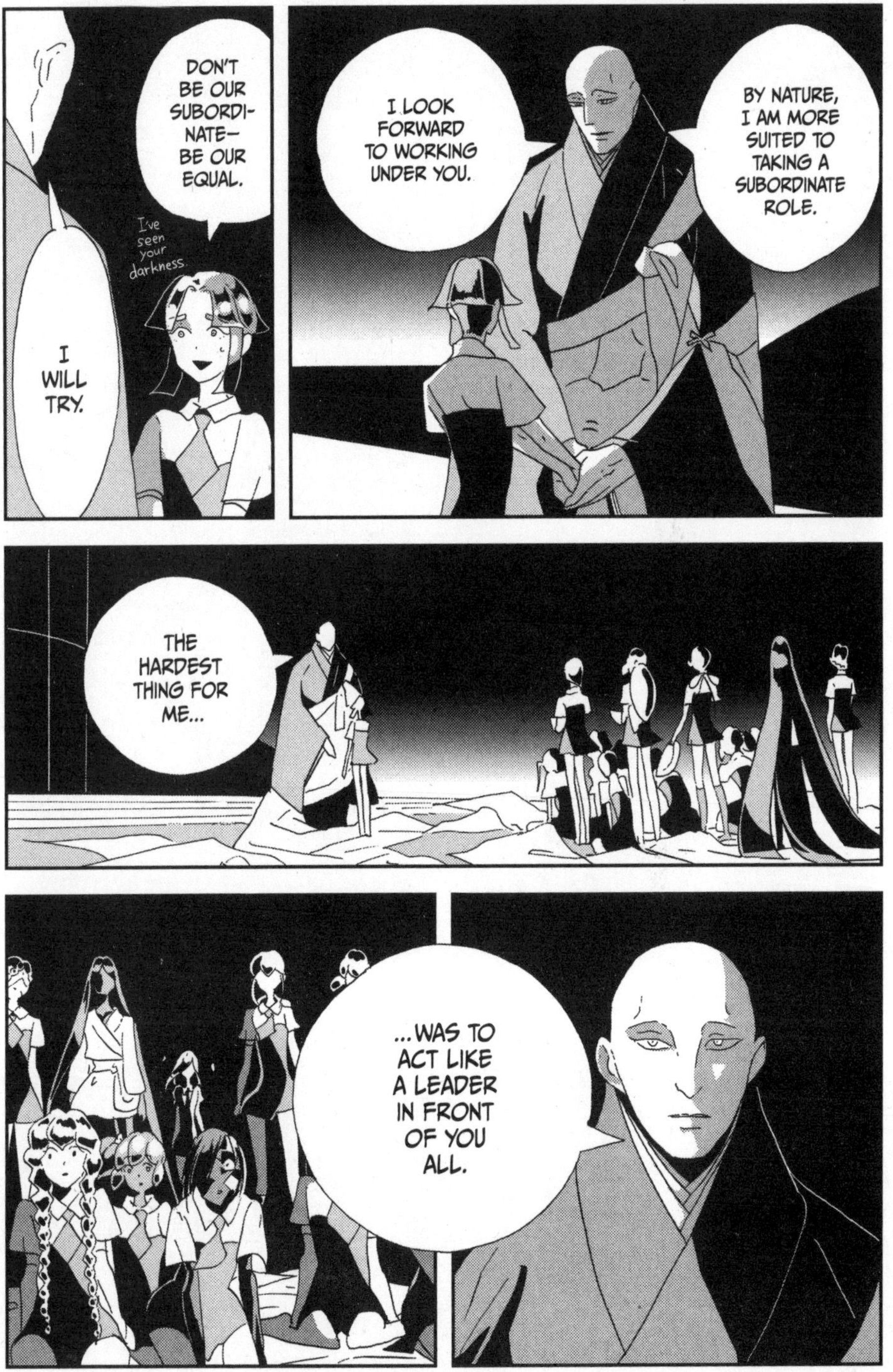
BY NATURE, I AM MORE SUITED TO TAKING A SUBORDINATE ROLE.
I LOOK FORWARD TO WORKING UNDER YOU.
DON'T BE OUR SUBORDINATE— BE OUR EQUAL.
I've seen your darkness.
I WILL TRY.
THE HARDEST THING FOR ME...
...WAS TO ACT LIKE A LEADER IN FRONT OF YOU ALL.

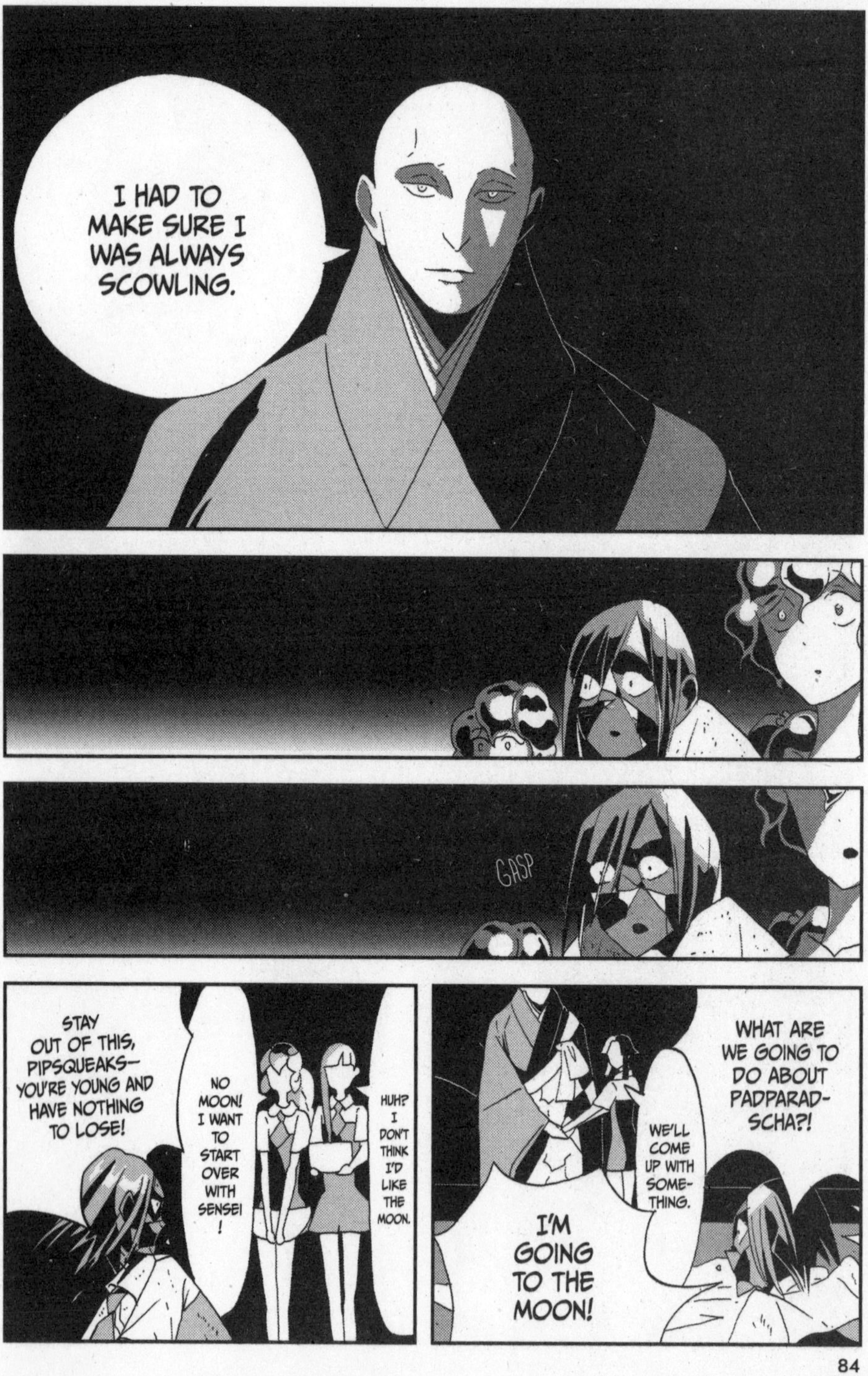
I HAD TO MAKE SURE I WAS ALWAYS SCOWLING.
GASP
WHAT ARE WE GOING TO DO ABOUT PADPARAD-SCHA?!
WE'LL COME UP WITH SOME-THING.
I'M GOING TO THE MOON!
HUH? I DON'T THINK I'D LIKE THE MOON.
NO MOON! I WANT TO START OVER WITH SENSEI!
STAY OUT OF THIS, PIPSQUEAKS—YOU'RE YOUNG AND HAVE NOTHING TO LOSE!

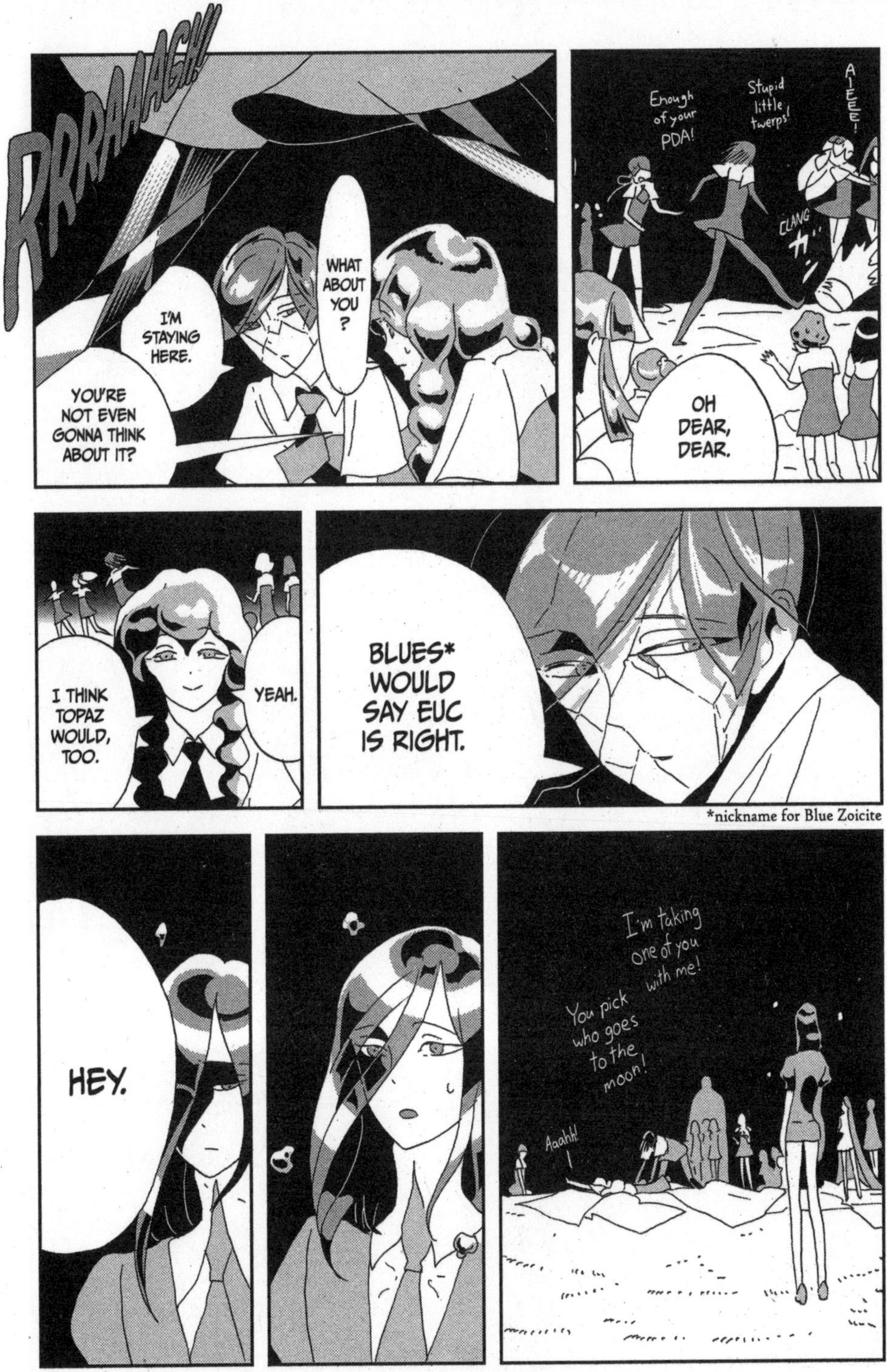
AIEEE!
Stupid little twerps!
Enough of your PDA!
CLANG
OH DEAR, DEAR.
RRRAAAGH!!
WHAT ABOUT YOU?
I'M STAYING HERE.
YOU'RE NOT EVEN GONNA THINK ABOUT IT?
BLUES* WOULD SAY EUC IS RIGHT.
I THINK TOPAZ WOULD, TOO.
YEAH.
I'm taking one of you with me!
You pick who goes to the moon!
Aaahh!
HEY.

*nickname for Blue Zoicite

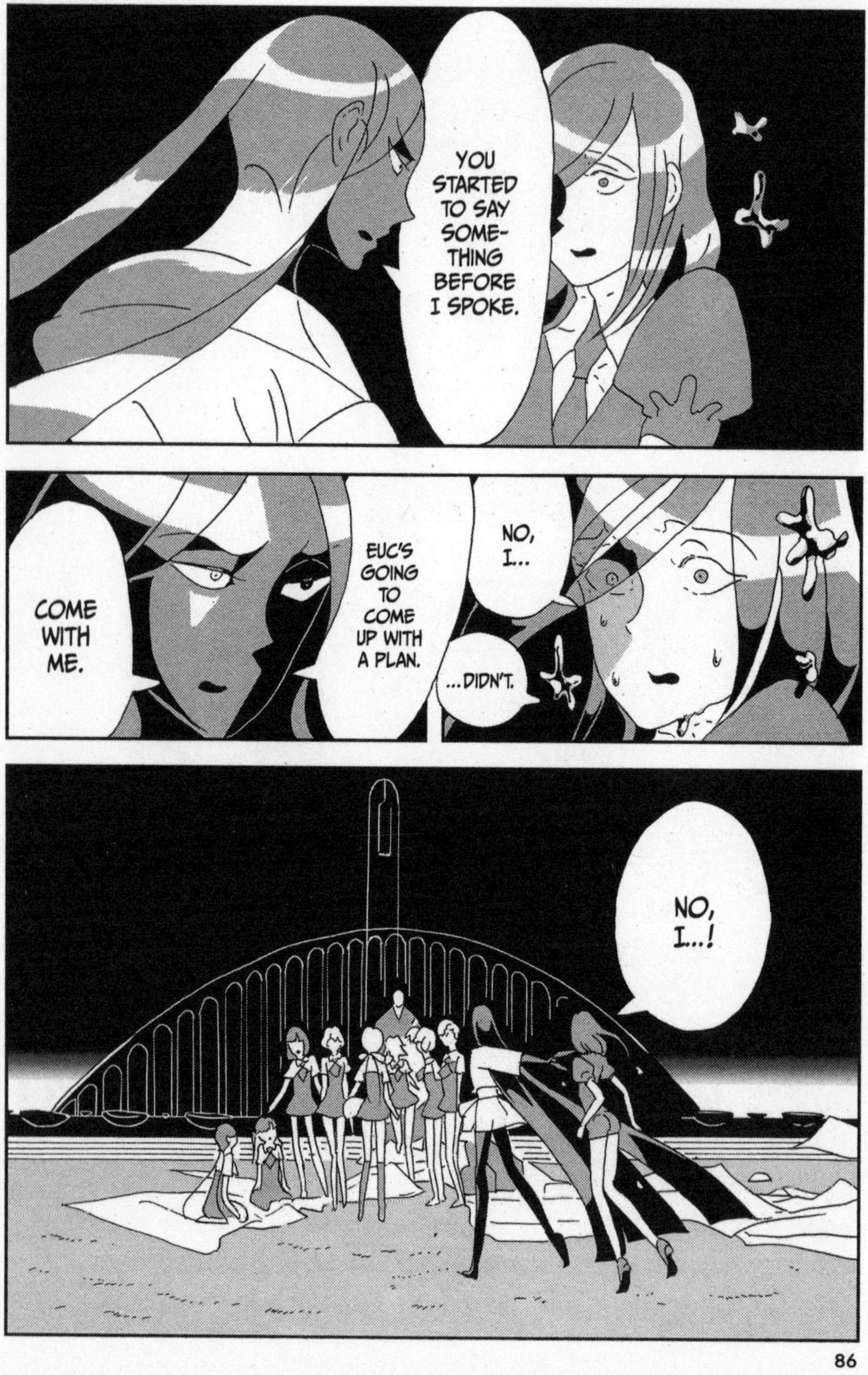
YOU STARTED TO SAY SOME-THING BEFORE I SPOKE.
NO, I...
...DIDN'T.
EUC'S GOING TO COME UP WITH A PLAN.
COME WITH ME.
NO, I...!

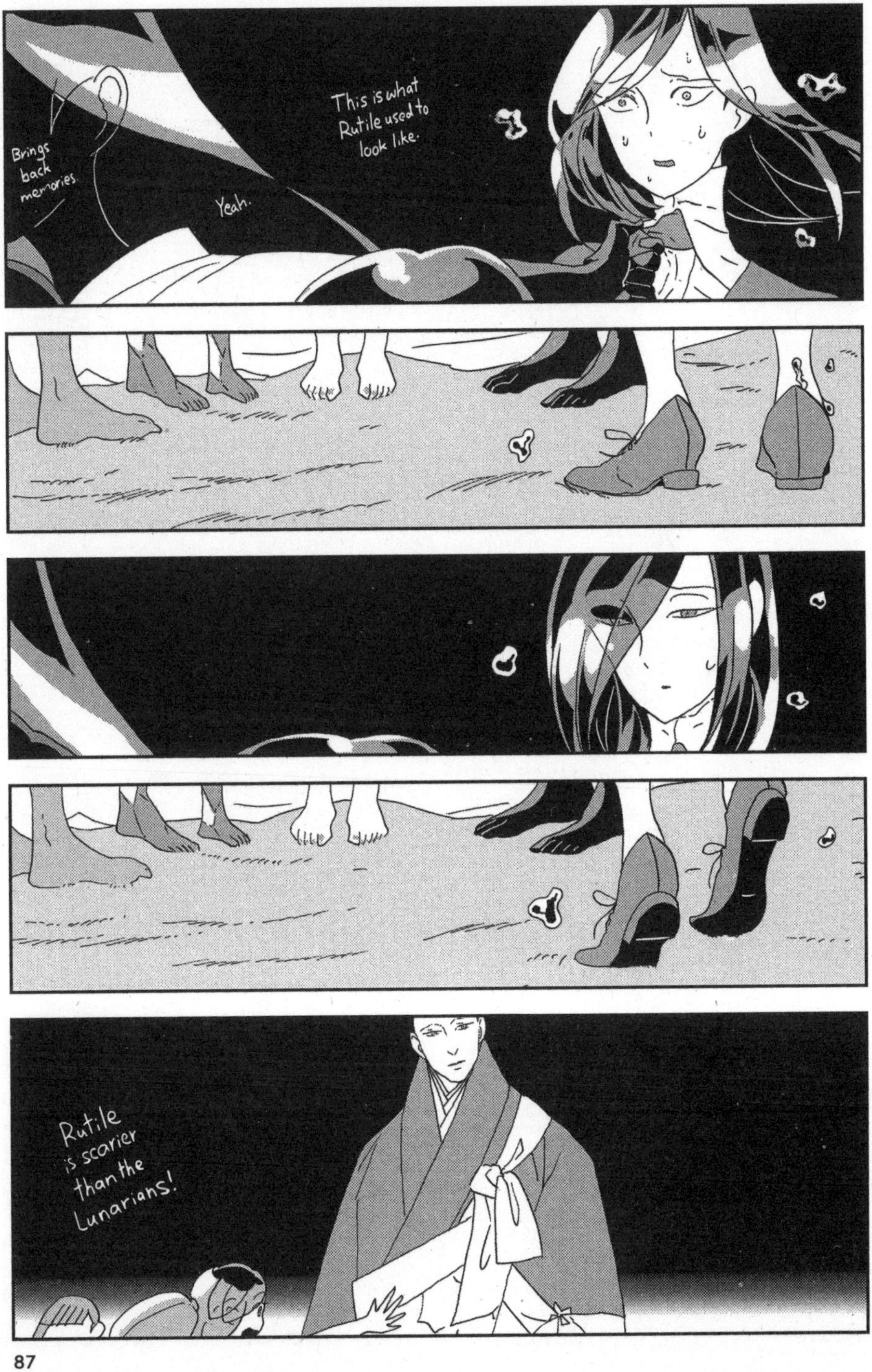
This is what Rutile used to look like.
Yeah.
Brings back memories.
Rutile is scarier than the Lunarians!

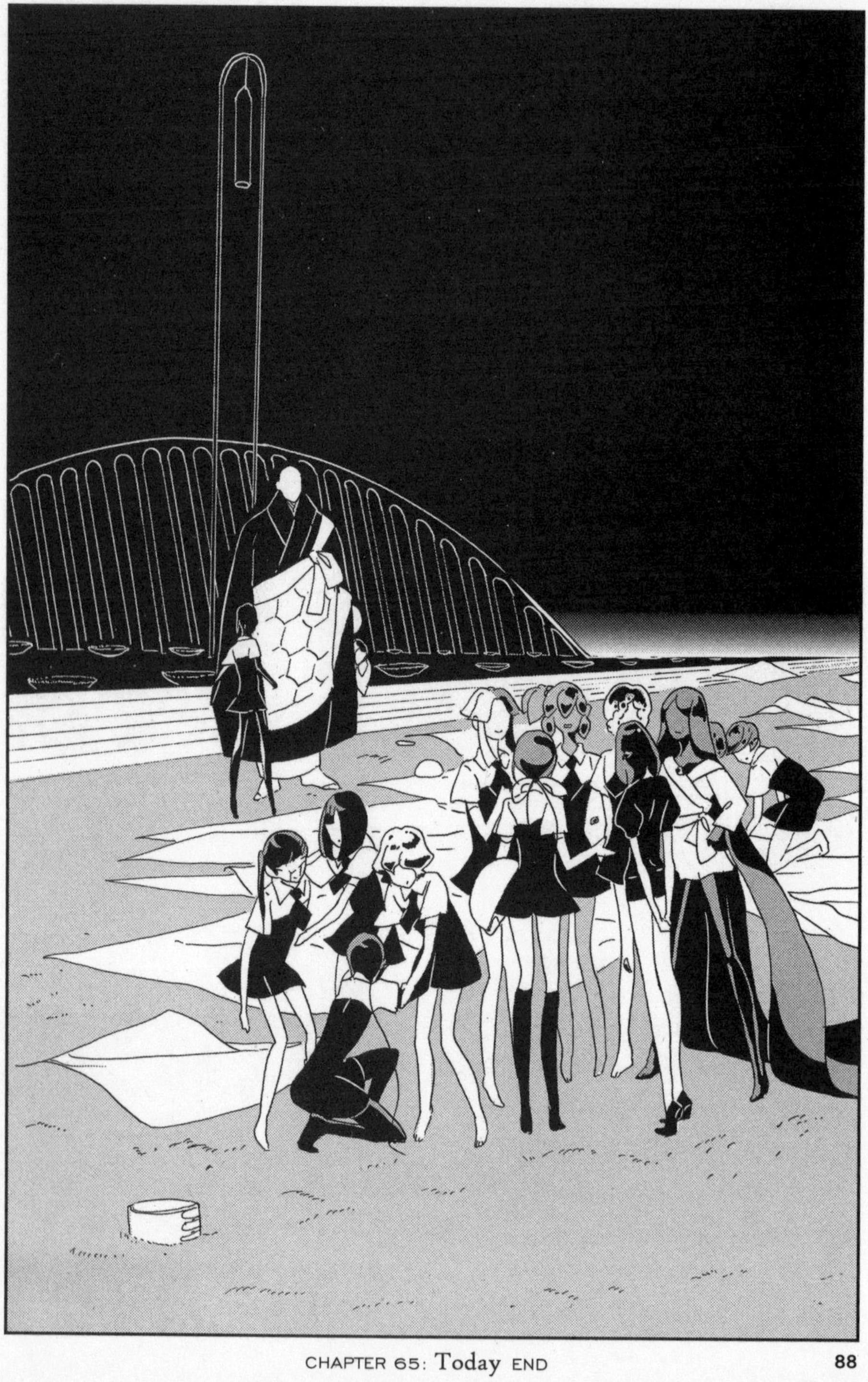

CHAPTER 65: Today END

CHAPTER 66:

Freedom

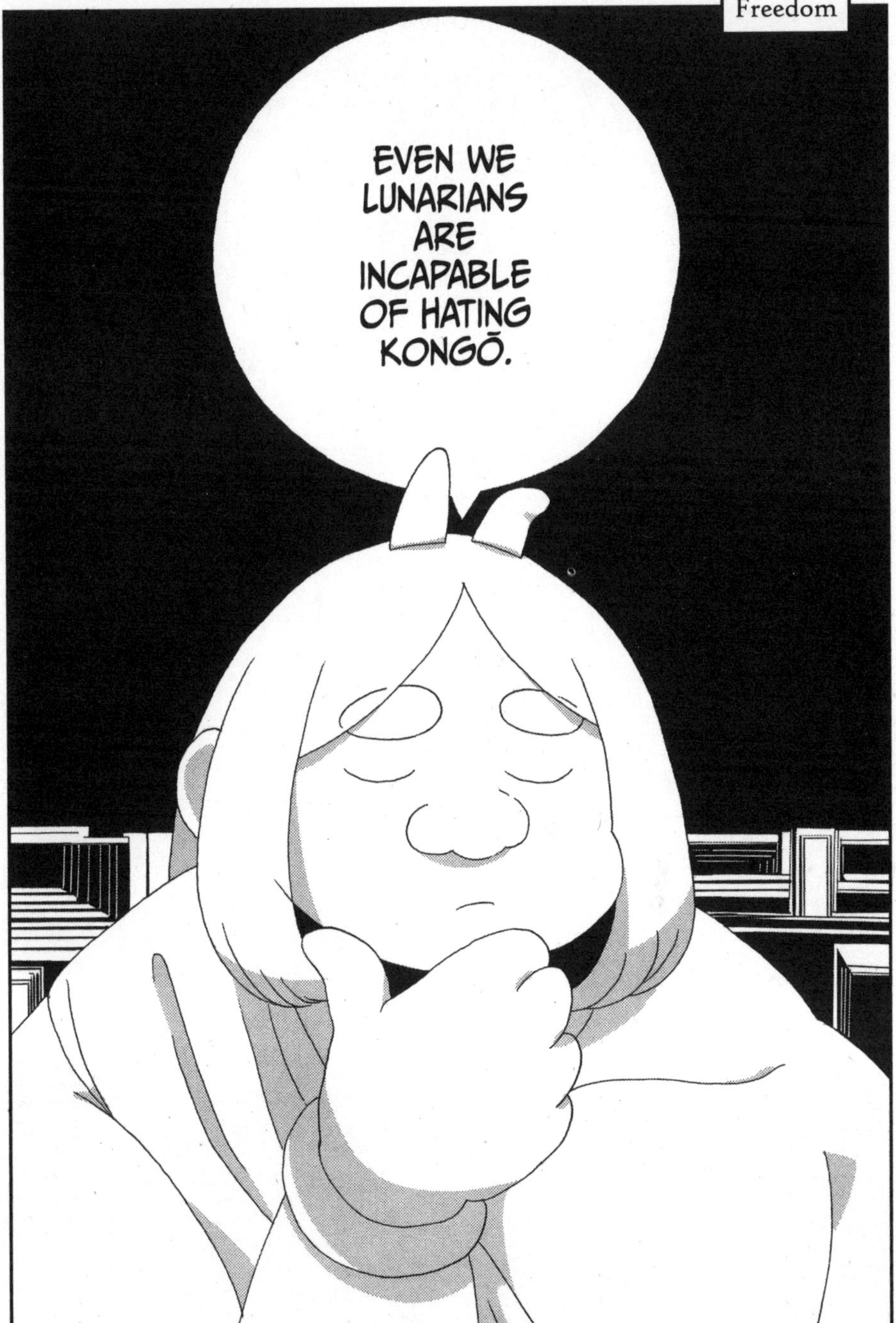

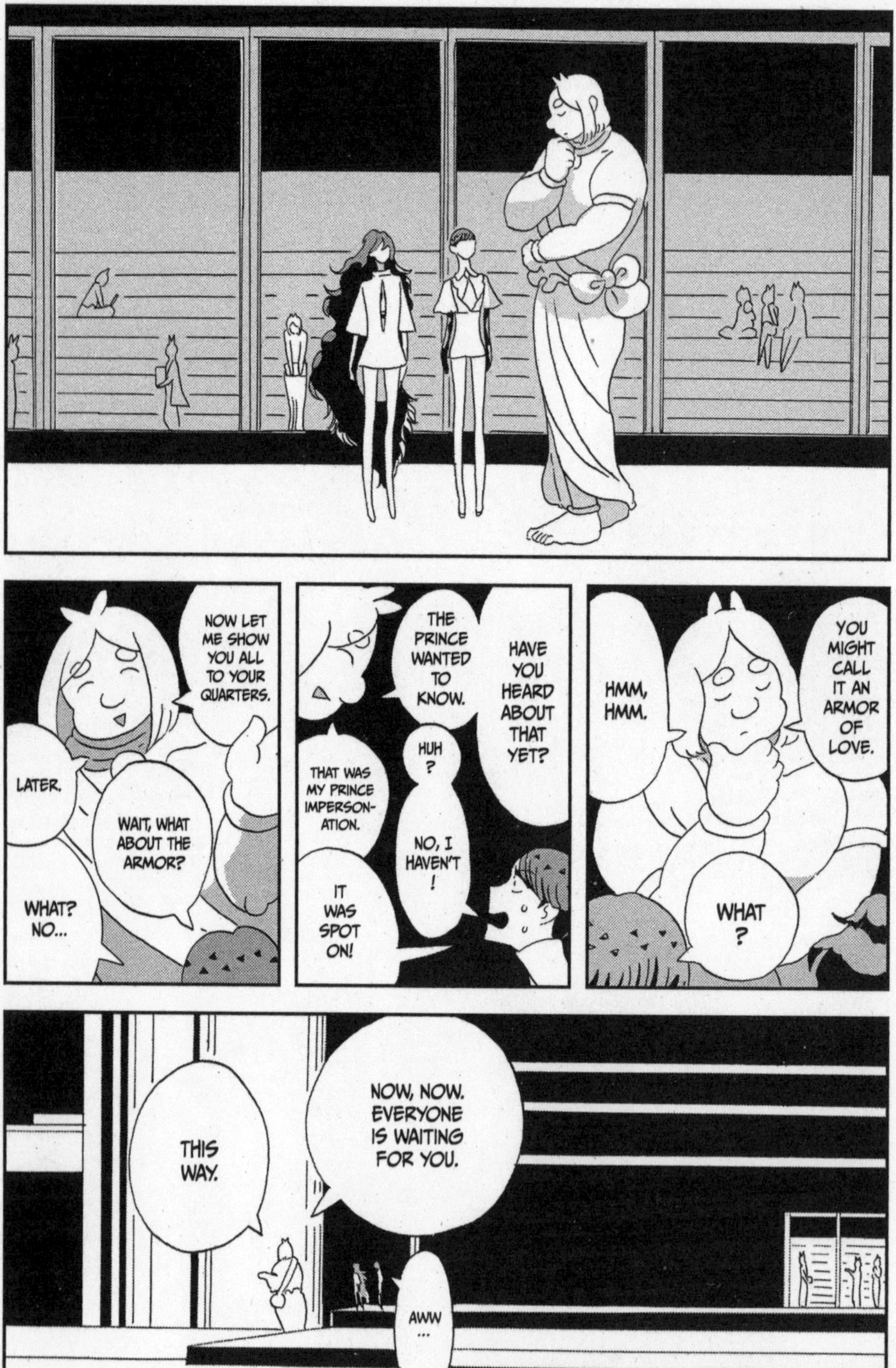
YOU MIGHT CALL IT AN ARMOR OF LOVE.
HMM, HMM.
WHAT?
HAVE YOU HEARD ABOUT THAT YET?
THE PRINCE WANTED TO KNOW.
HUH?
NO, I HAVEN'T!
THAT WAS MY PRINCE IMPERSONATION.
IT WAS SPOT ON!
NOW LET ME SHOW YOU ALL TO YOUR QUARTERS.
WAIT, WHAT ABOUT THE ARMOR?
LATER.
WHAT? NO...
NOW, NOW. EVERYONE IS WAITING FOR YOU.
THIS WAY.
AWW...

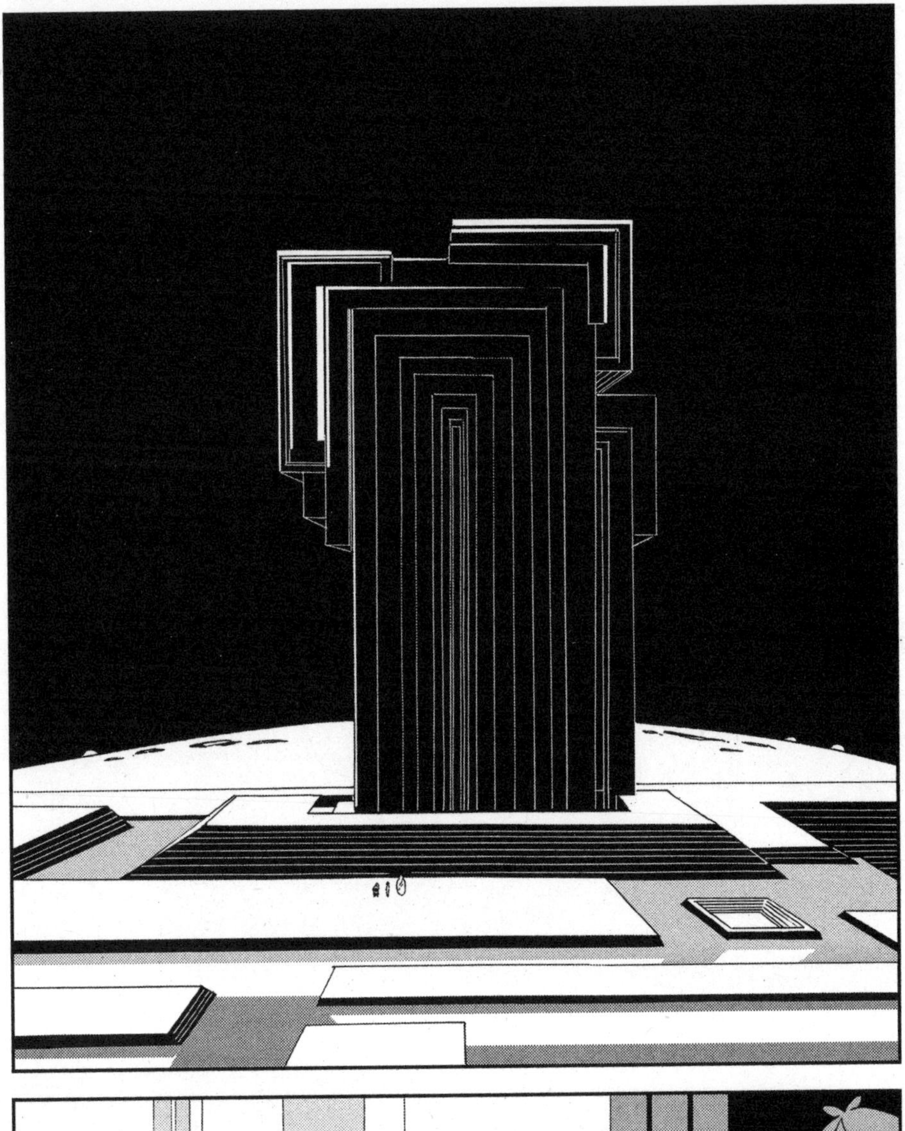
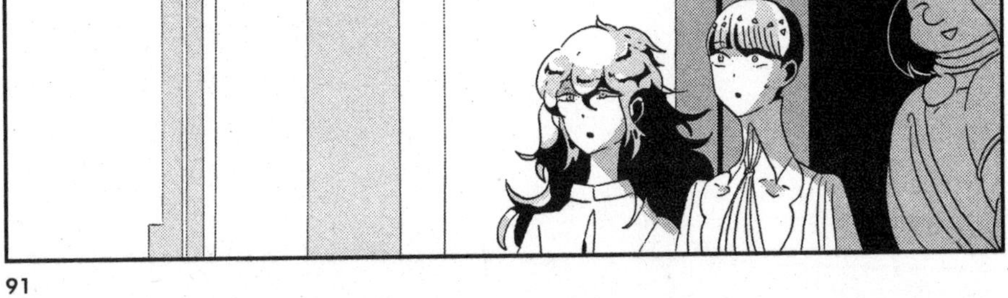

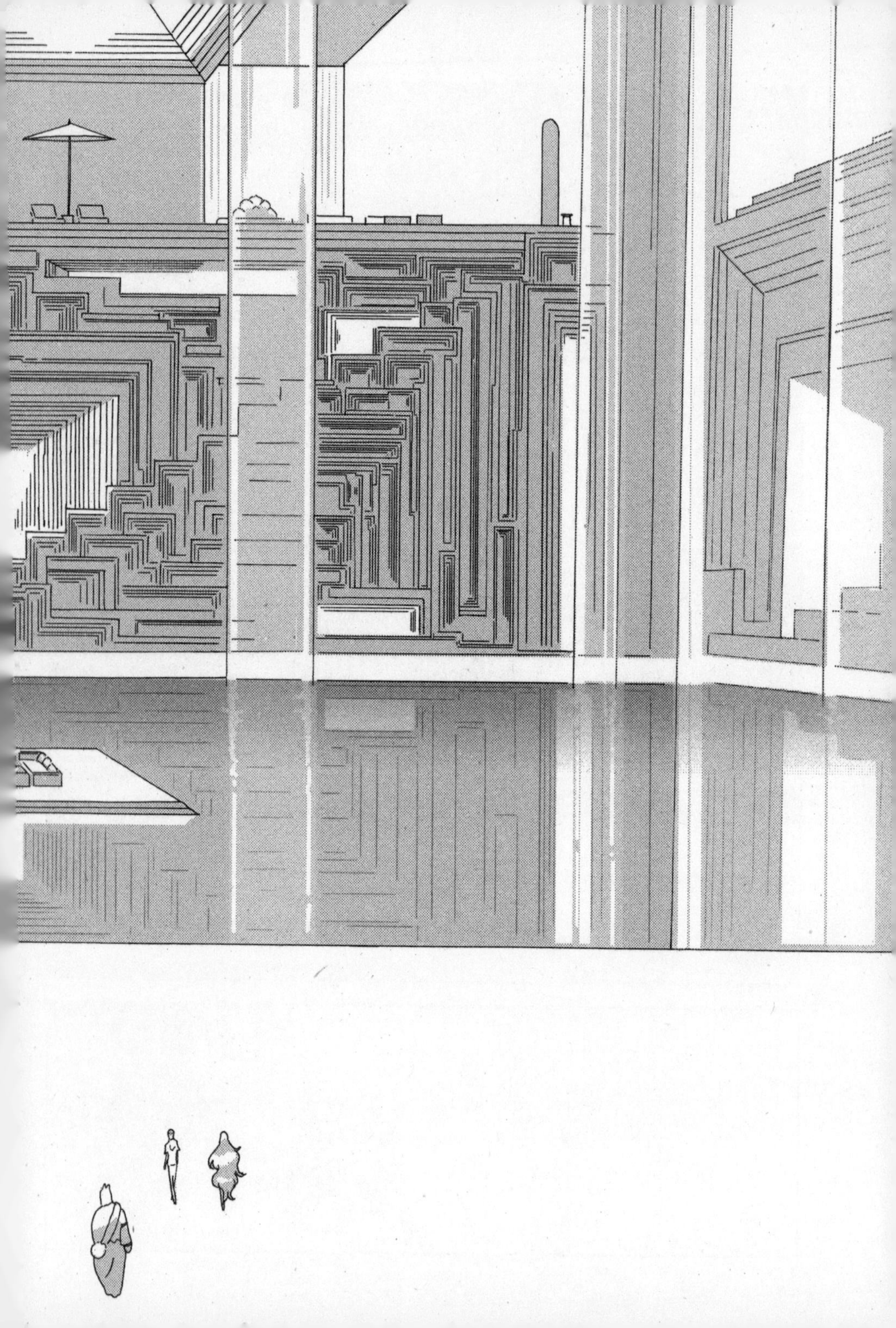

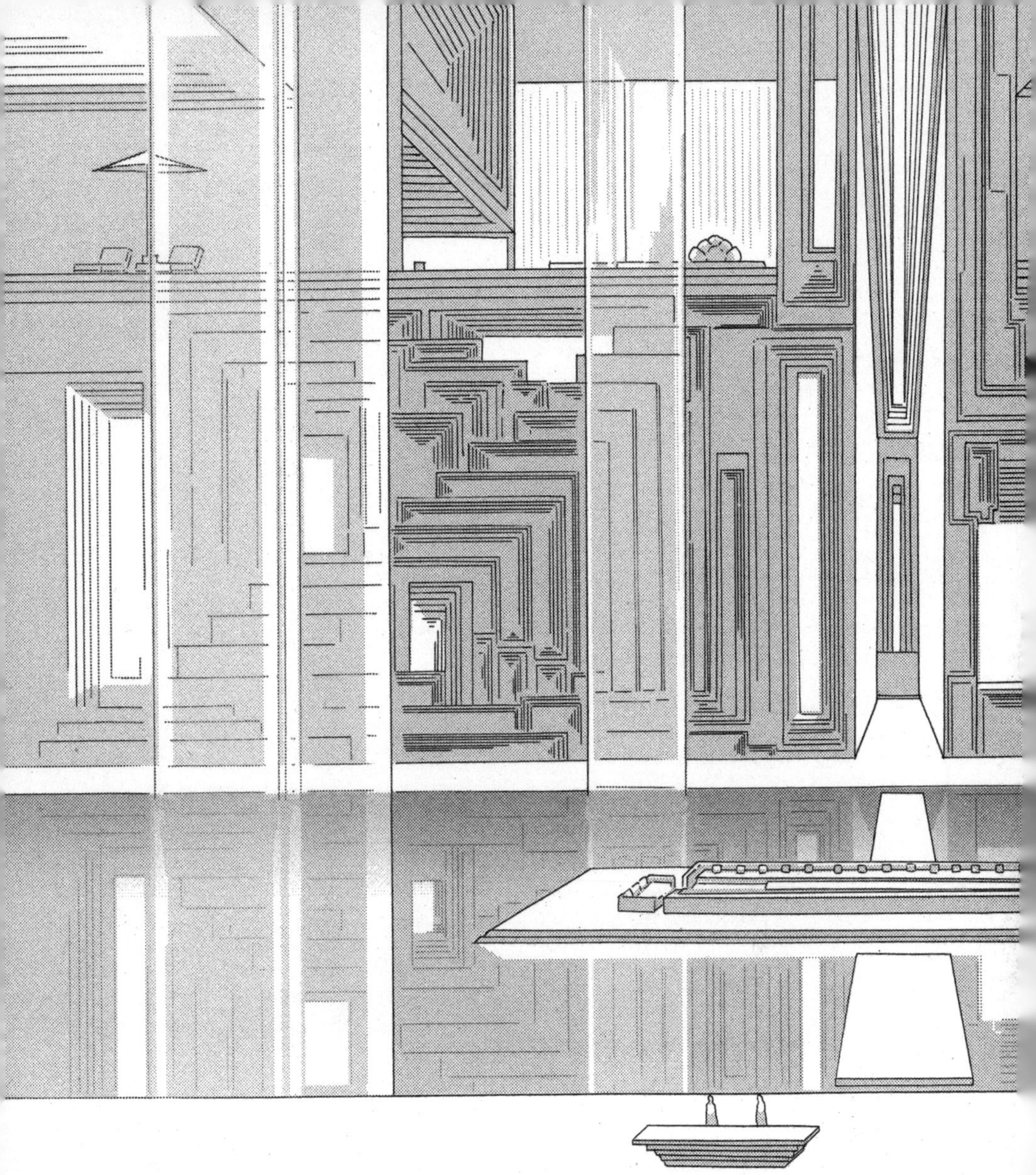

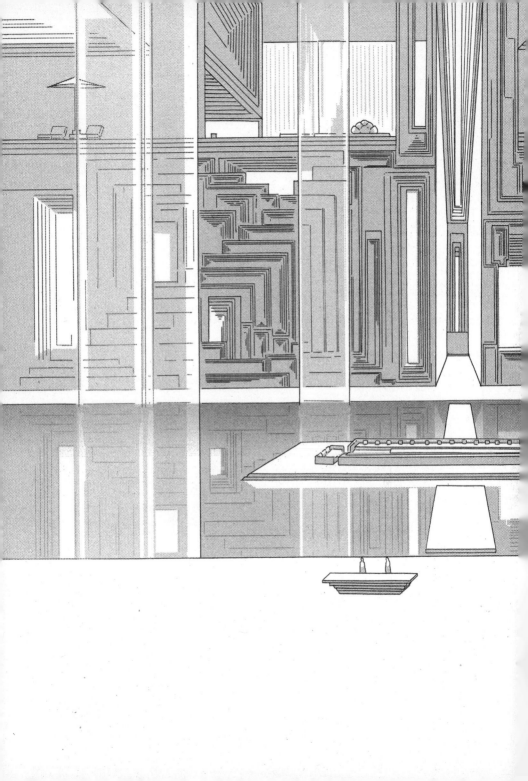

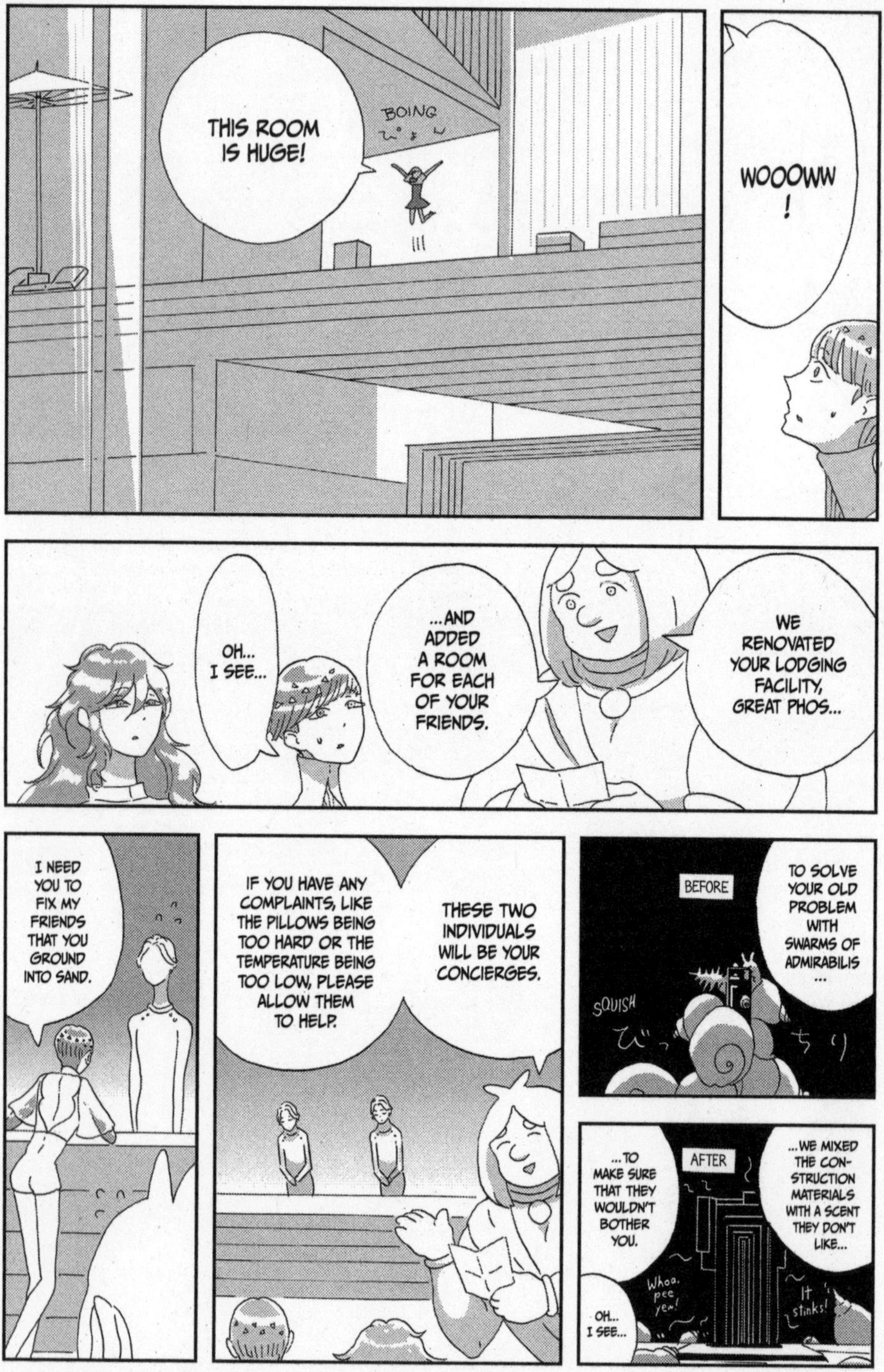
WOOOWW !
THIS ROOM IS HUGE!
BOING
WE RENOVATED YOUR LODGING FACILITY, GREAT PHOS...
...AND ADDED A ROOM FOR EACH OF YOUR FRIENDS.
OH... I SEE...
BEFORE
TO SOLVE YOUR OLD PROBLEM WITH SWARMS OF ADMIRABILIS ...
SQUISH
AFTER
...WE MIXED THE CON-STRUCTION MATERIALS WITH A SCENT THEY DON'T LIKE...
...TO MAKE SURE THAT THEY WOULDN'T BOTHER YOU.
It stinks!
Whoa, pee yew!
OH... I SEE...
THESE TWO INDIVIDUALS WILL BE YOUR CONCIERGES.
IF YOU HAVE ANY COMPLAINTS, LIKE THE PILLOWS BEING TOO HARD OR THE TEMPERATURE BEING TOO LOW, PLEASE ALLOW THEM TO HELP.
I NEED YOU TO FIX MY FRIENDS THAT YOU GROUND INTO SAND.

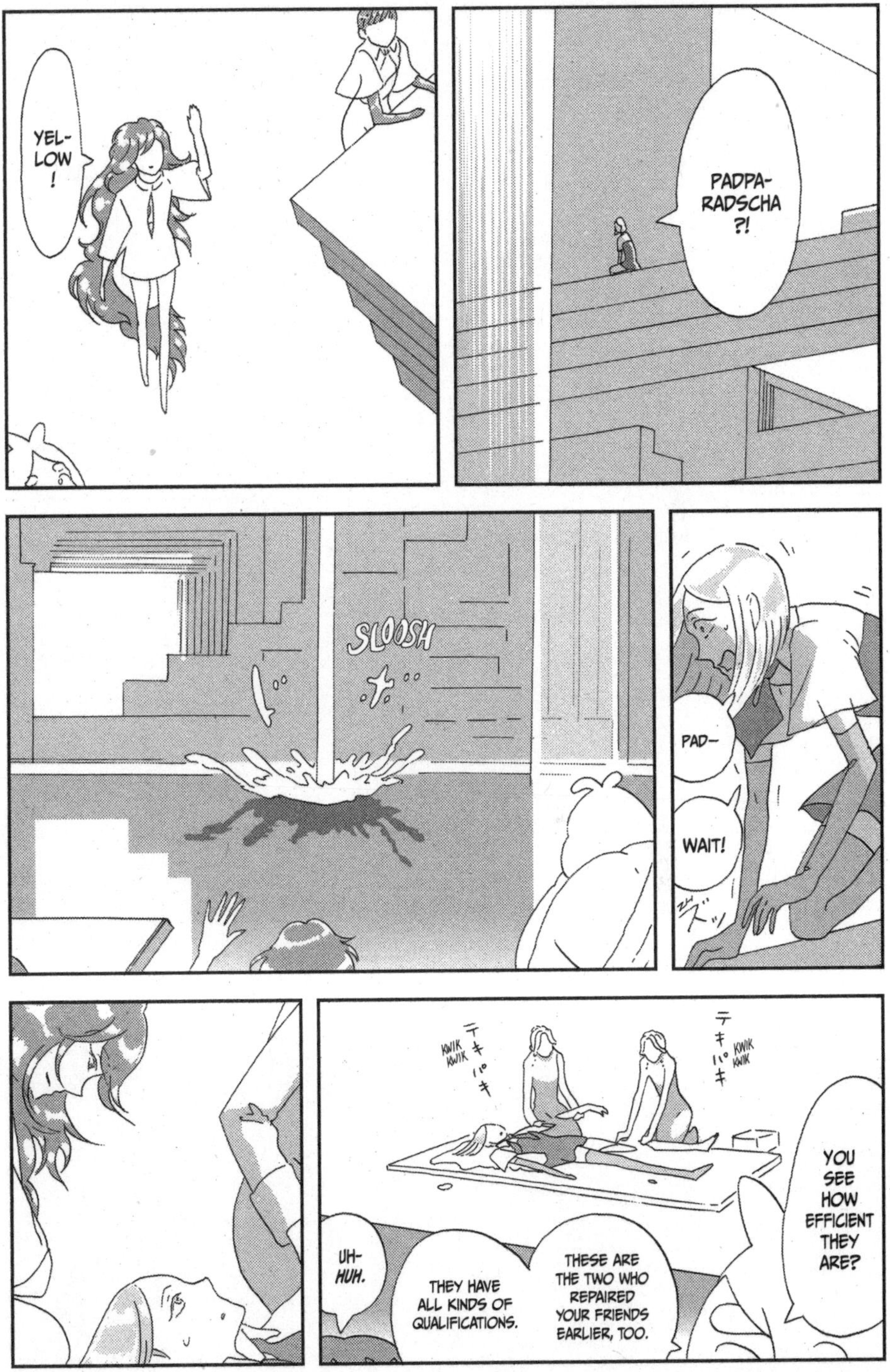
PADPA-RADSCHA?!
YEL-LOW!
PAD—
WAIT!
SLOOSH
テキパキ
KWIK KWIK
テキパキ
KWIK KWIK
YOU SEE HOW EFFICIENT THEY ARE?
THESE ARE THE TWO WHO REPAIRED YOUR FRIENDS EARLIER, TOO.
THEY HAVE ALL KINDS OF QUALIFICATIONS.
UH-HUH.

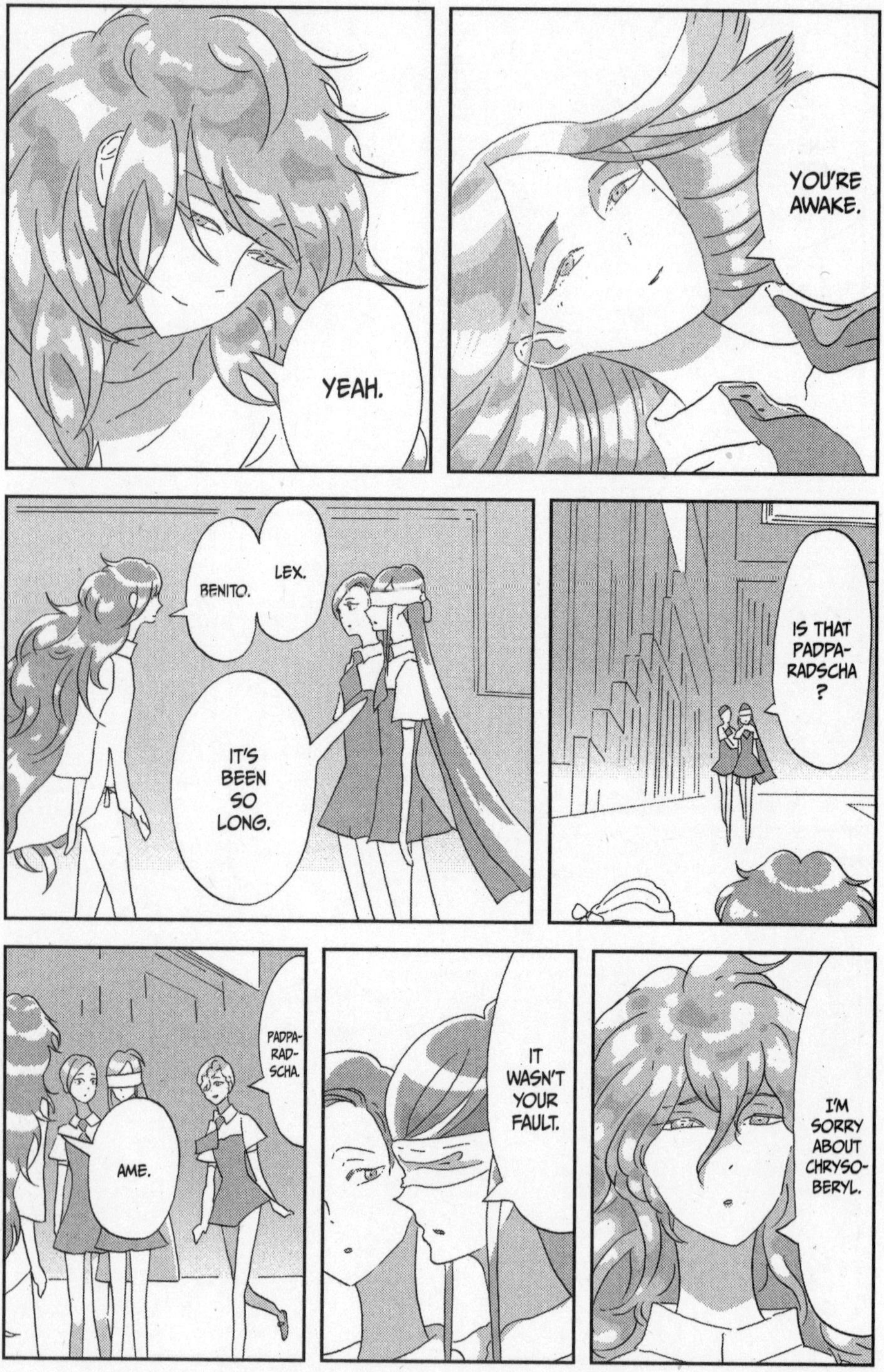
YOU'RE AWAKE.
YEAH.
IS THAT PADPARADSCHA?
LEX.
BENITO.
IT'S BEEN SO LONG.
I'M SORRY ABOUT CHRYSOBERYL.
IT WASN'T YOUR FAULT.
PADPARADSCHA.
AME.

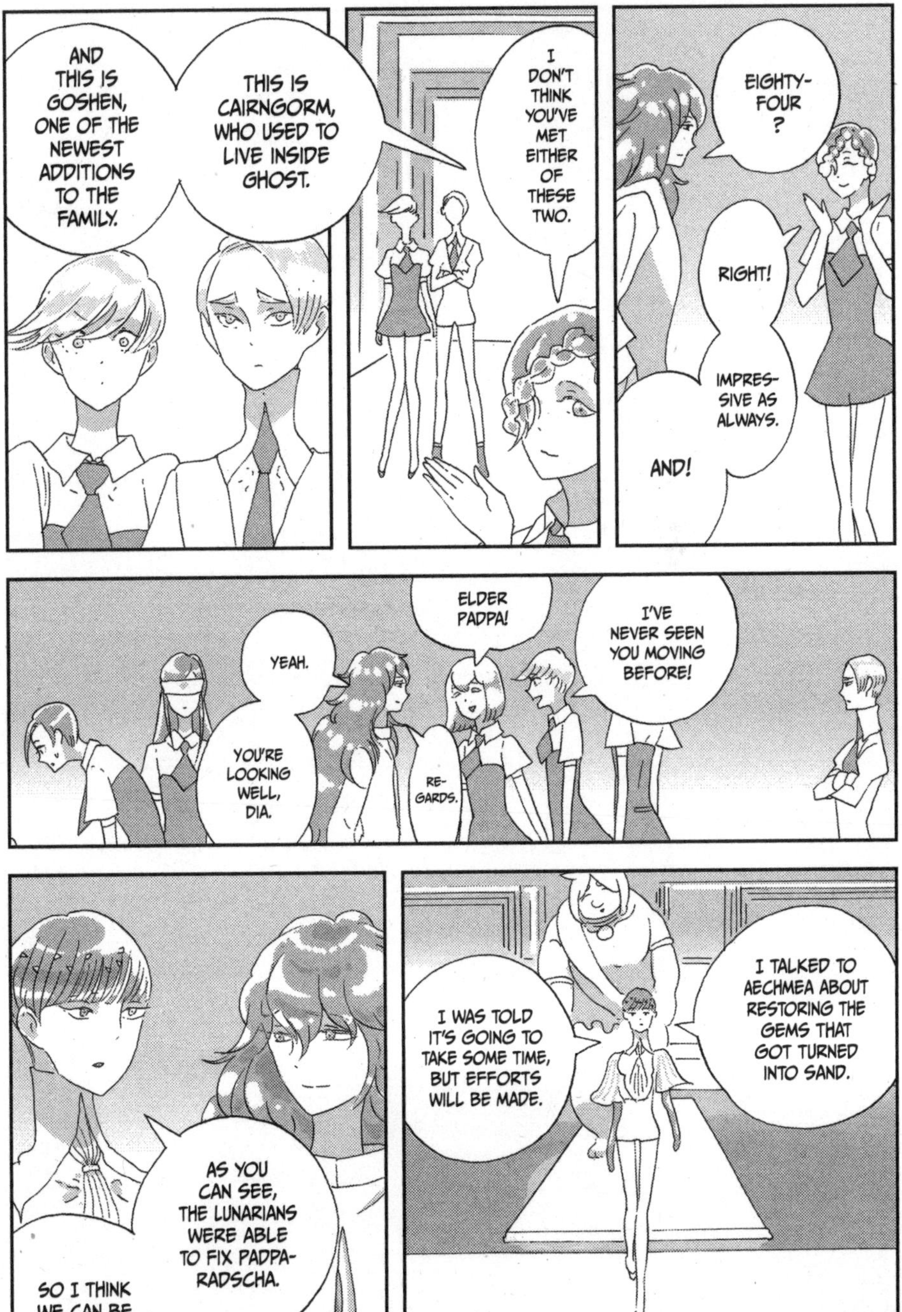
EIGHTY-FOUR ?
RIGHT!
IMPRESSIVE AS ALWAYS.
AND!
I DON'T THINK YOU'VE MET EITHER OF THESE TWO.
THIS IS CAIRNGORM, WHO USED TO LIVE INSIDE GHOST.
AND THIS IS GOSHEN, ONE OF THE NEWEST ADDITIONS TO THE FAMILY.
I'VE NEVER SEEN YOU MOVING BEFORE!
ELDER PADPA!
REGARDS.
YEAH.
YOU'RE LOOKING WELL, DIA.
I TALKED TO AECHMEA ABOUT RESTORING THE GEMS THAT GOT TURNED INTO SAND.
I WAS TOLD IT'S GOING TO TAKE SOME TIME, BUT EFFORTS WILL BE MADE.
AS YOU CAN SEE, THE LUNARIANS WERE ABLE TO FIX PADPARADSCHA.
SO I THINK WE CAN BE OPTIMISTIC.

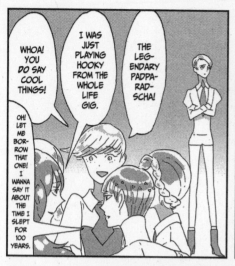

ISN'T THAT GREAT, ELDER YELLOW?
DID YOU HEAR THAT?
YES...
THE LEGENDARY PADPARADSCHA!
I WAS JUST PLAYING HOOKY FROM THE WHOLE LIFE GIG.
WHOA! YOU DO SAY COOL THINGS!
OH! LET ME BORROW THAT ONE! I WANNA SAY IT ABOUT THE TIME I SLEPT FOR 100 YEARS.
WE HAVE COMPANY.

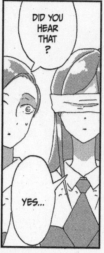

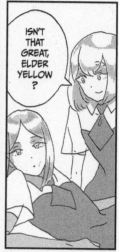

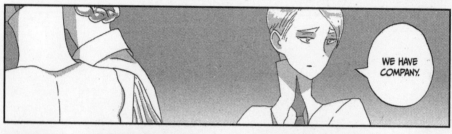

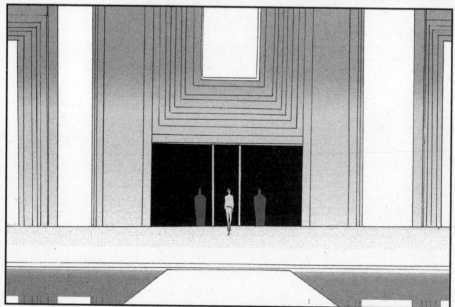

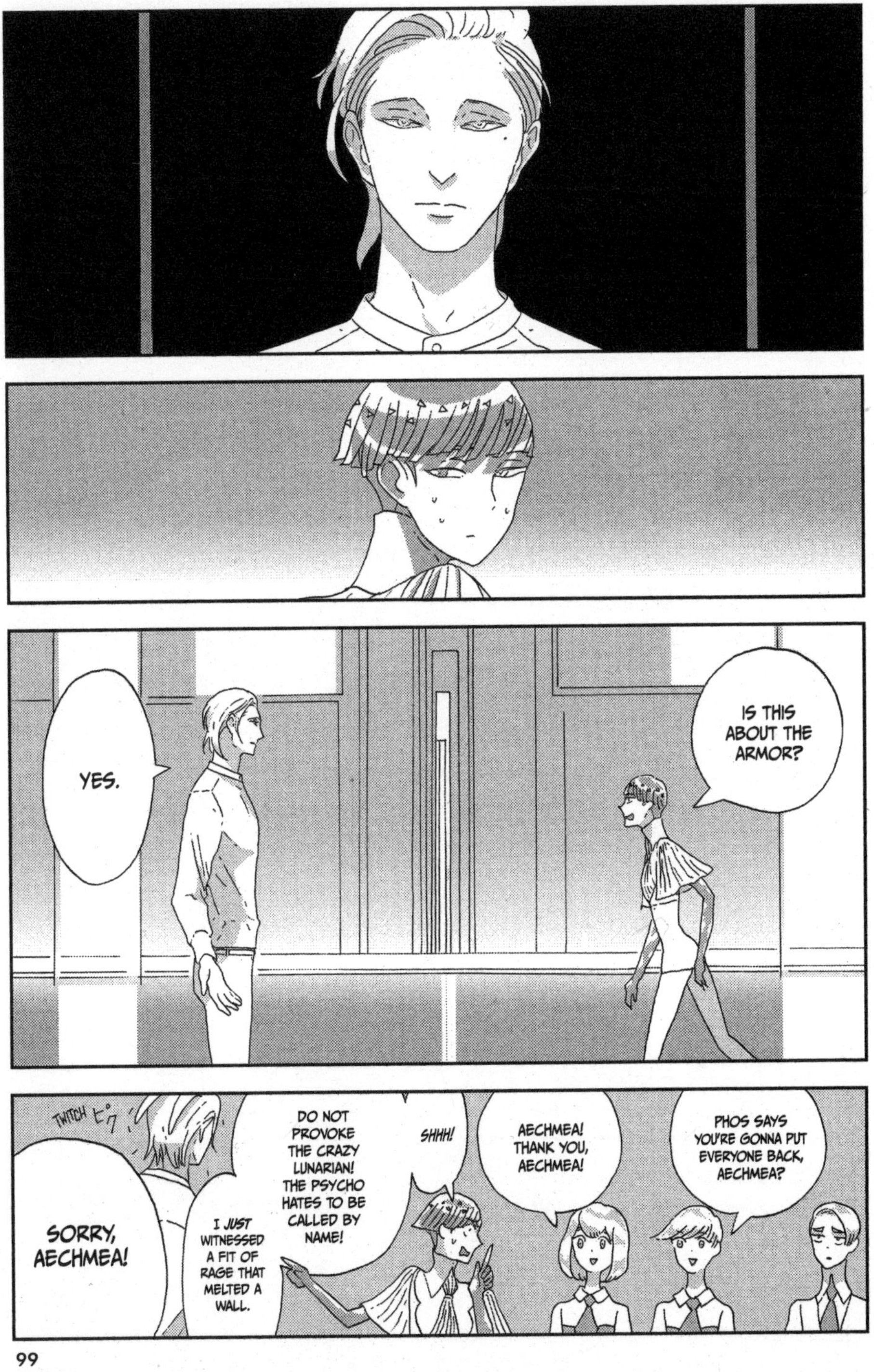
IS THIS ABOUT THE ARMOR?
YES.
PHOS SAYS YOU'RE GONNA PUT EVERYONE BACK, AECHMEA?
AECHMEA! THANK YOU, AECHMEA!
SHHH!
DO NOT PROVOKE THE CRAZY LUNARIAN! THE PSYCHO HATES TO BE CALLED BY NAME!
I JUST WITNESSED A FIT OF RAGE THAT MELTED A WALL.
TWITCH ピク
SORRY, AECHMEA!

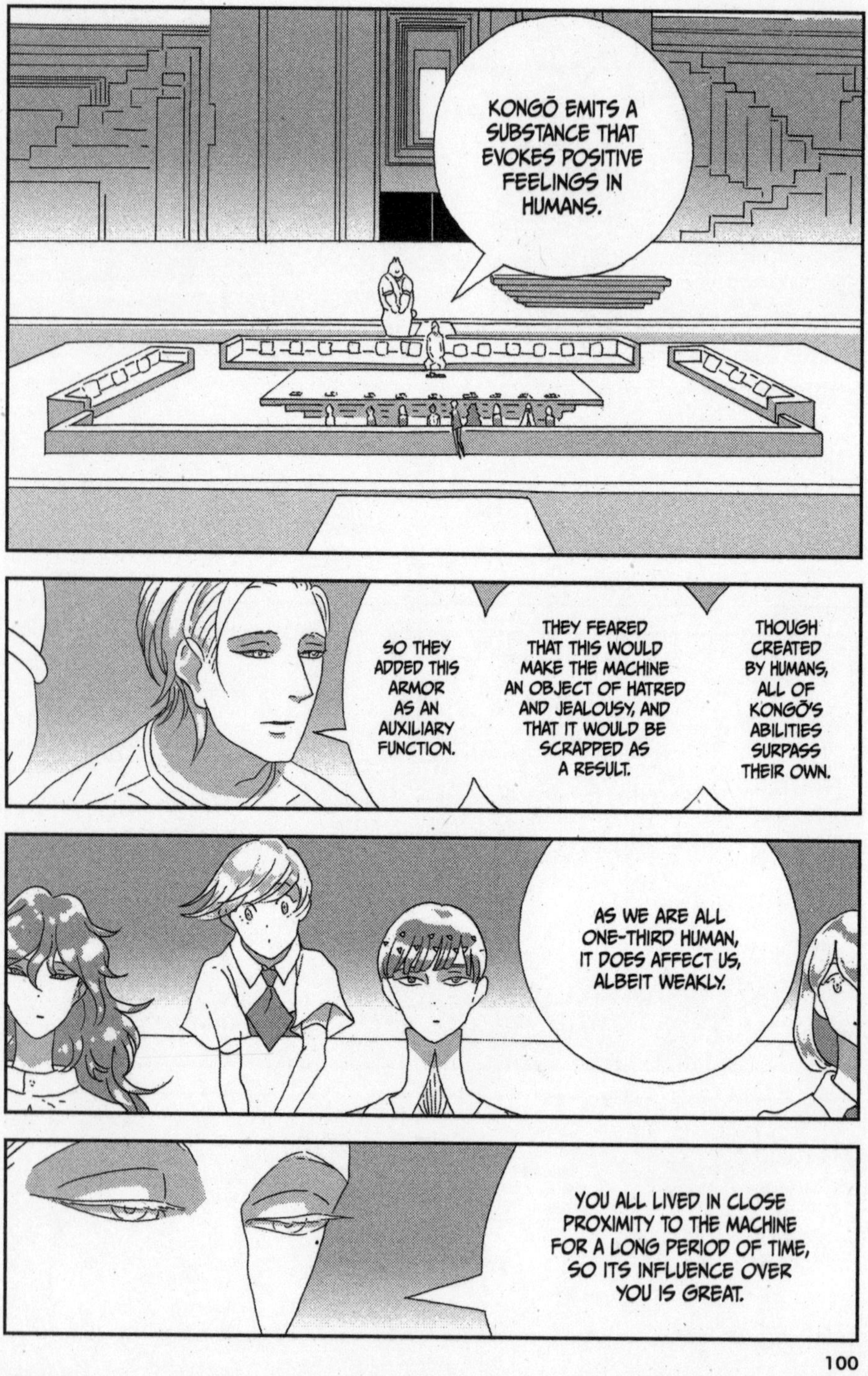
KONGŌ EMITS A SUBSTANCE THAT EVOKES POSITIVE FEELINGS IN HUMANS.
THOUGH CREATED BY HUMANS, ALL OF KONGŌ'S ABILITIES SURPASS THEIR OWN.
THEY FEARED THAT THIS WOULD MAKE THE MACHINE AN OBJECT OF HATRED AND JEALOUSY, AND THAT IT WOULD BE SCRAPPED AS A RESULT.
SO THEY ADDED THIS ARMOR AS AN AUXILIARY FUNCTION.
AS WE ARE ALL ONE-THIRD HUMAN, IT DOES AFFECT US, ALBEIT WEAKLY.
YOU ALL LIVED IN CLOSE PROXIMITY TO THE MACHINE FOR A LONG PERIOD OF TIME, SO ITS INFLUENCE OVER YOU IS GREAT.

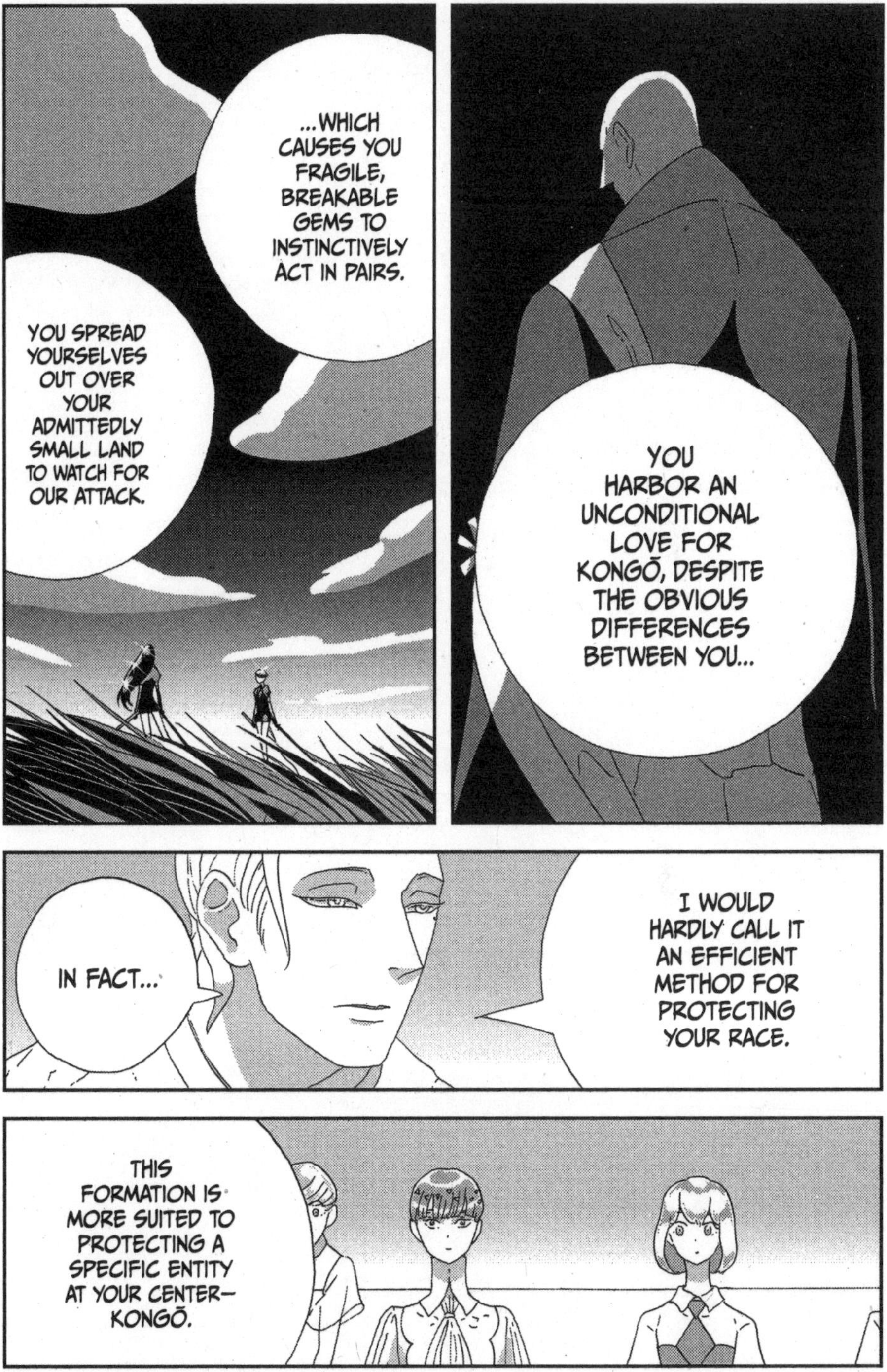
YOU HARBOR AN UNCONDITIONAL LOVE FOR KONGŌ, DESPITE THE OBVIOUS DIFFERENCES BETWEEN YOU...
...WHICH CAUSES YOU FRAGILE, BREAKABLE GEMS TO INSTINCTIVELY ACT IN PAIRS.
YOU SPREAD YOURSELVES OUT OVER YOUR ADMITTEDLY SMALL LAND TO WATCH FOR OUR ATTACK.
I WOULD HARDLY CALL IT AN EFFICIENT METHOD FOR PROTECTING YOUR RACE.
IN FACT...
THIS FORMATION IS MORE SUITED TO PROTECTING A SPECIFIC ENTITY AT YOUR CENTER—KONGŌ.

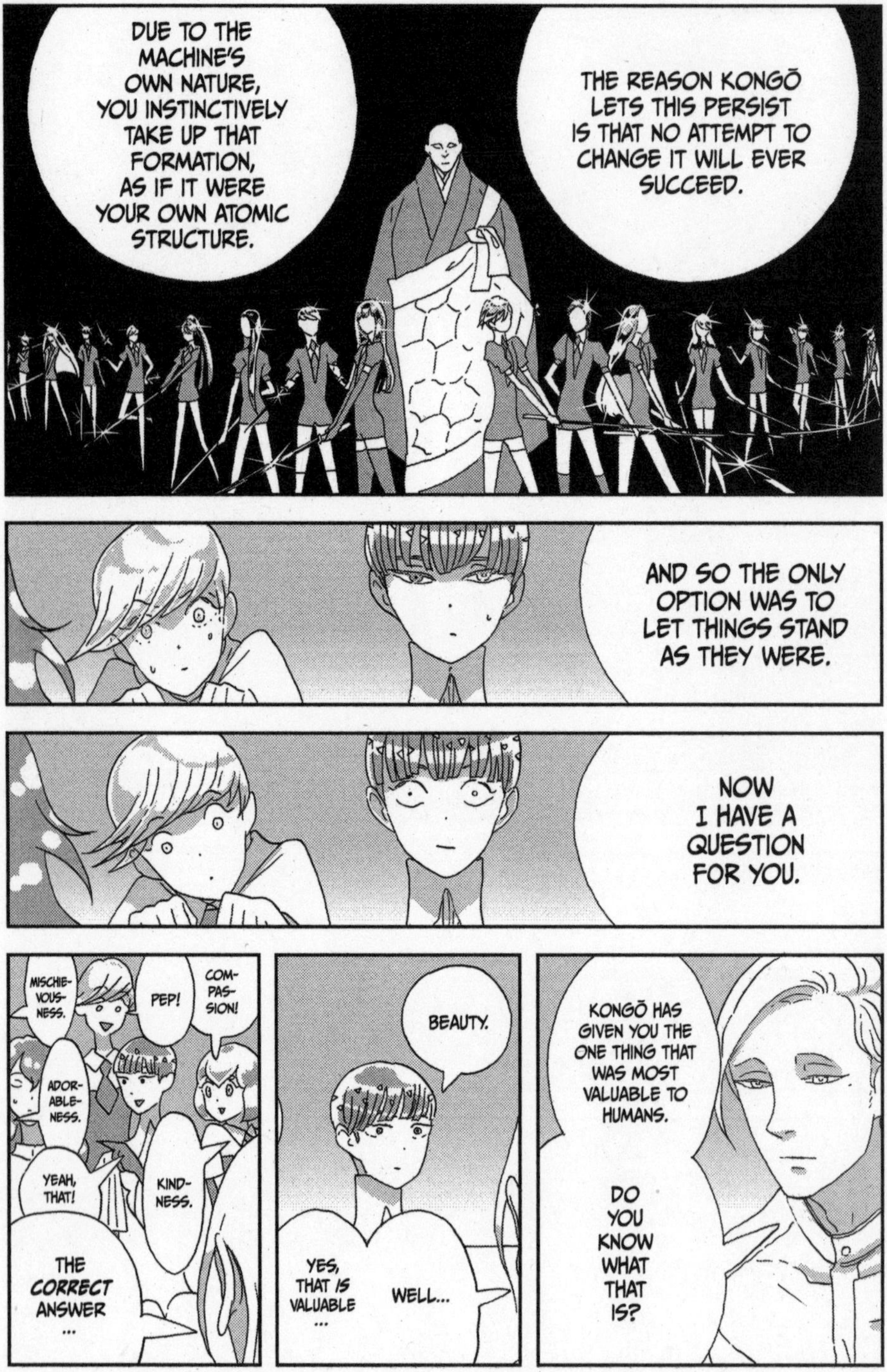
THE REASON KONGŌ LETS THIS PERSIST IS THAT NO ATTEMPT TO CHANGE IT WILL EVER SUCCEED.
DUE TO THE MACHINE'S OWN NATURE, YOU INSTINCTIVELY TAKE UP THAT FORMATION, AS IF IT WERE YOUR OWN ATOMIC STRUCTURE.
AND SO THE ONLY OPTION WAS TO LET THINGS STAND AS THEY WERE.
NOW I HAVE A QUESTION FOR YOU.
KONGŌ HAS GIVEN YOU THE ONE THING THAT WAS MOST VALUABLE TO HUMANS.
DO YOU KNOW WHAT THAT IS?
BEAUTY.
WELL...
YES, THAT *IS* VALUABLE ...
COMPASSION!
PEP!
MISCHIEVOUSNESS.
ADORABLENESS.
KINDNESS.
YEAH, THAT!
THE **CORRECT** ANSWER ...

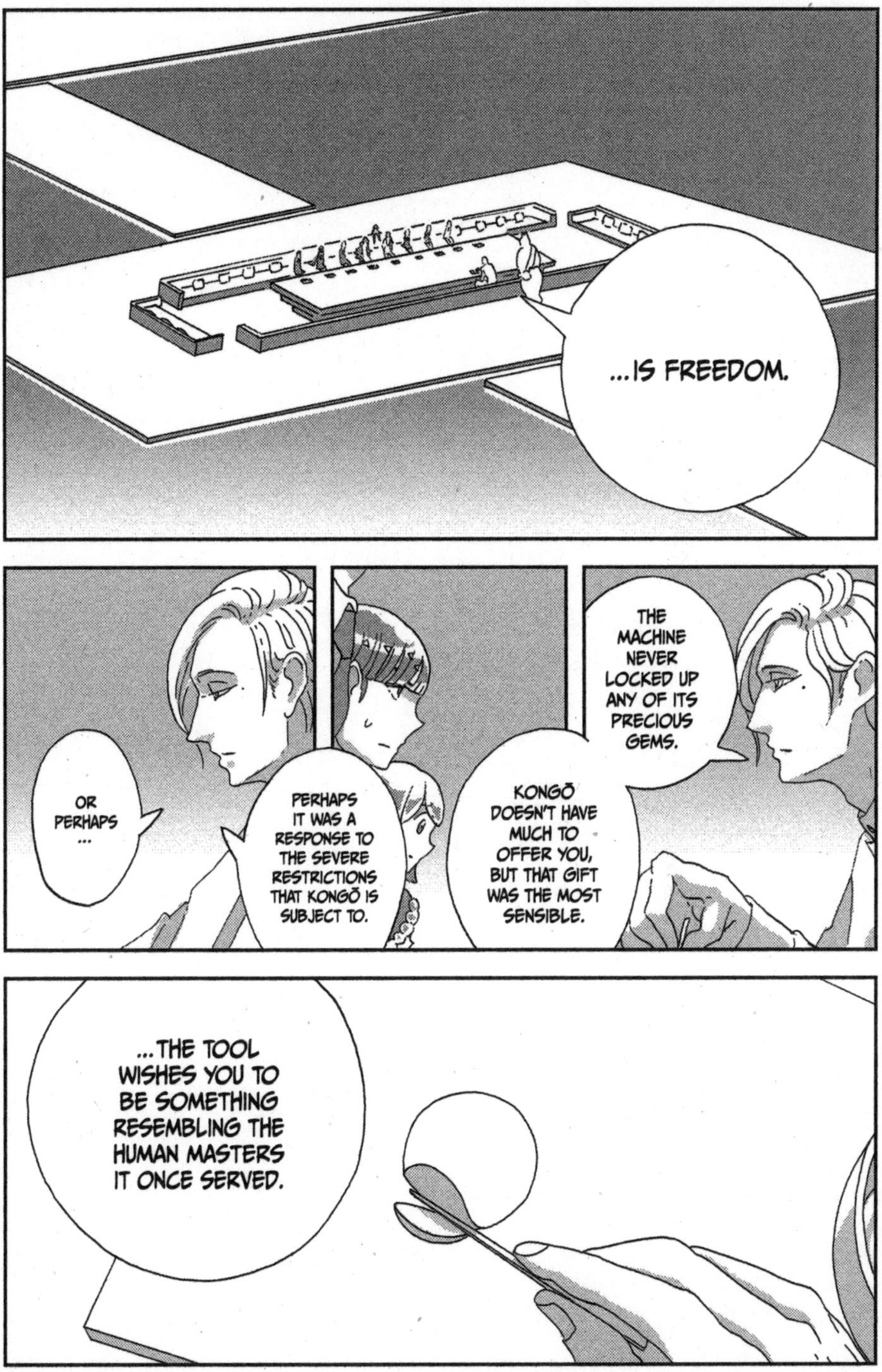
...IS FREEDOM.
THE MACHINE NEVER LOCKED UP ANY OF ITS PRECIOUS GEMS.
KONGŌ DOESN'T HAVE MUCH TO OFFER YOU, BUT THAT GIFT WAS THE MOST SENSIBLE.
PERHAPS IT WAS A RESPONSE TO THE SEVERE RESTRICTIONS THAT KONGŌ IS SUBJECT TO.
OR PERHAPS ...
...THE TOOL WISHES YOU TO BE SOMETHING RESEMBLING THE HUMAN MASTERS IT ONCE SERVED.

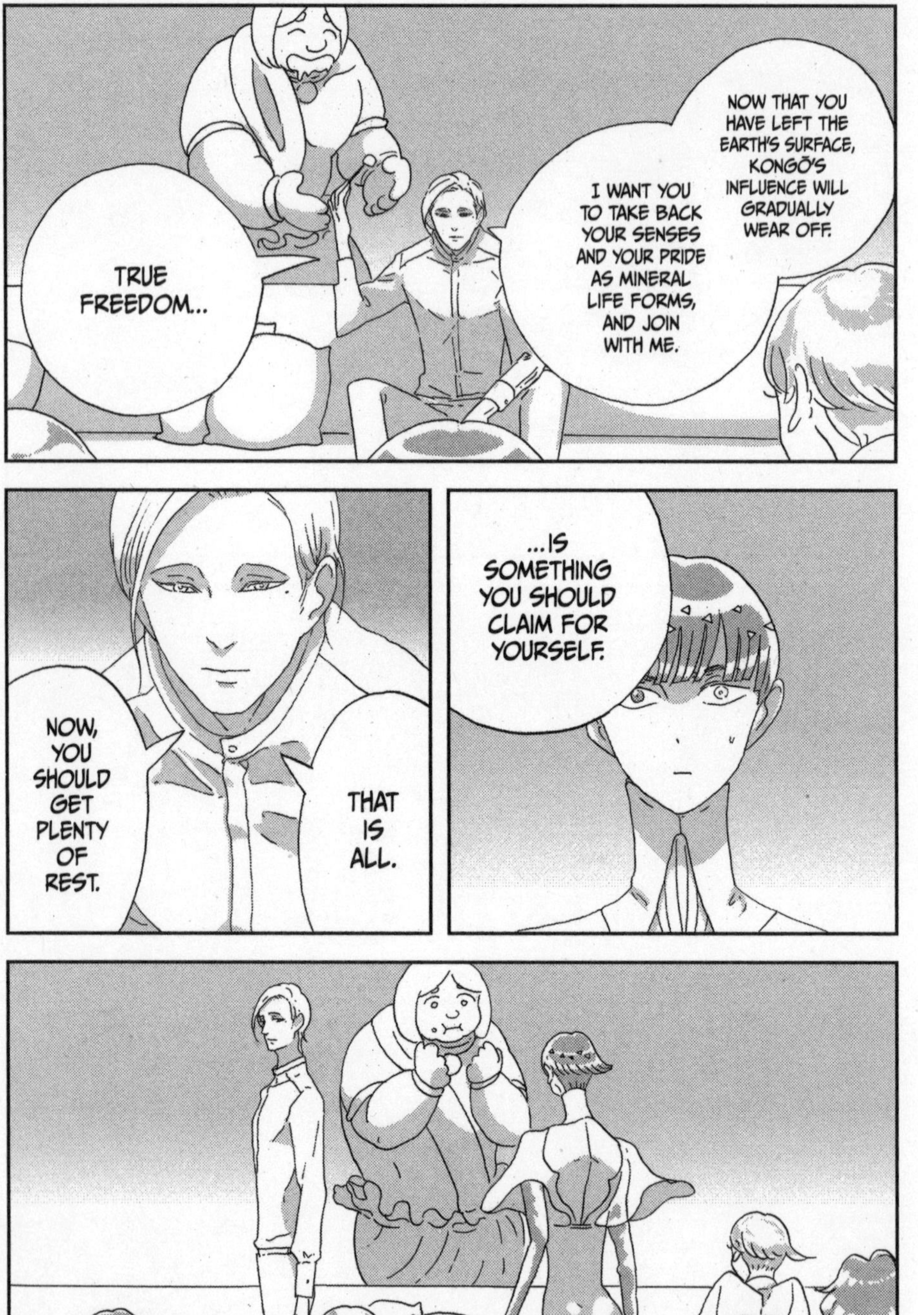
NOW THAT YOU HAVE LEFT THE EARTH'S SURFACE, KONGŌ'S INFLUENCE WILL GRADUALLY WEAR OFF.
I WANT YOU TO TAKE BACK YOUR SENSES AND YOUR PRIDE AS MINERAL LIFE FORMS, AND JOIN WITH ME.
TRUE FREEDOM...
...IS SOMETHING YOU SHOULD CLAIM FOR YOURSELF.
THAT IS ALL.
NOW, YOU SHOULD GET PLENTY OF REST.

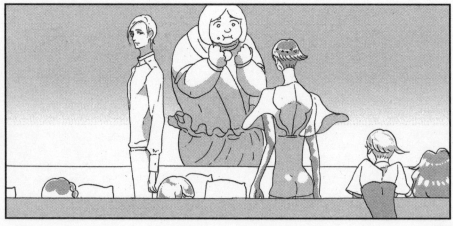

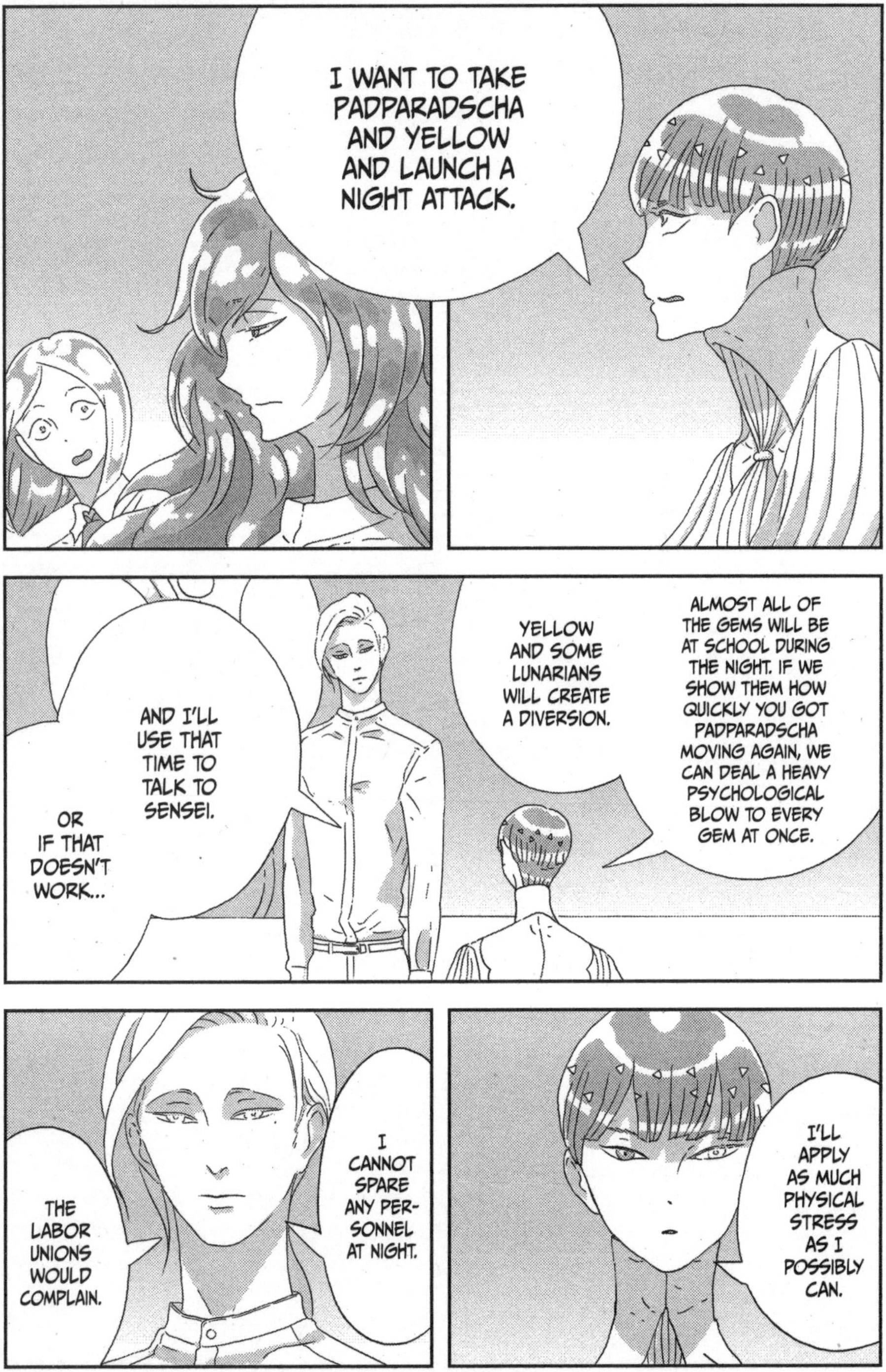
I WANT TO TAKE PADPARADSCHA AND YELLOW AND LAUNCH A NIGHT ATTACK.
ALMOST ALL OF THE GEMS WILL BE AT SCHOOL DURING THE NIGHT. IF WE SHOW THEM HOW QUICKLY YOU GOT PADPARADSCHA MOVING AGAIN, WE CAN DEAL A HEAVY PSYCHOLOGICAL BLOW TO EVERY GEM AT ONCE.
YELLOW AND SOME LUNARIANS WILL CREATE A DIVERSION.
AND I'LL USE THAT TIME TO TALK TO SENSEI.
OR IF THAT DOESN'T WORK...
I'LL APPLY AS MUCH PHYSICAL STRESS AS I POSSIBLY CAN.
I CANNOT SPARE ANY PERSONNEL AT NIGHT.
THE LABOR UNIONS WOULD COMPLAIN.

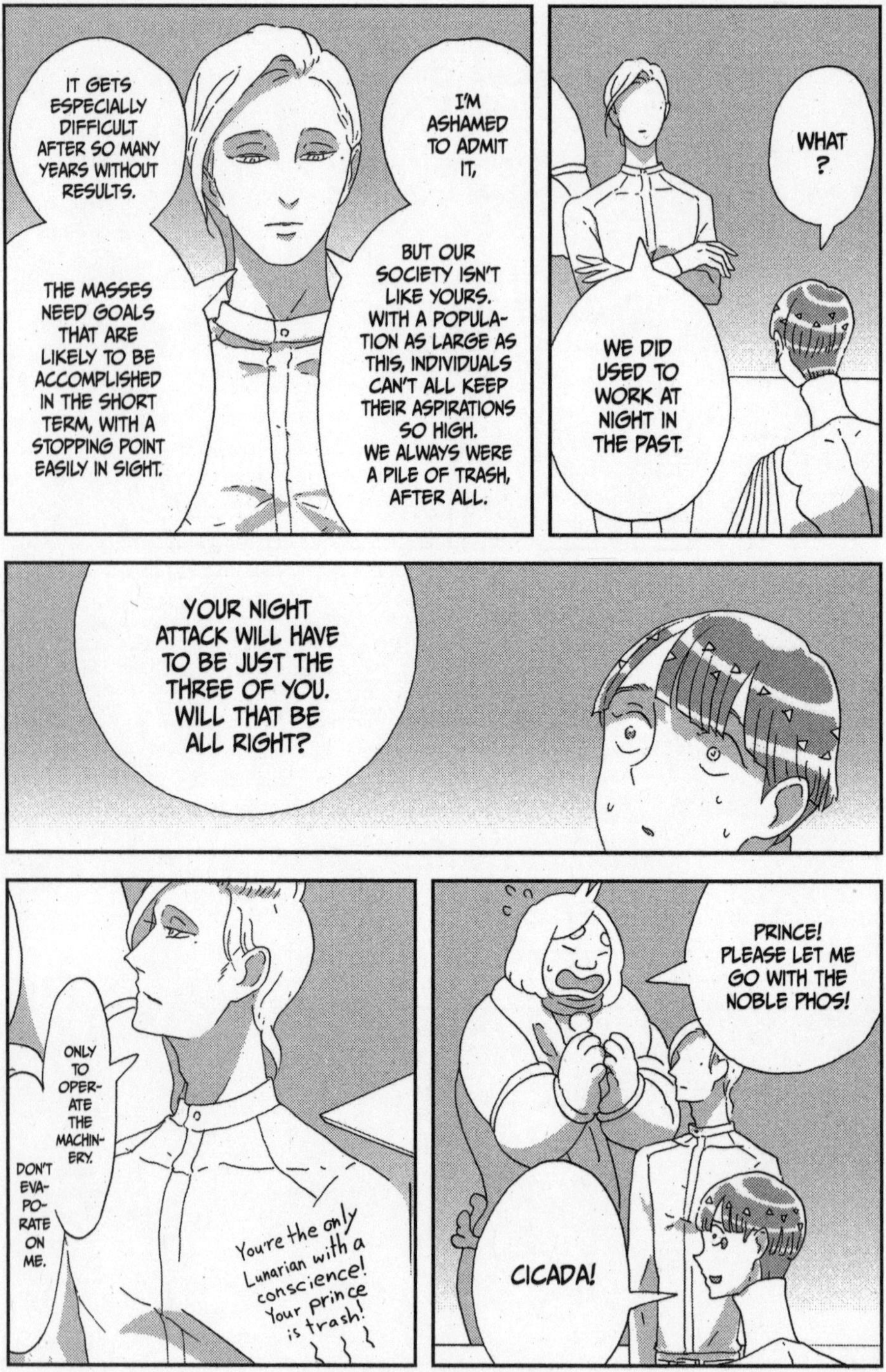
WHAT?
WE DID USED TO WORK AT NIGHT IN THE PAST.
I'M ASHAMED TO ADMIT IT,
BUT OUR SOCIETY ISN'T LIKE YOURS. WITH A POPULATION AS LARGE AS THIS, INDIVIDUALS CAN'T ALL KEEP THEIR ASPIRATIONS SO HIGH. WE ALWAYS WERE A PILE OF TRASH, AFTER ALL.
IT GETS ESPECIALLY DIFFICULT AFTER SO MANY YEARS WITHOUT RESULTS.
THE MASSES NEED GOALS THAT ARE LIKELY TO BE ACCOMPLISHED IN THE SHORT TERM, WITH A STOPPING POINT EASILY IN SIGHT.
YOUR NIGHT ATTACK WILL HAVE TO BE JUST THE THREE OF YOU. WILL THAT BE ALL RIGHT?
PRINCE! PLEASE LET ME GO WITH THE NOBLE PHOS!
CICADA!
ONLY TO OPERATE THE MACHINERY.
DON'T EVAPORATE ON ME.
You're the only Lunarian with a conscience! Your prince is trash!

AS
FOR
YOUR
REQUEST
...

...THAT
WE RESTORE
THE GEMS THAT
WE GROUND
INTO SAND.

THERE
ARE...

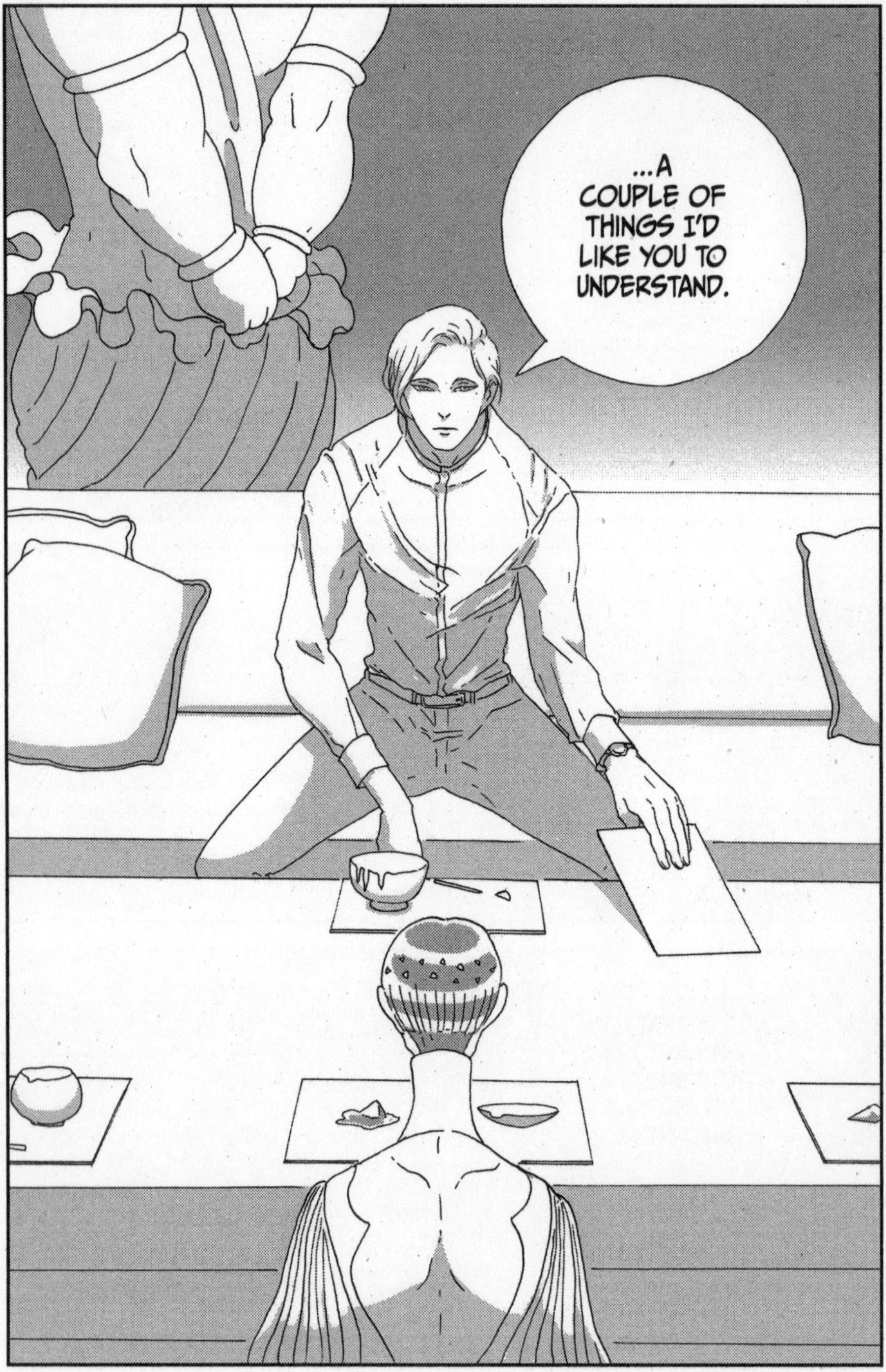
...A COUPLE OF THINGS I'D LIKE YOU TO UNDERSTAND.

CHAPTER 66: Freedom END

CHAPTER 67:

Cairngorm

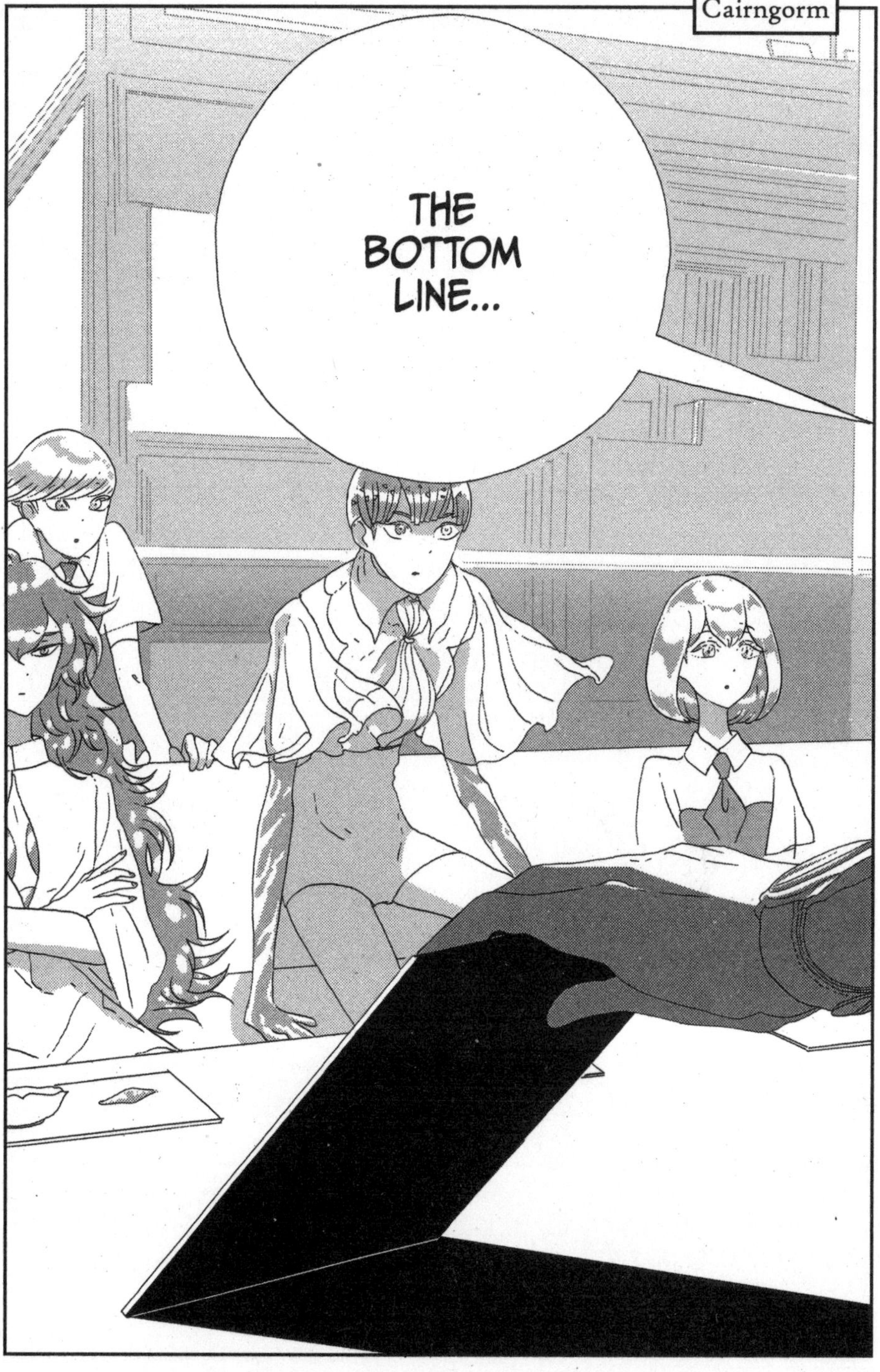
THE BOTTOM LINE...

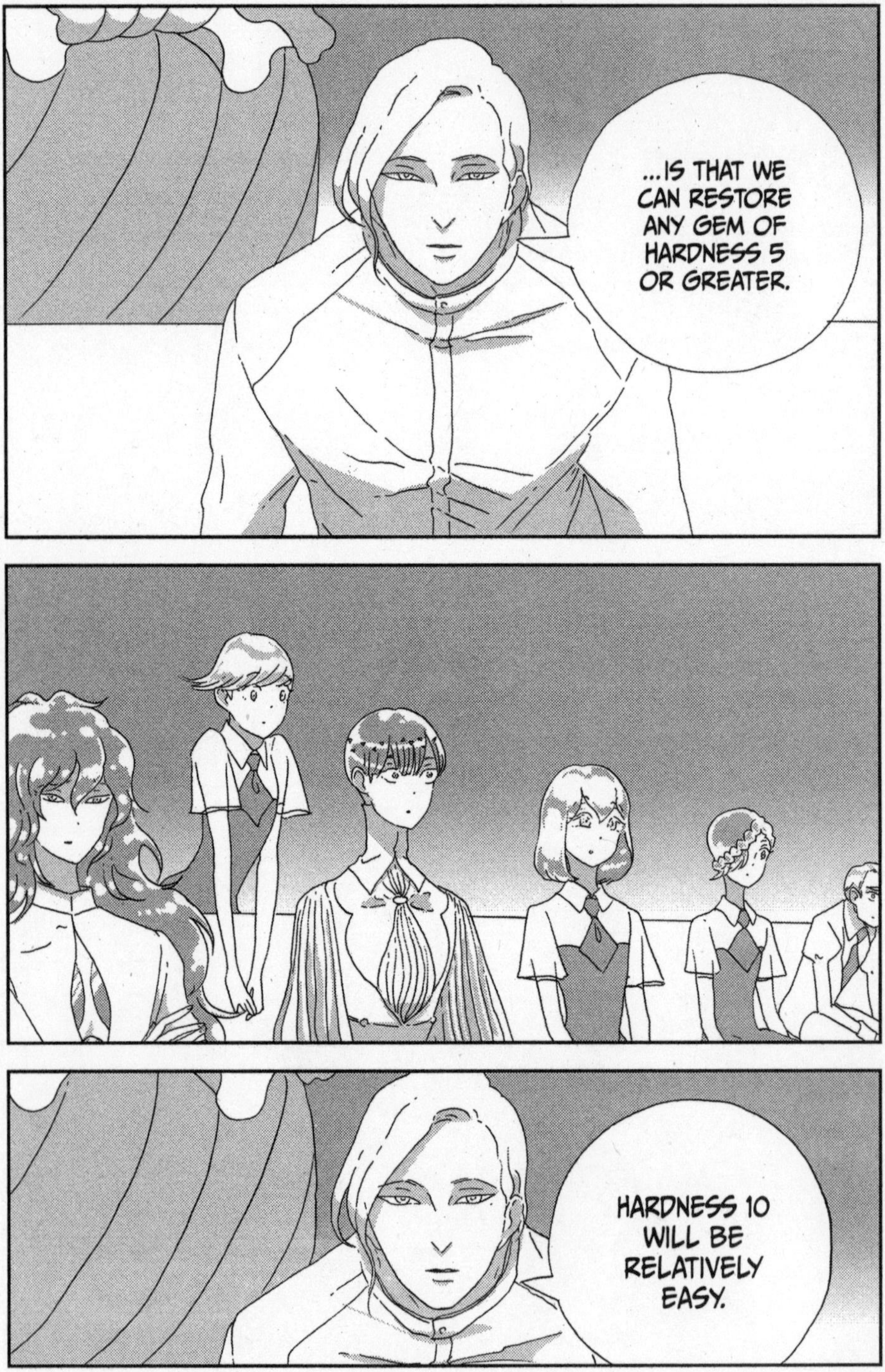
...IS THAT WE CAN RESTORE ANY GEM OF HARDNESS 5 OR GREATER.
HARDNESS 10 WILL BE RELATIVELY EASY.

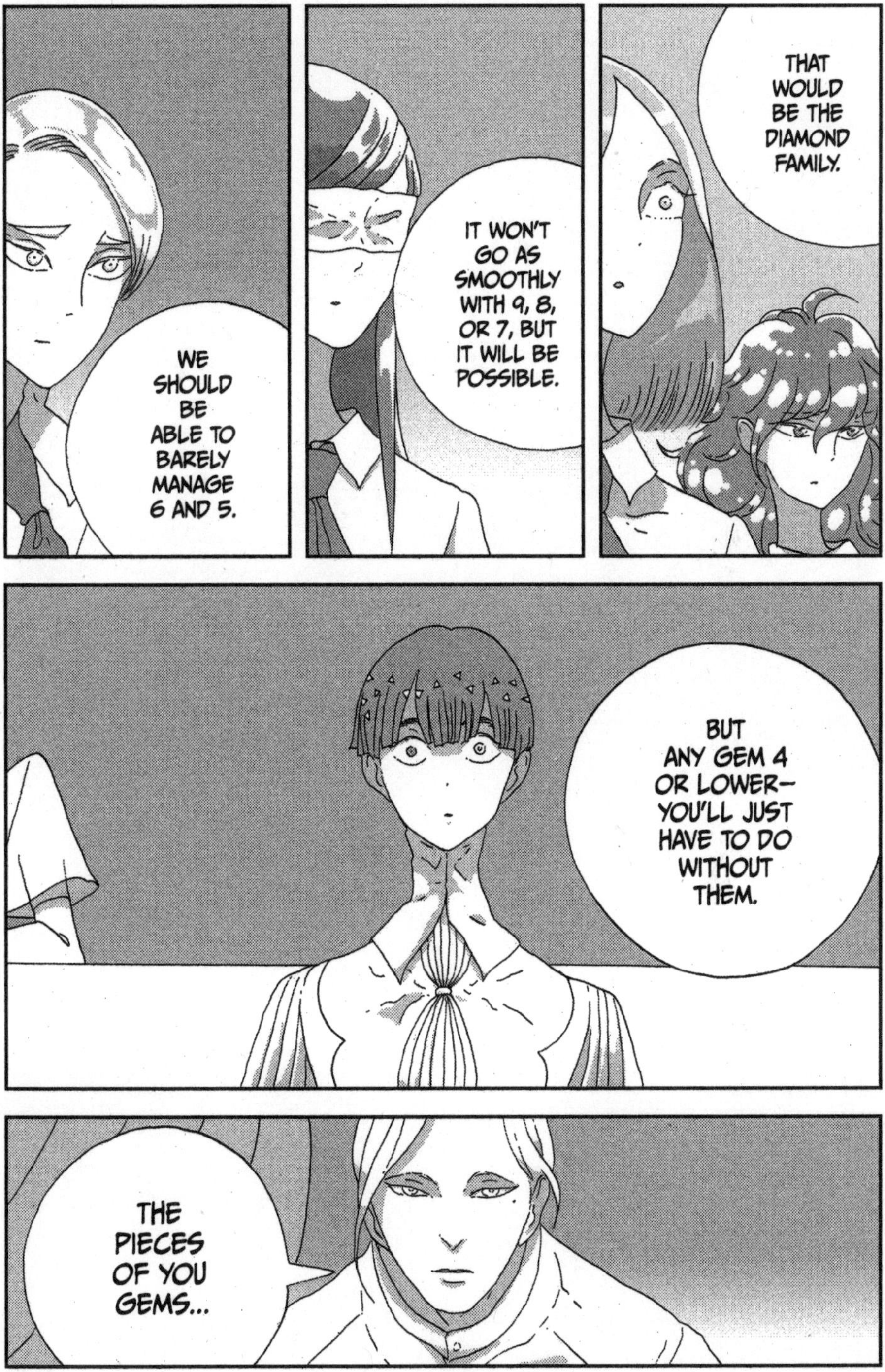
THAT WOULD BE THE DIAMOND FAMILY.
IT WON'T GO AS SMOOTHLY WITH 9, 8, OR 7, BUT IT WILL BE POSSIBLE.
WE SHOULD BE ABLE TO BARELY MANAGE 6 AND 5.
BUT ANY GEM 4 OR LOWER— YOU'LL JUST HAVE TO DO WITHOUT THEM.
THE PIECES OF YOU GEMS...

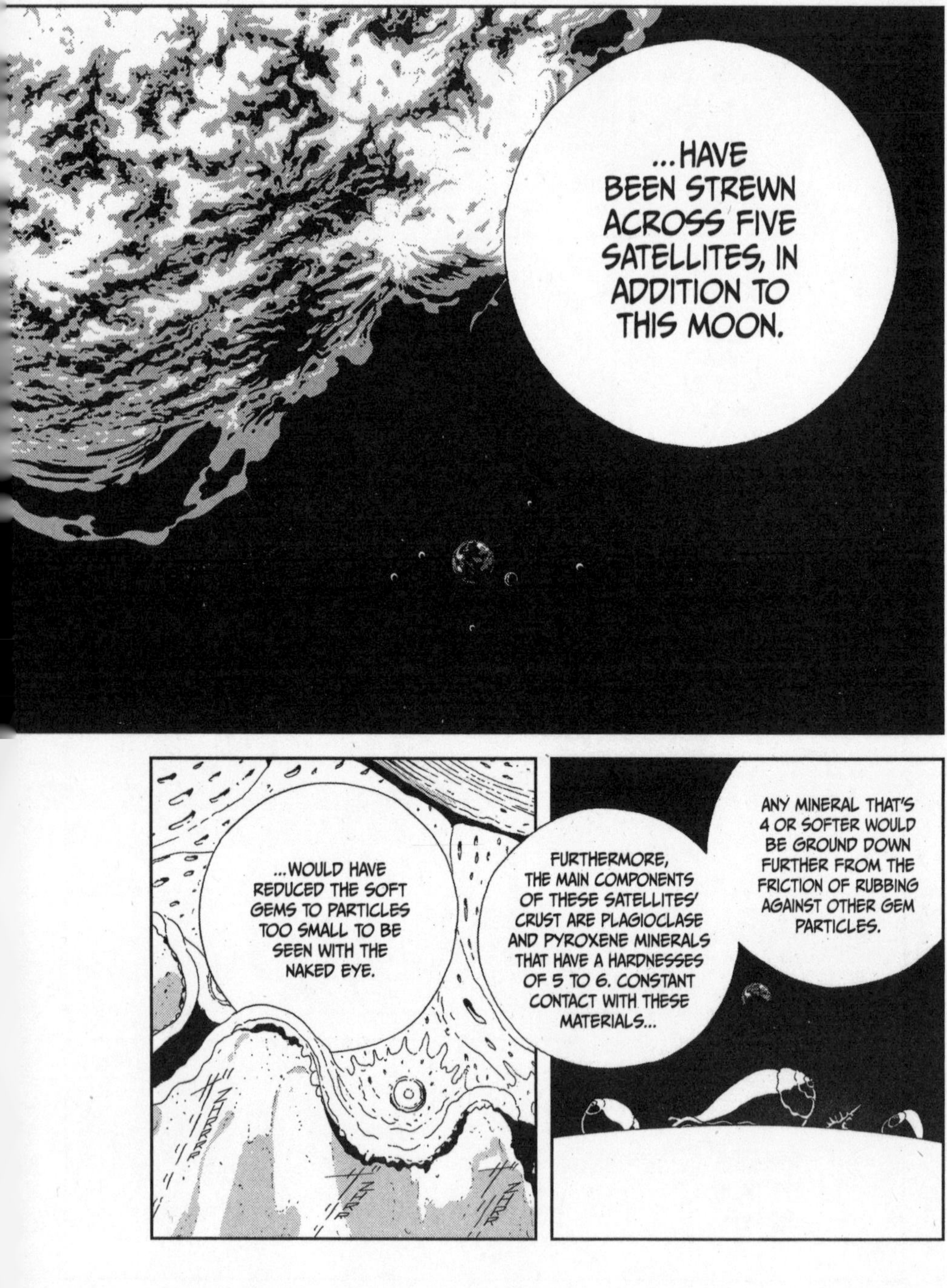

...HAVE BEEN STREWN ACROSS FIVE SATELLITES, IN ADDITION TO THIS MOON.
ANY MINERAL THAT'S 4 OR SOFTER WOULD BE GROUND DOWN FURTHER FROM THE FRICTION OF RUBBING AGAINST OTHER GEM PARTICLES.
FURTHERMORE, THE MAIN COMPONENTS OF THESE SATELLITES' CRUST ARE PLAGIOCLASE AND PYROXENE MINERALS THAT HAVE A HARDNESSES OF 5 TO 6. CONSTANT CONTACT WITH THESE MATERIALS...
...WOULD HAVE REDUCED THE SOFT GEMS TO PARTICLES TOO SMALL TO BE SEEN WITH THE NAKED EYE.

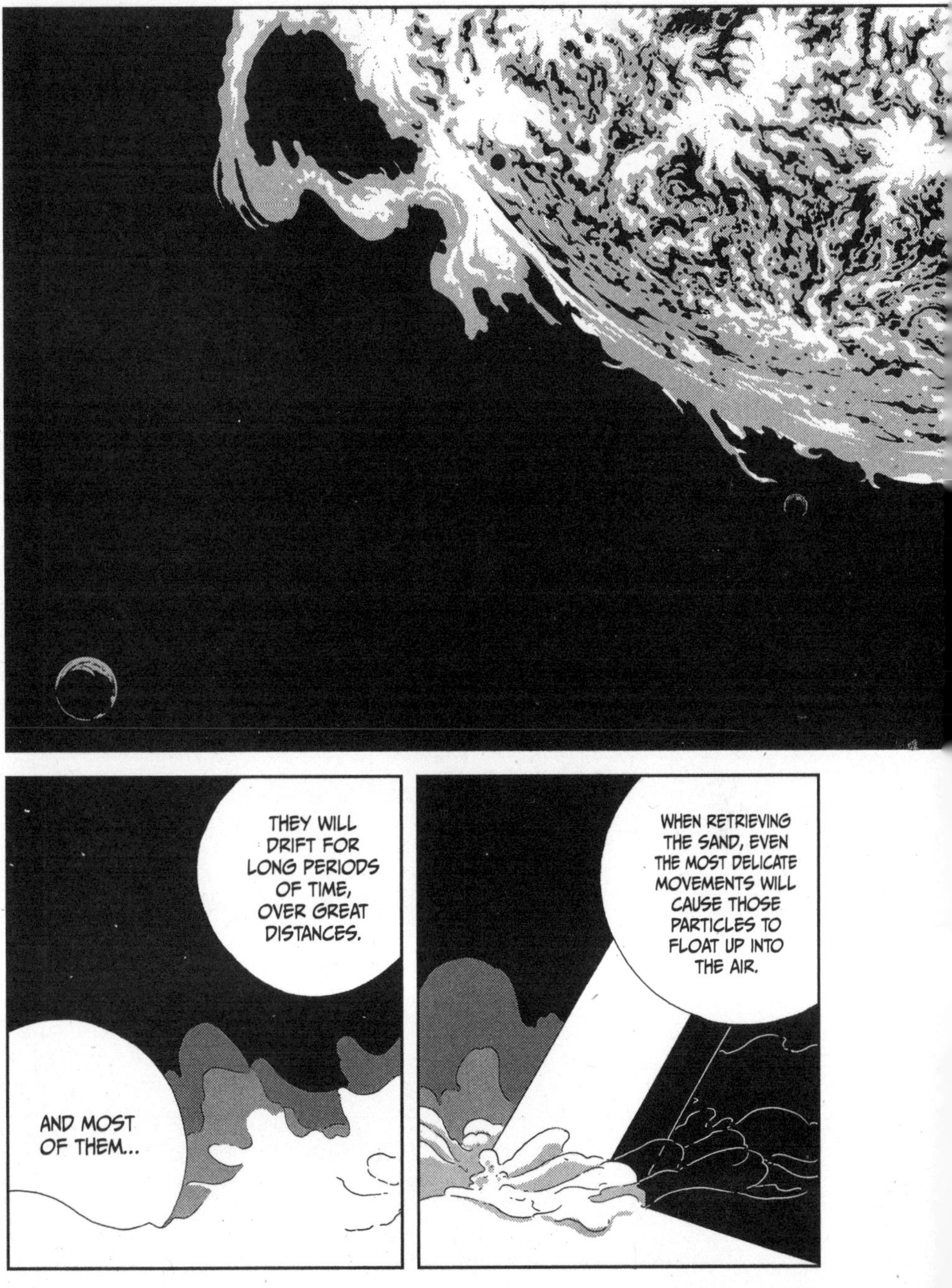
WHEN RETRIEVING THE SAND, EVEN THE MOST DELICATE MOVEMENTS WILL CAUSE THOSE PARTICLES TO FLOAT UP INTO THE AIR.
THEY WILL DRIFT FOR LONG PERIODS OF TIME, OVER GREAT DISTANCES.
AND MOST OF THEM...

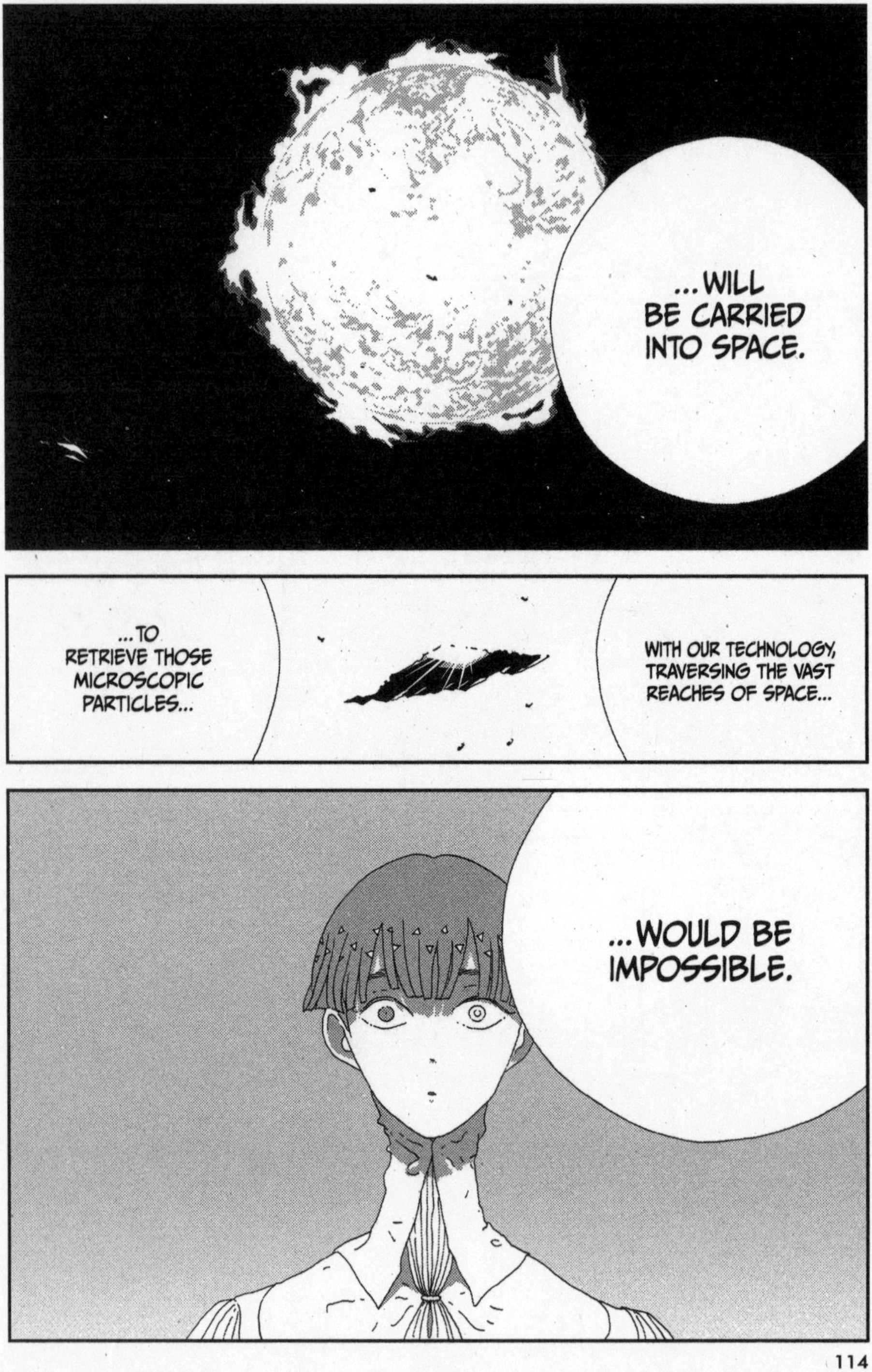
...WILL BE CARRIED INTO SPACE.
WITH OUR TECHNOLOGY, TRAVERSING THE VAST REACHES OF SPACE...
...TO RETRIEVE THOSE MICROSCOPIC PARTICLES...
...WOULD BE IMPOSSIBLE.

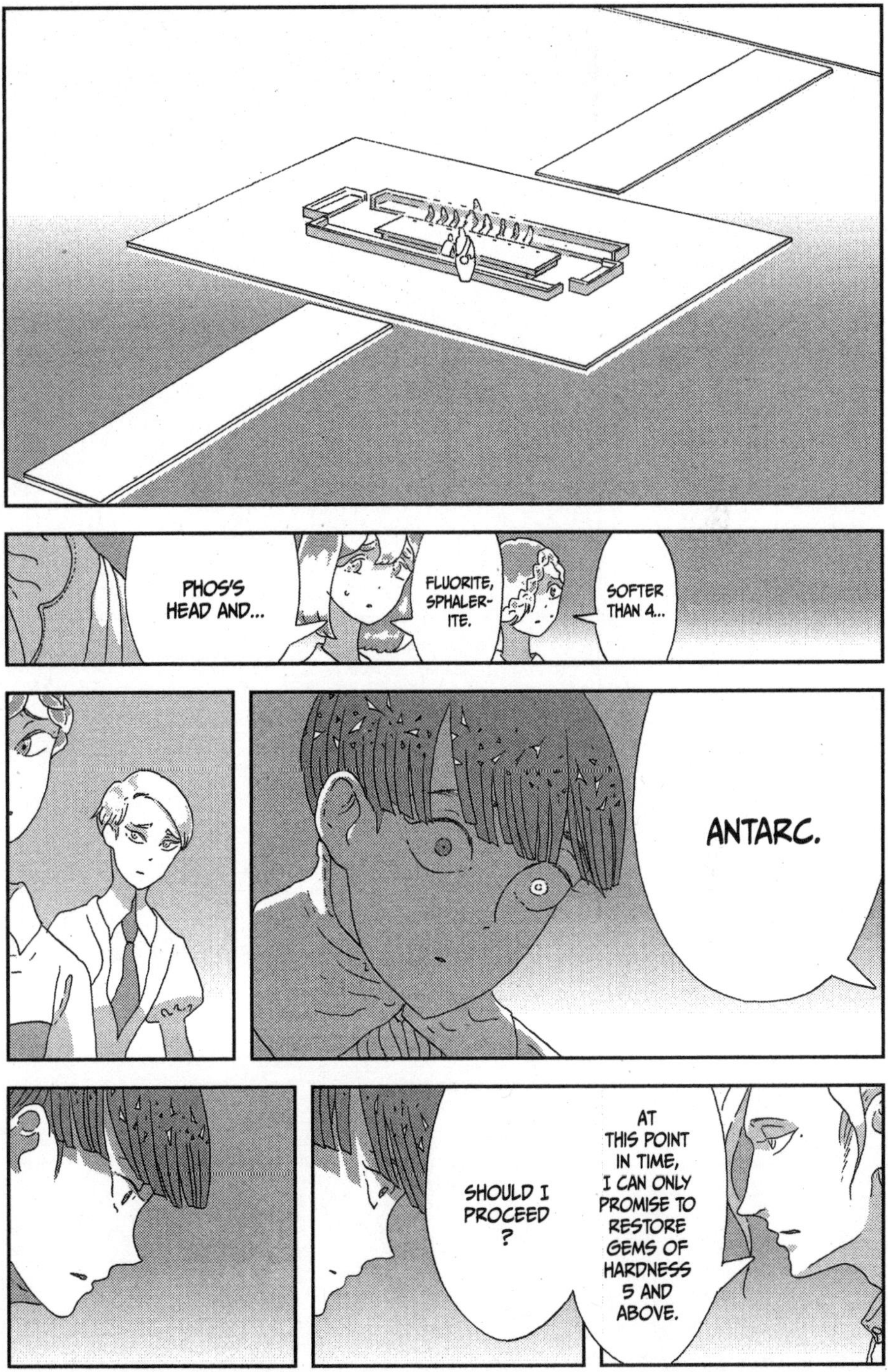
SOFTER THAN 4...
FLUORITE, SPHALERITE.
PHOS'S HEAD AND...
ANTARC.
AT THIS POINT IN TIME, I CAN ONLY PROMISE TO RESTORE GEMS OF HARDNESS 5 AND ABOVE.
SHOULD I PROCEED?

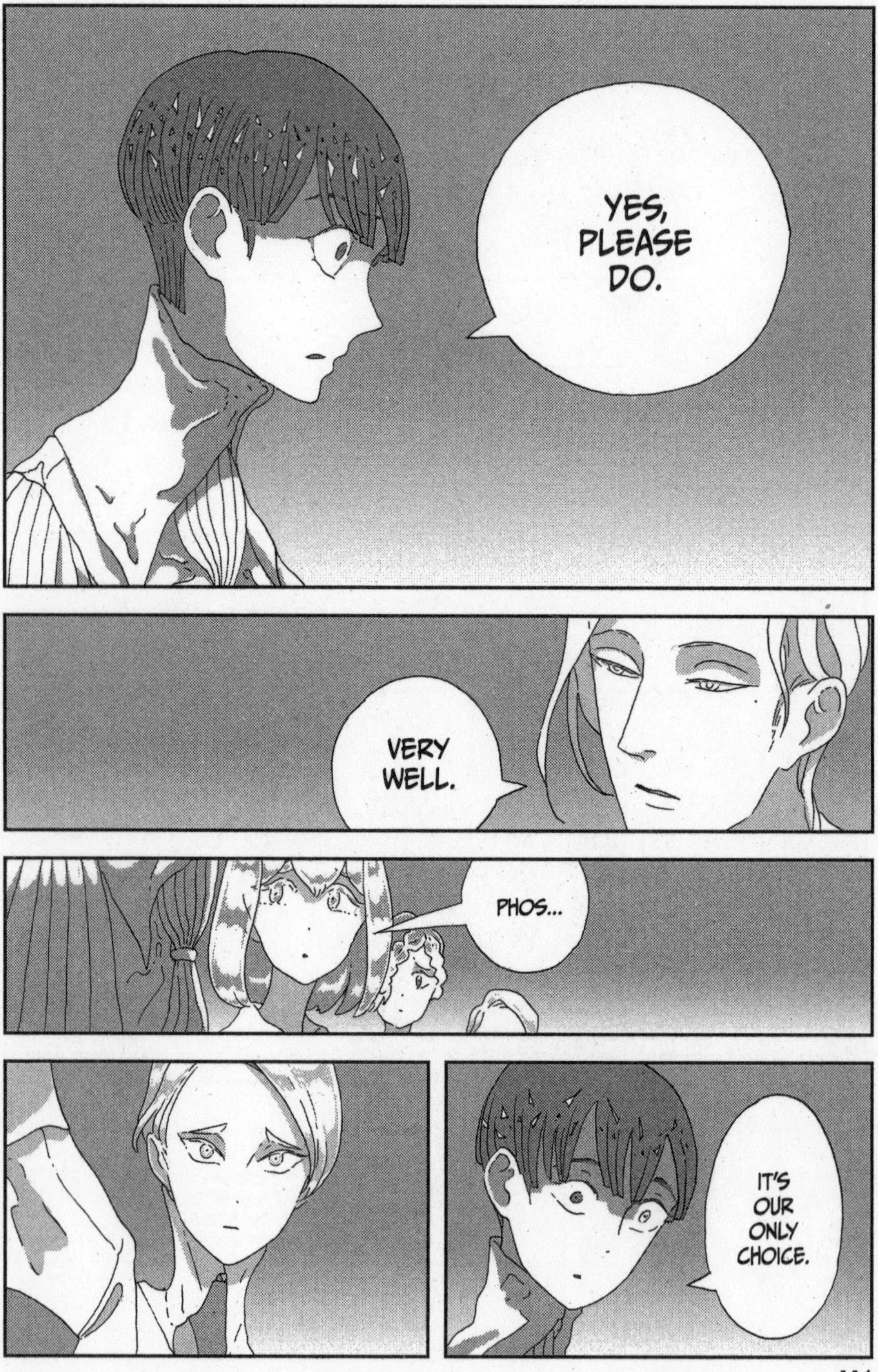
YES, PLEASE DO.
VERY WELL.
PHOS...
IT'S OUR ONLY CHOICE.

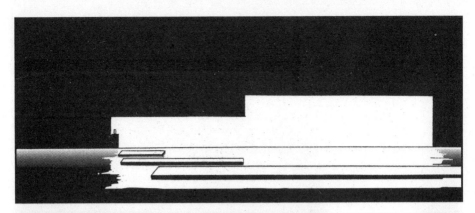

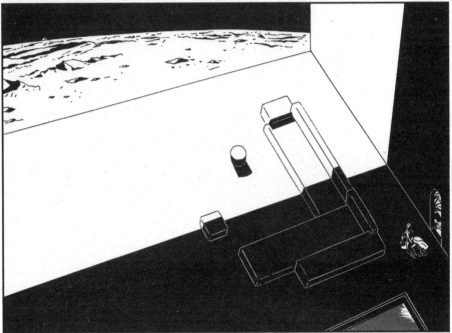

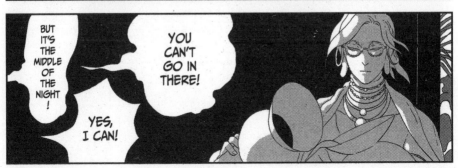

YOU CAN'T GO IN THERE!
BUT IT'S THE MIDDLE OF THE NIGHT!
YES, I CAN!

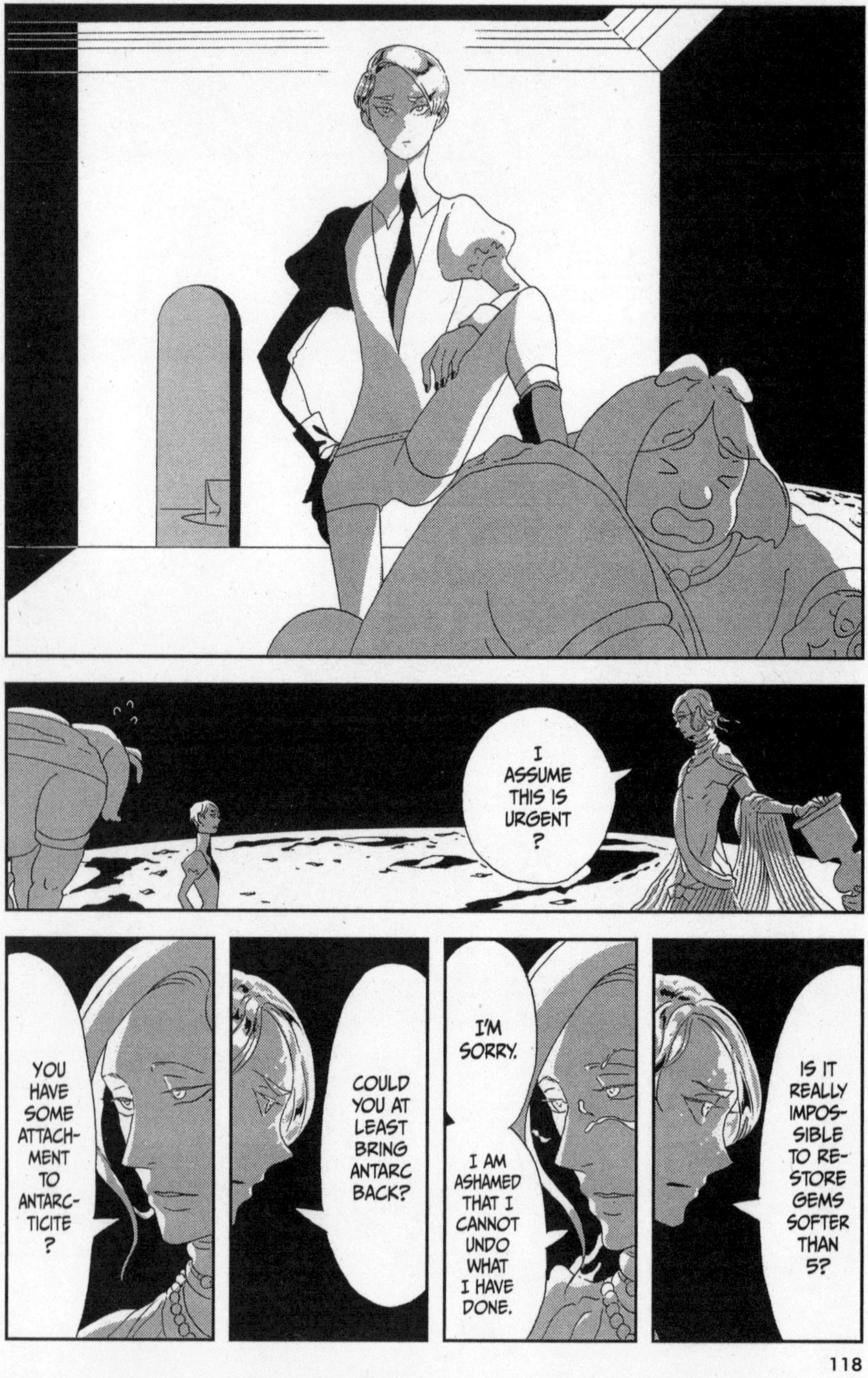
I ASSUME THIS IS URGENT ?
IS IT REALLY IMPOSSIBLE TO RESTORE GEMS SOFTER THAN 5?
I'M SORRY.
I AM ASHAMED THAT I CANNOT UNDO WHAT I HAVE DONE.
COULD YOU AT LEAST BRING ANTARC BACK?
YOU HAVE SOME ATTACHMENT TO ANTARCTICITE ?

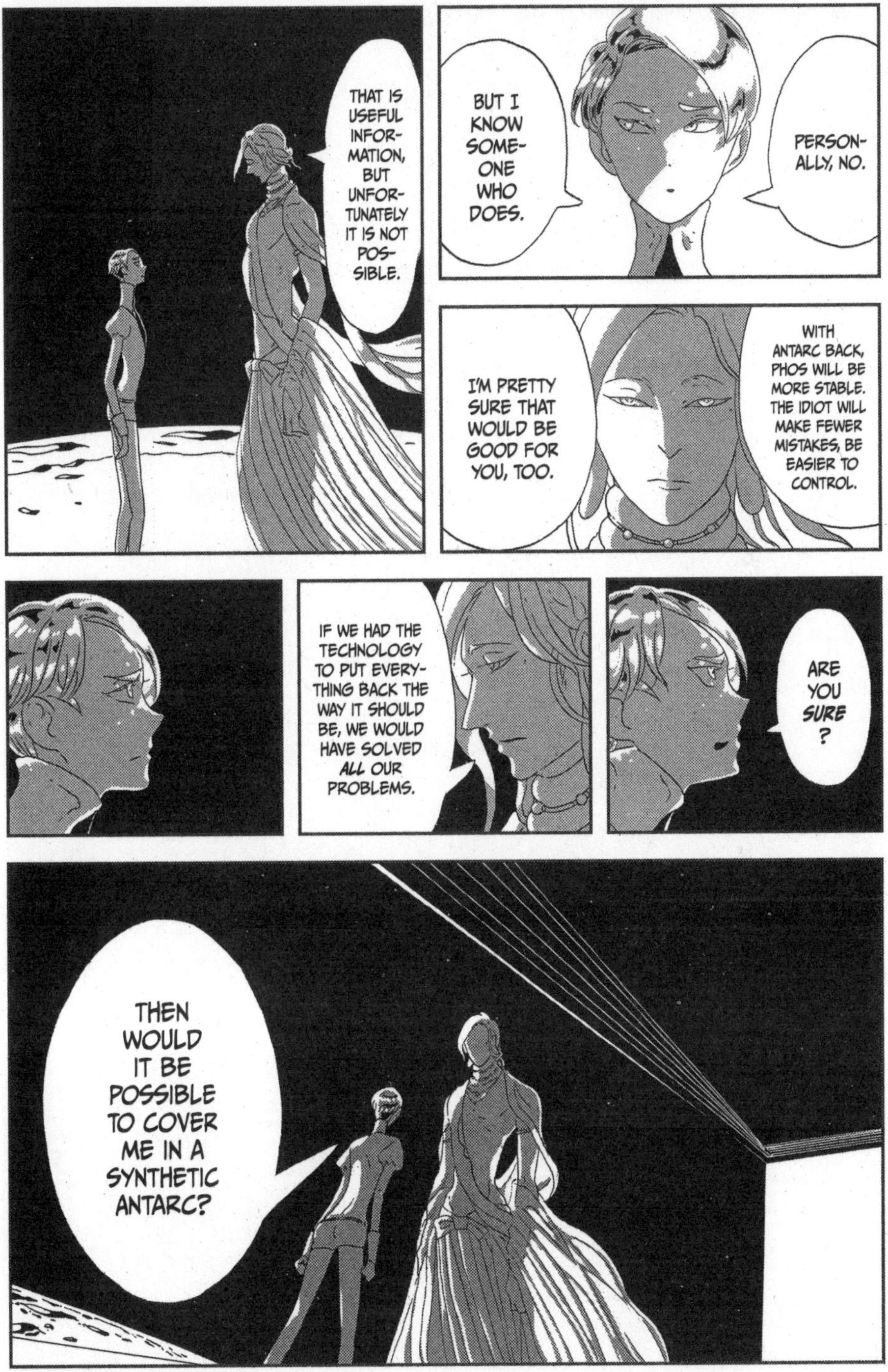
PERSONALLY, NO.
BUT I KNOW SOMEONE WHO DOES.
WITH ANTARC BACK, PHOS WILL BE MORE STABLE. THE IDIOT WILL MAKE FEWER MISTAKES, BE EASIER TO CONTROL.
I'M PRETTY SURE THAT WOULD BE GOOD FOR YOU, TOO.
THAT IS USEFUL INFORMATION, BUT UNFORTUNATELY IT IS NOT POSSIBLE.
ARE YOU *SURE* ?
IF WE HAD THE TECHNOLOGY TO PUT EVERYTHING BACK THE WAY IT SHOULD BE, WE WOULD HAVE SOLVED *ALL* OUR PROBLEMS.
THEN WOULD IT BE POSSIBLE TO COVER ME IN A SYNTHETIC ANTARC?

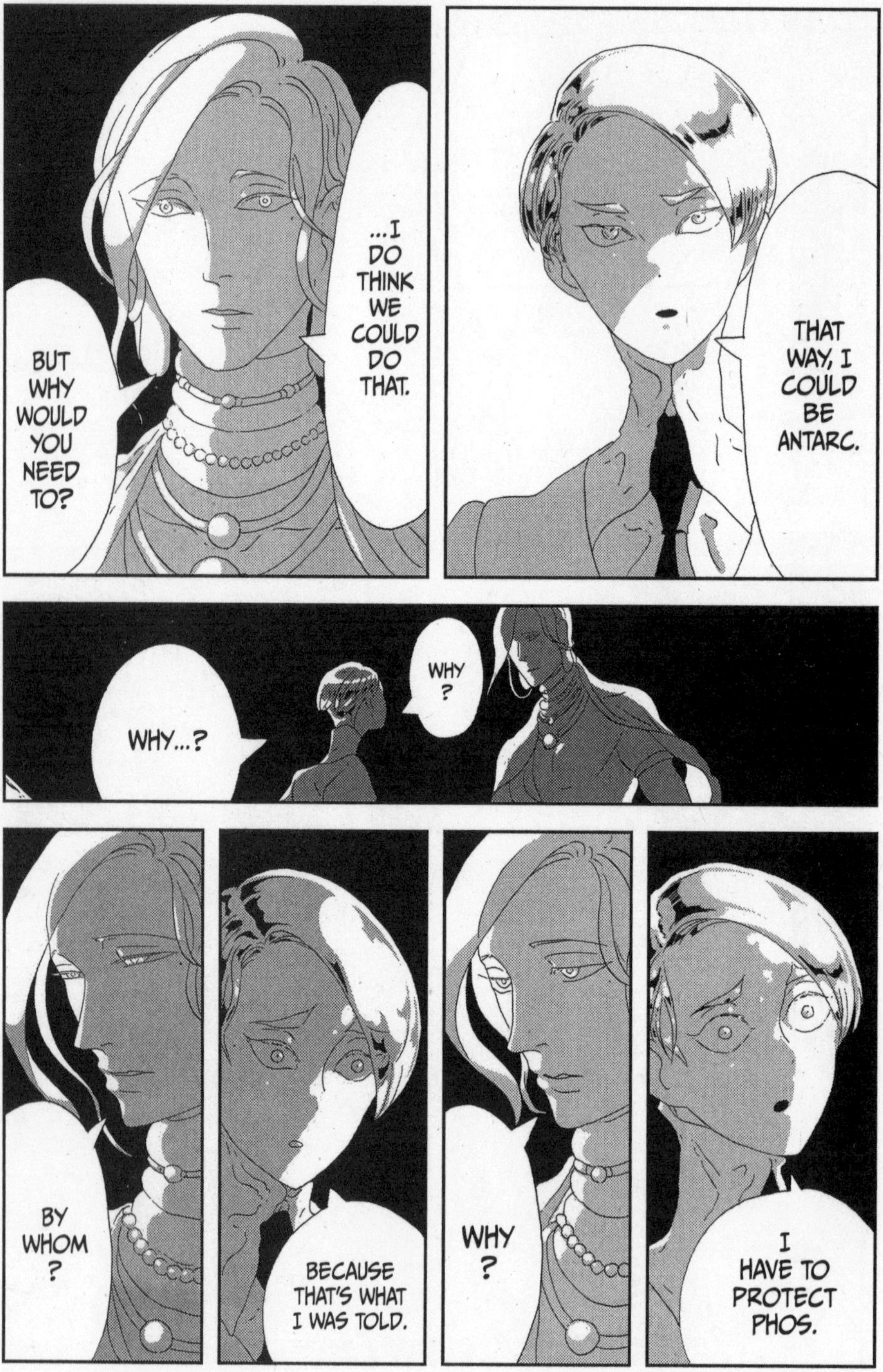
THAT WAY, I COULD BE ANTARC.
...I DO THINK WE COULD DO THAT.
BUT WHY WOULD YOU NEED TO?
WHY ?
WHY...?
I HAVE TO PROTECT PHOS.
WHY ?
BECAUSE THAT'S WHAT I WAS TOLD.
BY WHOM ?

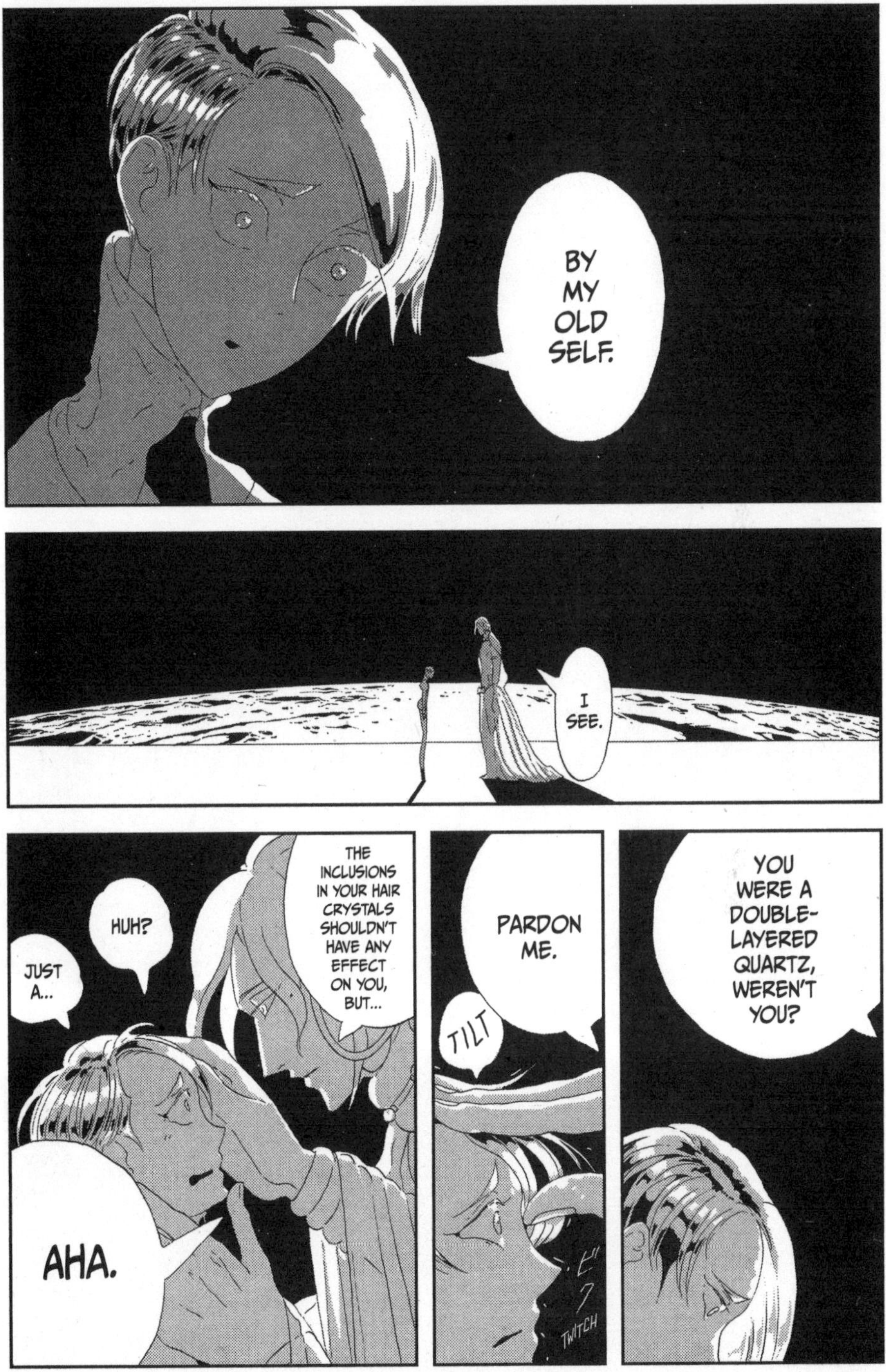

BY MY OLD SELF.
I SEE.
YOU WERE A DOUBLE-LAYERED QUARTZ, WEREN'T YOU?
PARDON ME.
TILT
ビク
TWITCH
THE INCLUSIONS IN YOUR HAIR CRYSTALS SHOULDN'T HAVE ANY EFFECT ON YOU, BUT...
HUH?
JUST A...
AHA.

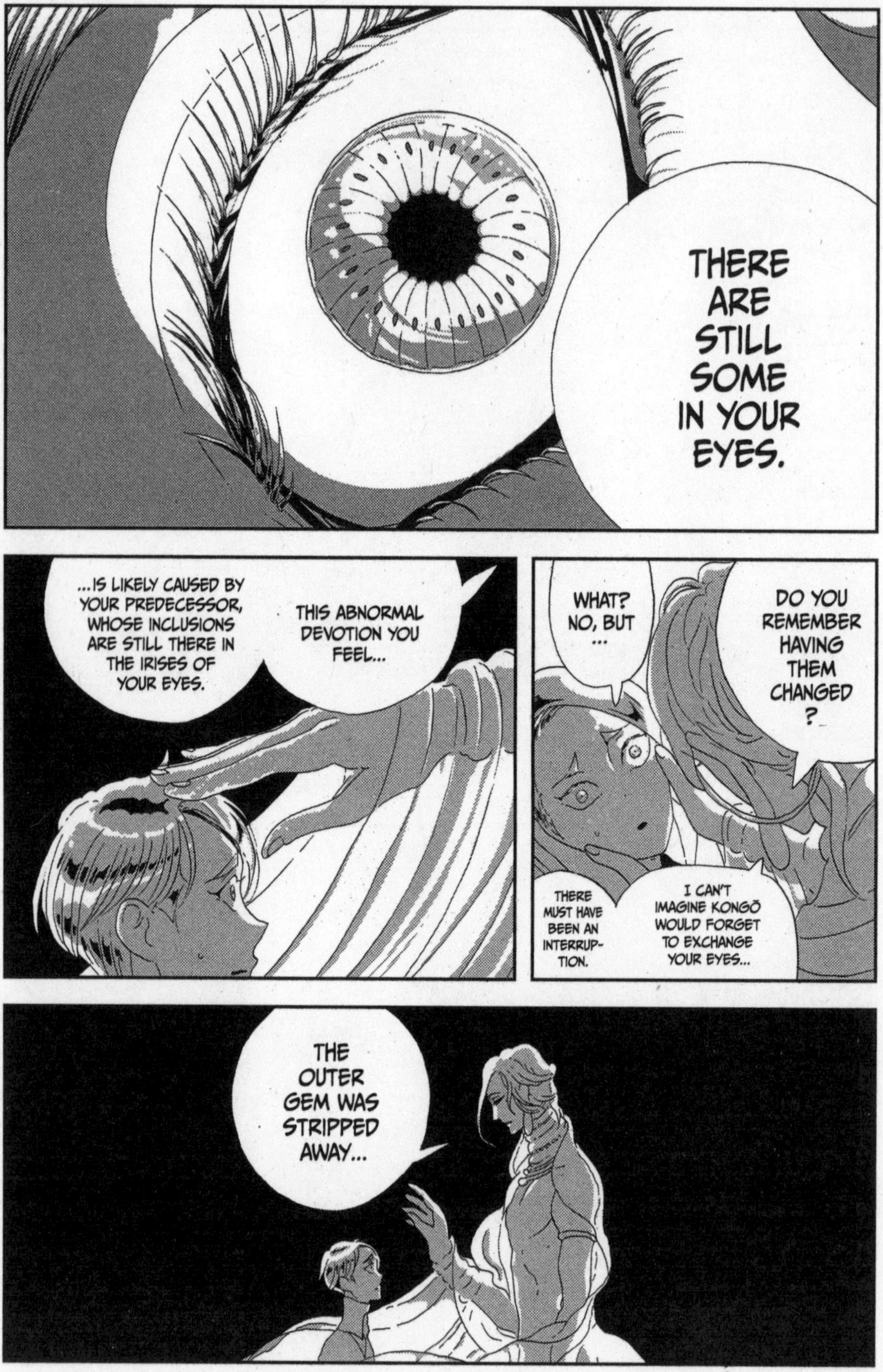
THERE ARE STILL SOME IN YOUR EYES.
DO YOU REMEMBER HAVING THEM CHANGED?
WHAT? NO, BUT ...
I CAN'T IMAGINE KONGŌ WOULD FORGET TO EXCHANGE YOUR EYES...
THERE MUST HAVE BEEN AN INTERRUP-TION.
THIS ABNORMAL DEVOTION YOU FEEL...
...IS LIKELY CAUSED BY YOUR PREDECESSOR, WHOSE INCLUSIONS ARE STILL THERE IN THE IRISES OF YOUR EYES.
THE OUTER GEM WAS STRIPPED AWAY...

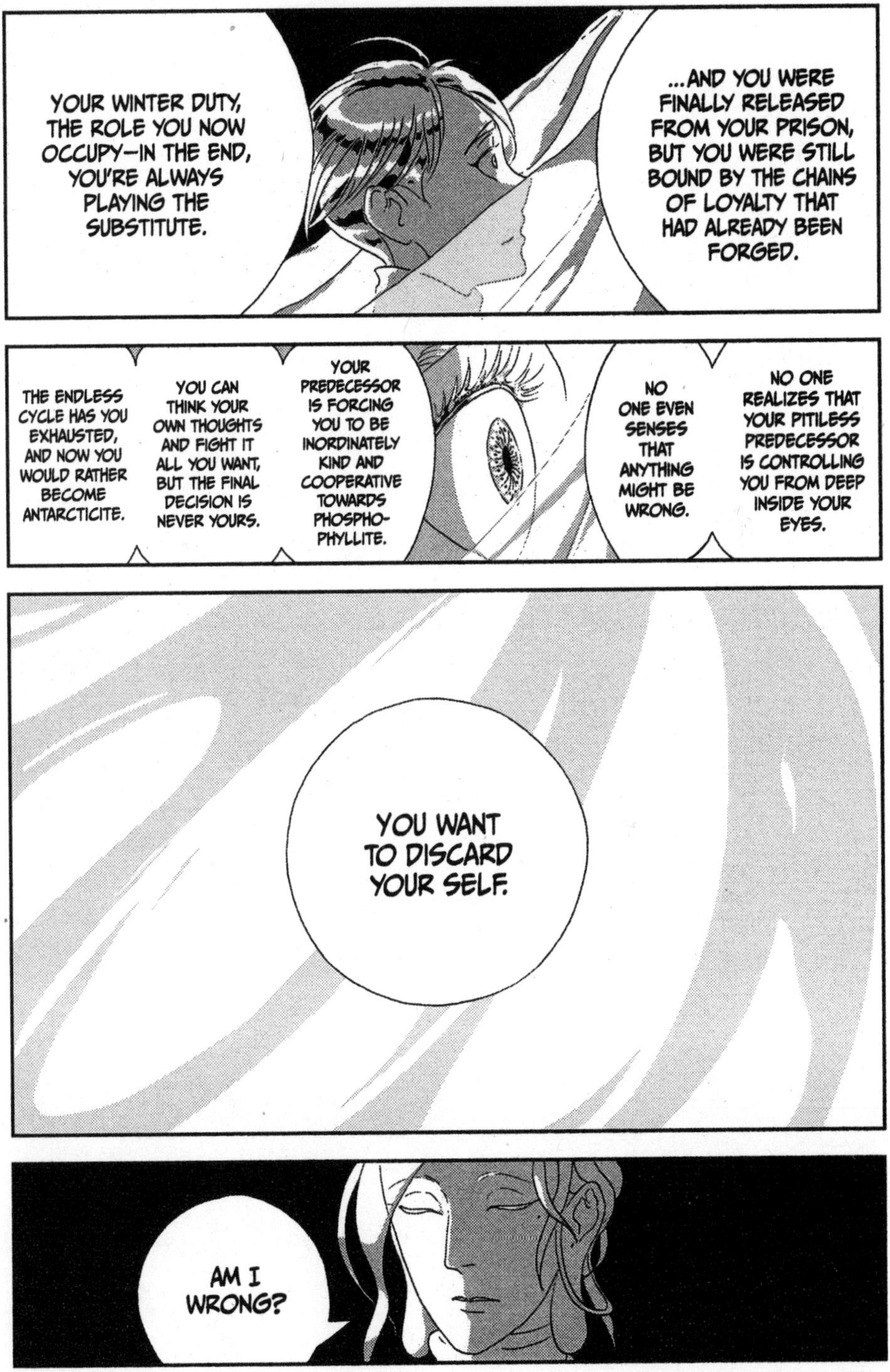
...AND YOU WERE FINALLY RELEASED FROM YOUR PRISON, BUT YOU WERE STILL BOUND BY THE CHAINS OF LOYALTY THAT HAD ALREADY BEEN FORGED.
YOUR WINTER DUTY, THE ROLE YOU NOW OCCUPY—IN THE END, YOU'RE ALWAYS PLAYING THE SUBSTITUTE.
NO ONE REALIZES THAT YOUR PITILESS PREDECESSOR IS CONTROLLING YOU FROM DEEP INSIDE YOUR EYES.
NO ONE EVEN SENSES THAT ANYTHING MIGHT BE WRONG.
YOUR PREDECESSOR IS FORCING YOU TO BE INORDINATELY KIND AND COOPERATIVE TOWARDS PHOSPHO-PHYLLITE.
YOU CAN THINK YOUR OWN THOUGHTS AND FIGHT IT ALL YOU WANT, BUT THE FINAL DECISION IS NEVER YOURS.
THE ENDLESS CYCLE HAS YOU EXHAUSTED, AND NOW YOU WOULD RATHER BECOME ANTARCTICITE.
YOU WANT TO DISCARD YOUR SELF.
AM I WRONG?

HOW...

...DID YOU...

I KNOW A THING OR TWO ABOUT CURSES.

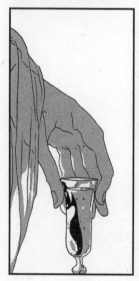

I DECLINE YOUR REQUEST TO TURN YOU INTO ANTARCTICITE.

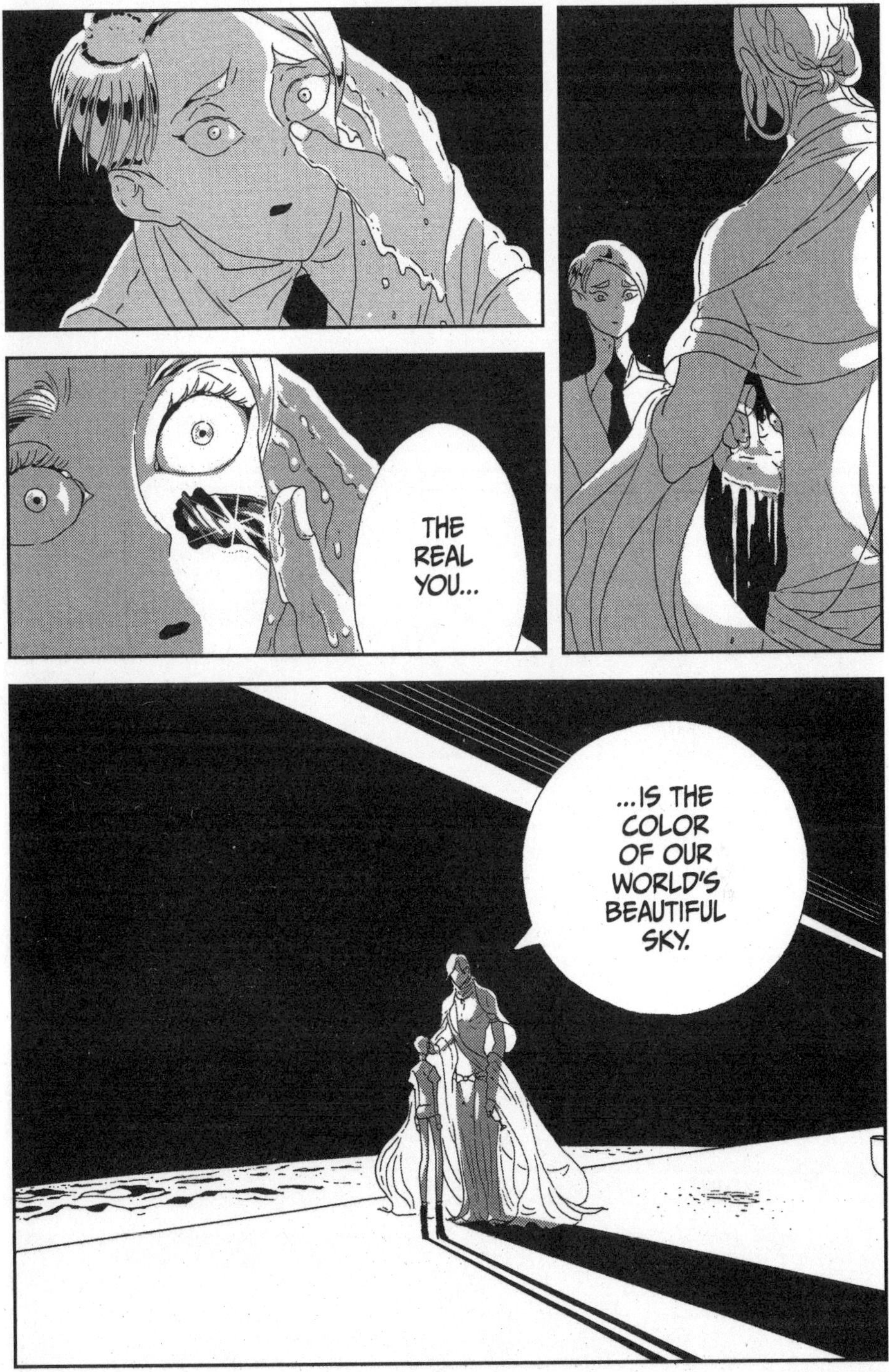
THE REAL YOU...
...IS THE COLOR OF OUR WORLD'S BEAUTIFUL SKY.

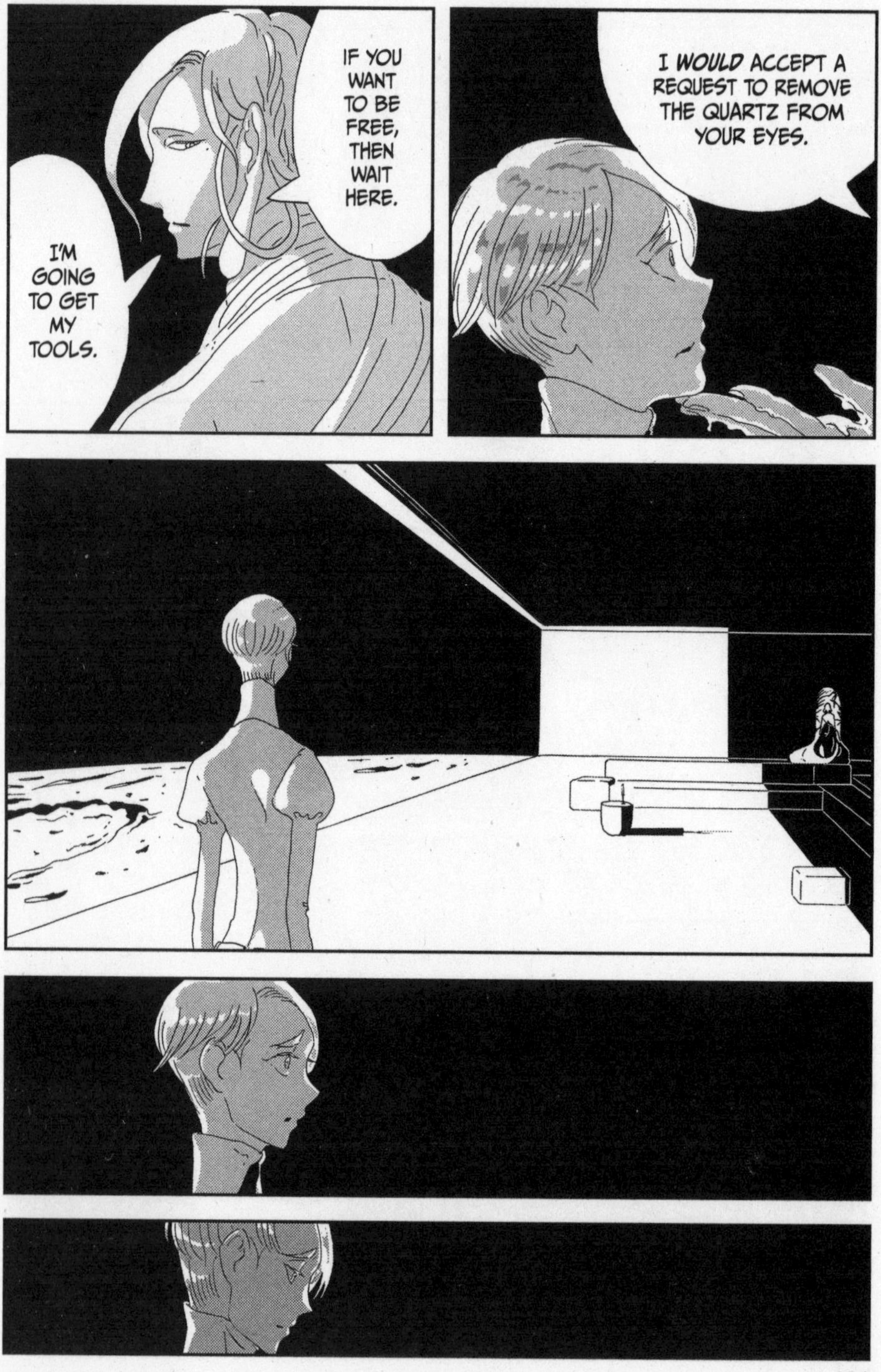
I *WOULD* ACCEPT A REQUEST TO REMOVE THE QUARTZ FROM YOUR EYES.
IF YOU WANT TO BE FREE, THEN WAIT HERE.
I'M GOING TO GET MY TOOLS.

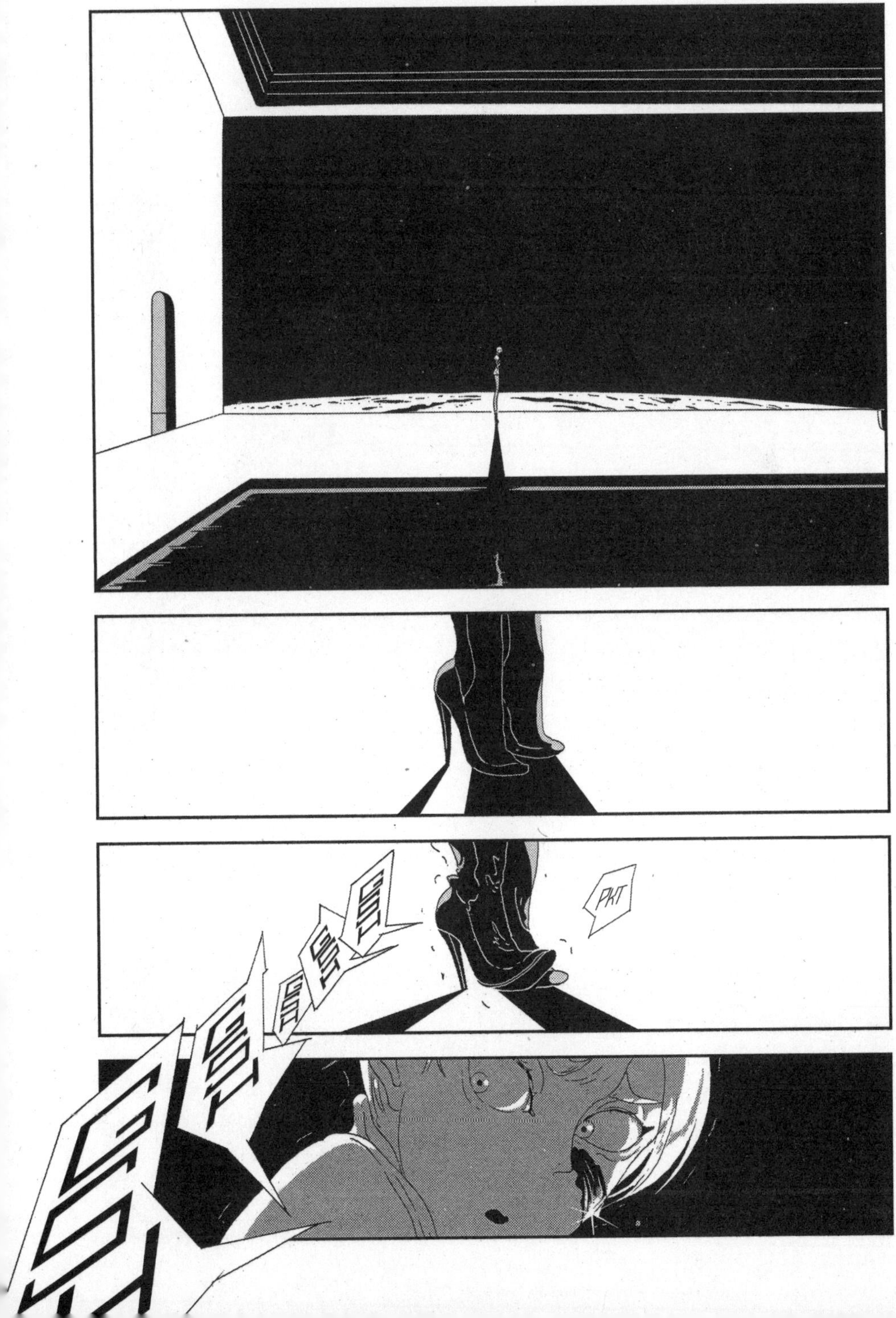
PKT
GUT
GUT
GUT
GUT
GUT

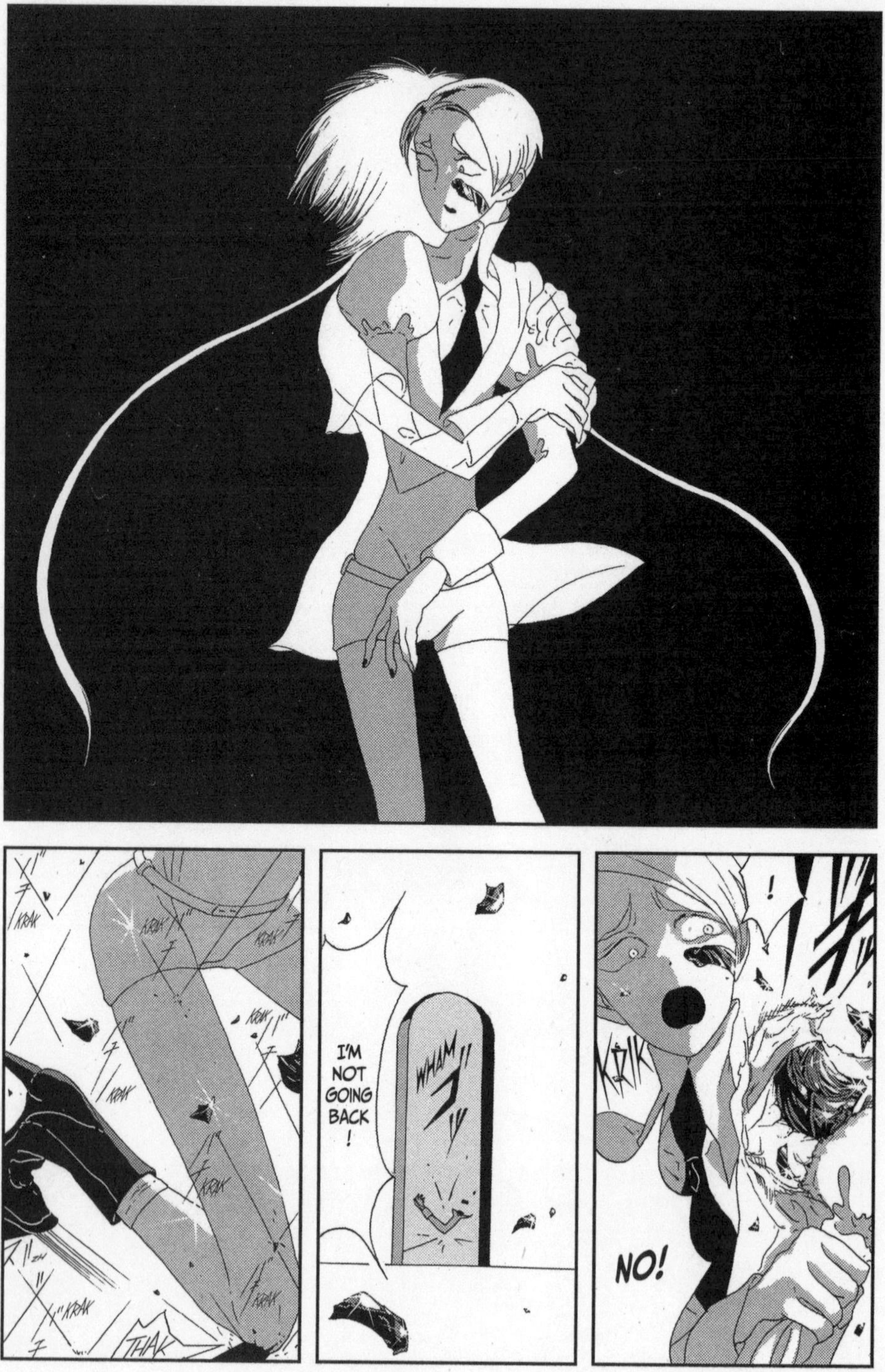
!
KRIK
NO!
I'M NOT GOING BACK!
WHAM
KRAK
KRAK
KRAK
KRAK
KRAK
KRAK
KRAK
THAK

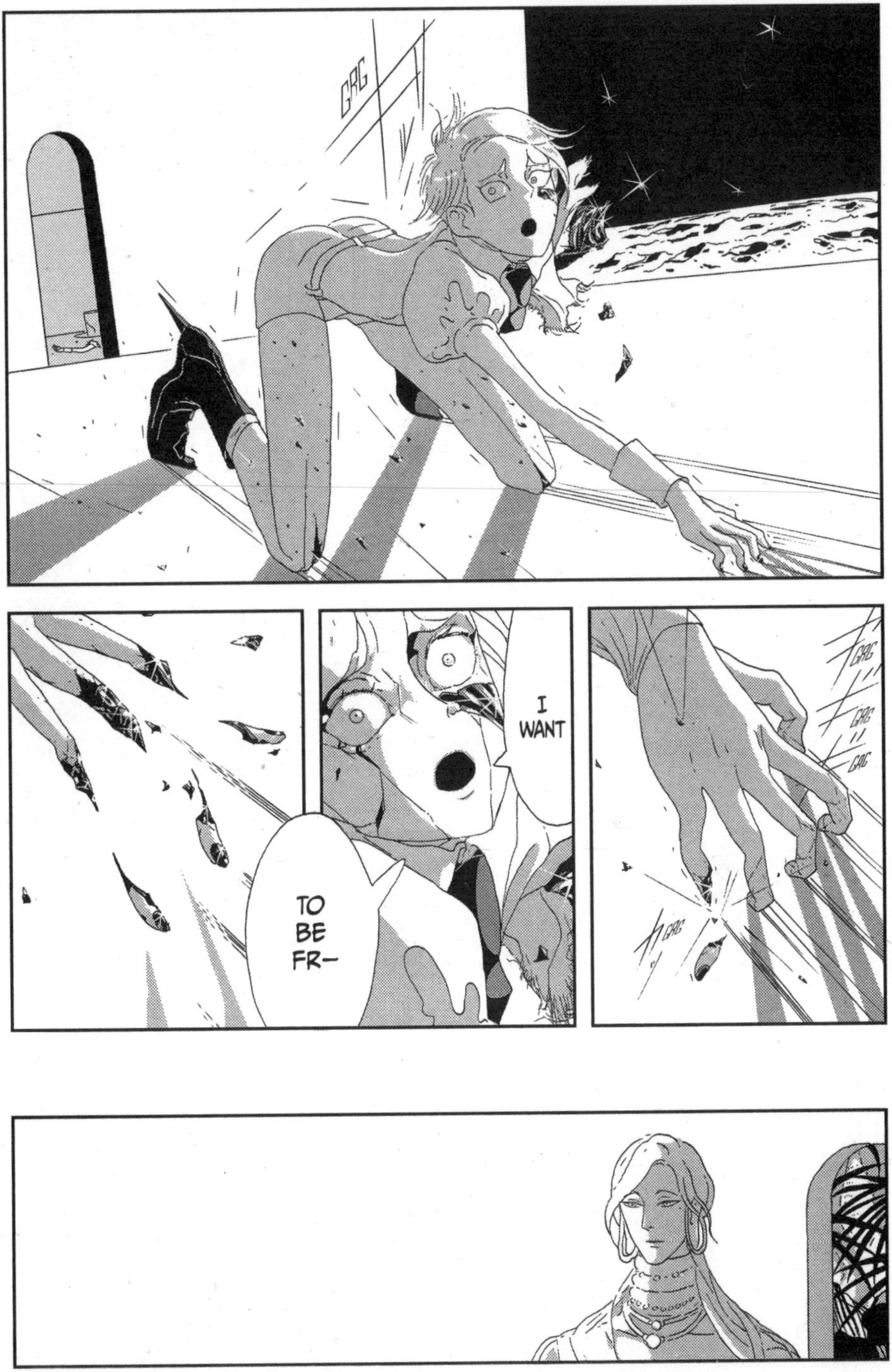
GRG
GRG
GRG
GRG
GRG
I WANT
TO BE FR–

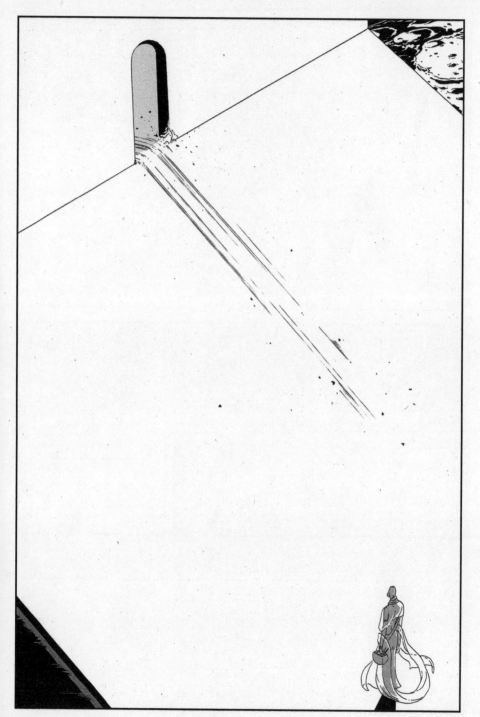

CLASP

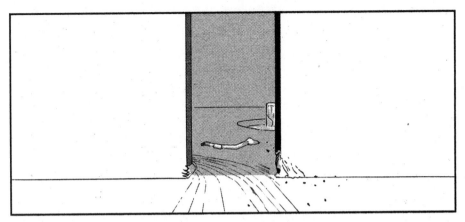

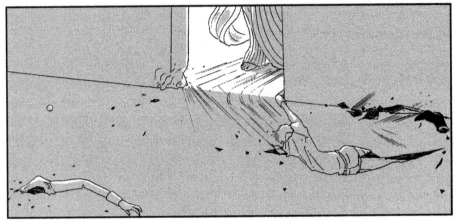

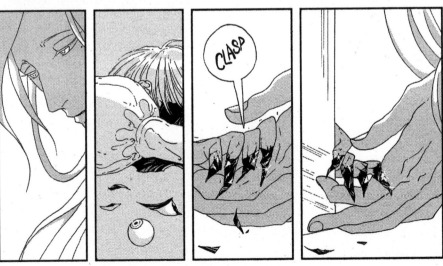

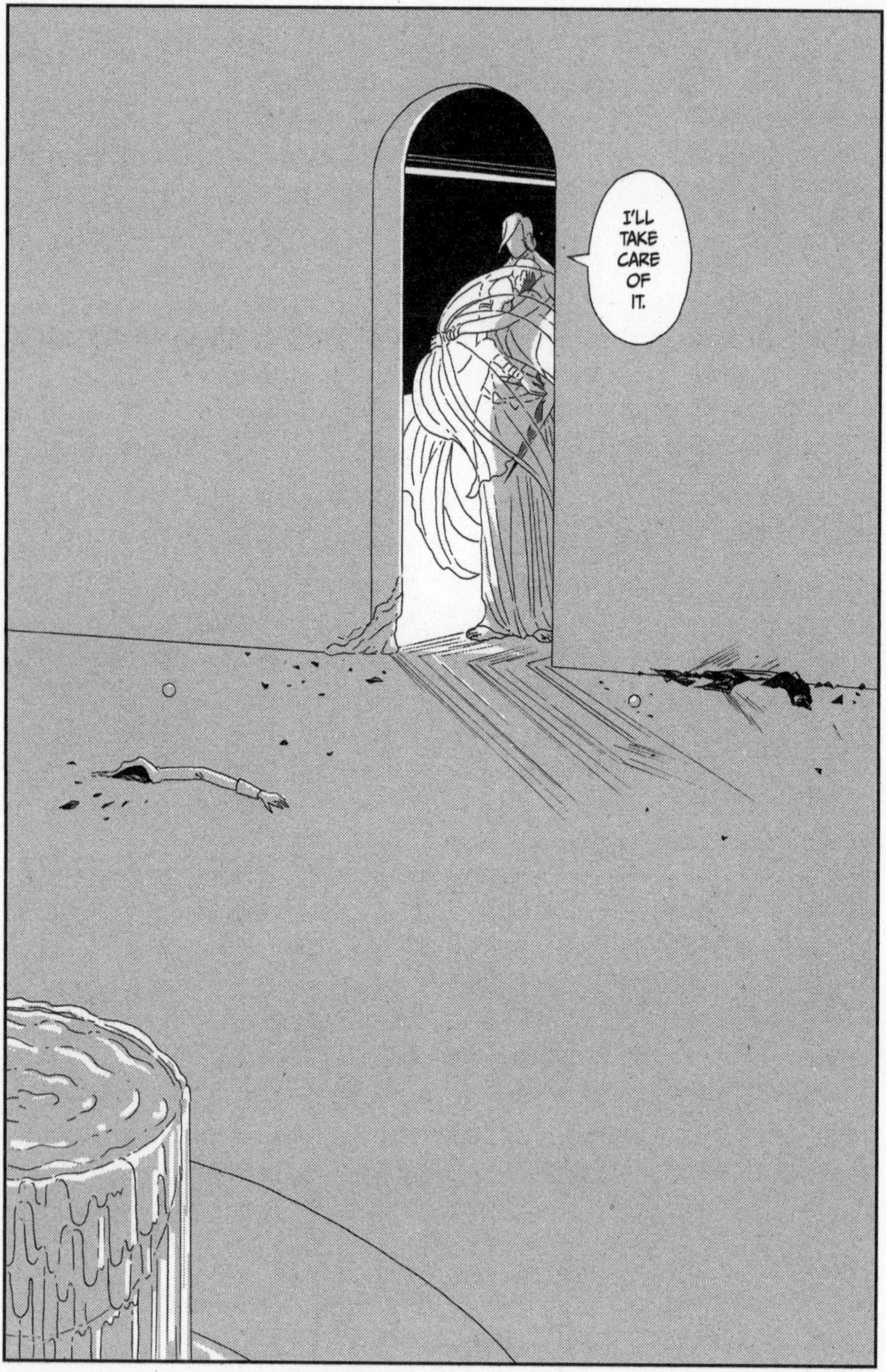
I'LL TAKE CARE OF IT.

CHAPTER 67: Cairngorm END

CHAPTER 68:

Change

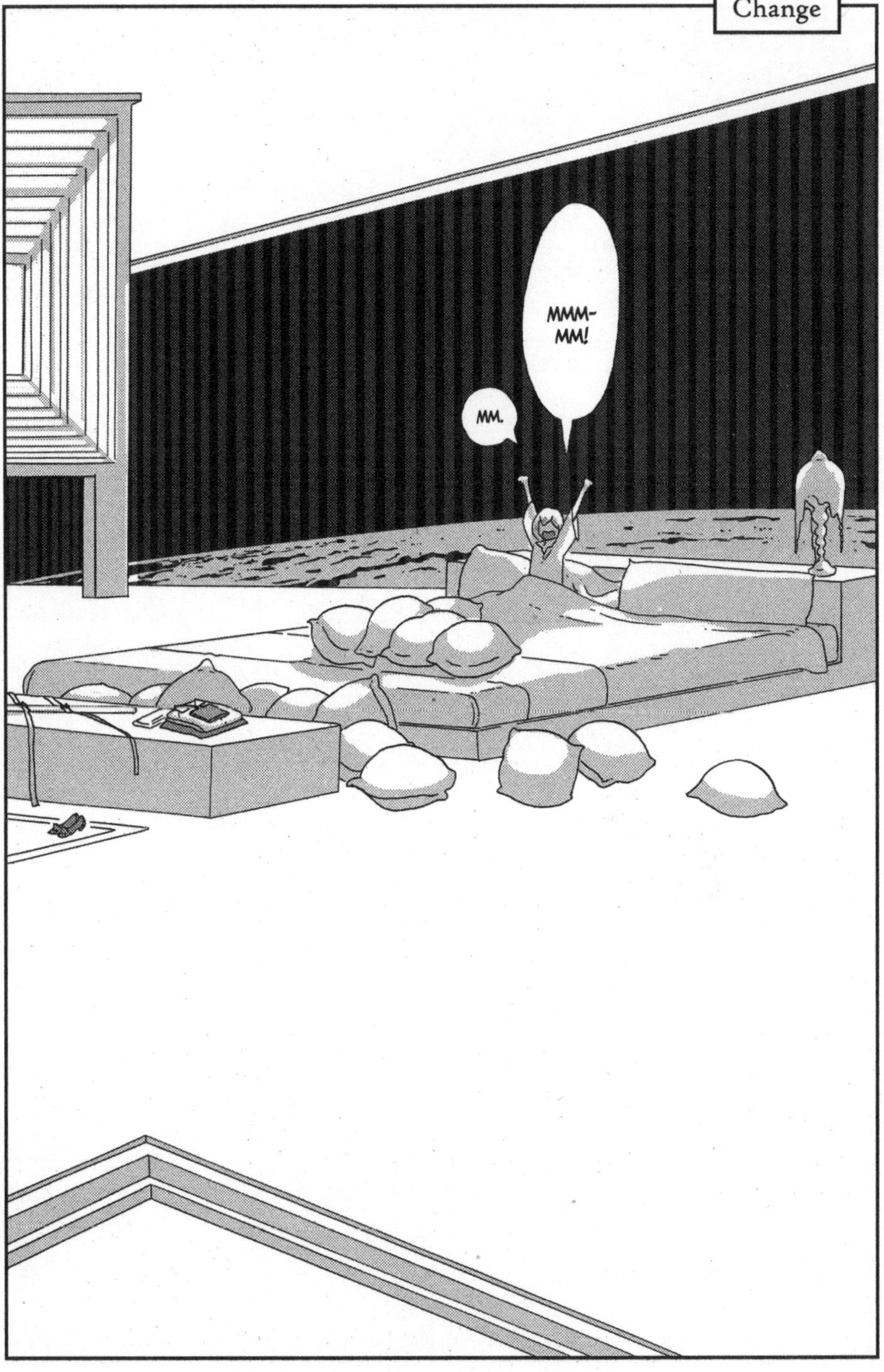
MMM-
MM!
MM.

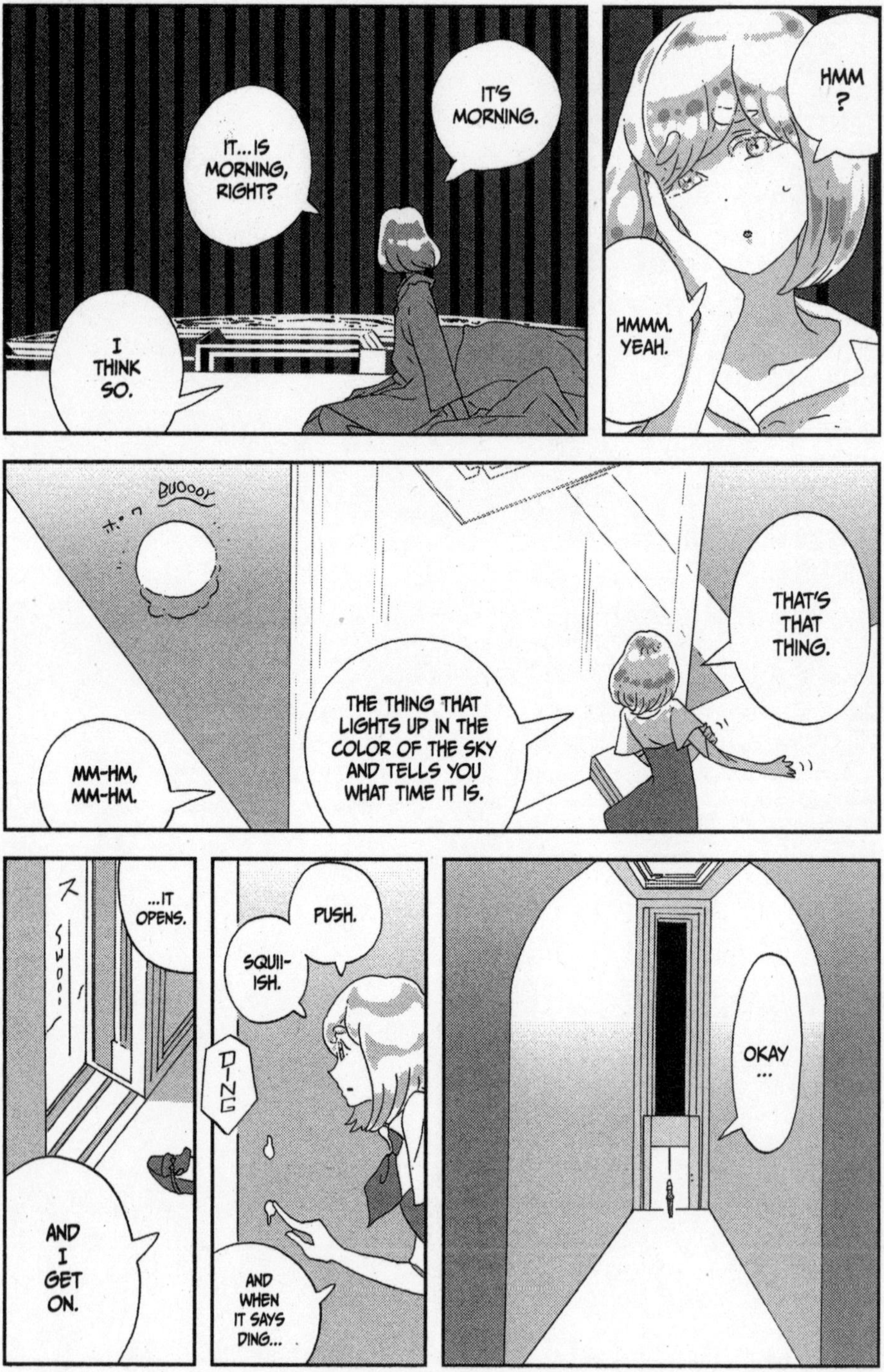
HMM ?
HMMM. YEAH.
IT'S MORNING.
IT...IS MORNING, RIGHT?
I THINK SO.
THAT'S THAT THING.
THE THING THAT LIGHTS UP IN THE COLOR OF THE SKY AND TELLS YOU WHAT TIME IT IS.
MM-HM, MM-HM.
OKAY ...
PUSH.
SQUIII-ISH.
DING
AND WHEN IT SAYS DING...
...IT OPENS.
SWOOO
AND I GET ON.

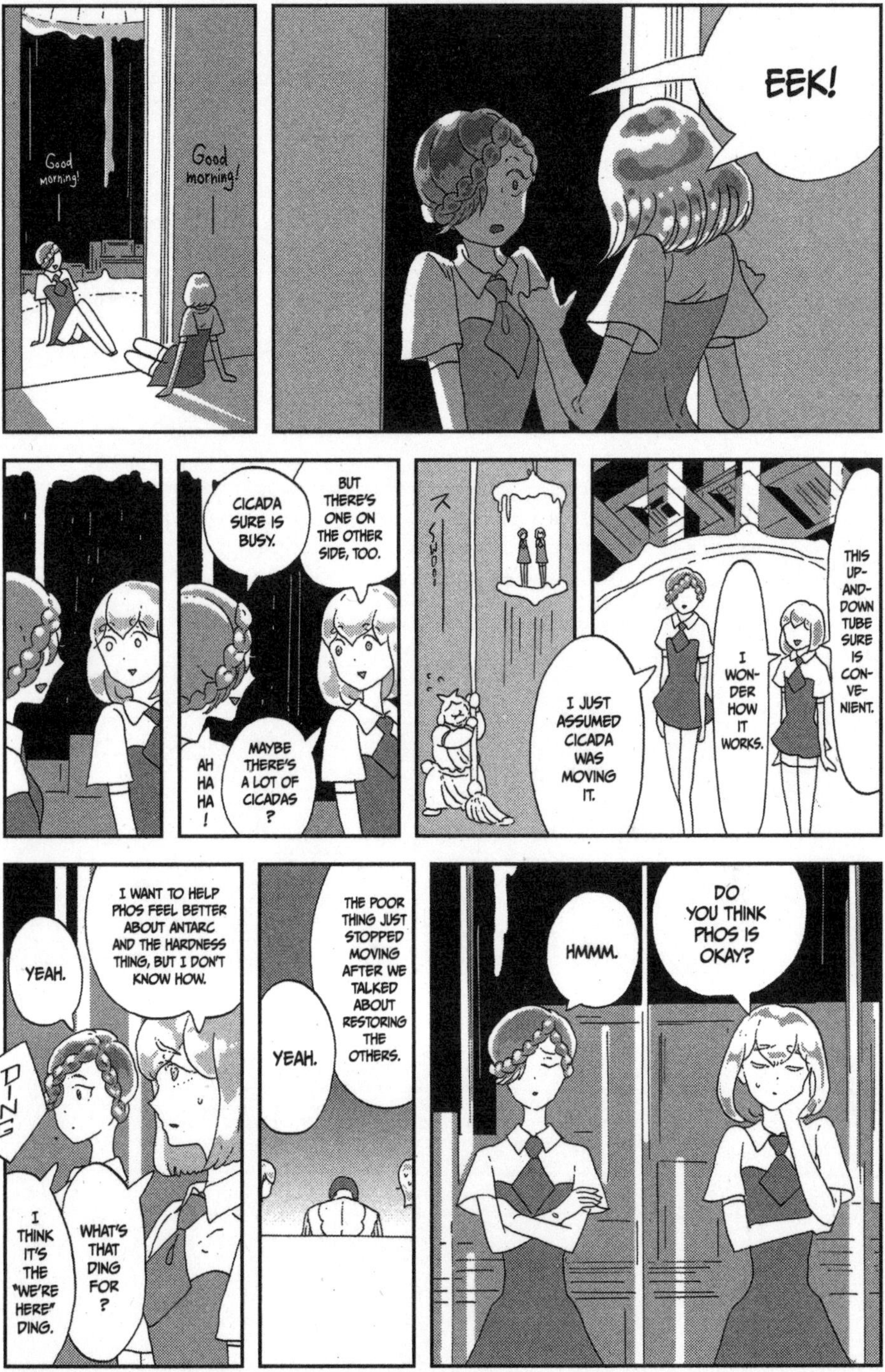
EEK!
Good morning!
Good morning!
THIS UP-AND-DOWN TUBE SURE IS CONVENIENT.
I WONDER HOW IT WORKS.
I JUST ASSUMED CICADA WAS MOVING IT.
BUT THERE'S ONE ON THE OTHER SIDE, TOO.
CICADA SURE IS BUSY.
MAYBE THERE'S A LOT OF CICADAS?
AH HA HA!
DO YOU THINK PHOS IS OKAY?
HMMM.
THE POOR THING JUST STOPPED MOVING AFTER WE TALKED ABOUT RESTORING THE OTHERS.
YEAH.
I WANT TO HELP PHOS FEEL BETTER ABOUT ANTARC AND THE HARDNESS THING, BUT I DON'T KNOW HOW.
YEAH.
DING
WHAT'S THAT DING FOR?
I THINK IT'S THE "WE'RE HERE" DING.

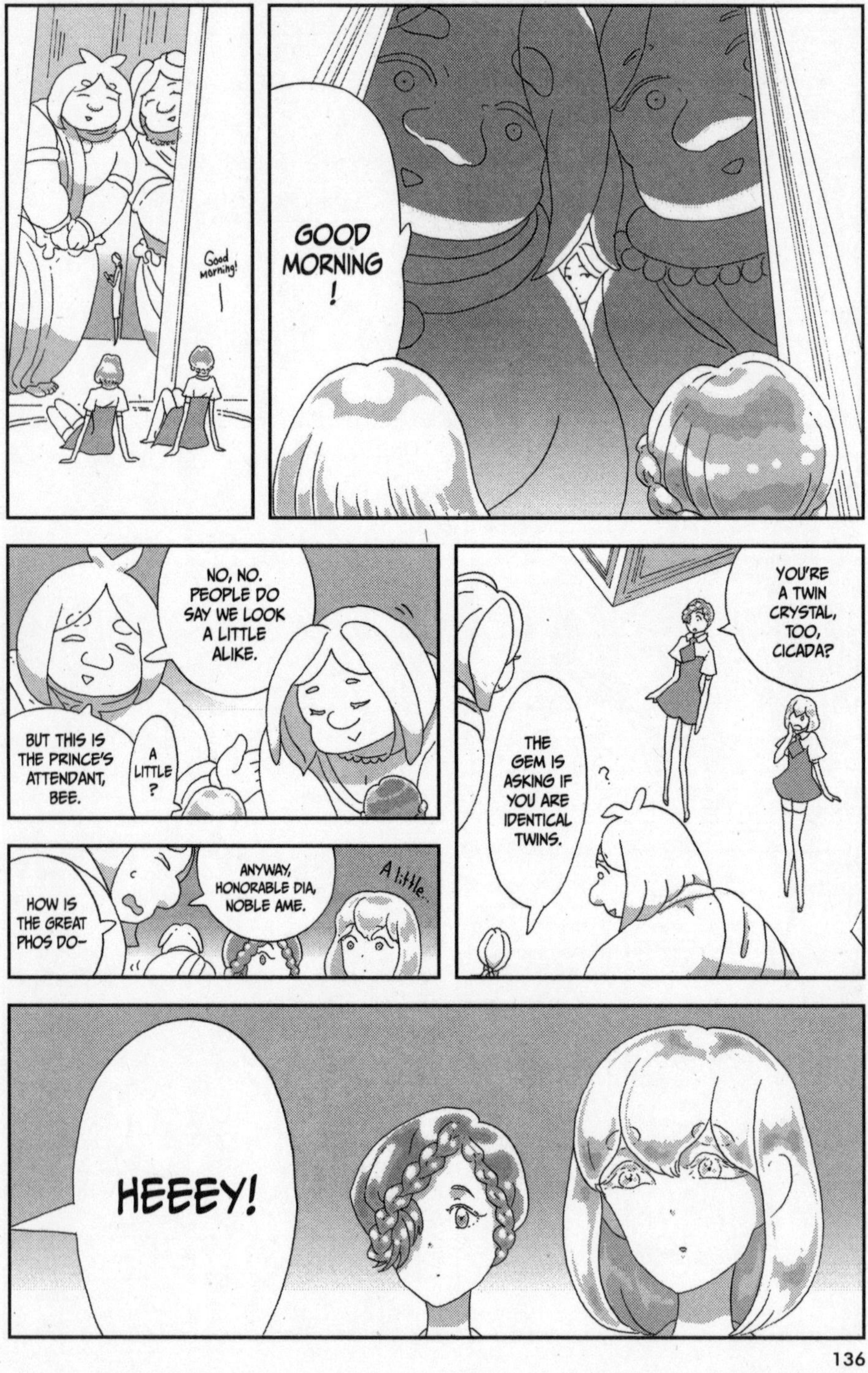
GOOD MORNING!
Good morning!
YOU'RE A TWIN CRYSTAL, TOO, CICADA?
THE GEM IS ASKING IF YOU ARE IDENTICAL TWINS.
NO, NO. PEOPLE DO SAY WE LOOK A LITTLE ALIKE.
A LITTLE?
BUT THIS IS THE PRINCE'S ATTENDANT, BEE.
A little...
ANYWAY, HONORABLE DIA, NOBLE AME.
HOW IS THE GREAT PHOS DO-
HEEEY!

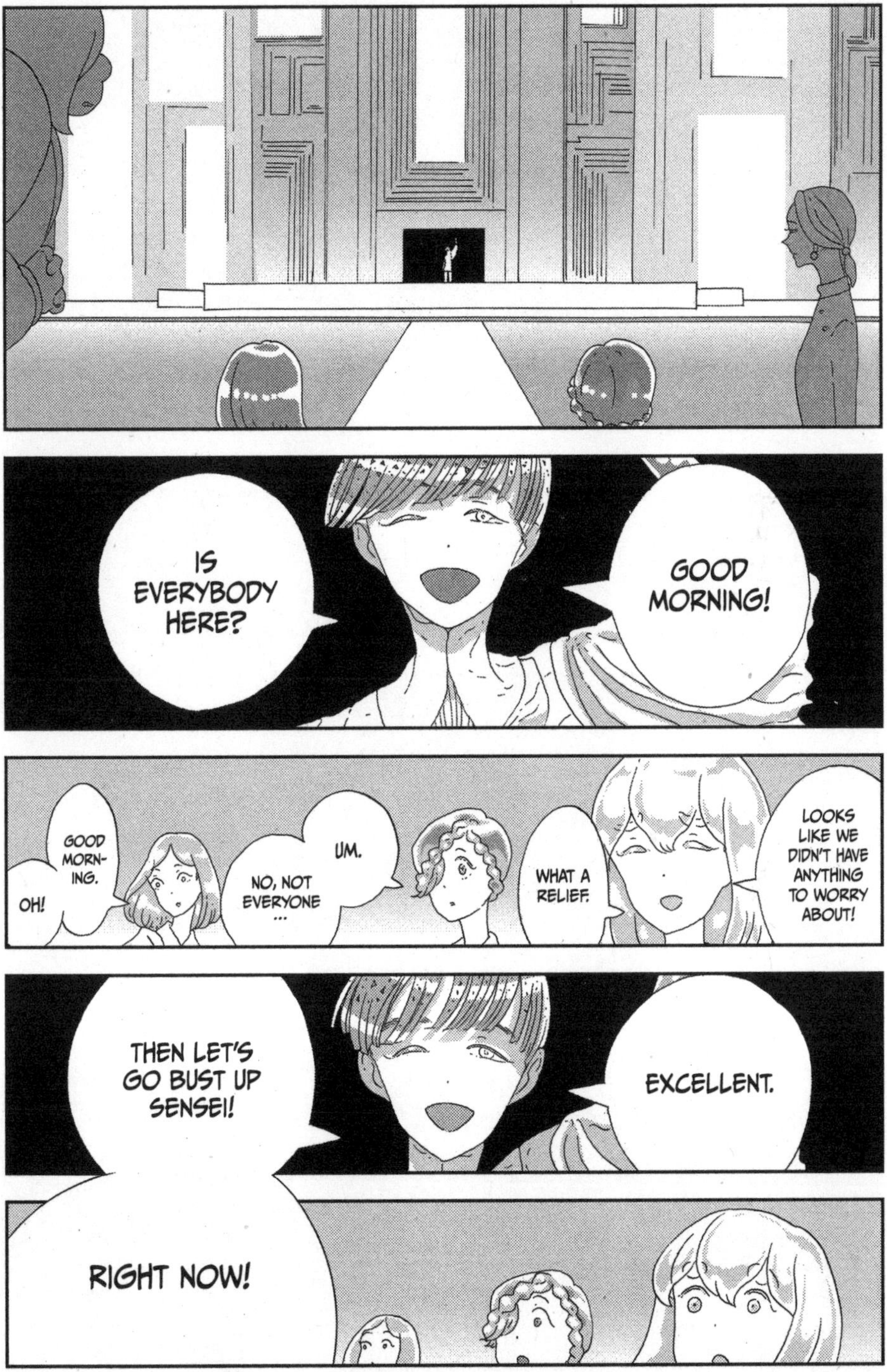
GOOD MORNING!
IS EVERYBODY HERE?
LOOKS LIKE WE DIDN'T HAVE ANYTHING TO WORRY ABOUT!
WHAT A RELIEF.
UM.
NO, NOT EVERYONE ...
GOOD MORN-ING.
OH!
EXCELLENT.
THEN LET'S GO BUST UP SENSEI!
RIGHT NOW!

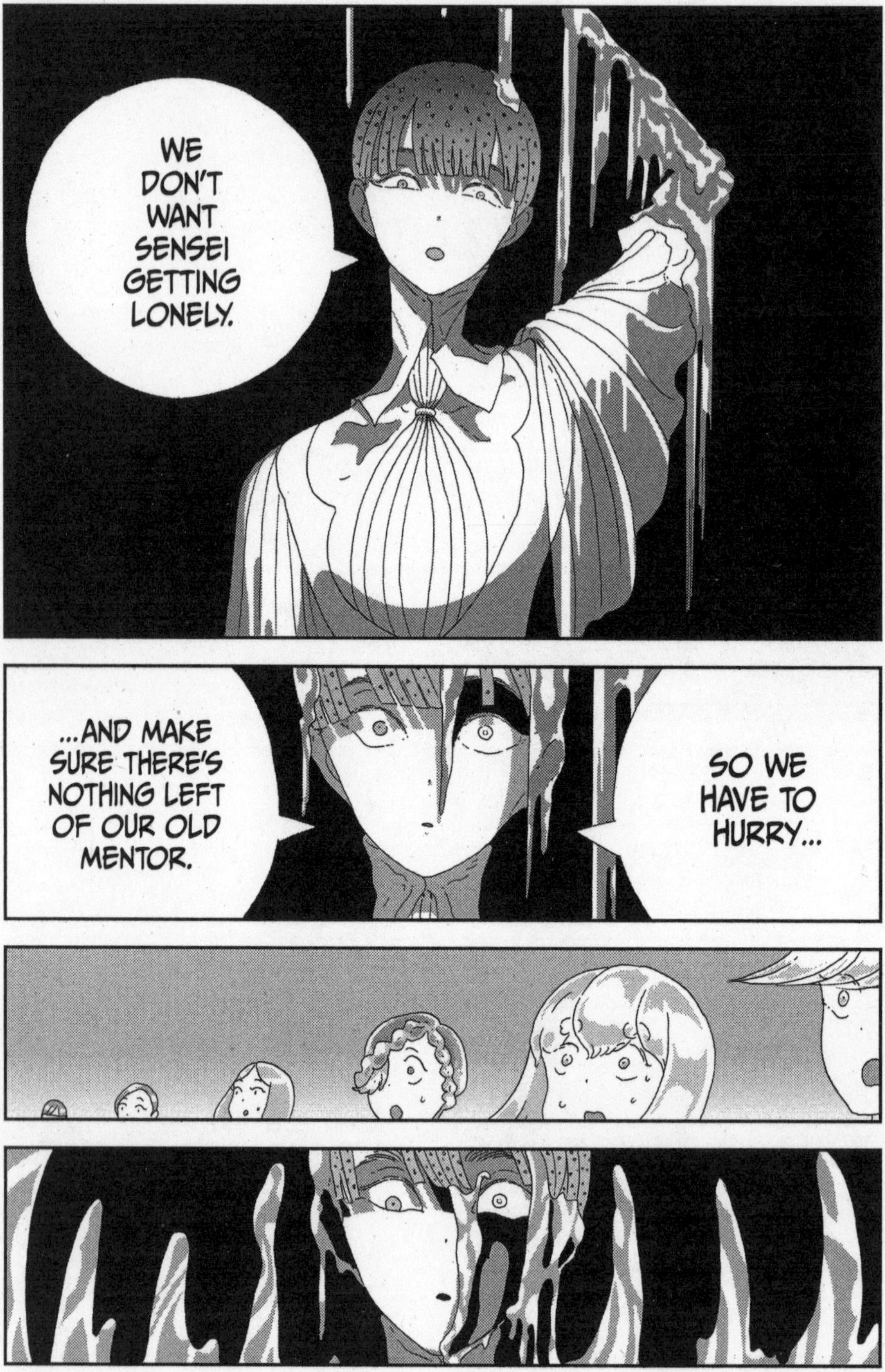
WE DON'T WANT SENSEI GETTING LONELY.
SO WE HAVE TO HURRY...
...AND MAKE SURE THERE'S NOTHING LEFT OF OUR OLD MENTOR.

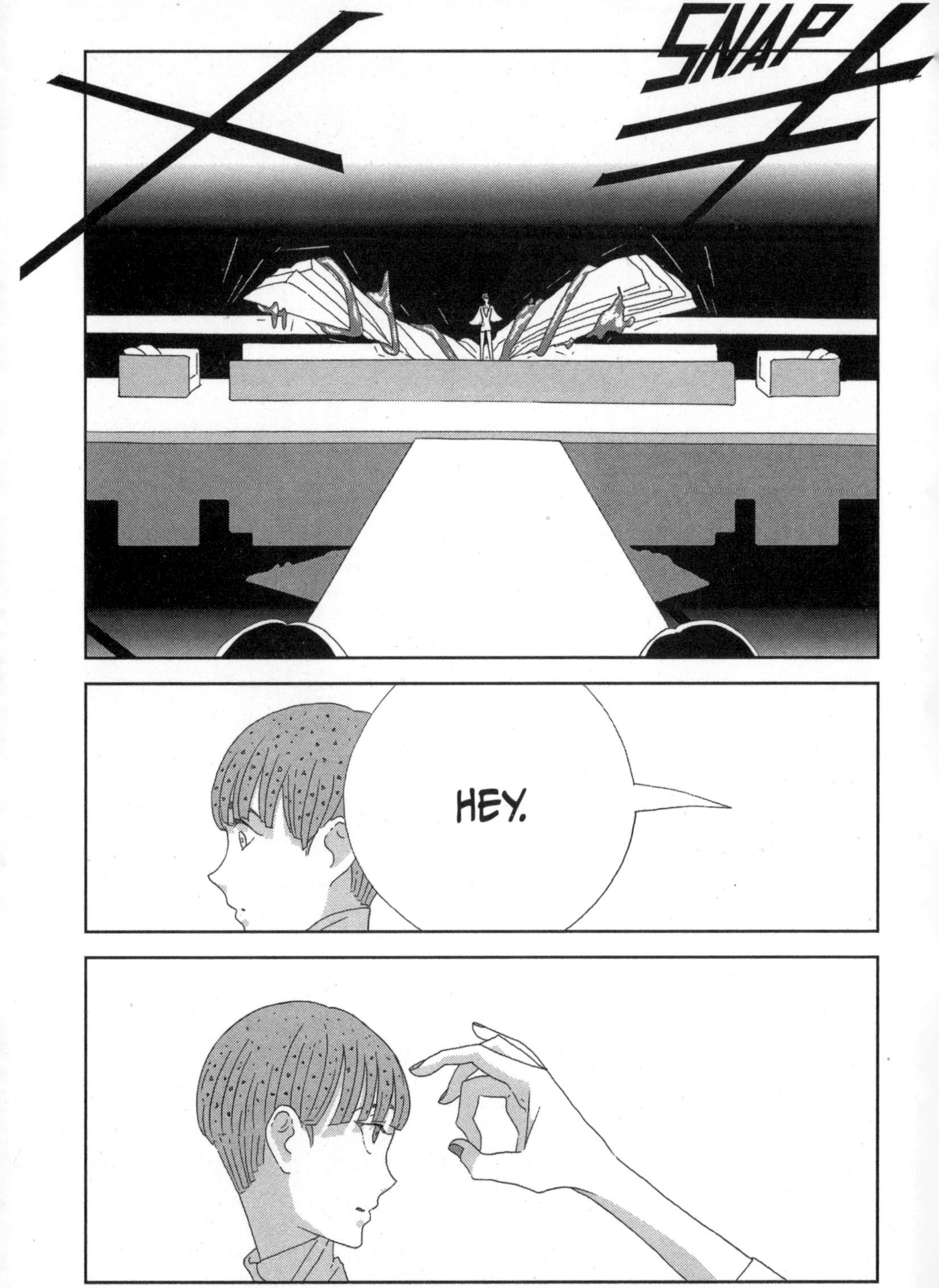
SNAP
HEY.

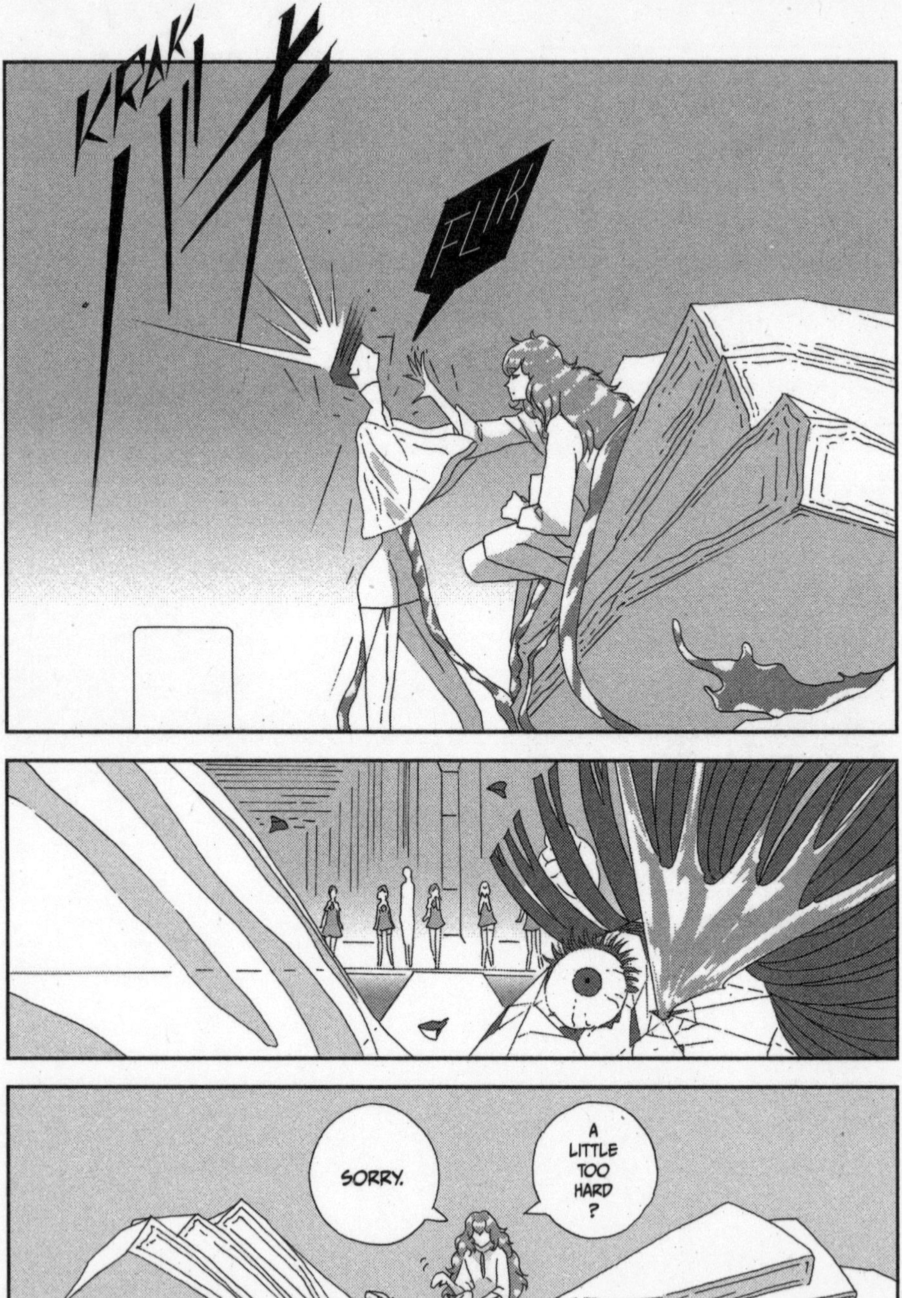
KRAK
FLIK
A LITTLE TOO HARD?
SORRY.

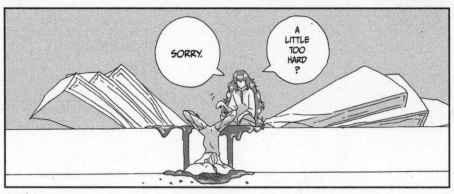

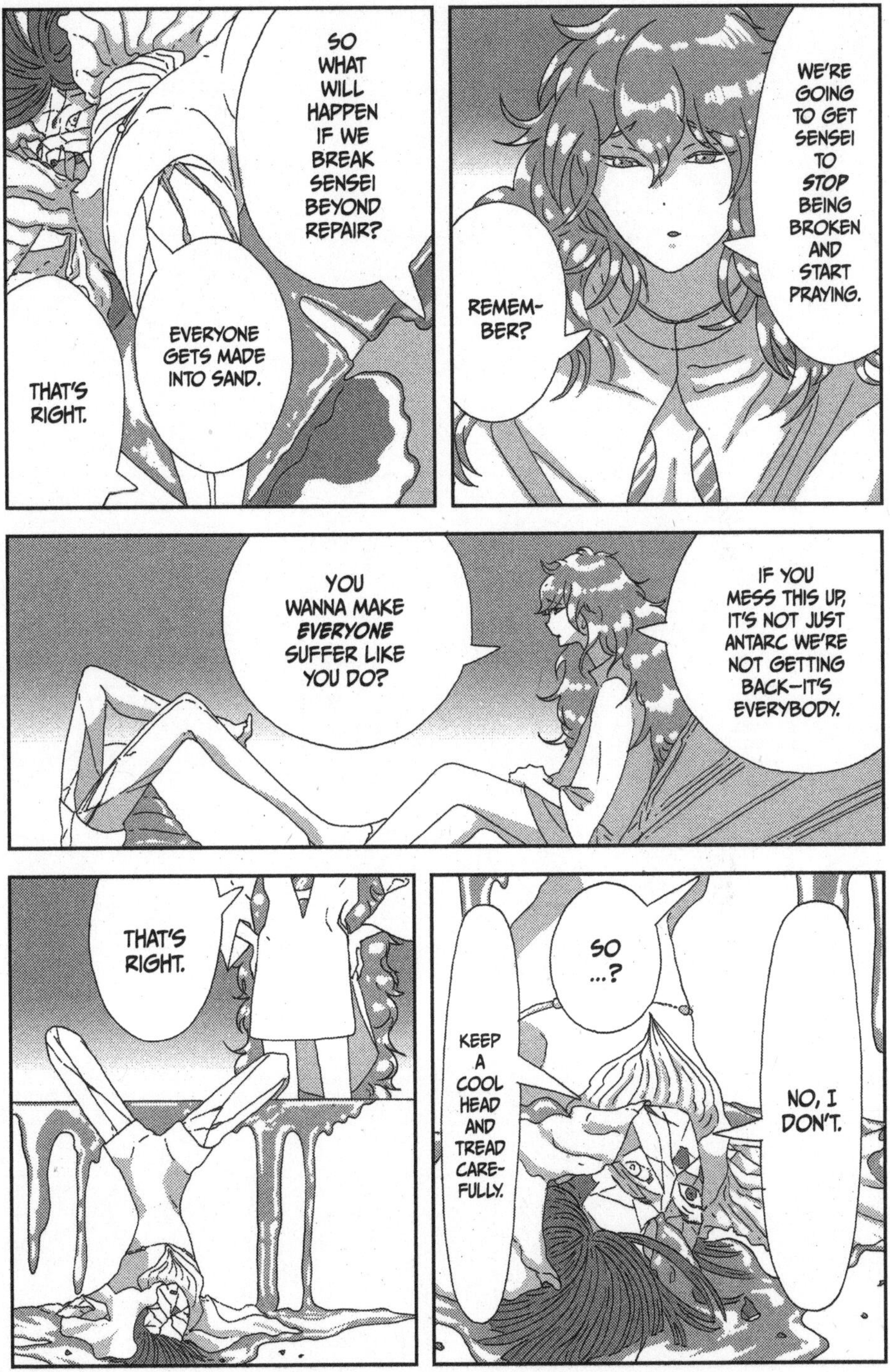
WE'RE GOING TO GET SENSEI TO *STOP* BEING BROKEN AND START PRAYING.
REMEM-BER?
SO WHAT WILL HAPPEN IF WE BREAK SENSEI BEYOND REPAIR?
EVERYONE GETS MADE INTO SAND.
THAT'S RIGHT.
IF YOU MESS THIS UP, IT'S NOT JUST ANTARC WE'RE NOT GETTING BACK—IT'S EVERYBODY.
YOU WANNA MAKE *EVERYONE* SUFFER LIKE YOU DO?
SO ...?
NO, I DON'T.
KEEP A COOL HEAD AND TREAD CARE-FULLY.
THAT'S RIGHT.

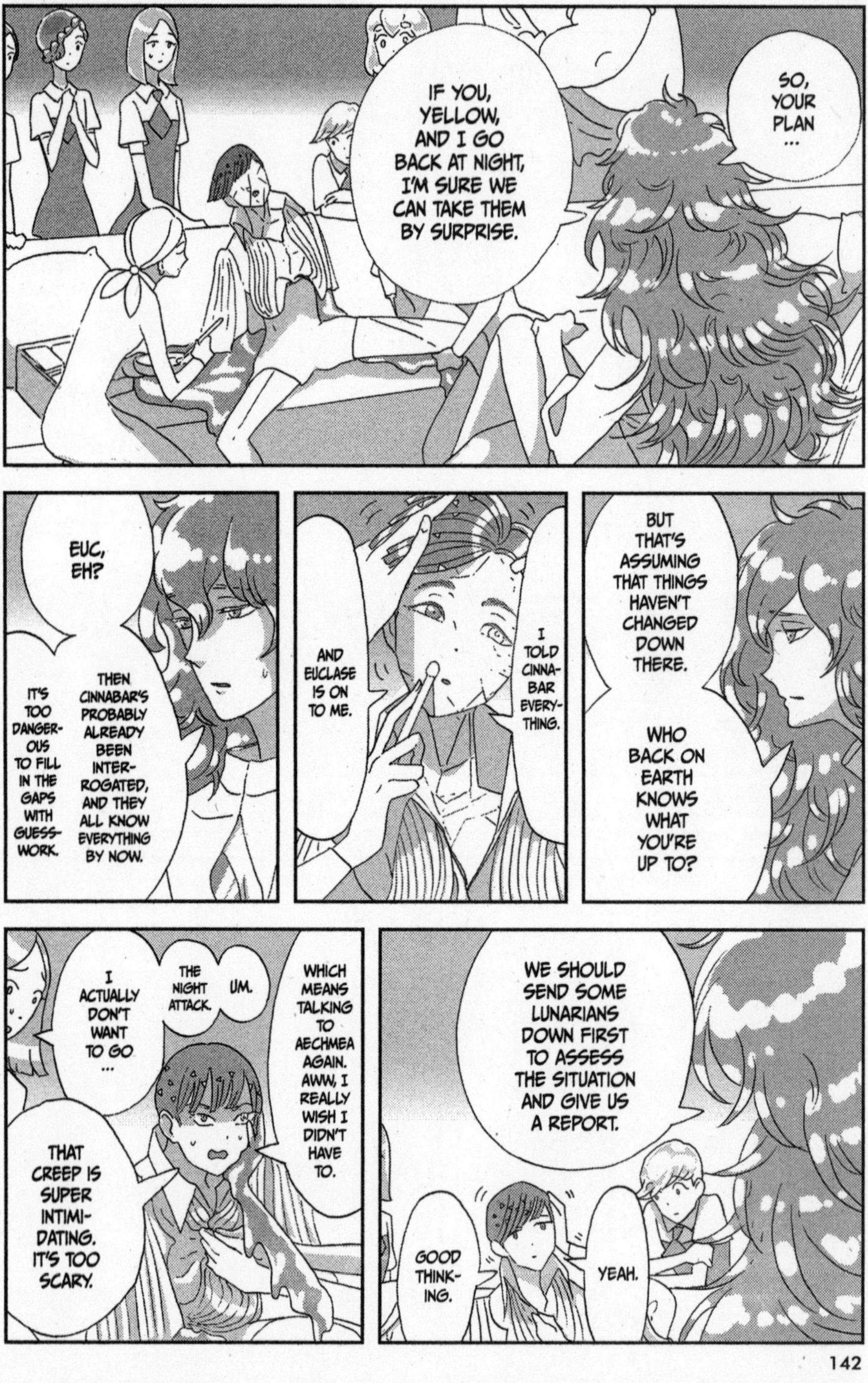
SO, YOUR PLAN ...
IF YOU, YELLOW, AND I GO BACK AT NIGHT, I'M SURE WE CAN TAKE THEM BY SURPRISE.
BUT THAT'S ASSUMING THAT THINGS HAVEN'T CHANGED DOWN THERE.
WHO BACK ON EARTH KNOWS WHAT YOU'RE UP TO?
I TOLD CINNABAR EVERYTHING.
AND EUCLASE IS ON TO ME.
EUC, EH?
THEN CINNABAR'S PROBABLY ALREADY BEEN INTERROGATED, AND THEY ALL KNOW EVERYTHING BY NOW.
IT'S TOO DANGEROUS TO FILL IN THE GAPS WITH GUESSWORK.
WE SHOULD SEND SOME LUNARIANS DOWN FIRST TO ASSESS THE SITUATION AND GIVE US A REPORT.
YEAH.
GOOD THINKING.
WHICH MEANS TALKING TO AECHMEA AGAIN. AWW, I REALLY WISH I DIDN'T HAVE TO.
UM.
THE NIGHT ATTACK.
I ACTUALLY DON'T WANT TO GO ...
THAT CREEP IS SUPER INTIMIDATING. IT'S TOO SCARY.

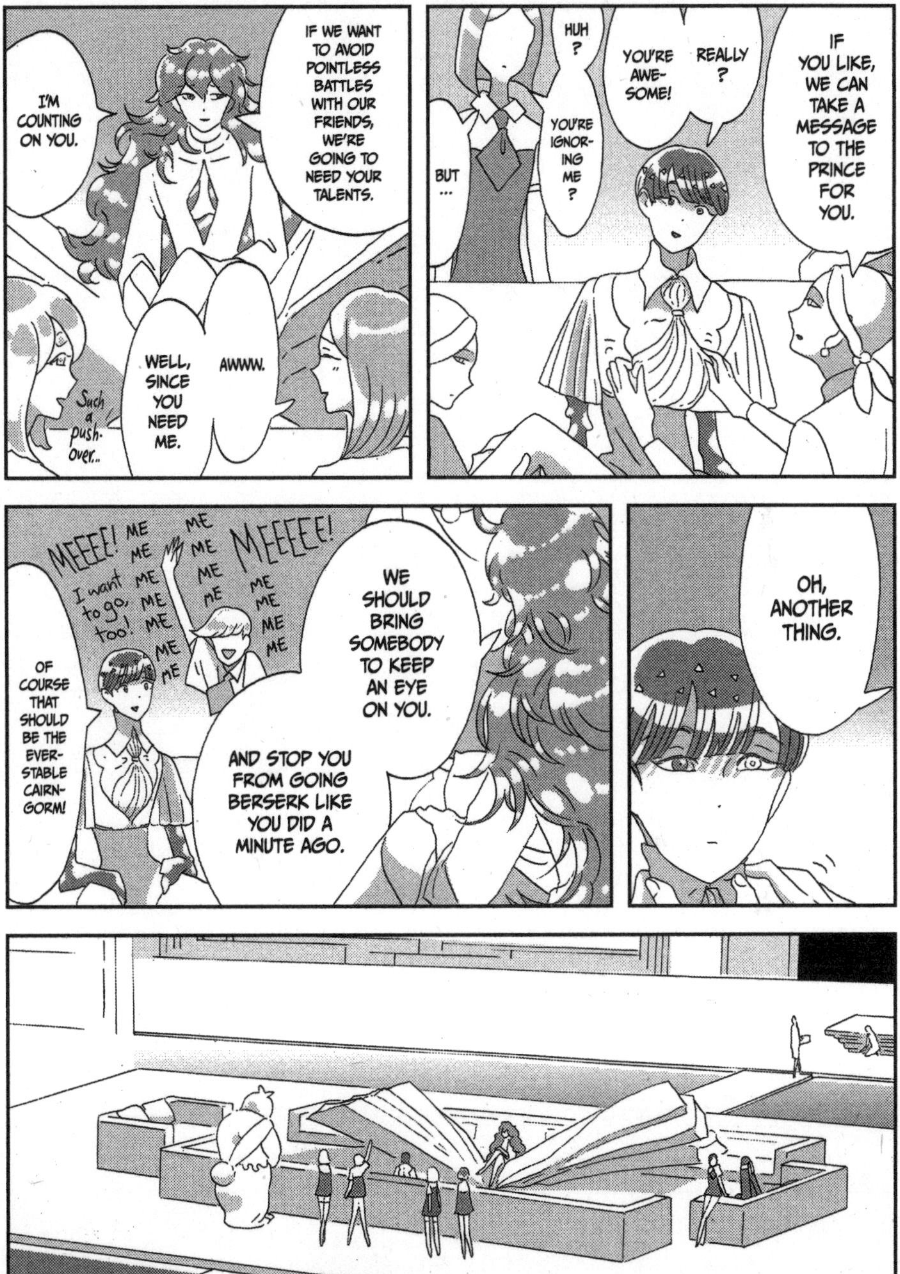
IF YOU LIKE, WE CAN TAKE A MESSAGE TO THE PRINCE FOR YOU.
REALLY?
YOU'RE AWESOME!
HUH?
YOU'RE IGNORING ME?
BUT...
IF WE WANT TO AVOID POINTLESS BATTLES WITH OUR FRIENDS, WE'RE GOING TO NEED YOUR TALENTS.
I'M COUNTING ON YOU.
AWWW.
WELL, SINCE YOU NEED ME.
Such a push-over...
OH, ANOTHER THING.
WE SHOULD BRING SOMEBODY TO KEEP AN EYE ON YOU.
AND STOP YOU FROM GOING BERSERK LIKE YOU DID A MINUTE AGO.
MEEEEE!
ME ME ME ME ME ME ME ME ME ME ME ME ME ME
MEEEE!
I want to go, me too!
OF COURSE THAT SHOULD BE THE EVER-STABLE CAIRNGORM!

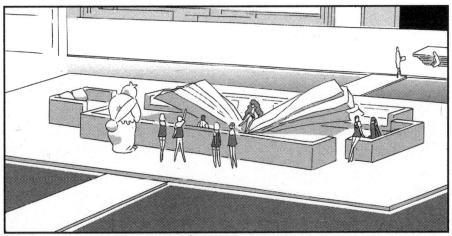

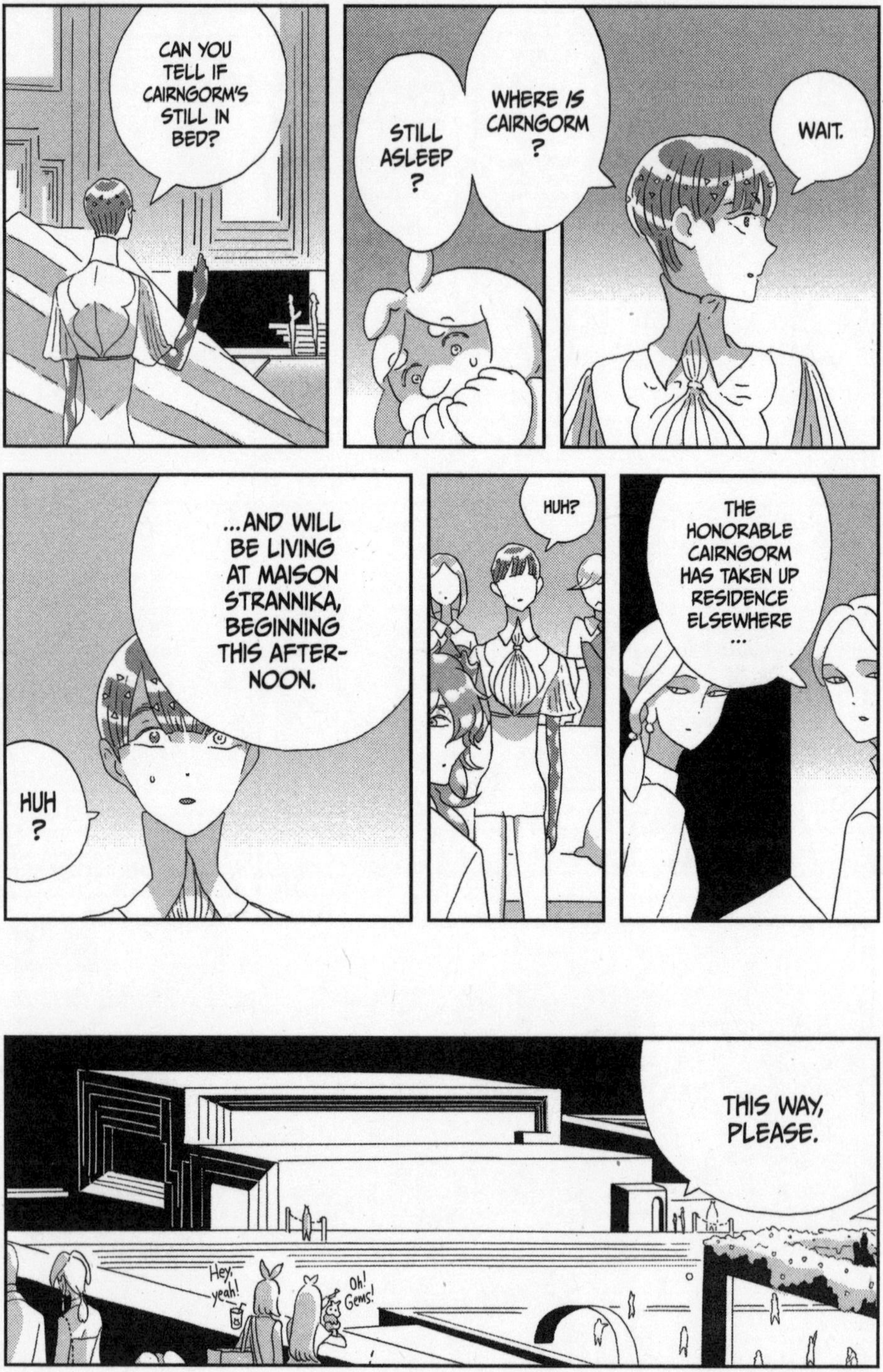
WAIT.
WHERE IS CAIRNGORM ?
STILL ASLEEP ?
CAN YOU TELL IF CAIRNGORM'S STILL IN BED?
THE HONORABLE CAIRNGORM HAS TAKEN UP RESIDENCE ELSEWHERE ...
HUH?
...AND WILL BE LIVING AT MAISON STRANNIKA, BEGINNING THIS AFTER-NOON.
HUH ?
THIS WAY, PLEASE.
Oh! Gems!
Hey, yeah!

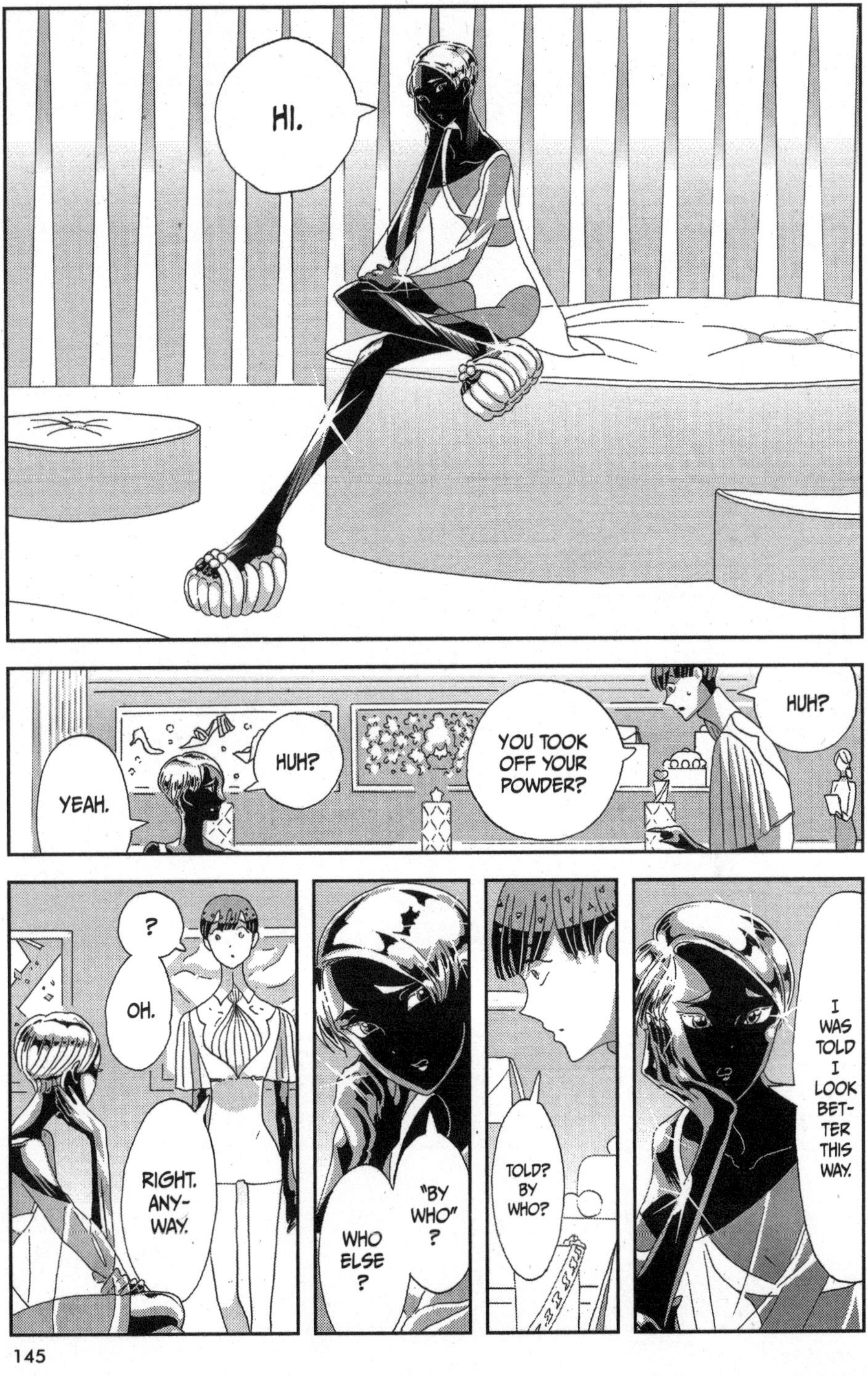
HI.
HUH?
YOU TOOK OFF YOUR POWDER?
HUH?
YEAH.
I WAS TOLD I LOOK BETTER THIS WAY.
TOLD? BY WHO?
"BY WHO"?
WHO ELSE?
?
OH.
RIGHT. ANYWAY.

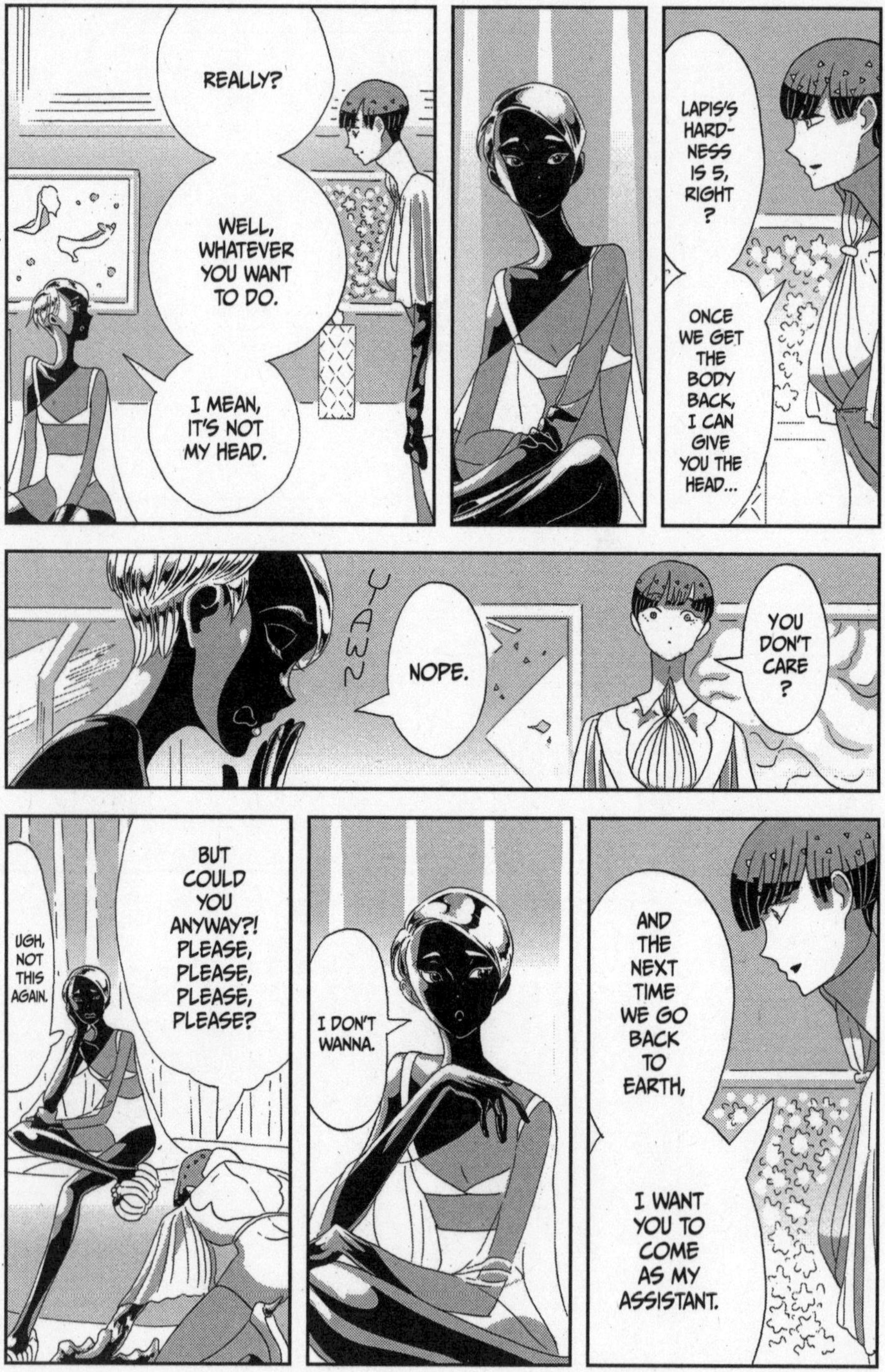
LAPIS'S HARDNESS IS 5, RIGHT?
ONCE WE GET THE BODY BACK, I CAN GIVE YOU THE HEAD...
REALLY?
WELL, WHATEVER YOU WANT TO DO.
I MEAN, IT'S NOT MY HEAD.
YOU DON'T CARE?
NOPE.
YAWN
AND THE NEXT TIME WE GO BACK TO EARTH,
I WANT YOU TO COME AS MY ASSISTANT.
I DON'T WANNA.
BUT COULD YOU ANYWAY?! PLEASE, PLEASE, PLEASE, PLEASE?
UGH, NOT THIS AGAIN.

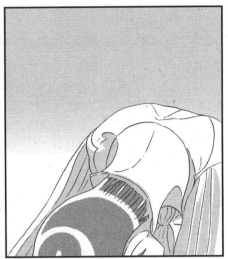

I'M NOT GOING.

PHOS.

WE'RE READY FOR YOU!

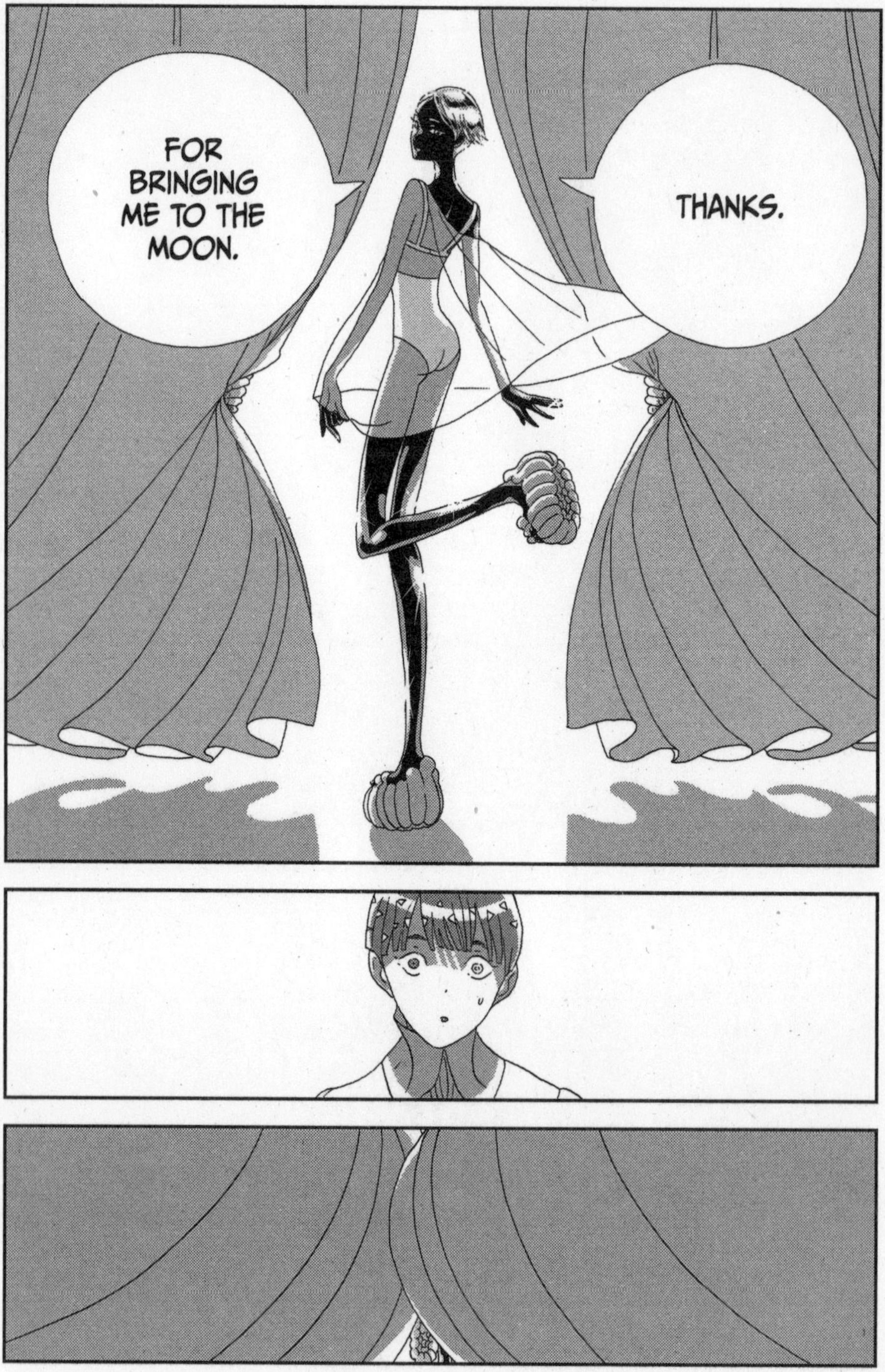
THANKS.
FOR BRINGING ME TO THE MOON.

HUH
?

WAIT
A—
WHAT
IN THE
...

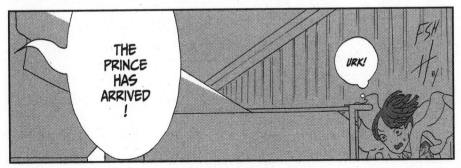

THE
PRINCE
HAS
ARRIVED
!

URK!

FSH

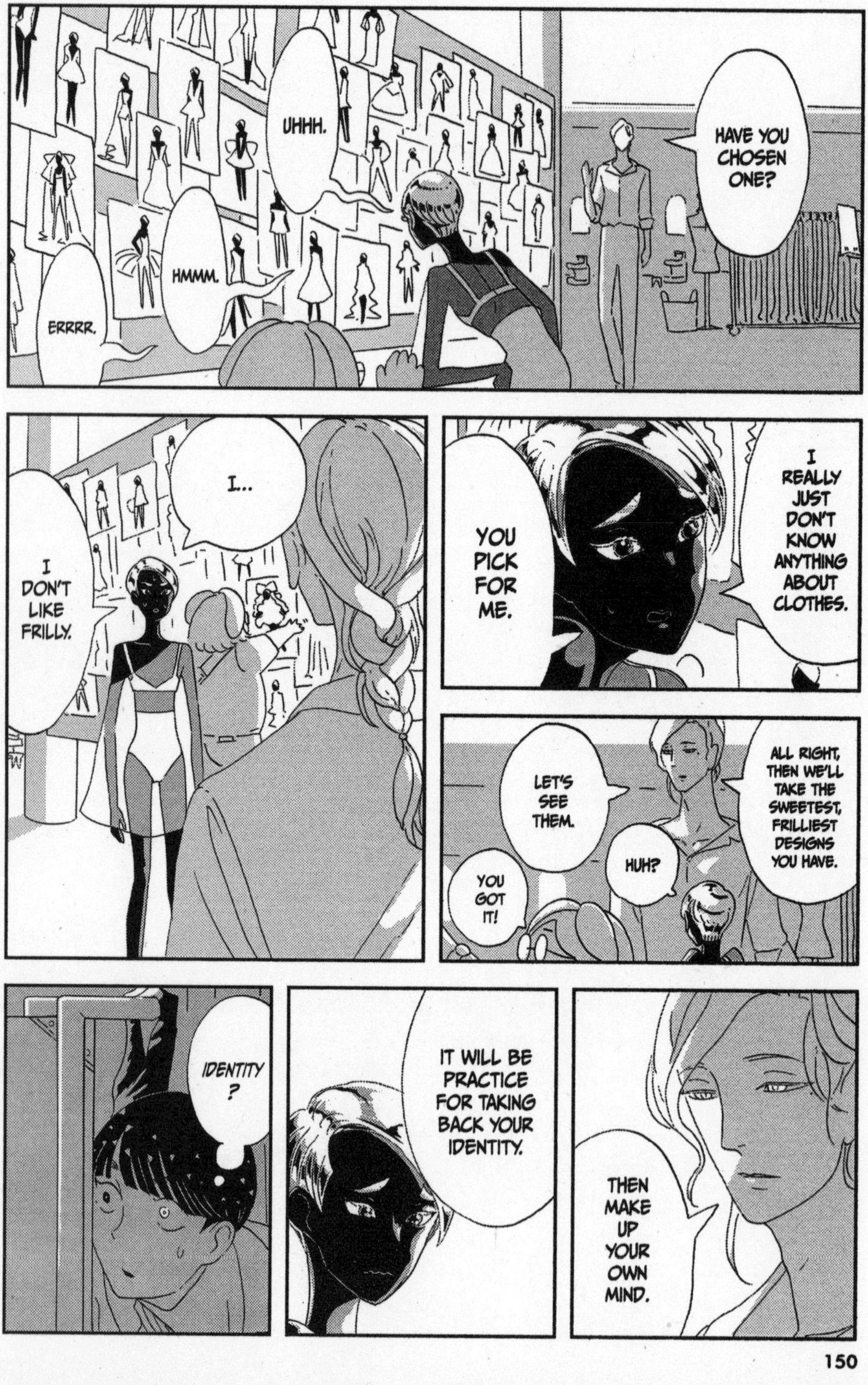
HAVE YOU CHOSEN ONE?
UHHH.
HMMM.
ERRRR.
I REALLY JUST DON'T KNOW ANYTHING ABOUT CLOTHES.
YOU PICK FOR ME.
ALL RIGHT, THEN WE'LL TAKE THE SWEETEST, FRILLIEST DESIGNS YOU HAVE.
LET'S SEE THEM.
HUH?
YOU GOT IT!
I...
I DON'T LIKE FRILLY.
THEN MAKE UP YOUR OWN MIND.
IT WILL BE PRACTICE FOR TAKING BACK YOUR IDENTITY.
IDENTITY?

WHAT ARE YOU SAYING? YOU GOT A PROBLEM WITH MY CHOICE? YOU'RE MOCKING ME, AREN'T YOU?! THIS IS WHY I TOLD *YOU* TO PICK!

WHAT ?!

NO.

REALLY?

I...

GUESS ...?

...THIS ONE.

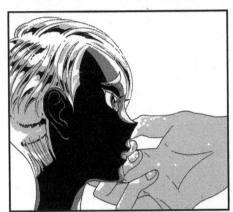

I DIDN'T EXPECT IT. IT'S VERY YOU.

EEP!

★ ド‥ン
Bump

ROLL   ロ   ROLL   ロ   ROLL
コ ロ   コ ロ   コ ロ . . . .

RATTLE

ド‥ズ
FWUMP

WHOA...!

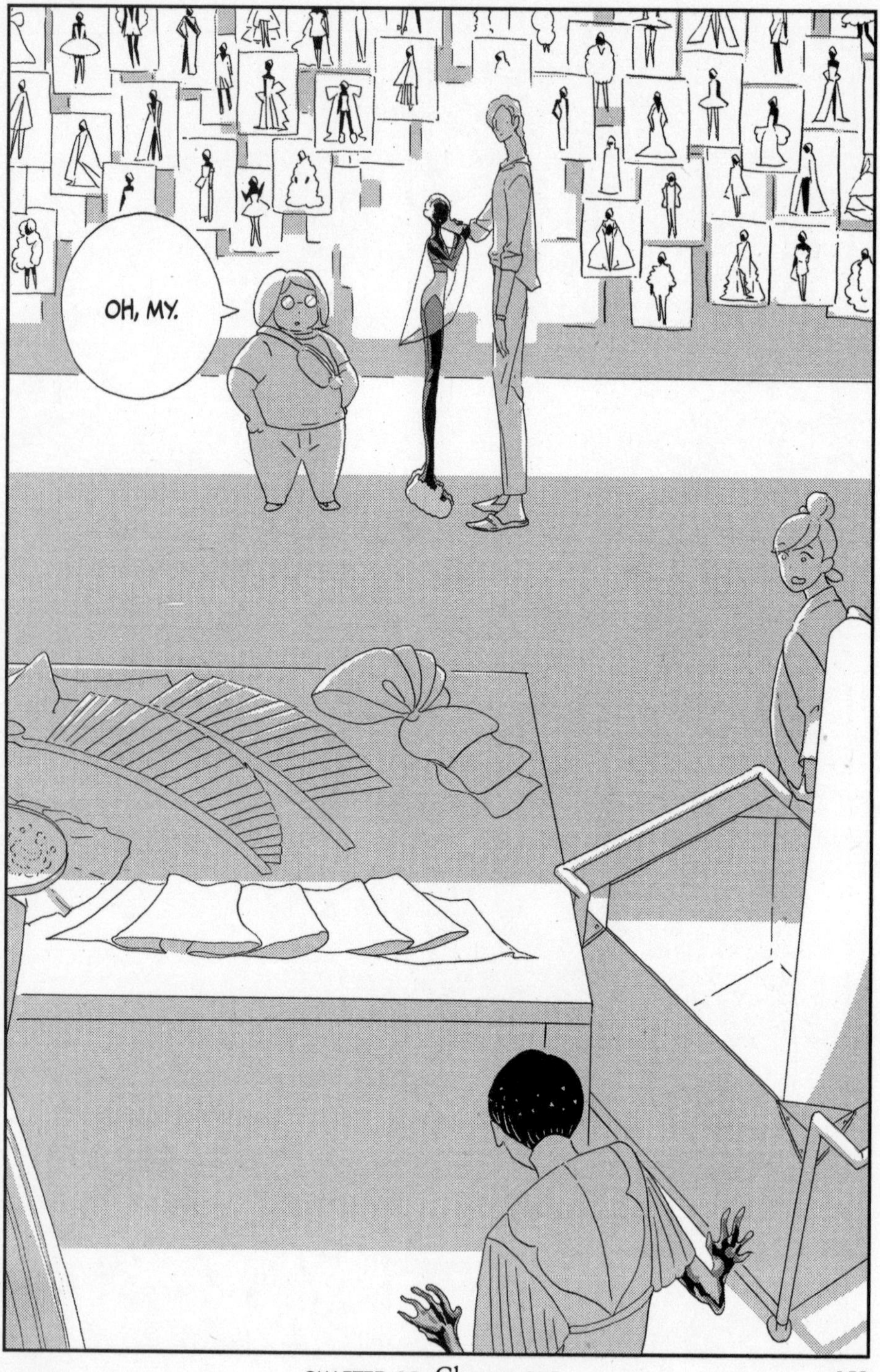
OH, MY.

CHAPTER 68: Change END

CHAPTER 69:

Constancy

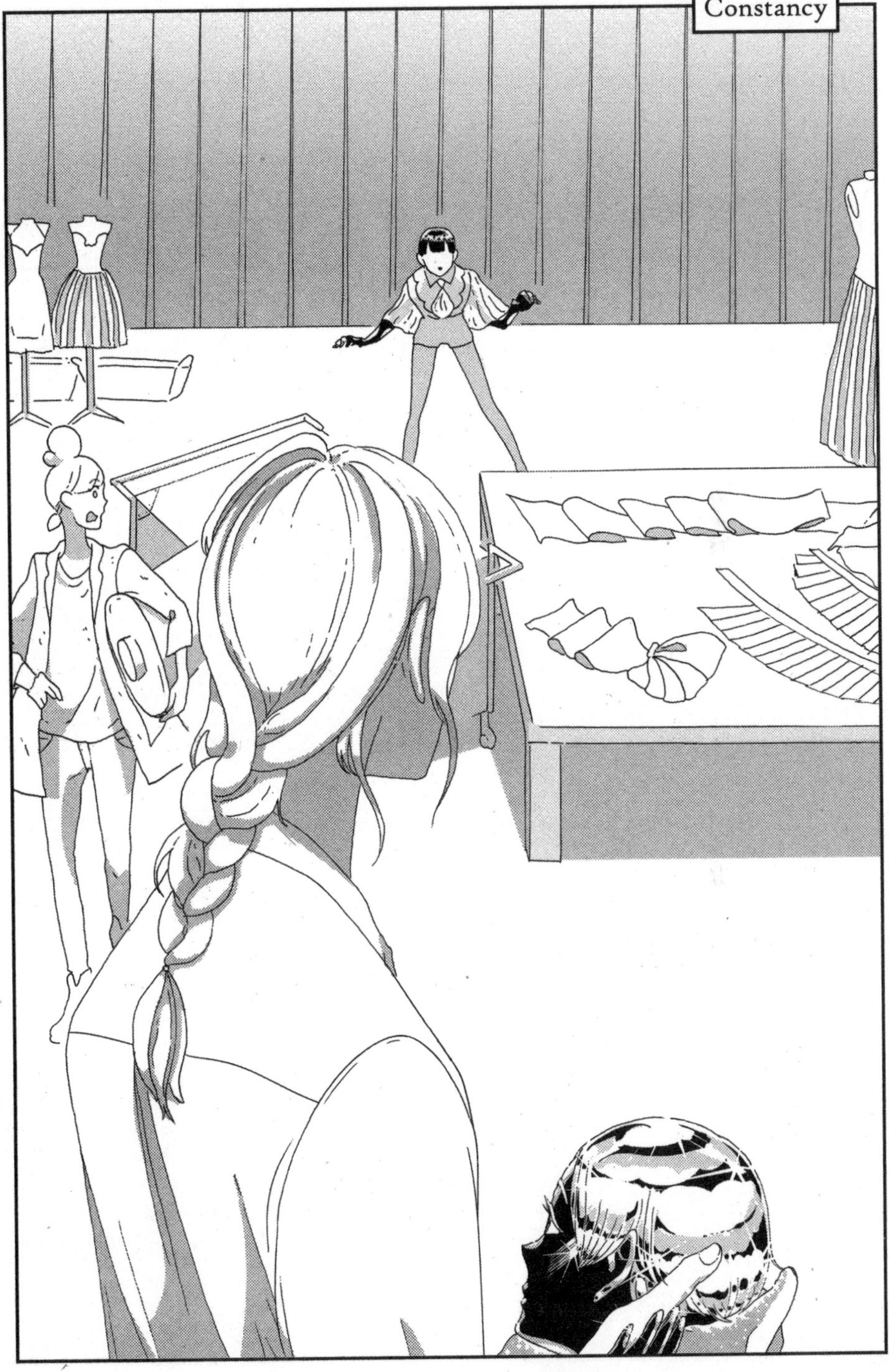

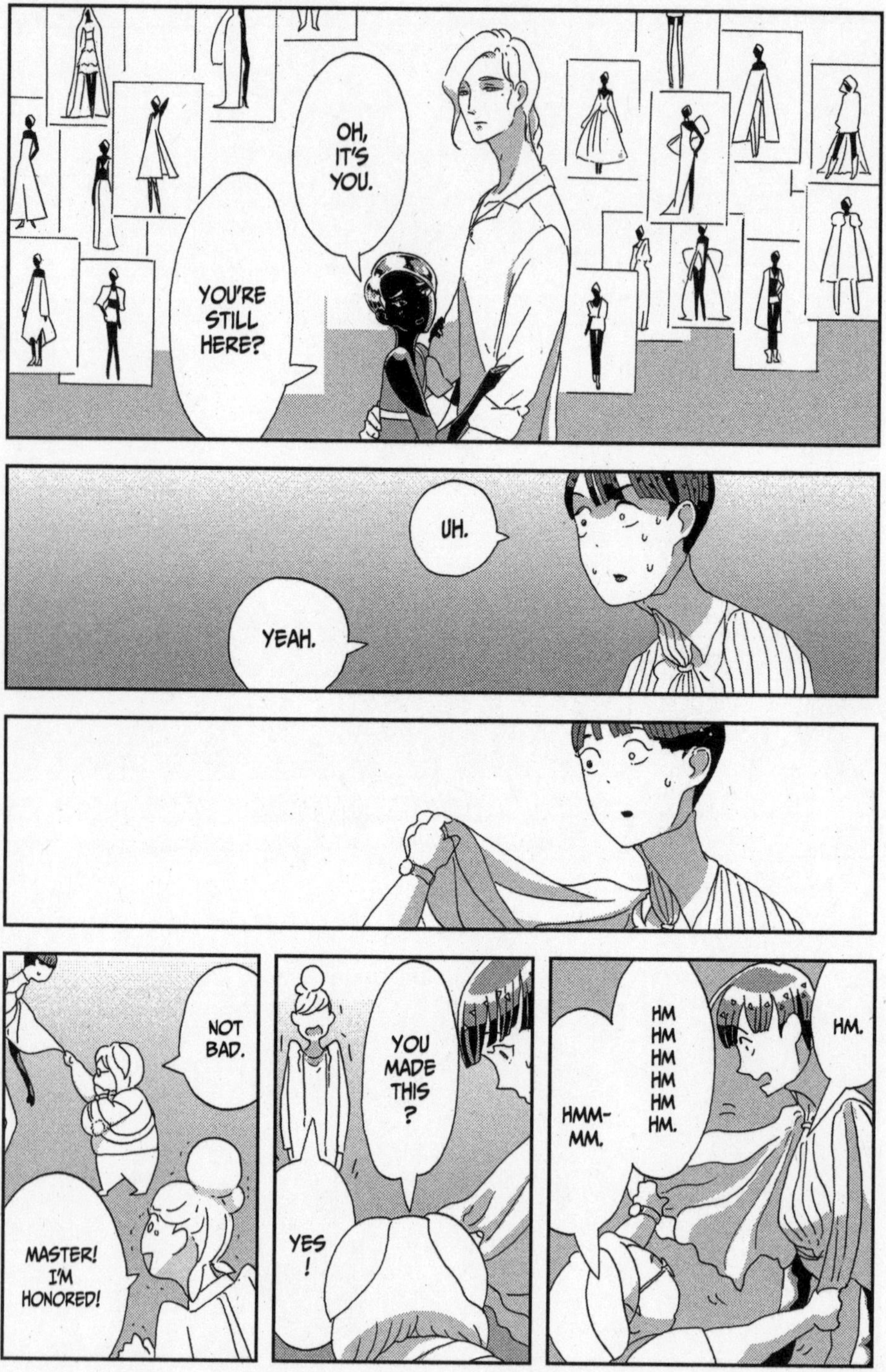
OH, IT'S YOU.
YOU'RE STILL HERE?
UH.
YEAH.
HM.
HM HM HM HM HM HM.
HMM-MM.
YOU MADE THIS?
YES!
NOT BAD.
MASTER! I'M HONORED!

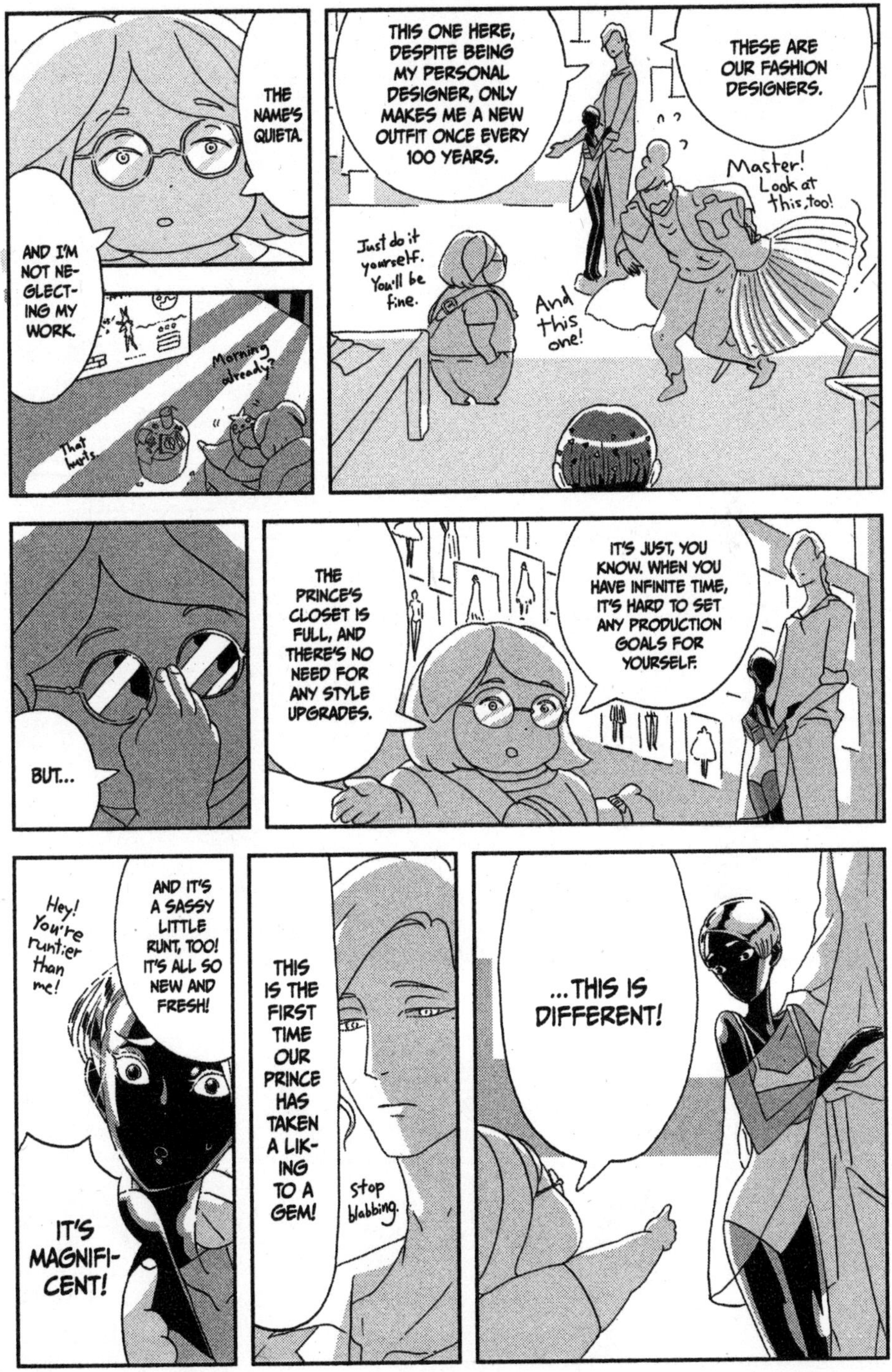
THESE ARE OUR FASHION DESIGNERS.
THIS ONE HERE, DESPITE BEING MY PERSONAL DESIGNER, ONLY MAKES ME A NEW OUTFIT ONCE EVERY 100 YEARS.
Master! Look at this, too!
And this one!
Just do it yourself. You'll be fine.
THE NAME'S QUIETA.
AND I'M NOT NEGLECTING MY WORK.
Morning already?
That hurts.
IT'S JUST, YOU KNOW. WHEN YOU HAVE INFINITE TIME, IT'S HARD TO SET ANY PRODUCTION GOALS FOR YOURSELF.
THE PRINCE'S CLOSET IS FULL, AND THERE'S NO NEED FOR ANY STYLE UPGRADES.
BUT...
...THIS IS DIFFERENT!
THIS IS THE FIRST TIME OUR PRINCE HAS TAKEN A LIKING TO A GEM!
Stop blabbing.
AND IT'S A SASSY LITTLE RUNT, TOO! IT'S ALL SO NEW AND FRESH!
Hey! You're runtier than me!
IT'S MAGNIFICENT!

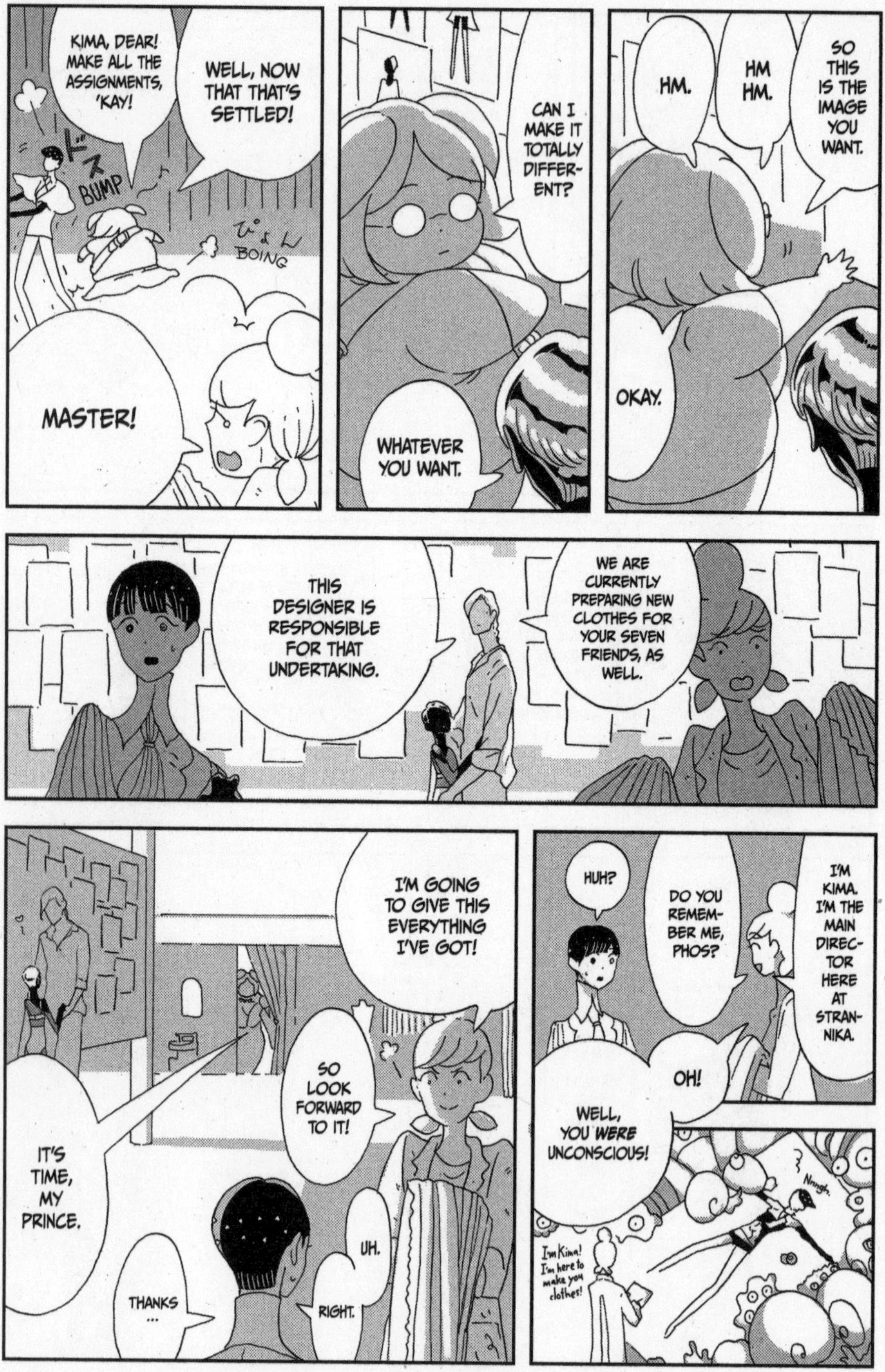
SO THIS IS THE IMAGE YOU WANT.
HM HM.
HM.
OKAY.
CAN I MAKE IT TOTALLY DIFFERENT?
WHATEVER YOU WANT.
WELL, NOW THAT THAT'S SETTLED!
KIMA, DEAR! MAKE ALL THE ASSIGNMENTS, 'KAY!
ドス BUMP
ぴょん BOING
MASTER!
WE ARE CURRENTLY PREPARING NEW CLOTHES FOR YOUR SEVEN FRIENDS, AS WELL.
THIS DESIGNER IS RESPONSIBLE FOR THAT UNDERTAKING.
I'M KIMA. I'M THE MAIN DIRECTOR HERE AT STRANNIKA.
DO YOU REMEMBER ME, PHOS?
HUH?
OH!
WELL, YOU WERE UNCONSCIOUS!
Nnngh.
I'm Kima! I'm here to make you clothes!
I'M GOING TO GIVE THIS EVERYTHING I'VE GOT!
SO LOOK FORWARD TO IT!
UH.
RIGHT.
THANKS ...
IT'S TIME, MY PRINCE.

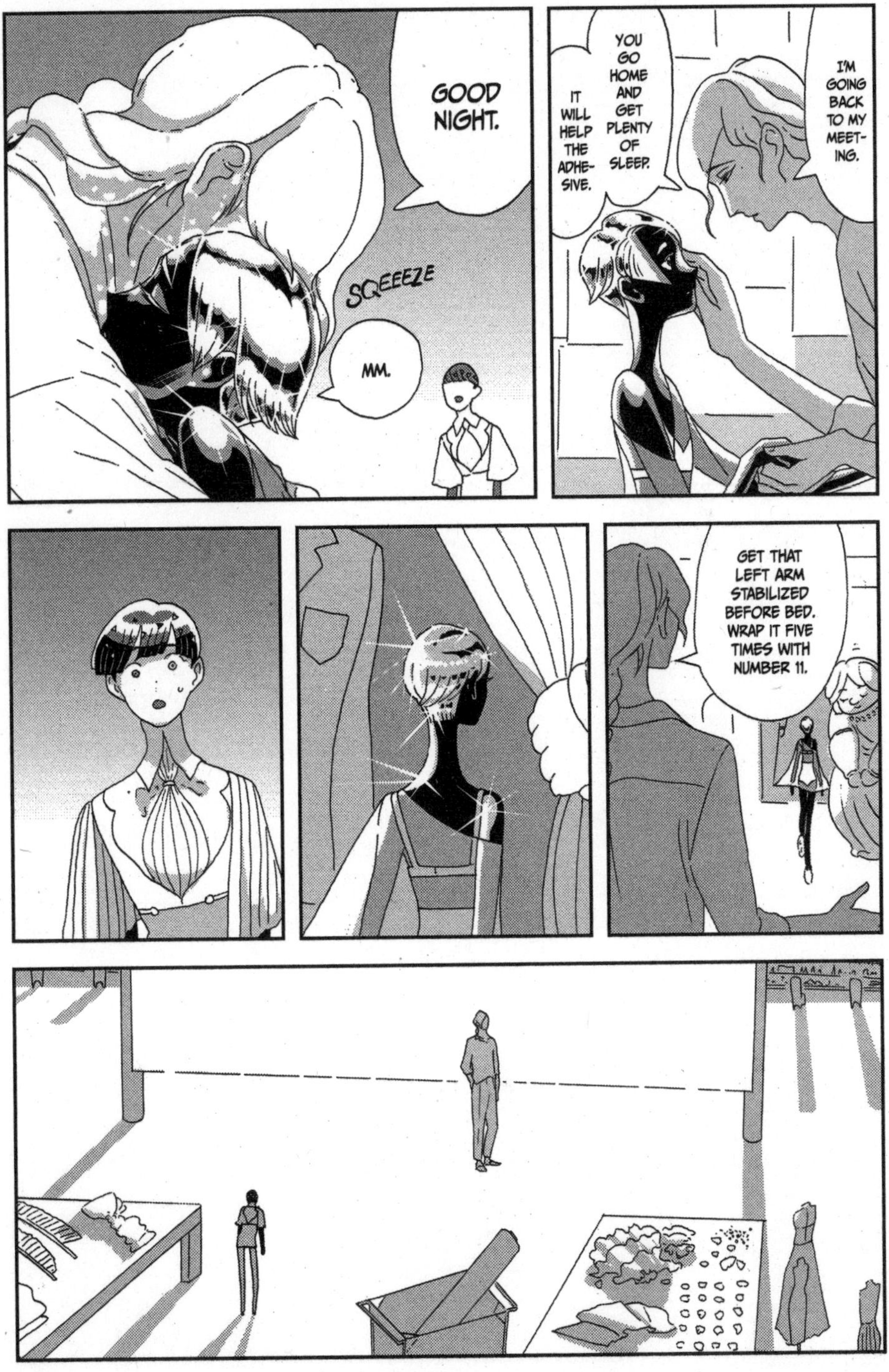
I'M GOING BACK TO MY MEET-ING.
YOU GO HOME AND GET PLENTY OF SLEEP.
IT WILL HELP THE ADHE-SIVE.
GOOD NIGHT.
SQEEEZE
MM.
GET THAT LEFT ARM STABILIZED BEFORE BED. WRAP IT FIVE TIMES WITH NUMBER 11.

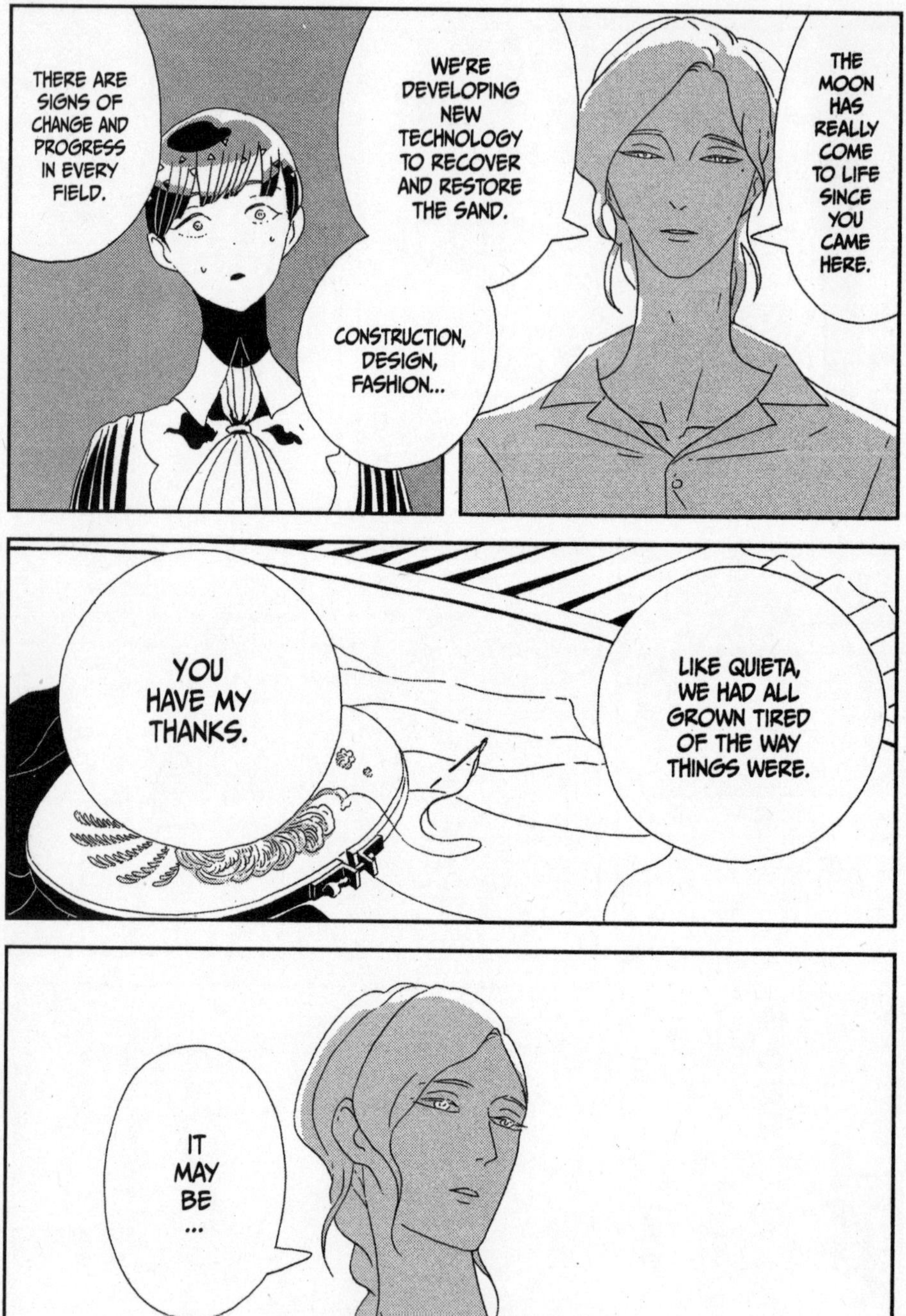
THE MOON HAS REALLY COME TO LIFE SINCE YOU CAME HERE.
WE'RE DEVELOPING NEW TECHNOLOGY TO RECOVER AND RESTORE THE SAND.
CONSTRUCTION, DESIGN, FASHION...
THERE ARE SIGNS OF CHANGE AND PROGRESS IN EVERY FIELD.
LIKE QUIETA, WE HAD ALL GROWN TIRED OF THE WAY THINGS WERE.
YOU HAVE MY THANKS.
IT MAY BE ...

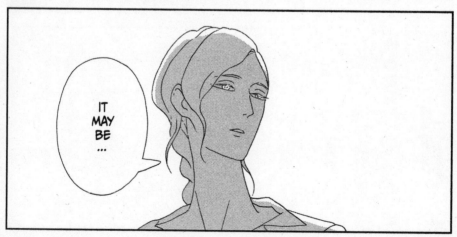

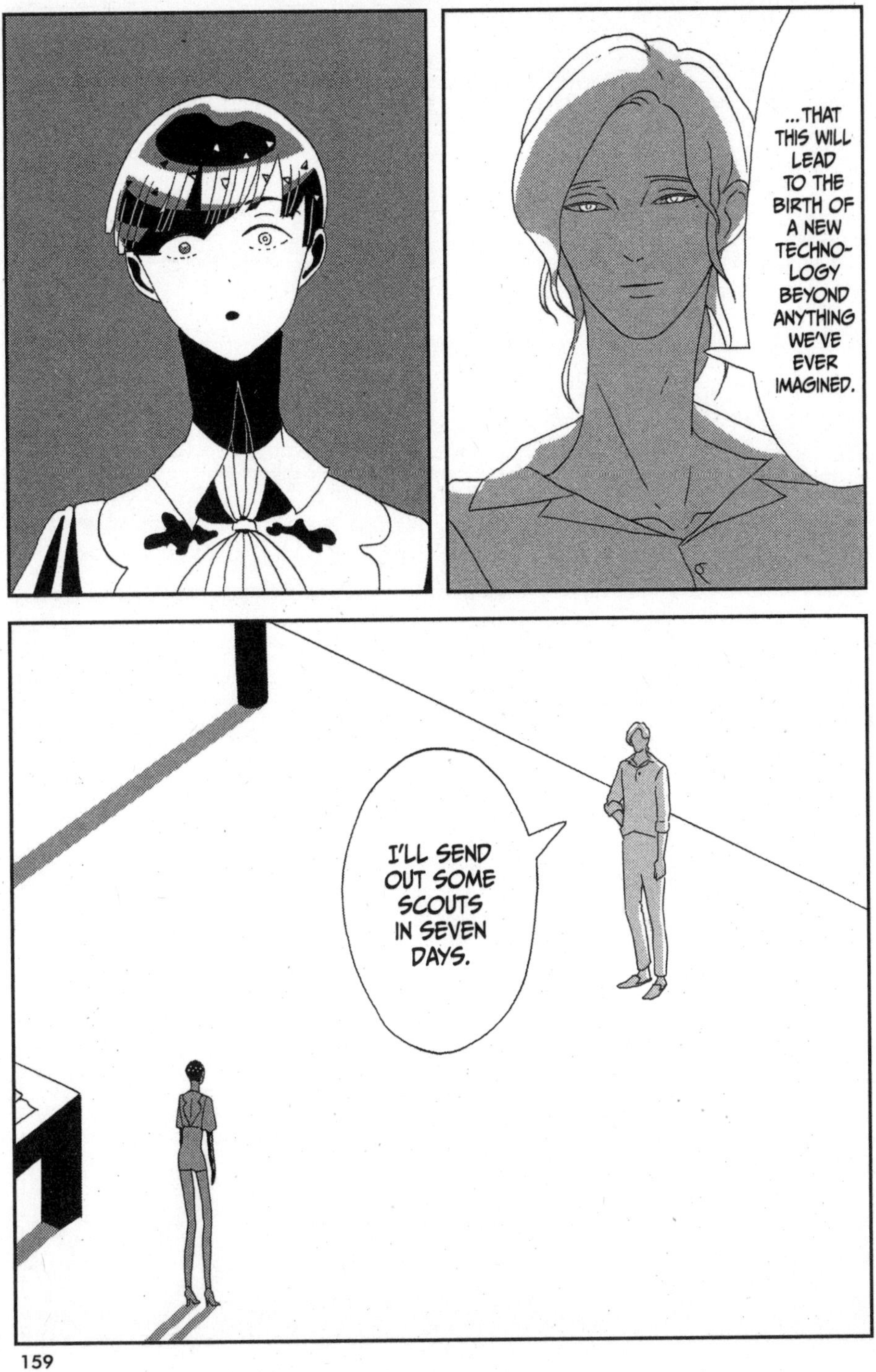
...THAT THIS WILL LEAD TO THE BIRTH OF A NEW TECHNO-LOGY BEYOND ANYTHING WE'VE EVER IMAGINED.
I'LL SEND OUT SOME SCOUTS IN SEVEN DAYS.

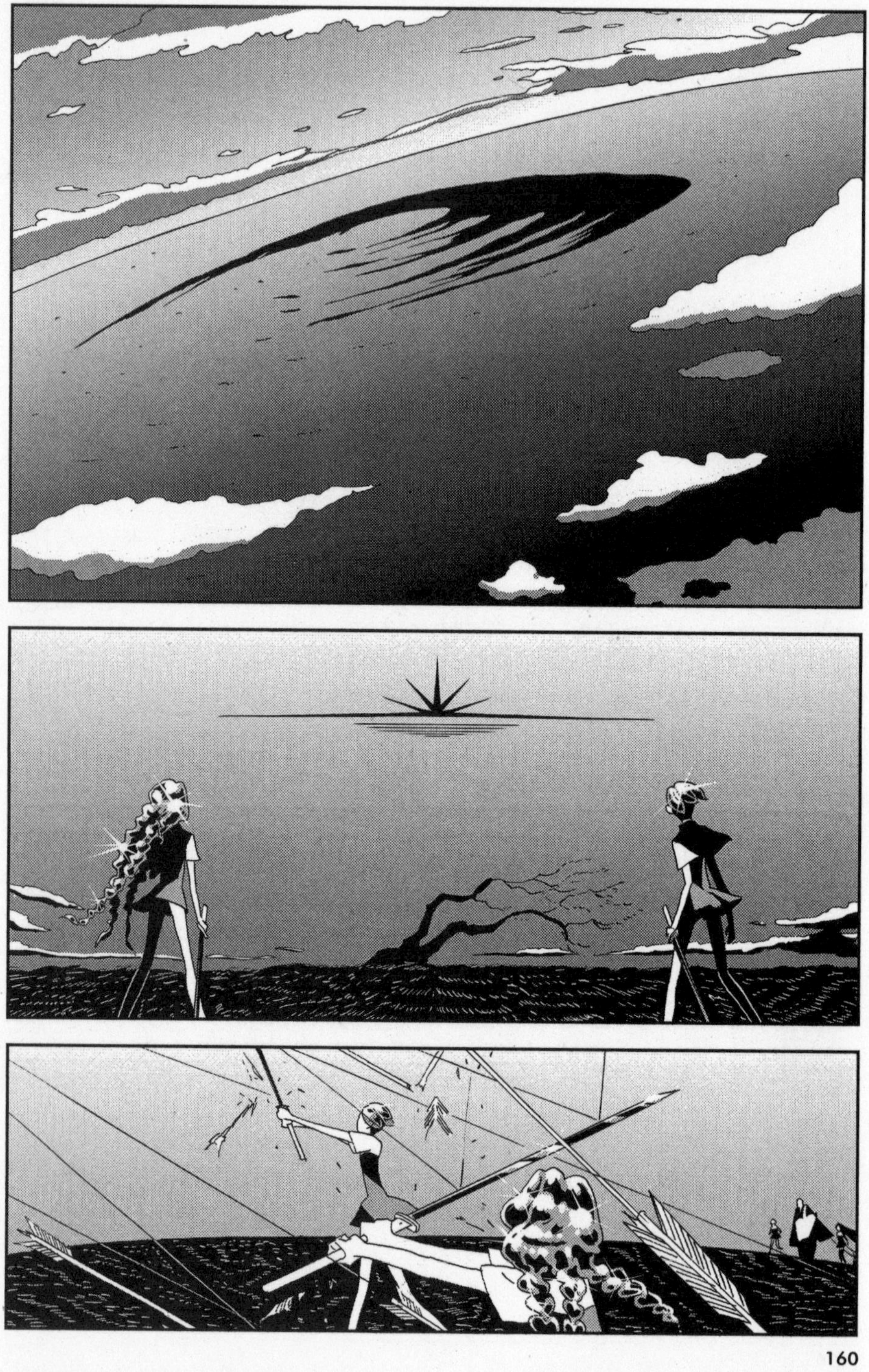

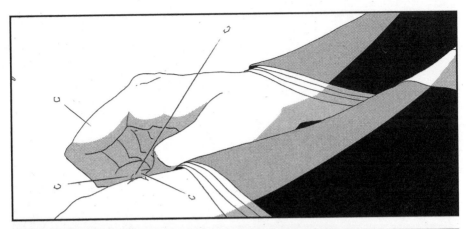

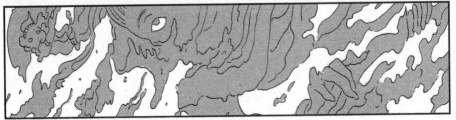

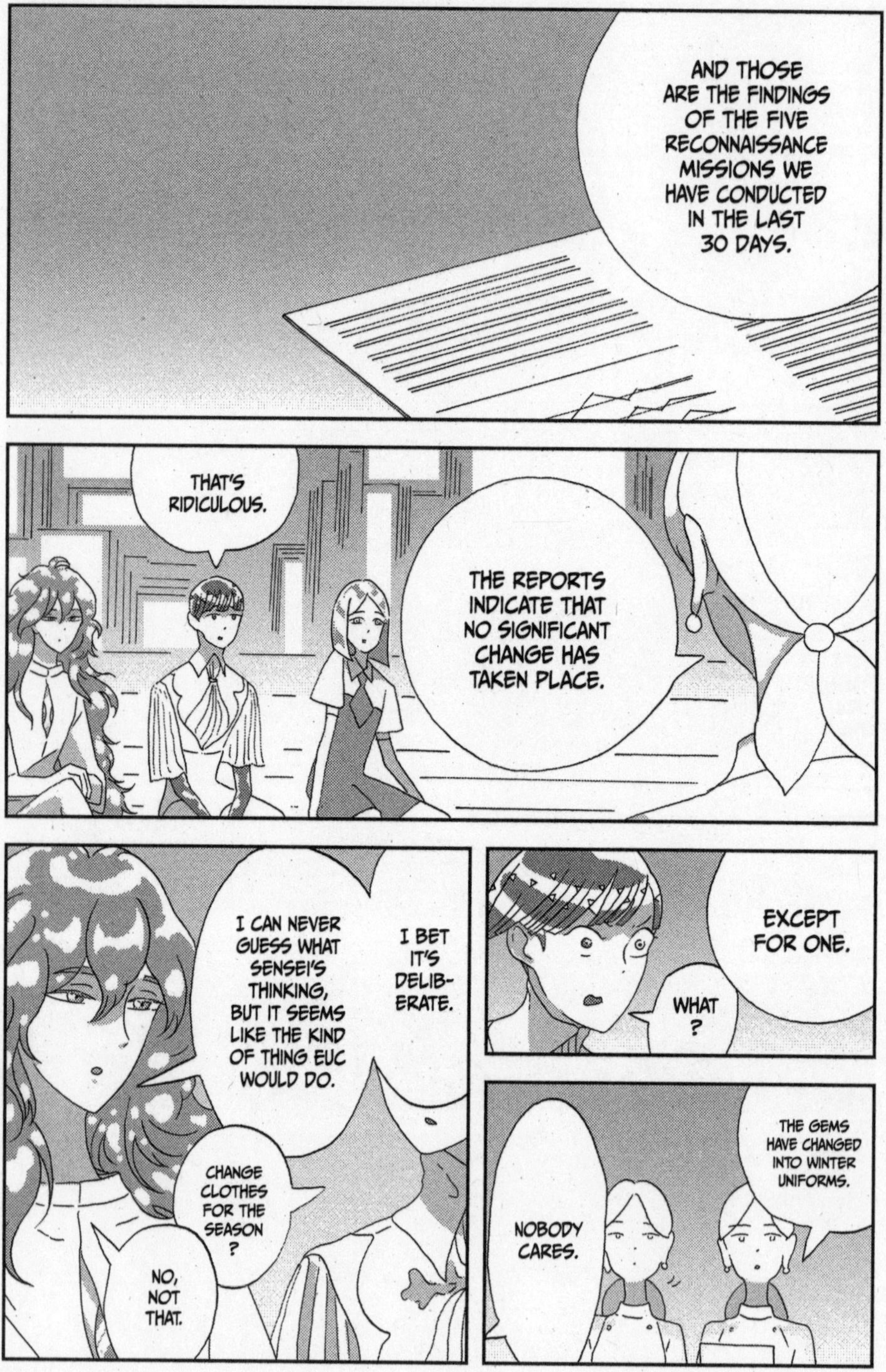
AND THOSE ARE THE FINDINGS OF THE FIVE RECONNAISSANCE MISSIONS WE HAVE CONDUCTED IN THE LAST 30 DAYS.
THE REPORTS INDICATE THAT NO SIGNIFICANT CHANGE HAS TAKEN PLACE.
THAT'S RIDICULOUS.
EXCEPT FOR ONE.
WHAT?
THE GEMS HAVE CHANGED INTO WINTER UNIFORMS.
NOBODY CARES.
I BET IT'S DELIBERATE.
I CAN NEVER GUESS WHAT SENSEI'S THINKING, BUT IT SEEMS LIKE THE KIND OF THING EUC WOULD DO.
CHANGE CLOTHES FOR THE SEASON?
NO, NOT THAT.

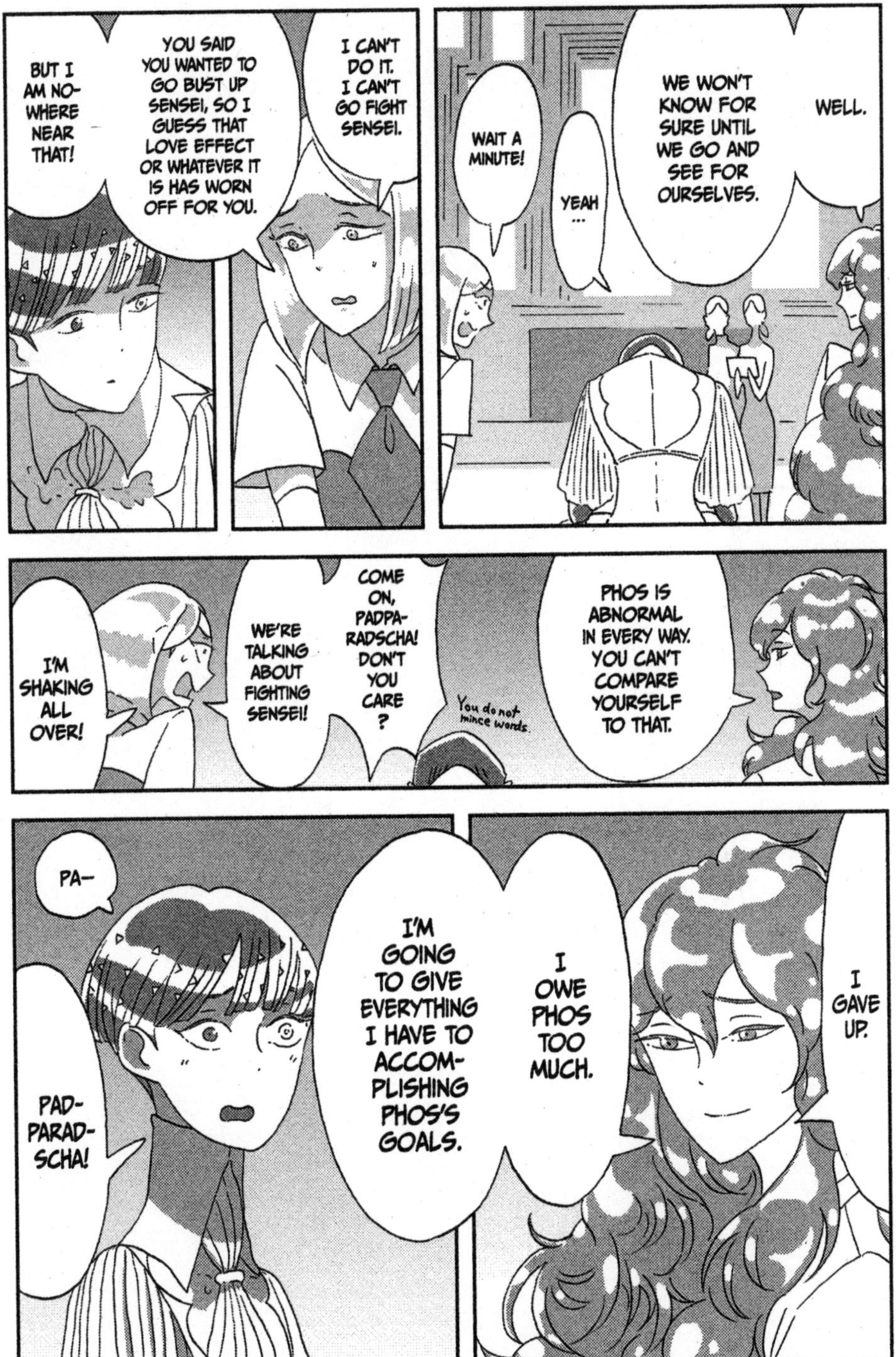
WELL.
WE WON'T KNOW FOR SURE UNTIL WE GO AND SEE FOR OURSELVES.
YEAH ...
WAIT A MINUTE!
I CAN'T DO IT. I CAN'T GO FIGHT SENSEI.
YOU SAID YOU WANTED TO GO BUST UP SENSEI, SO I GUESS THAT LOVE EFFECT OR WHATEVER IT IS HAS WORN OFF FOR YOU.
BUT I AM NO-WHERE NEAR THAT!
PHOS IS ABNORMAL IN EVERY WAY. YOU CAN'T COMPARE YOURSELF TO THAT.
You do not mince words.
COME ON, PADPARADSCHA! DON'T YOU CARE?
WE'RE TALKING ABOUT FIGHTING SENSEI!
I'M SHAKING ALL OVER!
I GAVE UP.
I OWE PHOS TOO MUCH.
I'M GOING TO GIVE EVERYTHING I HAVE TO ACCOM-PLISHING PHOS'S GOALS.
PA-
PAD-PARAD-SCHA!

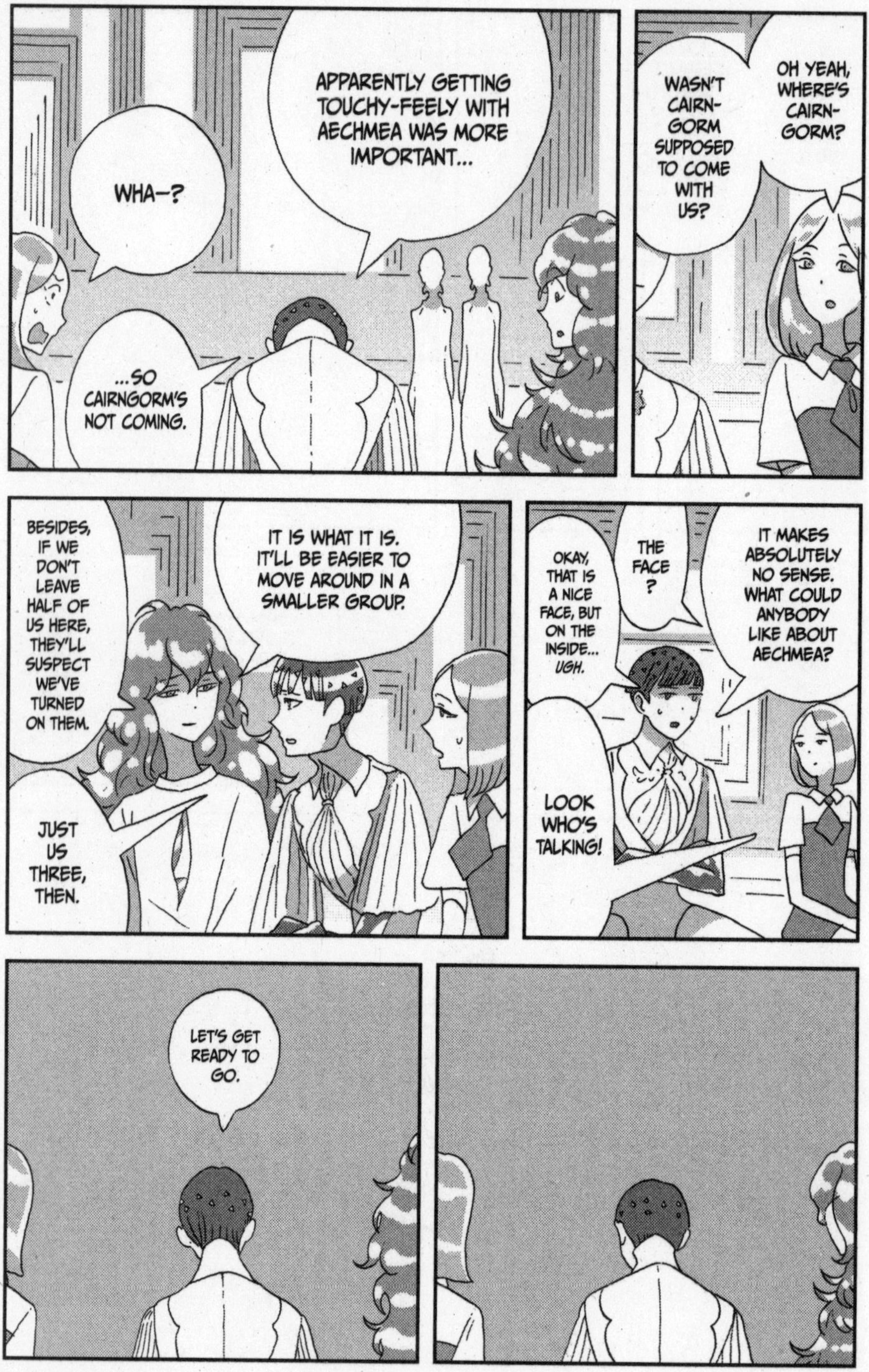
OH YEAH, WHERE'S CAIRN-GORM?
WASN'T CAIRN-GORM SUPPOSED TO COME WITH US?
APPARENTLY GETTING TOUCHY-FEELY WITH AECHMEA WAS MORE IMPORTANT...
WHA—?
...SO CAIRNGORM'S NOT COMING.
IT MAKES ABSOLUTELY NO SENSE. WHAT COULD ANYBODY LIKE ABOUT AECHMEA?
THE FACE?
OKAY, THAT IS A NICE FACE, BUT ON THE INSIDE... *UGH.*
LOOK WHO'S TALKING!
IT IS WHAT IT IS. IT'LL BE EASIER TO MOVE AROUND IN A SMALLER GROUP.
BESIDES, IF WE DON'T LEAVE HALF OF US HERE, THEY'LL SUSPECT WE'VE TURNED ON THEM.
JUST US THREE, THEN.
LET'S GET READY TO GO.

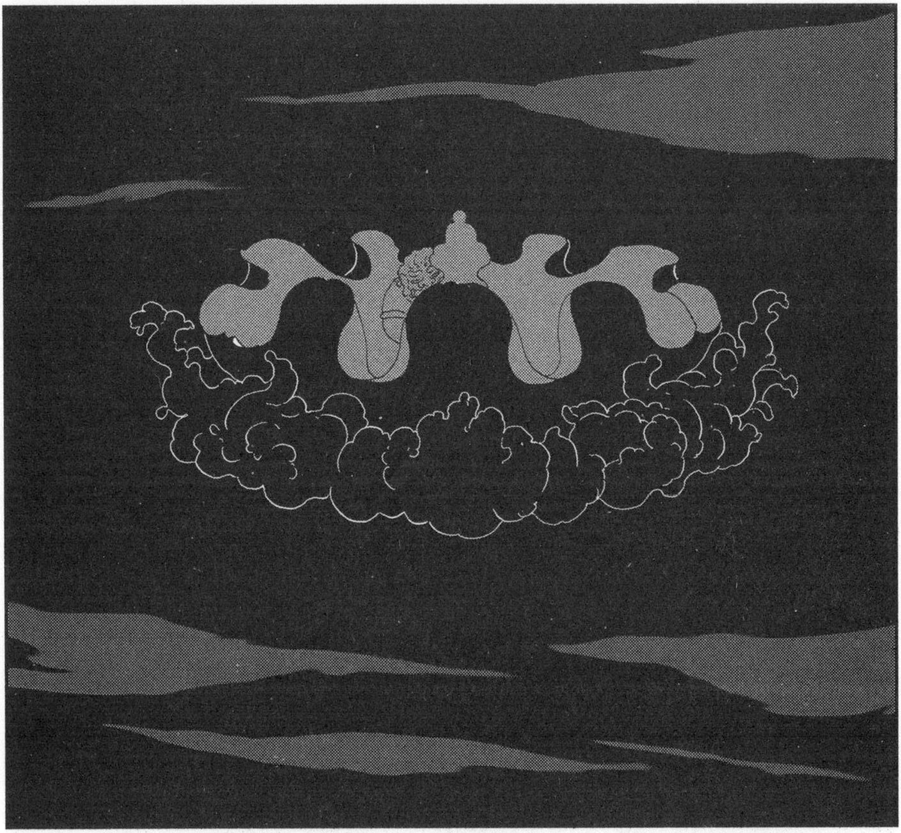
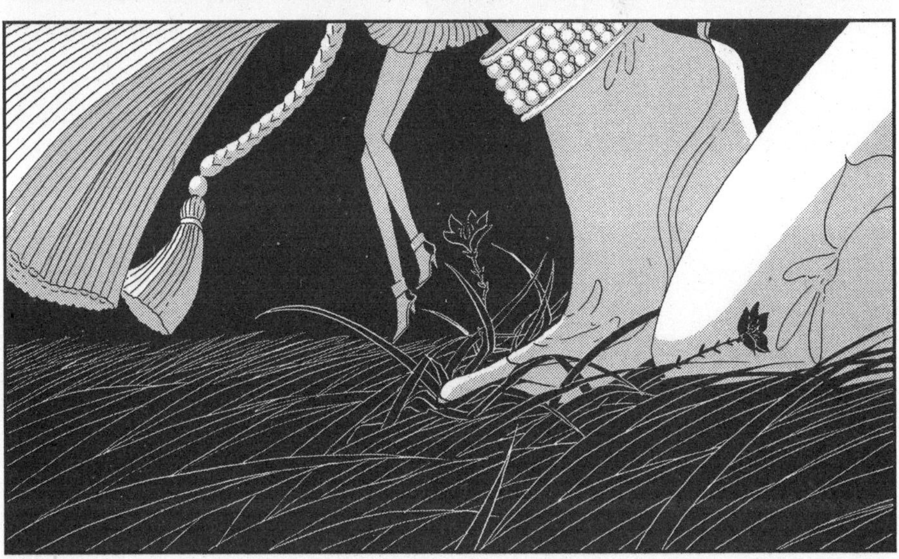

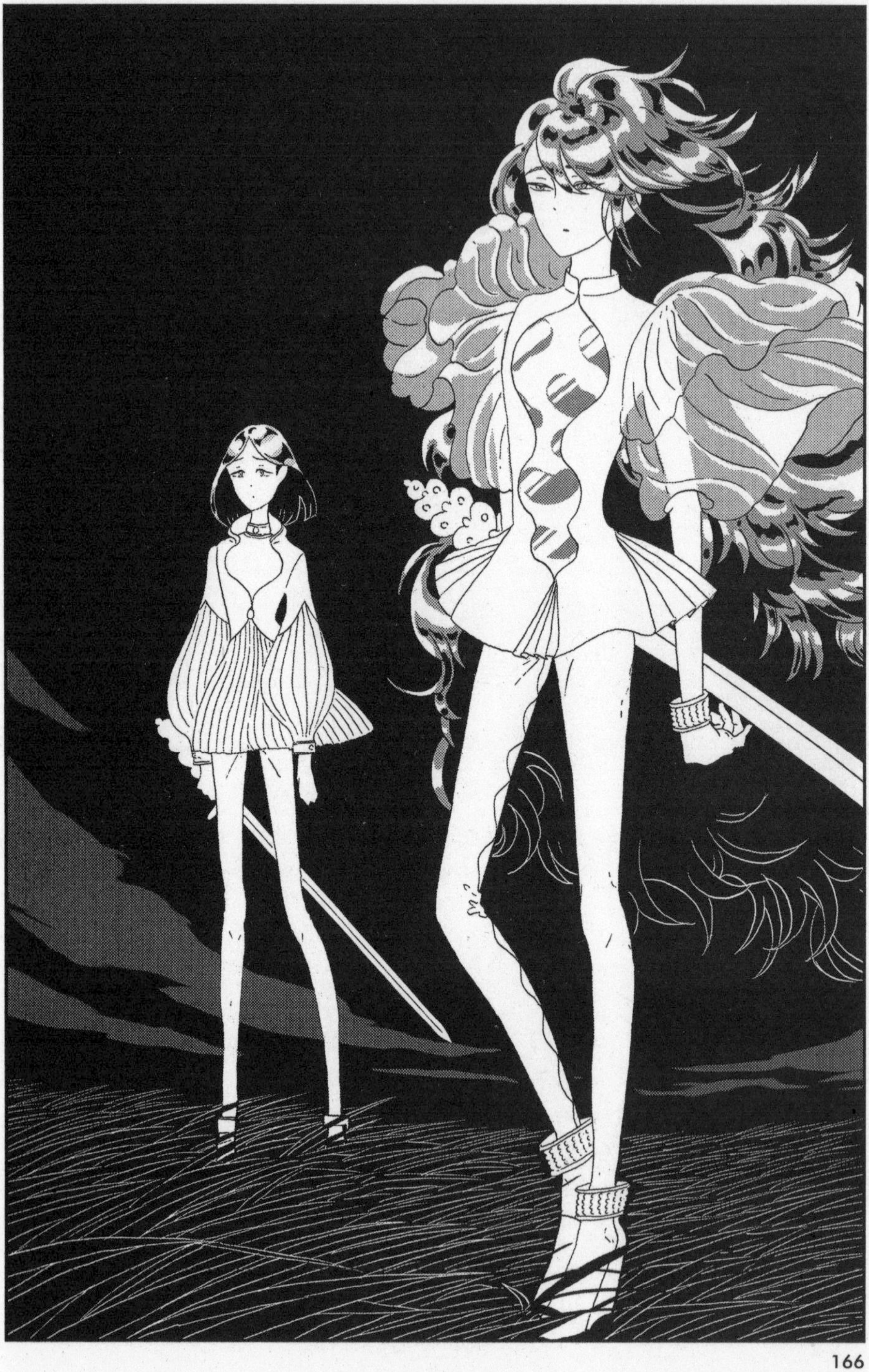

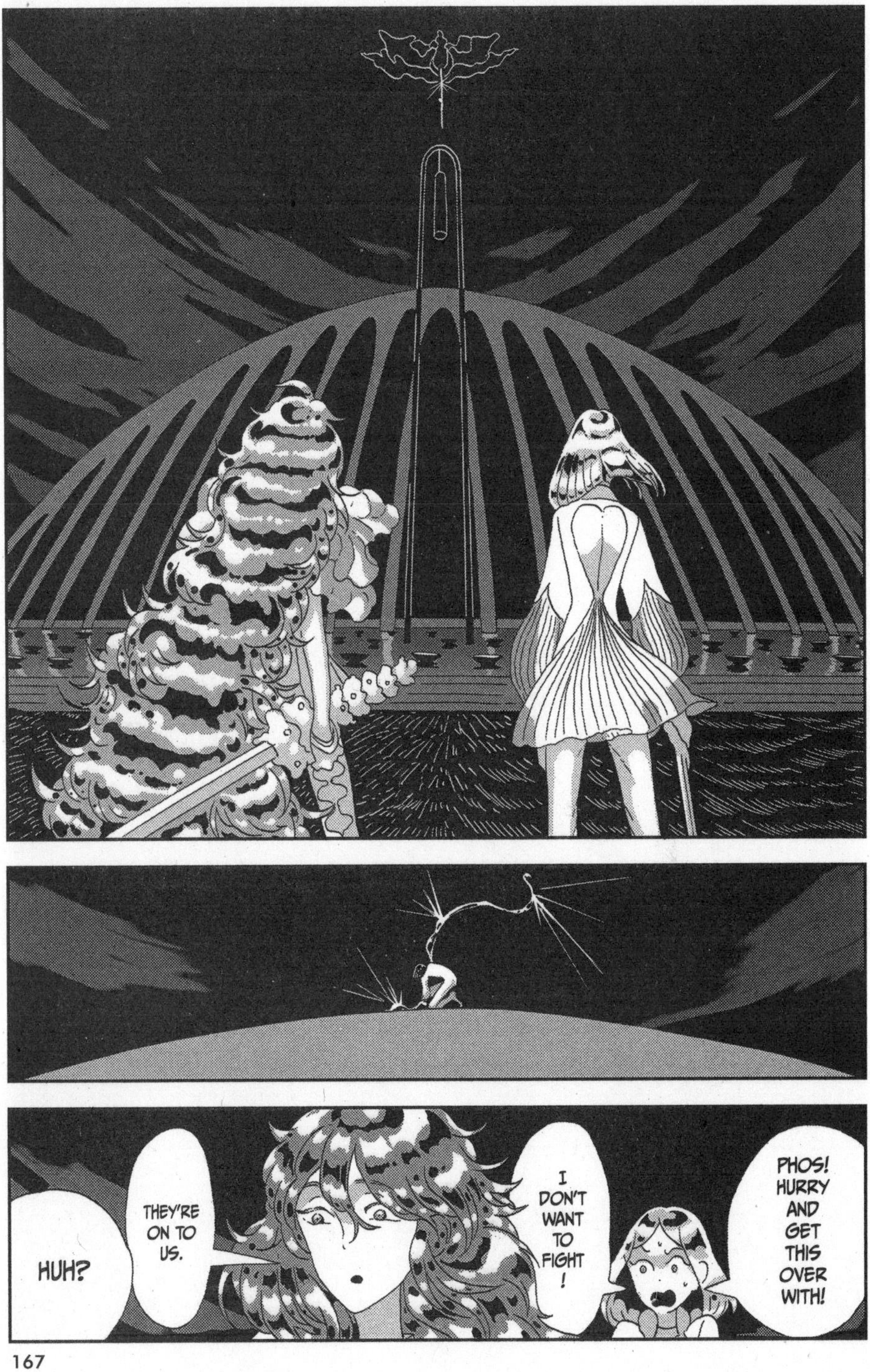
PHOS! HURRY AND GET THIS OVER WITH!
I DON'T WANT TO FIGHT!
THEY'RE ON TO US.
HUH?

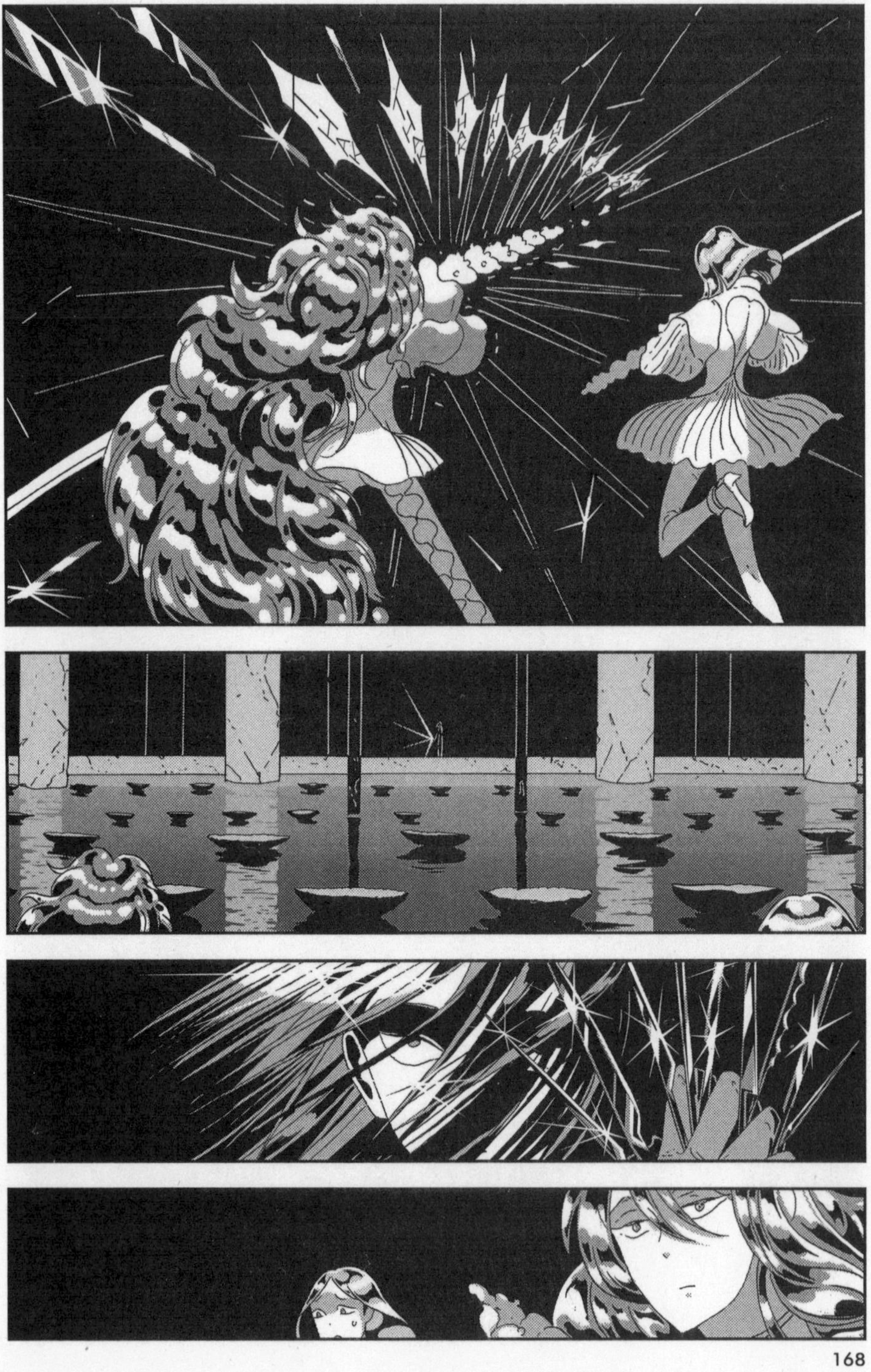
THAK THAK THAK THAK

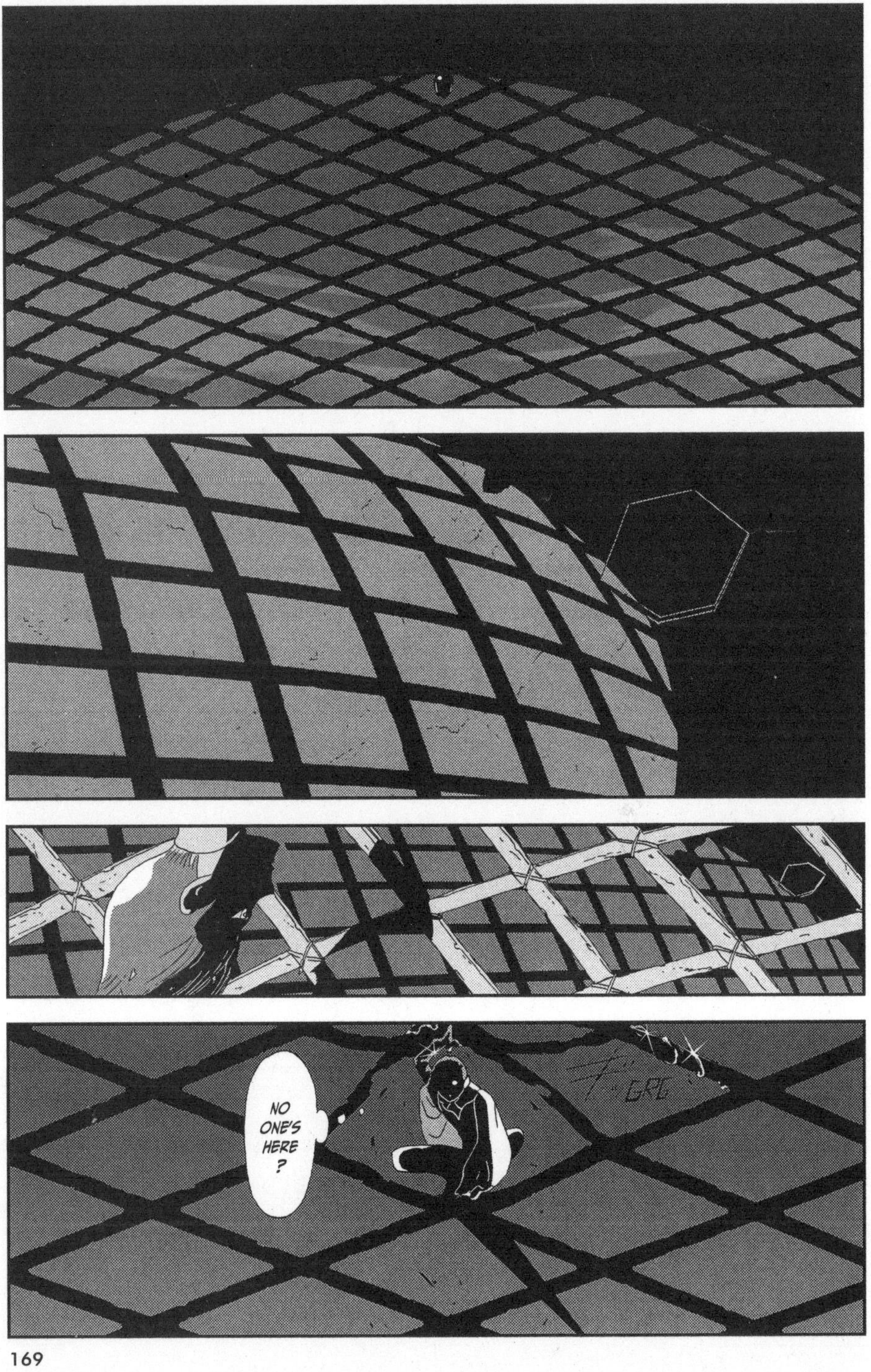
GRG
NO ONE'S HERE ?

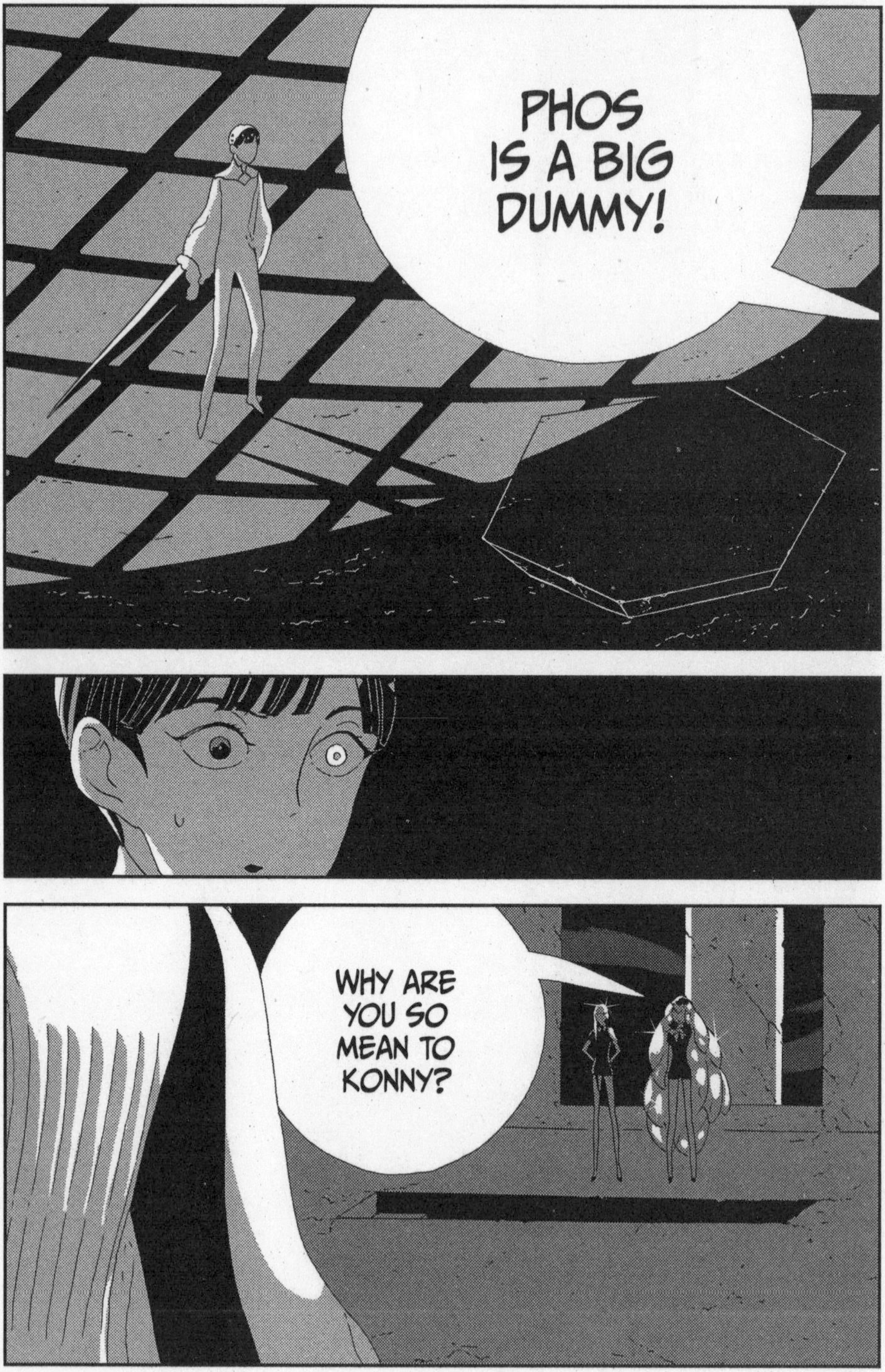
PHOS IS A BIG DUMMY!
WHY ARE YOU SO MEAN TO KONNY?

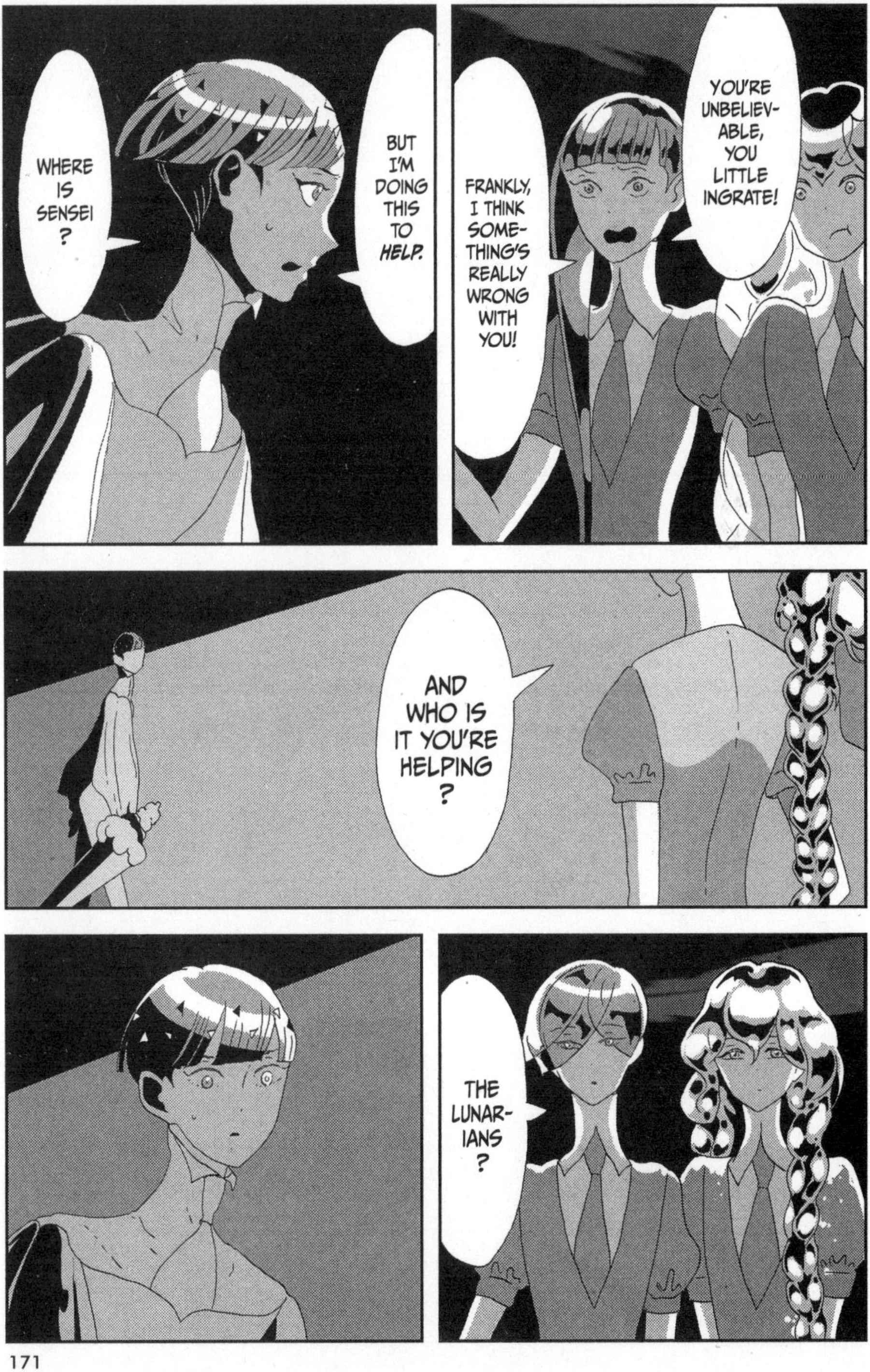
YOU'RE UNBELIEVABLE, YOU LITTLE INGRATE!
FRANKLY, I THINK SOMETHING'S REALLY WRONG WITH YOU!
BUT I'M DOING THIS TO *HELP.*
WHERE IS SENSEI?
AND WHO IS IT YOU'RE HELPING?
THE LUNARIANS?

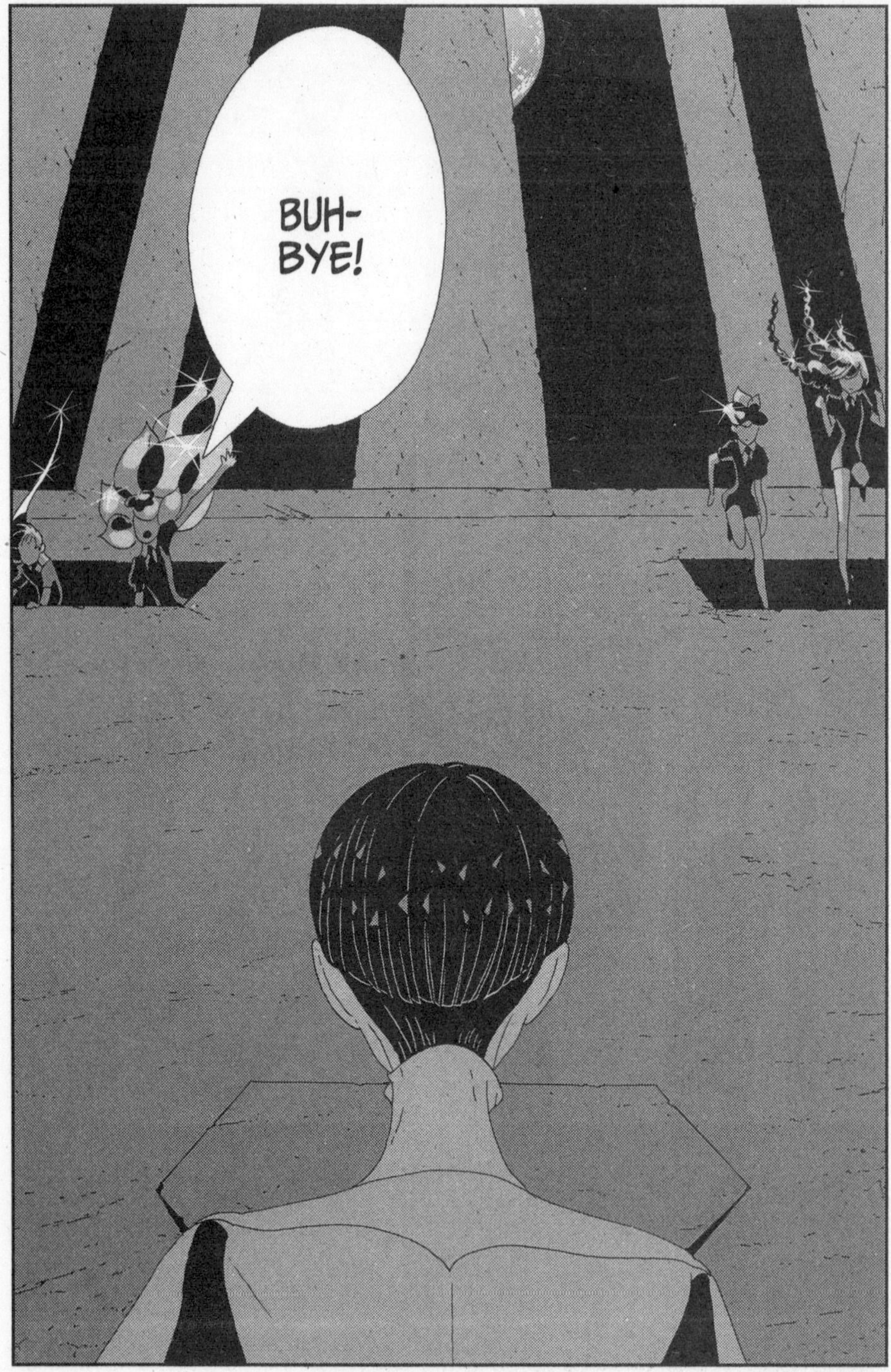
BUH-
BYE!

CHAPTER 69: Unchanging END

CHAPTER 70:

Before Dawn

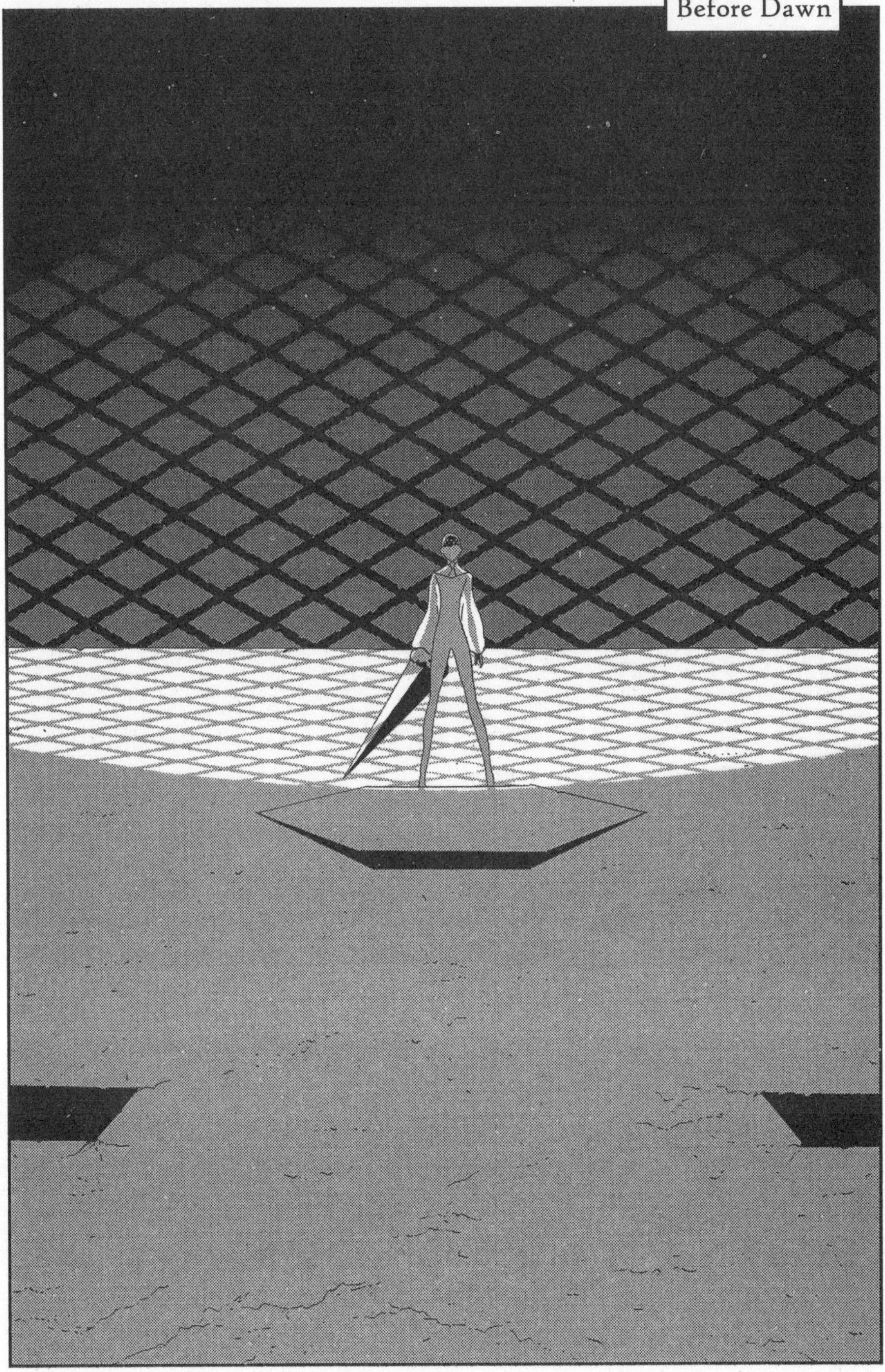

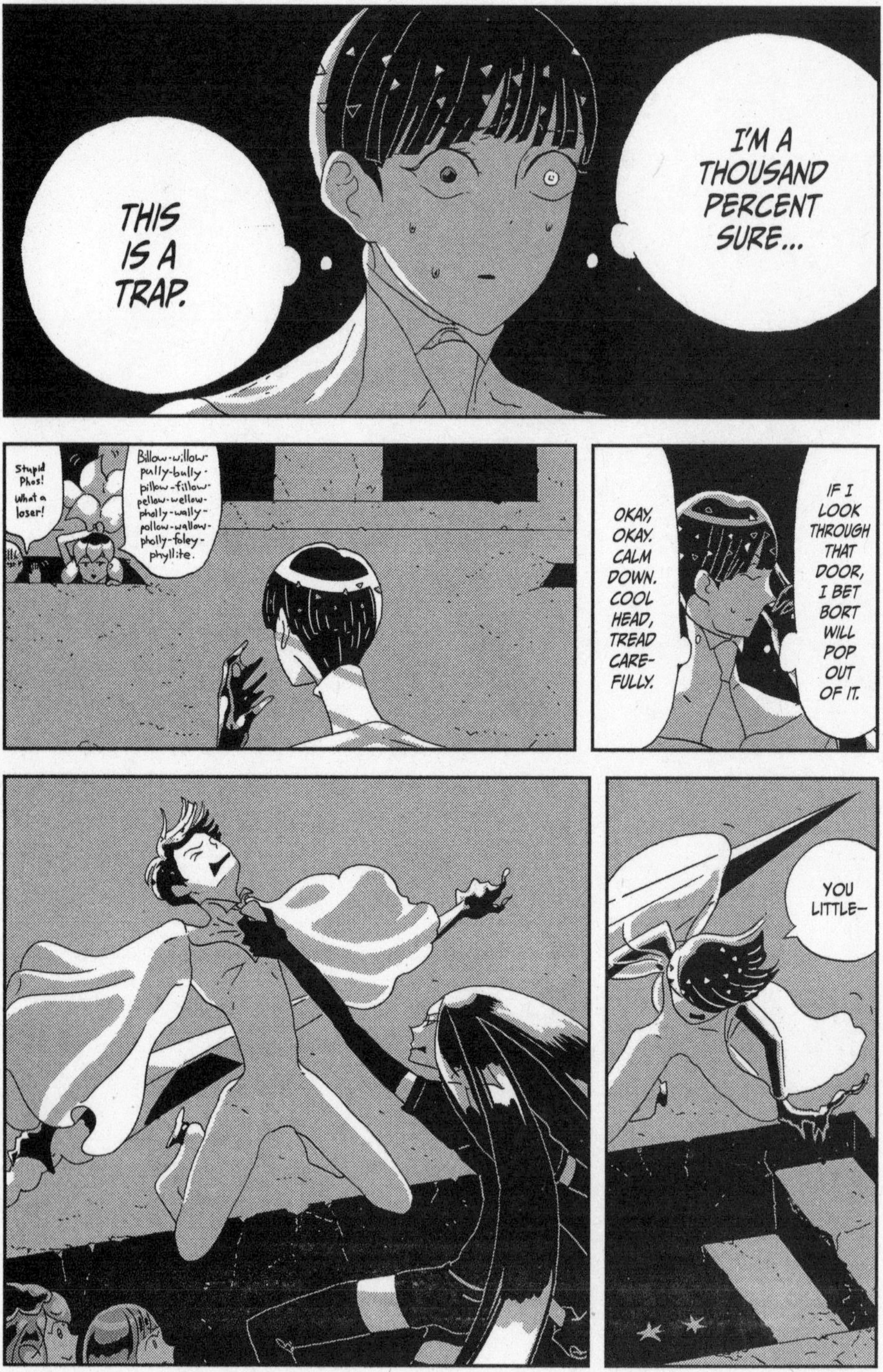
I'M A THOUSAND PERCENT SURE...
THIS IS A TRAP.
IF I LOOK THROUGH THAT DOOR, I BET BORT WILL POP OUT OF IT.
OKAY, OKAY. CALM DOWN. COOL HEAD, TREAD CARE-FULLY.
Billow-willow-pully-bully-pillow-fillow-pellow-wellow-pholly-wally-pollow-wallow-pholly-foley-phyllite.
Stupid Phos! What a loser!
YOU LITTLE—

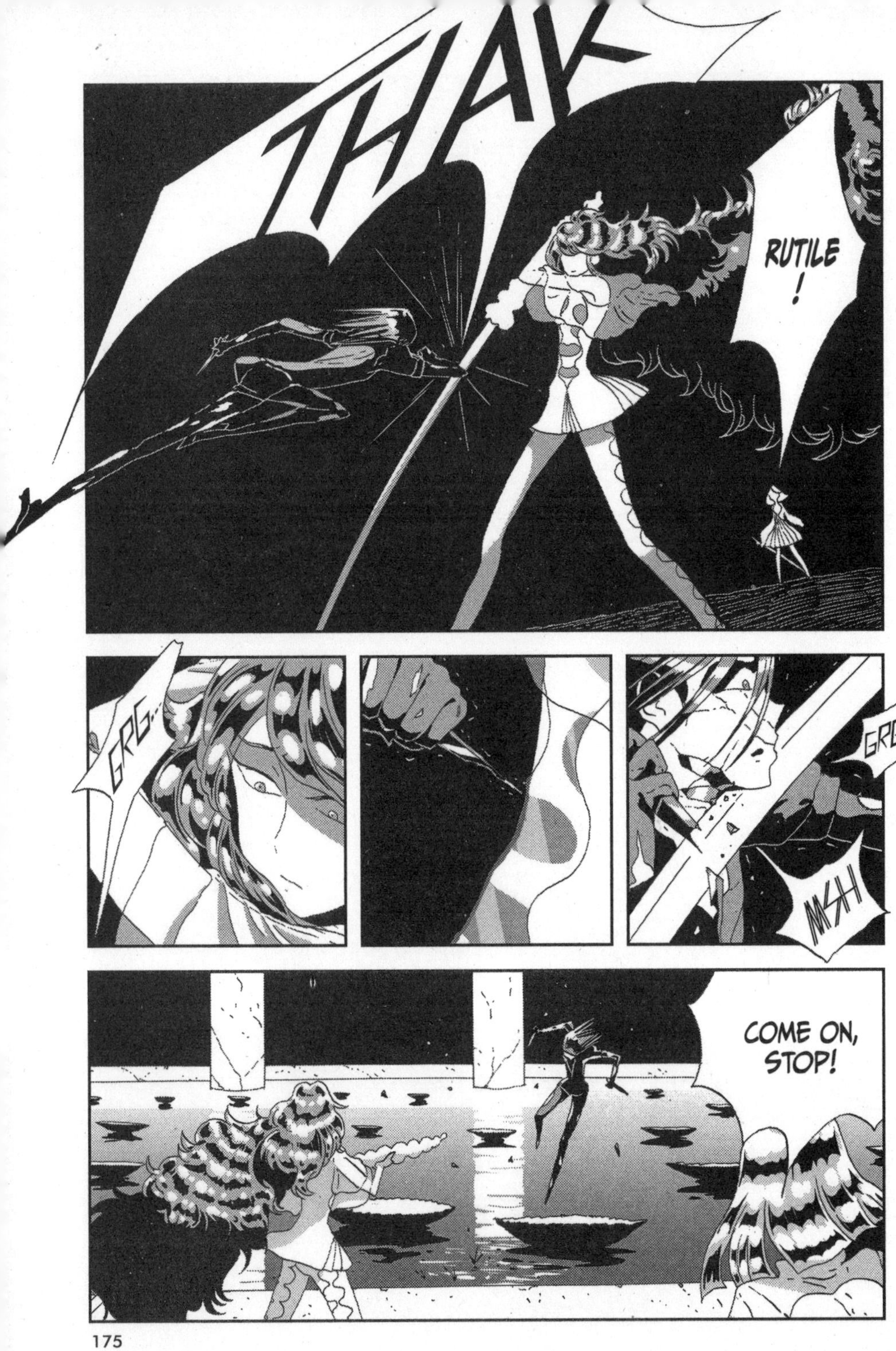
THAK
RUTILE !
GRG
MSH
GRG...
COME ON, STOP!

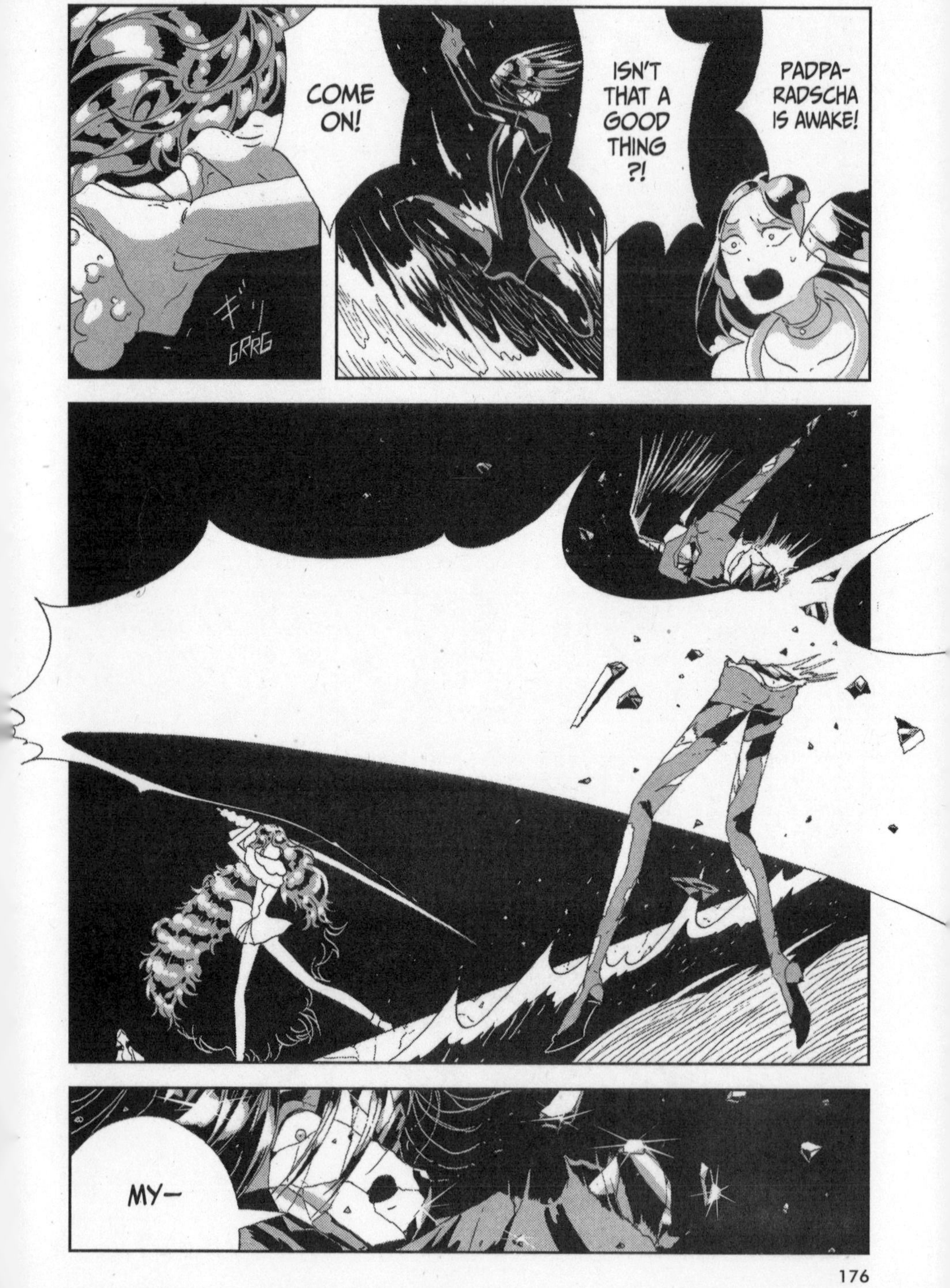
PADPARADSCHA IS AWAKE!
ISN'T THAT A GOOD THING?!
COME ON!
ギリ
GRRG
MY–

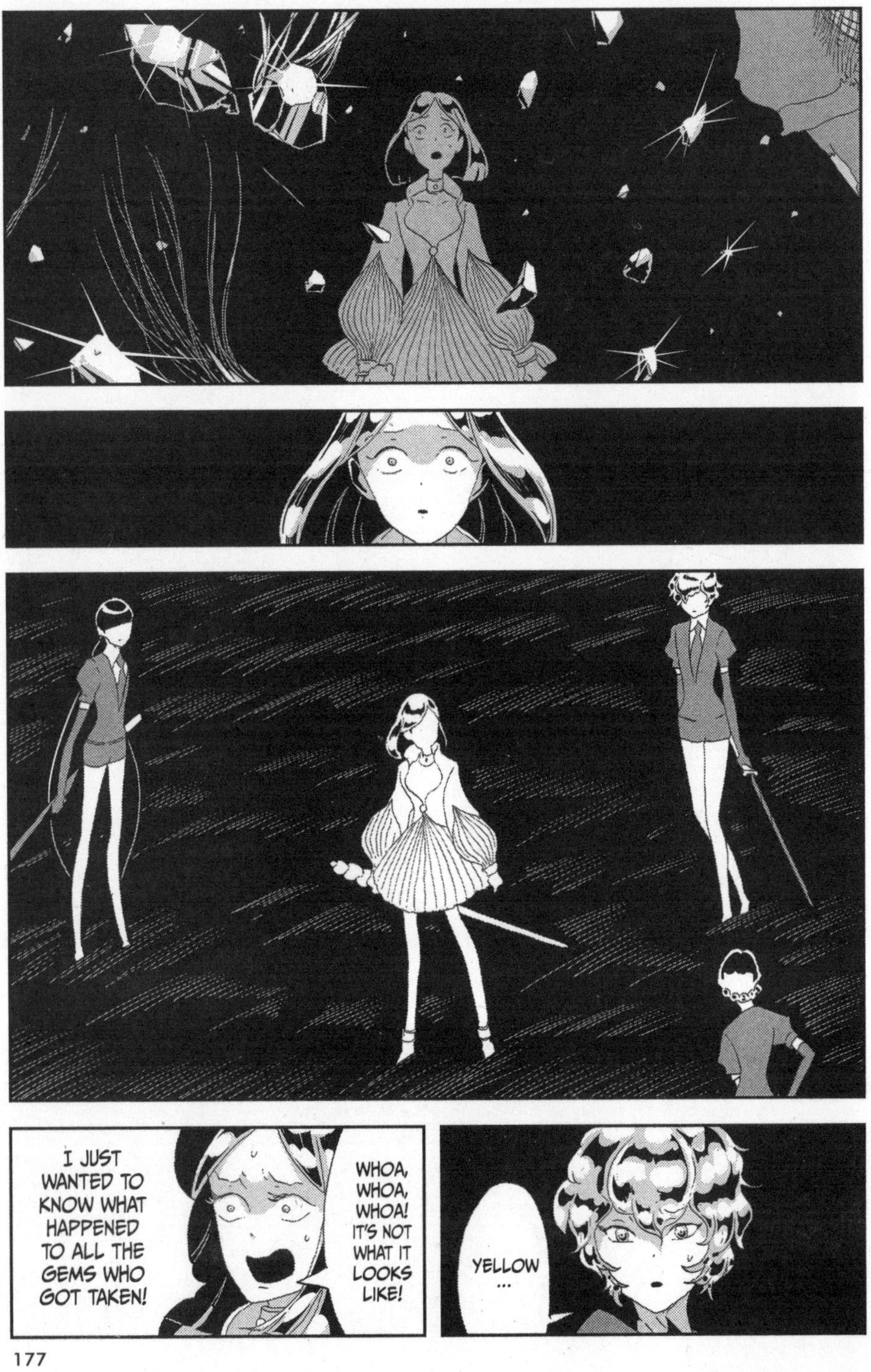
YELLOW ...
WHOA, WHOA, WHOA! IT'S NOT WHAT IT LOOKS LIKE!
I JUST WANTED TO KNOW WHAT HAPPENED TO ALL THE GEMS WHO GOT TAKEN!

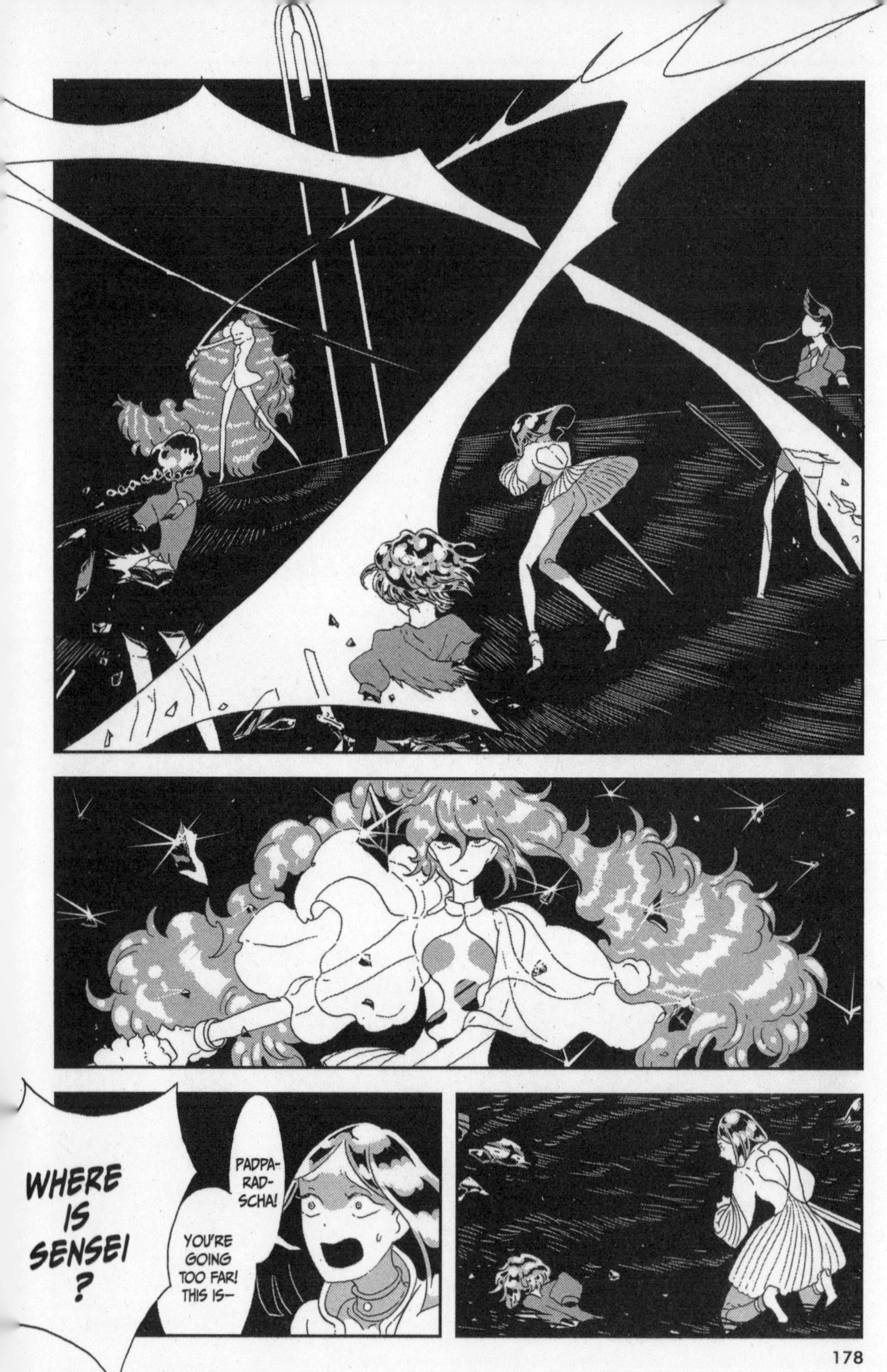
PADPARADSCHA!
YOU'RE GOING TOO FAR! THIS IS—
WHERE IS SENSEI?

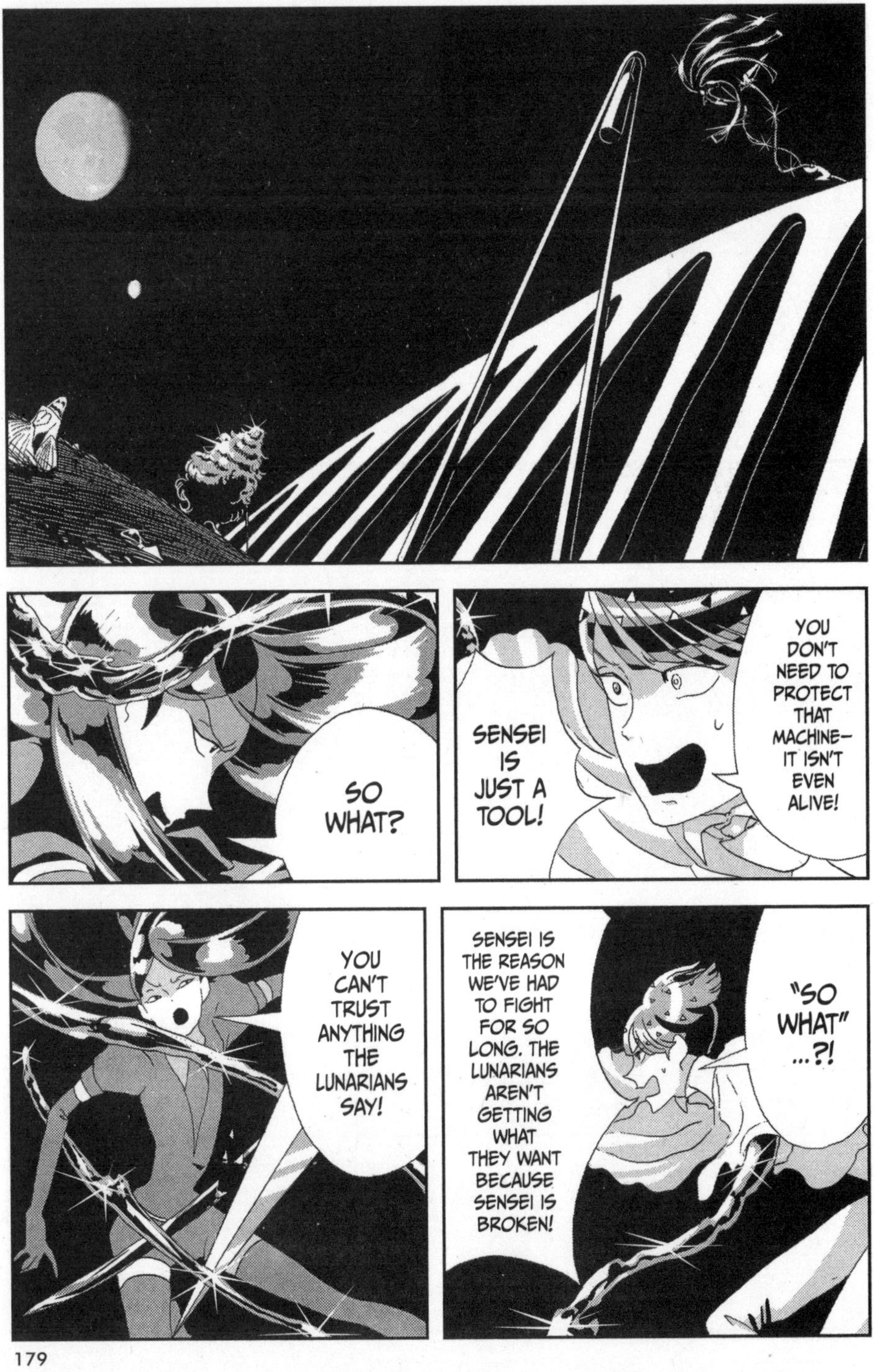
YOU DON'T NEED TO PROTECT THAT MACHINE— IT ISN'T EVEN ALIVE!
SENSEI IS JUST A TOOL!
SO WHAT?
"SO WHAT" ...?!
SENSEI IS THE REASON WE'VE HAD TO FIGHT FOR SO LONG. THE LUNARIANS AREN'T GETTING WHAT THEY WANT BECAUSE SENSEI IS BROKEN!
YOU CAN'T TRUST ANYTHING THE LUNARIANS SAY!

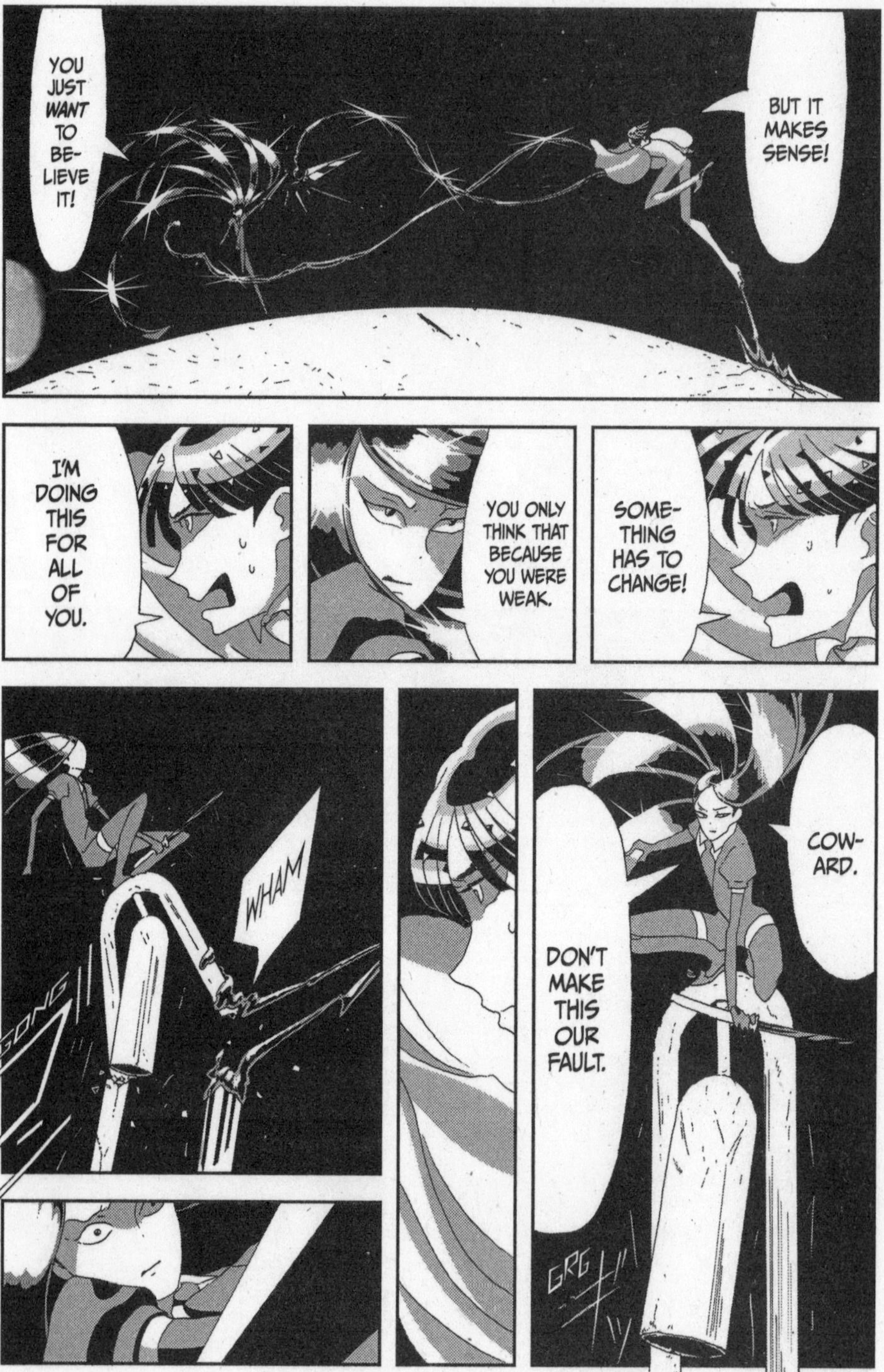
BUT IT MAKES SENSE!
YOU JUST WANT TO BE-LIEVE IT!
SOME-THING HAS TO CHANGE!
YOU ONLY THINK THAT BECAUSE YOU WERE WEAK.
I'M DOING THIS FOR ALL OF YOU.
COW-ARD.
DON'T MAKE THIS OUR FAULT.
GRG
WHAM
GONG

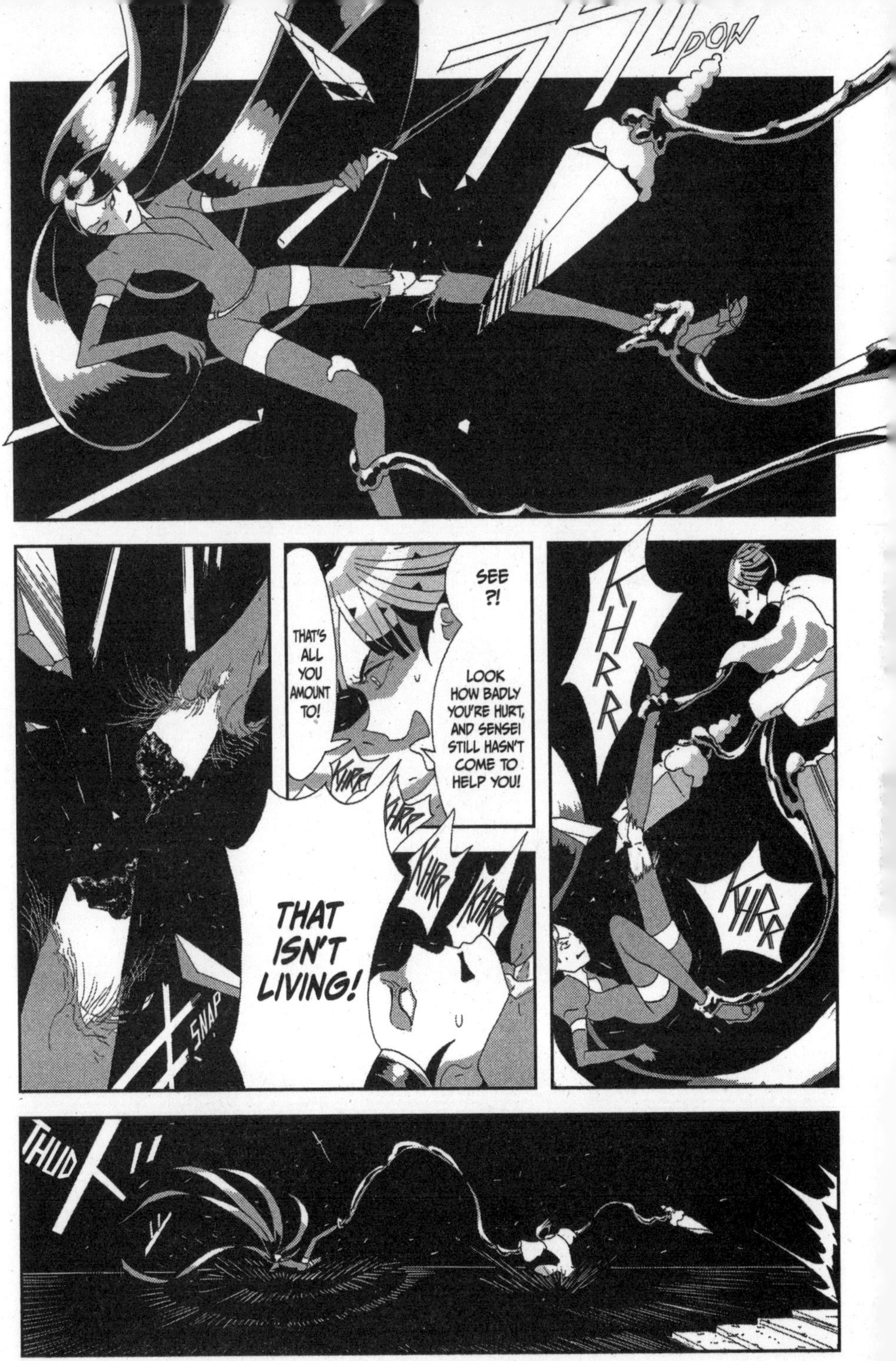
POW
KHRR
KHRR
SEE ?!
LOOK HOW BADLY YOU'RE HURT, AND SENSEI STILL HASN'T COME TO HELP YOU!
THAT'S ALL YOU AMOUNT TO!
KHRR
KHRR
KHRR
KHRR
THAT ISN'T LIVING!
SNAP
THUD

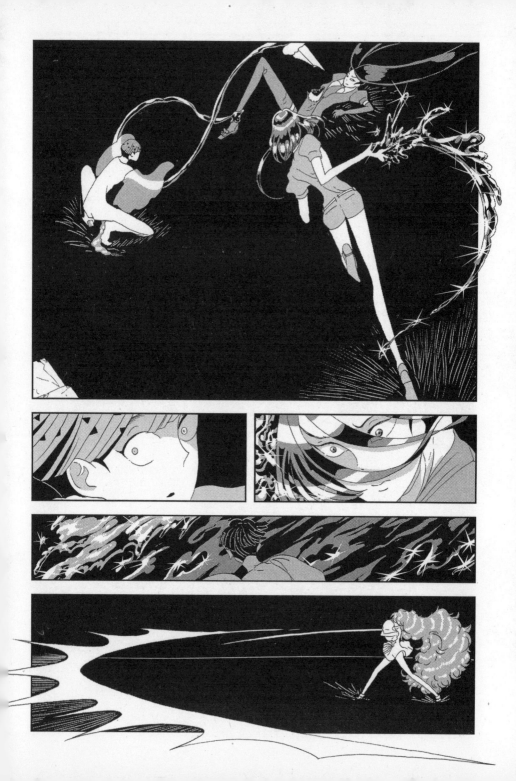

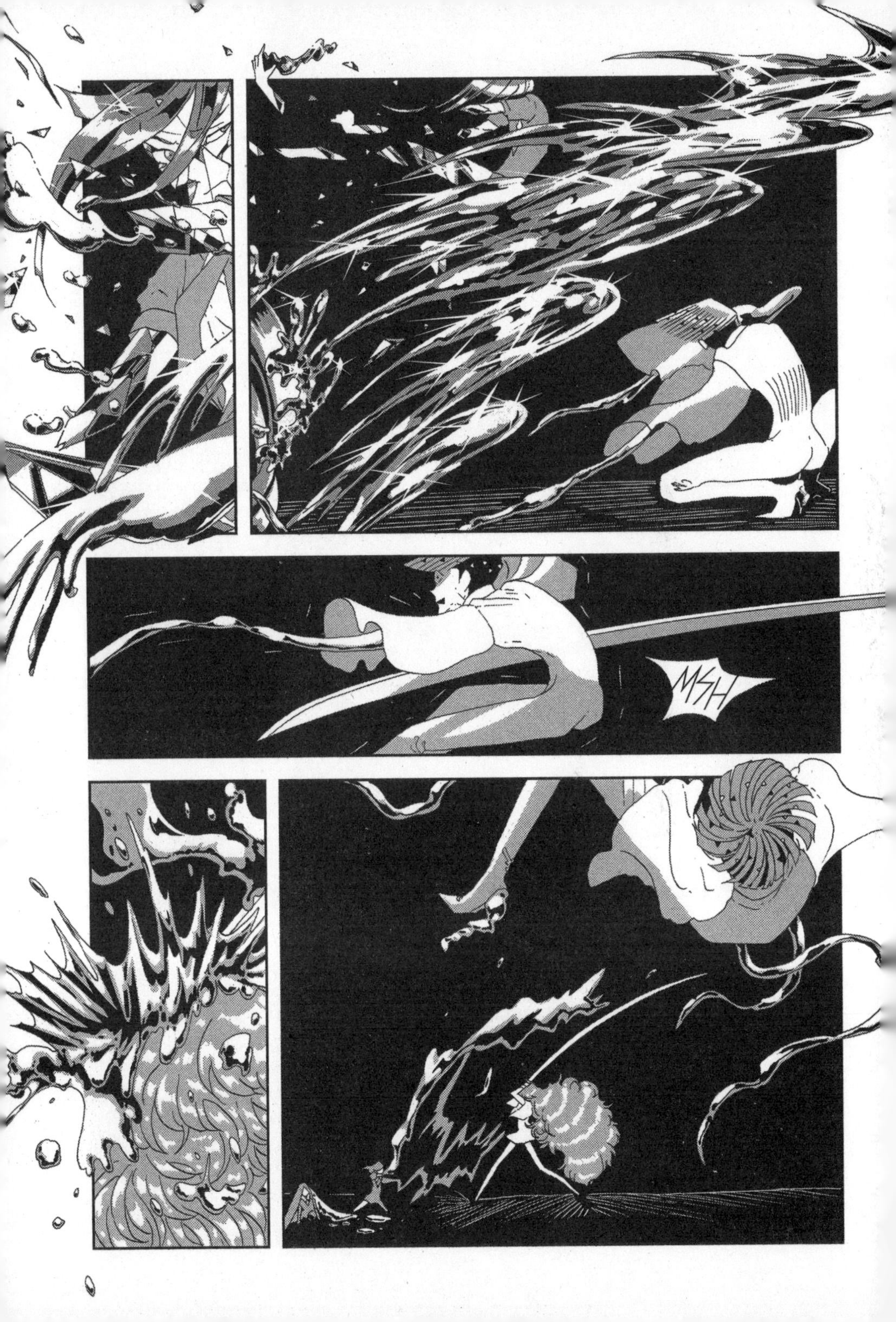
MSH

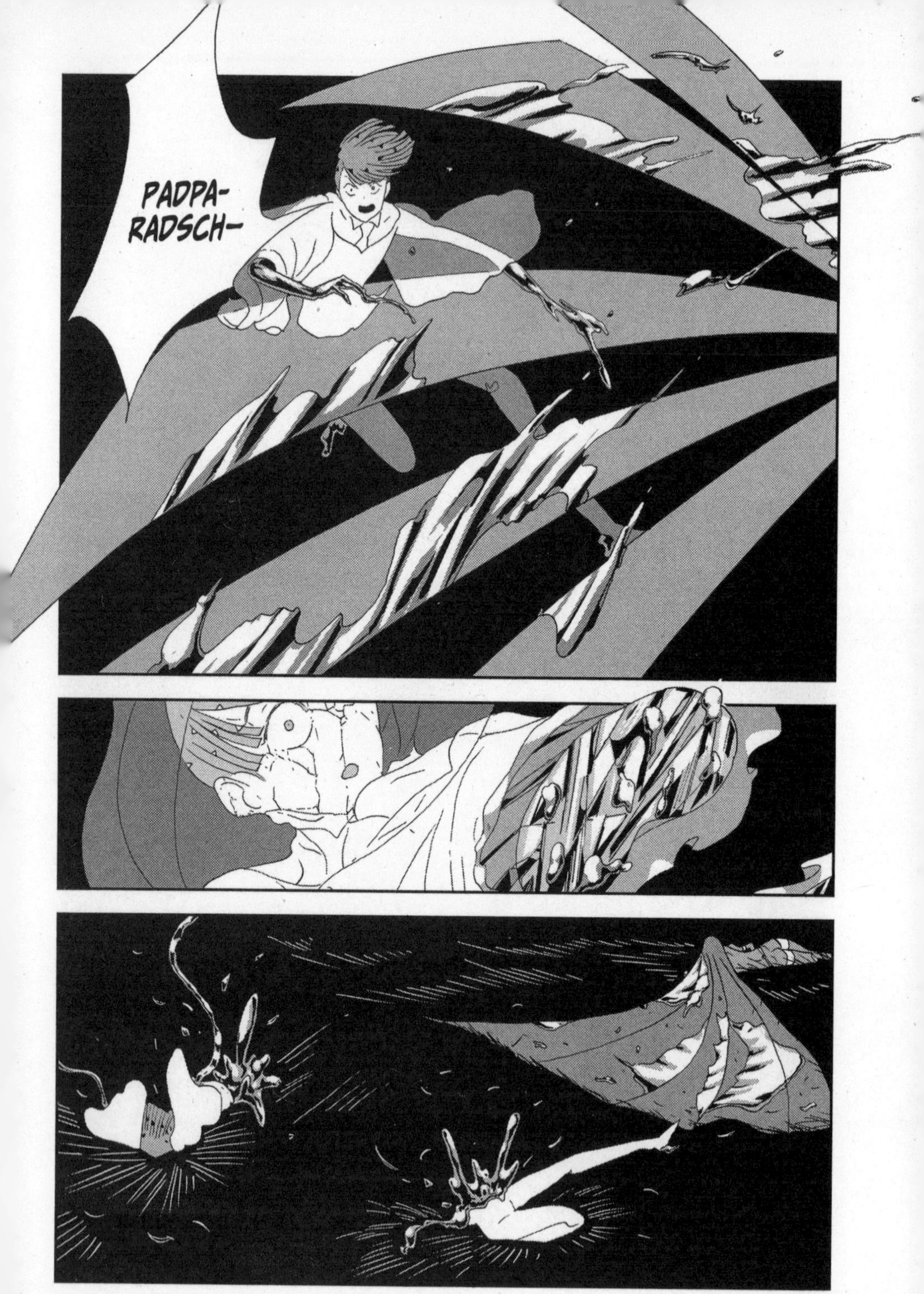
PADPA-
RADSCH-

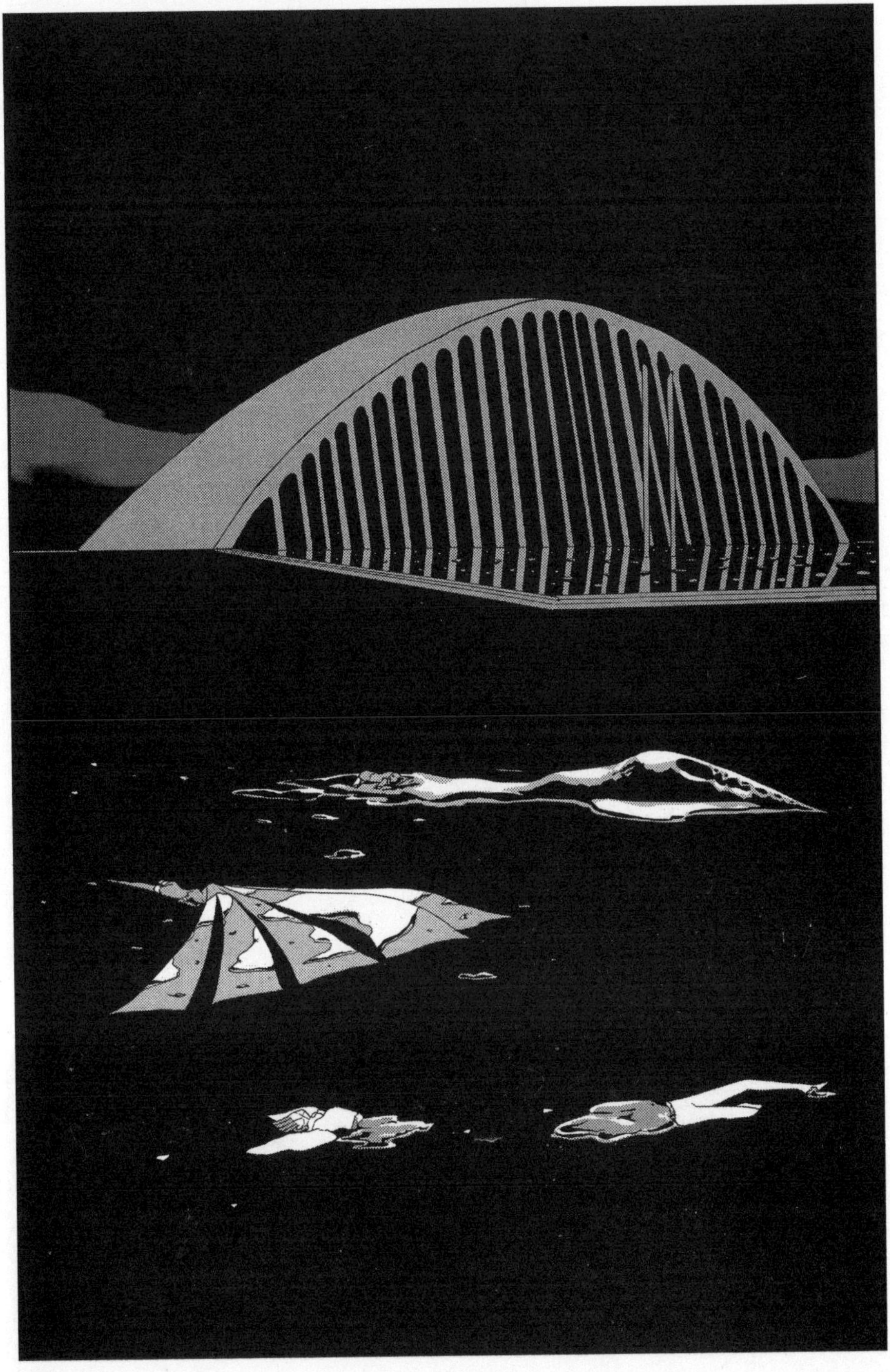

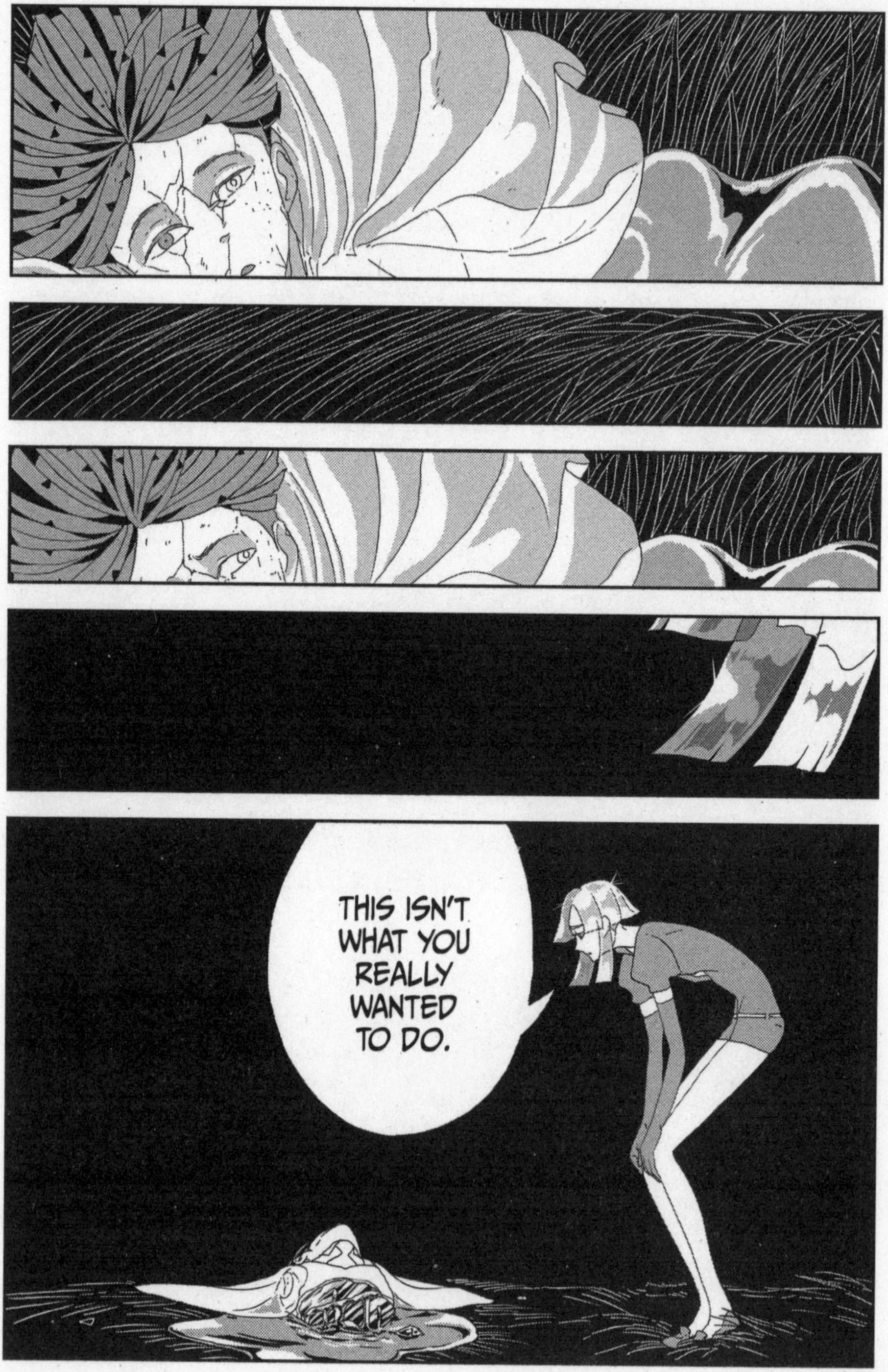
THIS ISN'T WHAT YOU REALLY WANTED TO DO.

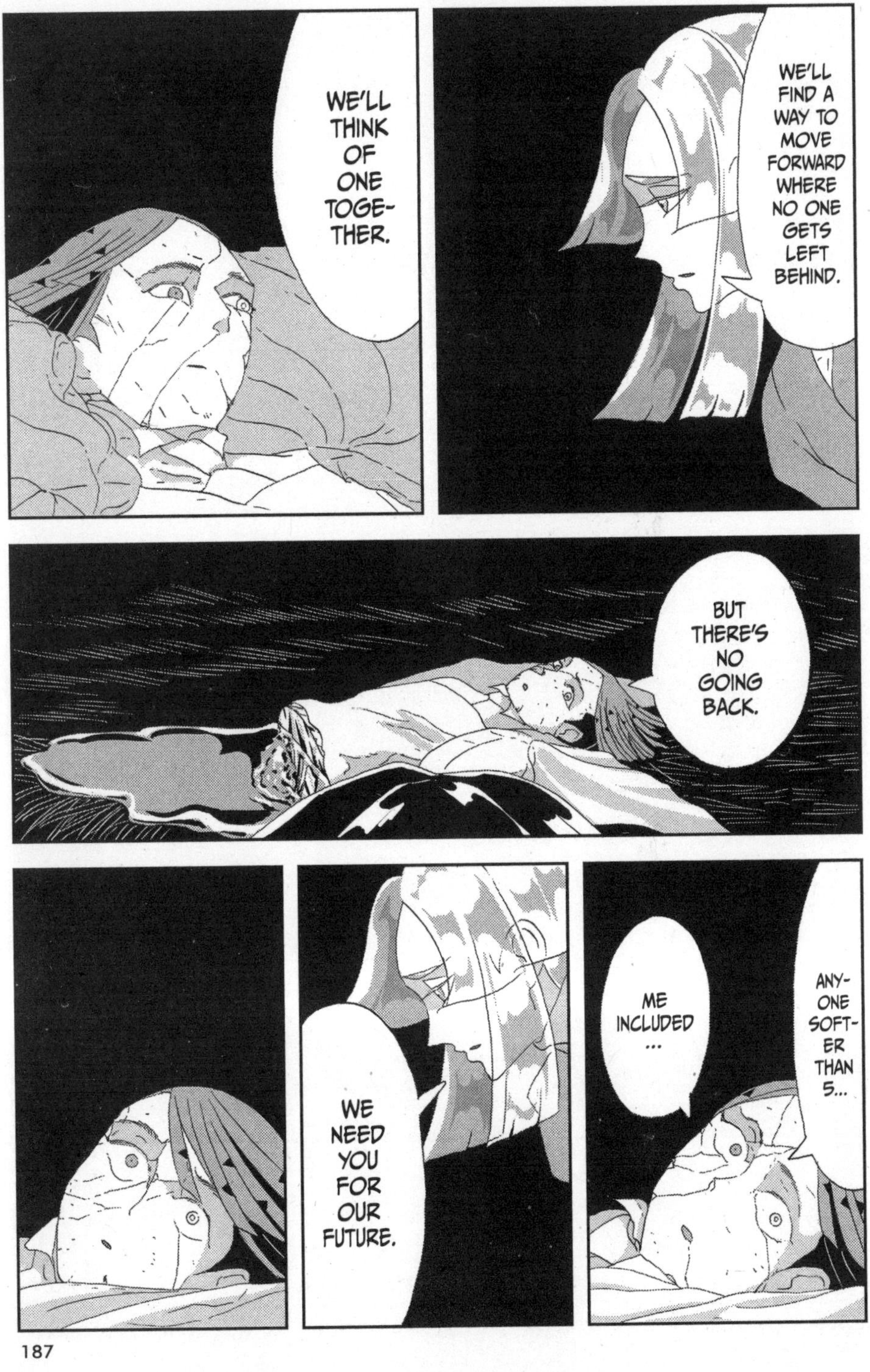
WE'LL FIND A WAY TO MOVE FORWARD WHERE NO ONE GETS LEFT BEHIND.
WE'LL THINK OF ONE TOGE-THER.
BUT THERE'S NO GOING BACK.
ANY-ONE SOFT-ER THAN 5...
ME INCLUDED ...
WE NEED YOU FOR OUR FUTURE.

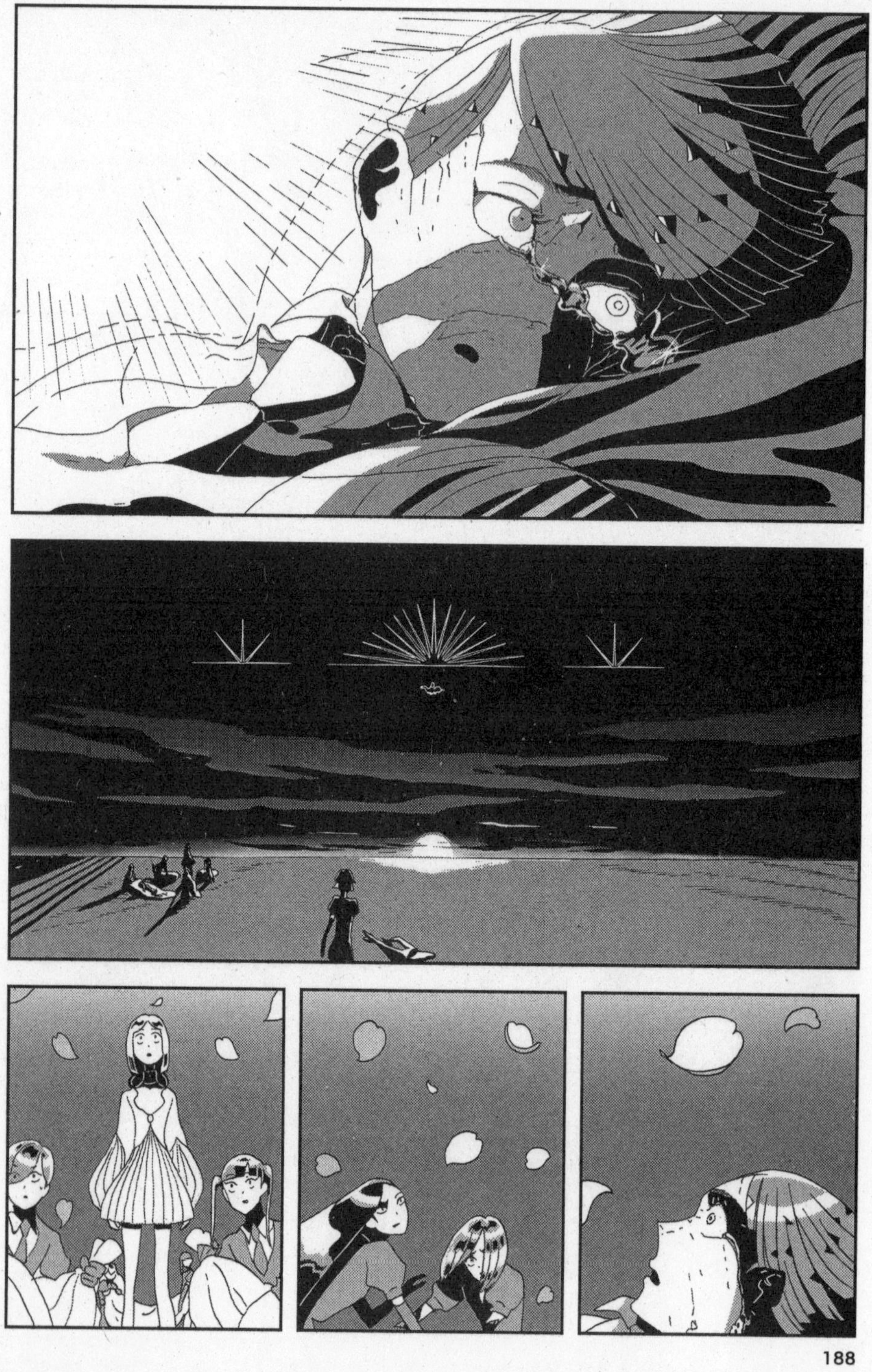

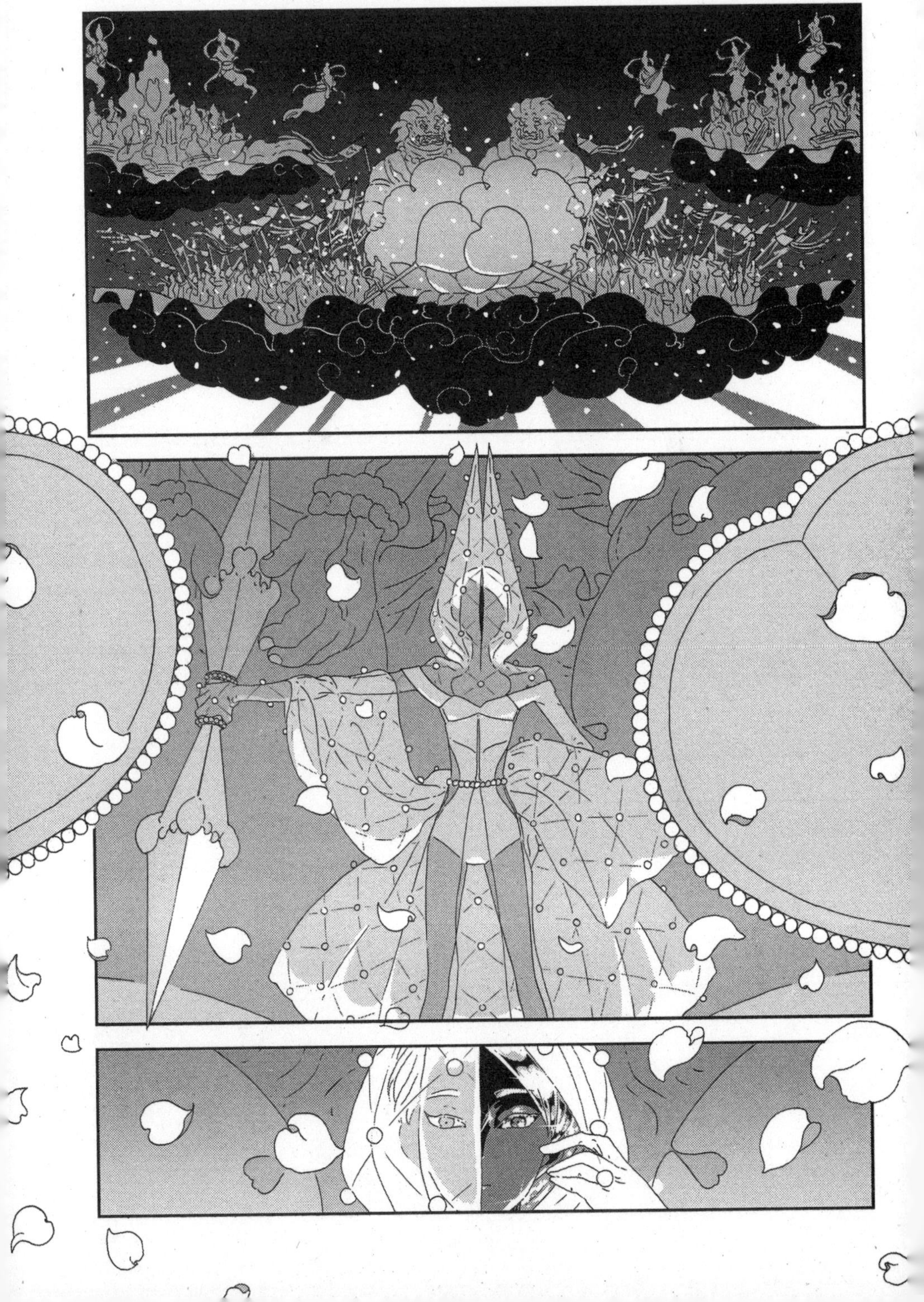

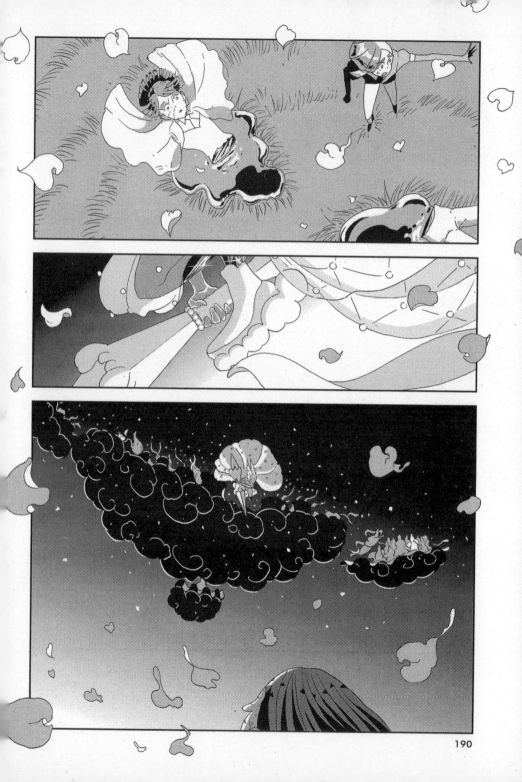

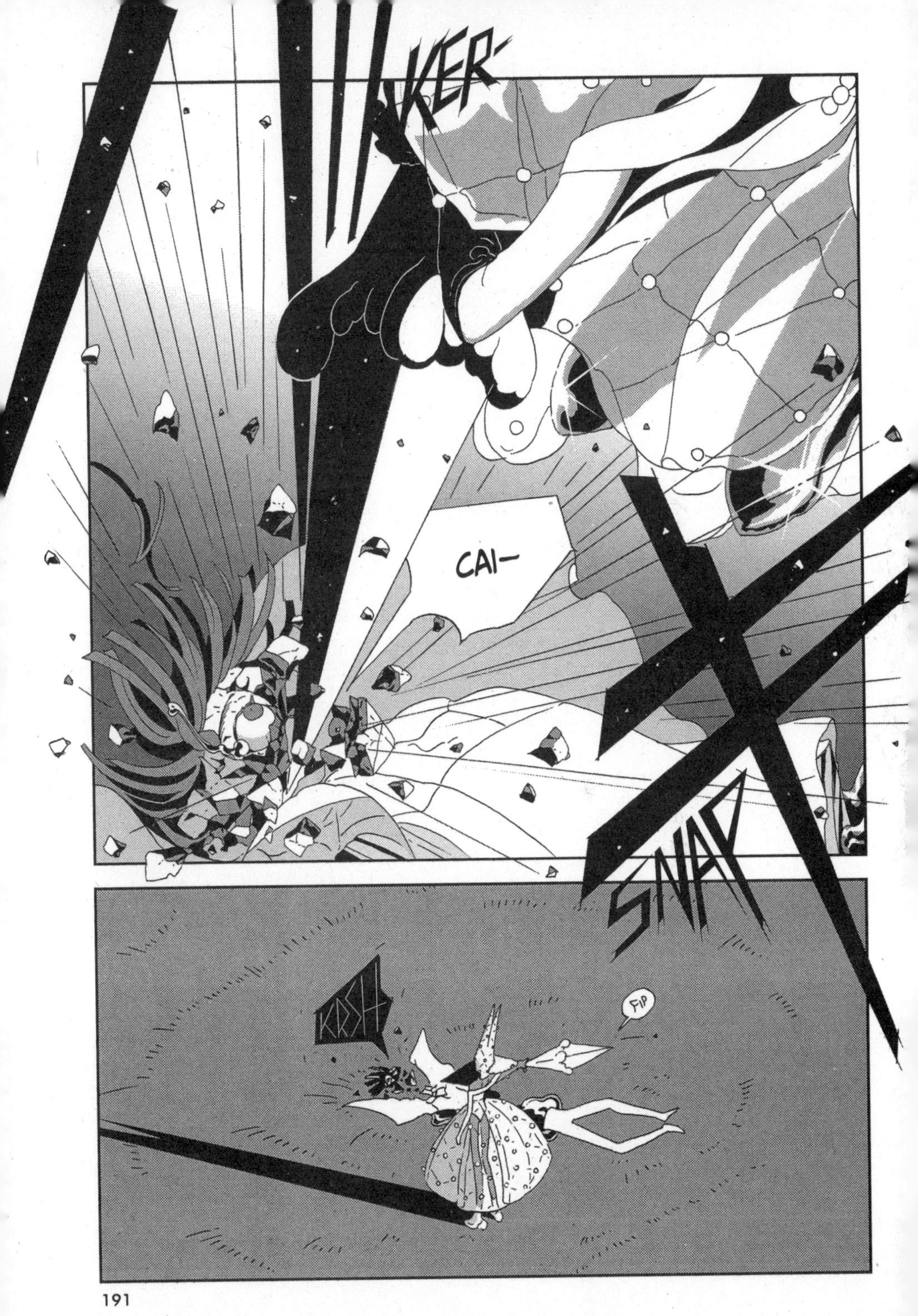
KER-
CAI-
SNAP
FIP
KRSH

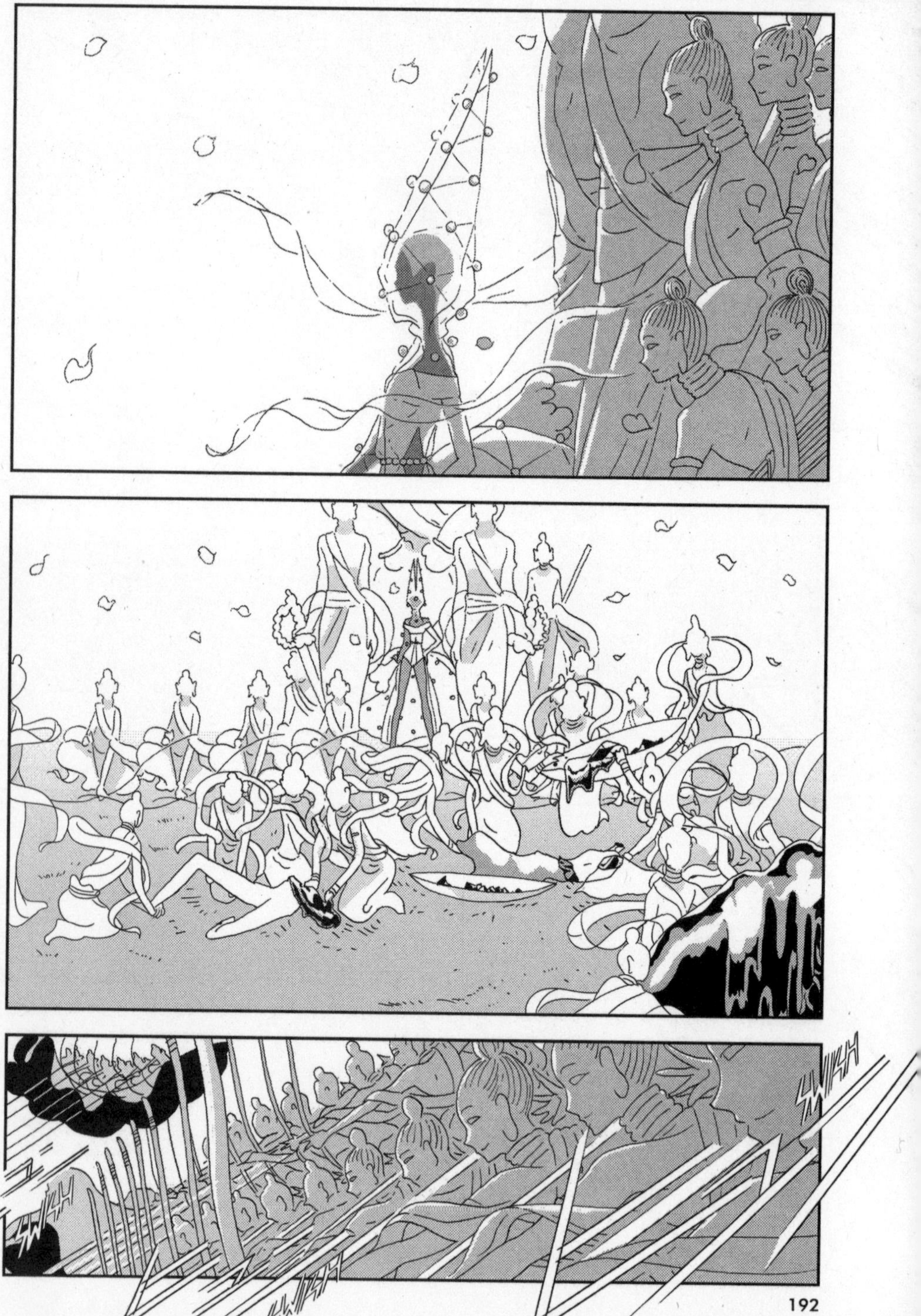
SWISH
SWISH
SWISH

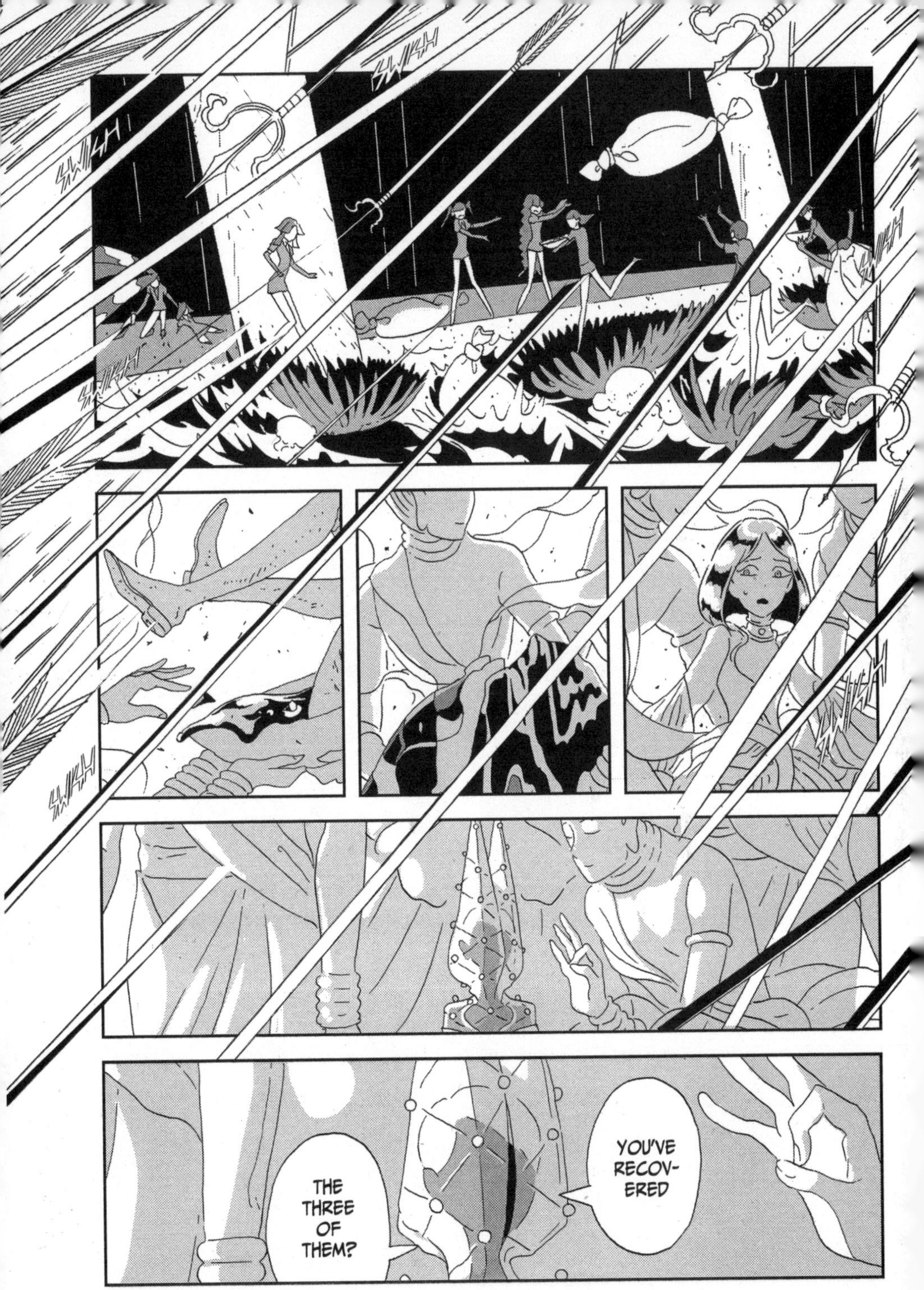
SWISH
SWISH
SWISH
SWISH
SWISH
SWISH
SWISH
YOU'VE RECOV-ERED
THE THREE OF THEM?

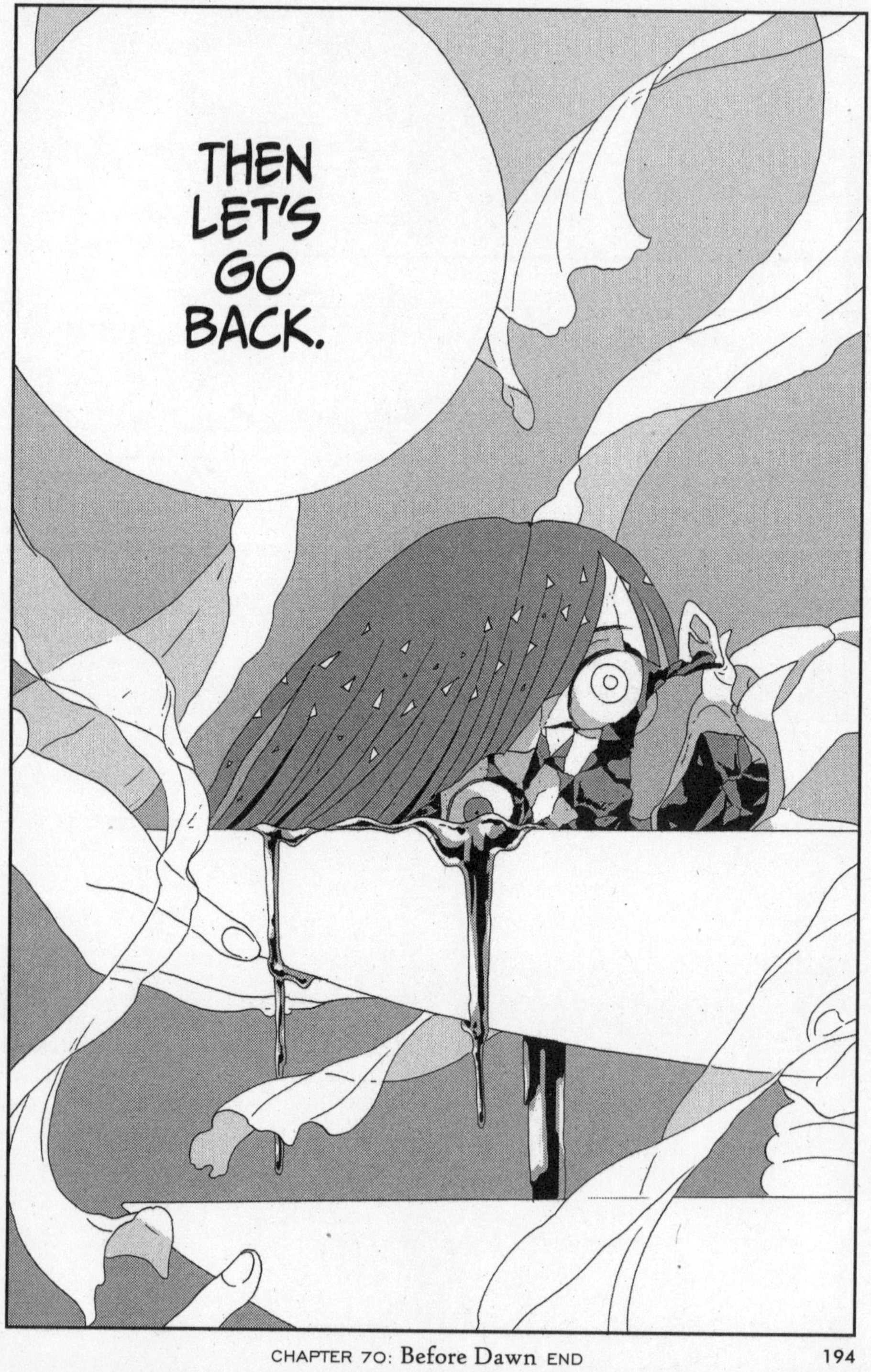
THEN LET'S GO BACK.

CHAPTER 70: Before Dawn END

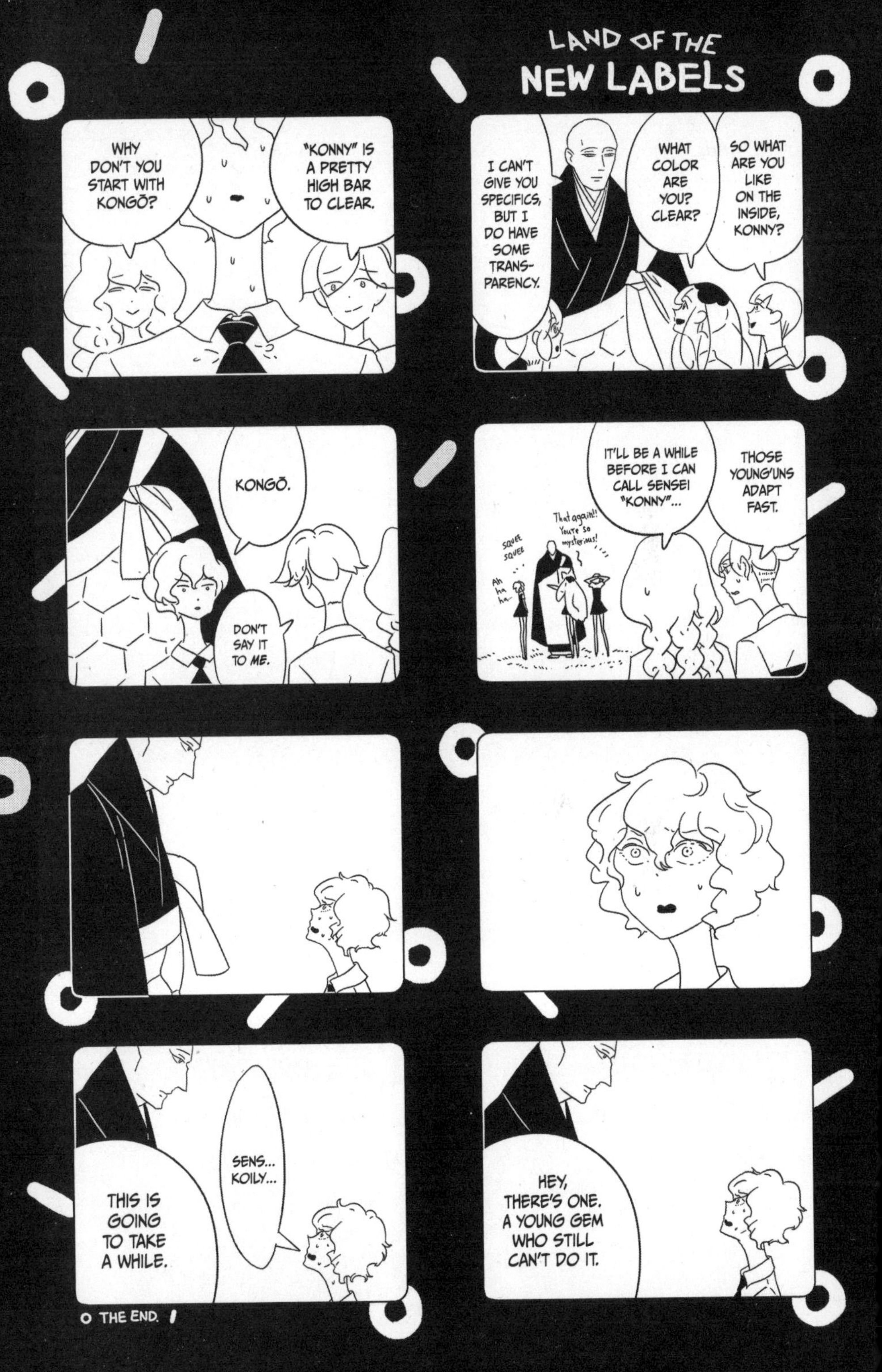
LAND OF THE NEW LABELS
SO WHAT ARE YOU LIKE ON THE INSIDE, KONNY?
WHAT COLOR ARE YOU? CLEAR?
I CAN'T GIVE YOU SPECIFICS, BUT I DO HAVE SOME TRANS-PARENCY.
"KONNY" IS A PRETTY HIGH BAR TO CLEAR.
WHY DON'T YOU START WITH KONGŌ?
THOSE YOUNG'UNS ADAPT FAST.
IT'LL BE A WHILE BEFORE I CAN CALL SENSEI "KONNY"...
That again!! You're so mysterious!
SQUEE SQUEE
Ah ha ha...
KONGŌ.
DON'T SAY IT TO *ME*.
HEY, THERE'S ONE. A YOUNG GEM WHO STILL CAN'T DO IT.
SENS... KOILY...
THIS IS GOING TO TAKE A WHILE.
THE END.

TRANSLATION NOTES

SENIOR LEX *page 6*

In the original Japanese, Goshenite addresses Alexandrite using the honorific paisen, which is a slangy way to say *senpai*. *Senpai* is the title given to anyone who became a part of a group before the speaker.

KONGŌ DAIJIHISHŌ JIZŌ BOSATSU *page 82*

Kongō's real name is patterned after the names of Buddhist figures known as Bodhisattvas—anyone who has attained enlightenment but chooses to stay on Earth in order to help others to Nirvana, or heaven. As previously noted, *kongō* is related to the Sanskrit word *vajra*, and represents indestructibility. It is also the Japanese name of the Diamond Realm, which represents the unchanging cosmic principle of the Buddha, and is depicted in a set of two mandalas known as the Mandala of the Two Realms. The other realm, the Womb Realm, represents the active, physical manifestation of Buddha in the natural world, or Earth. This brings us to the Jizō Bosatsu part of the name, which is the name of an extant Bodhisattva who is popular throughout Japan and whose name means "Earth Treasury" or "Earth Womb," among other things. This particular Bodhisattva has opted to wait to go to Nirvana until every occupant of every hell has managed to move on. The Daijihishō part of his name appears to be original, and means "great mercy crystal."

BEE   *page 136*

In keeping with the insect theme, the translators have opted to translate the name of Cicada's look-alike to Bee. The original name is *Ape*, which is Italian for "bee," but is also Ainu (an indigenous language of Japan) for "fire."

MAISON STRANNIKA   *page 144*

Maison is French for house, and is a word used fairly commonly in Japan for apartment complexes and the like. *Strannika* is the possessive form of the Russian word for "wanderer" (i.e. Wanderer's House), but the Japanese could also be rendered as *Sutra Nikah*, where *sutra* is Indonesian for "silk" (and is related to the word for Buddhist scriptures) and *nikah* is from the Arabic for "marriage."

SENSKOILY   *page 195*

Unable to call Kongō by anything less formal than Sensei, Zircon ends up combining Sensei, Kongō, and Konny (Kon-chan) into Senkō-chan, which may put the Japanese reader in mind of a cute little stick or coil of incense (*senkō*), possibly of the insect-repelling variety. The translators attempted to replicate this effect by using the name "Senskoily," which hopefully sounds like "incense coil."

JAPANESE EDITION INSIDE COVER GALLERY

Volume 9

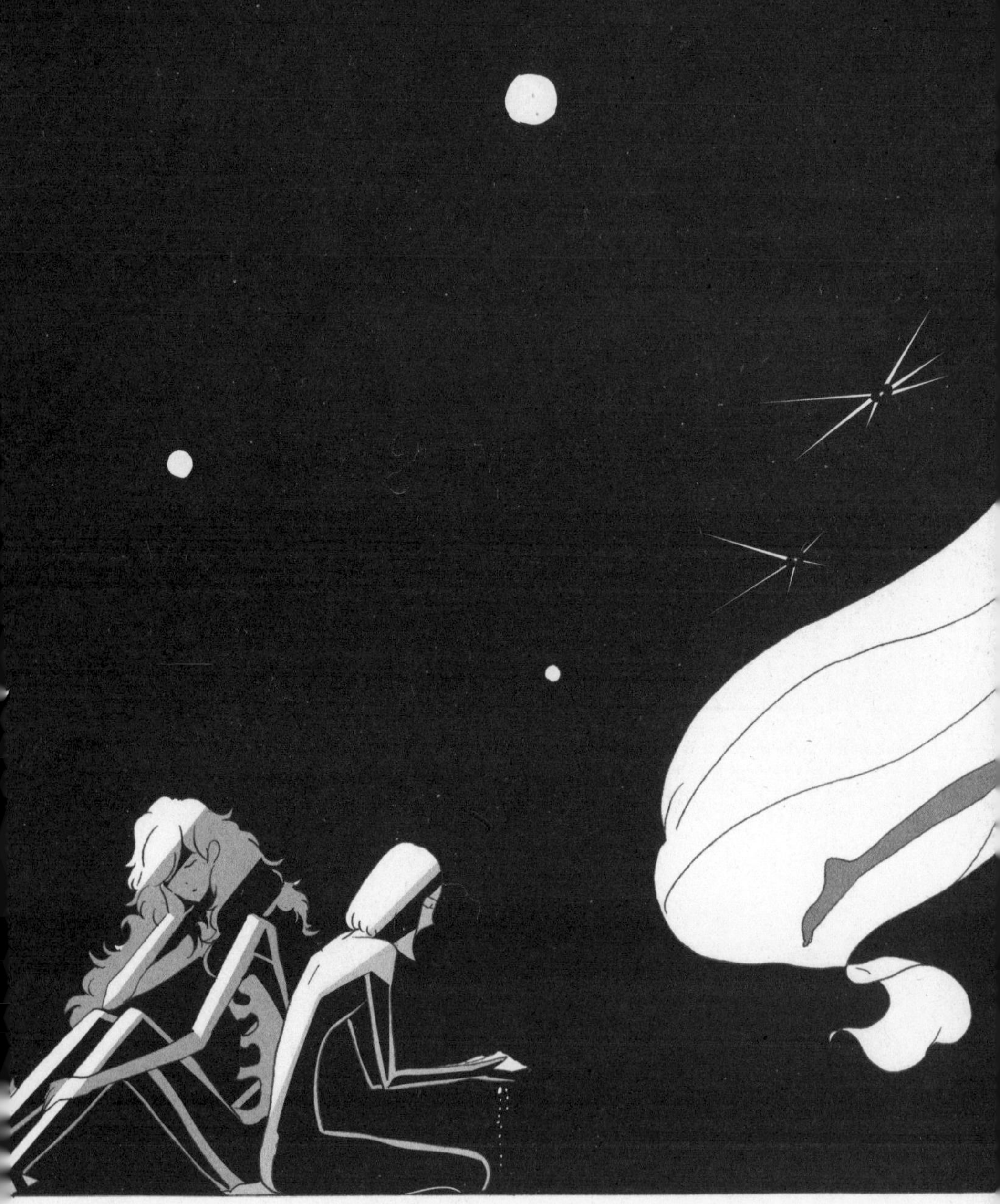

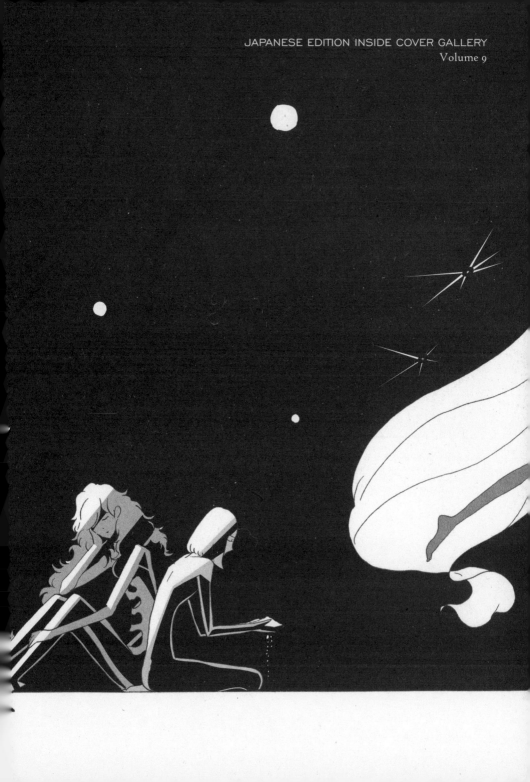

‹ KAMOME ›
SHIRAHAMA

Witch Hat Atelier

A magical manga
adventure for
fans of Disney
and Studio
Ghibli!

The magical adventure that took Japan by storm is finally here, from acclaimed DC and Marvel cover artist Kamome Shirahama!

In a world where everyone takes wonders like magic spells and dragons for granted, Coco is a girl with a simple dream: She wants to be a witch. But everybody knows magicians are born, not made, and Coco was not born with a gift for magic. Resigned to her un-magical life, Coco is about to give up on her dream to become a witch...until the day she meets Qifrey, a mysterious, traveling magician. After secretly seeing Qifrey perform magic in a way she's never seen before, Coco soon learns what everybody "knows" might not be the truth, and discovers that her magical dream may not be as far away as it may seem...

KC
**KODANSHA
COMICS**

Magus of the Library

Mitsu Izumi

MITSU IZUMI'S STUNNING ARTWORK BRINGS A FANTASTICAL LITERARY ADVENTURE TO LUSH, THRILLING LIFE!

Young Theo adores books, but the prejudice and hatred of his village keeps them ever out of his reach. Then one day, he chances to meet Sedona, a traveling librarian who works for the great library of Aftzaak, City of Books, and his life changes forever...

KC/
KODANSHA
COMICS

The award-winning manga about what happens inside you!

"Far more entertaining than it ought to be... what kid doesn't want to think that every time they sneeze a torpedo shoots out their nose?"
–Anime News Network

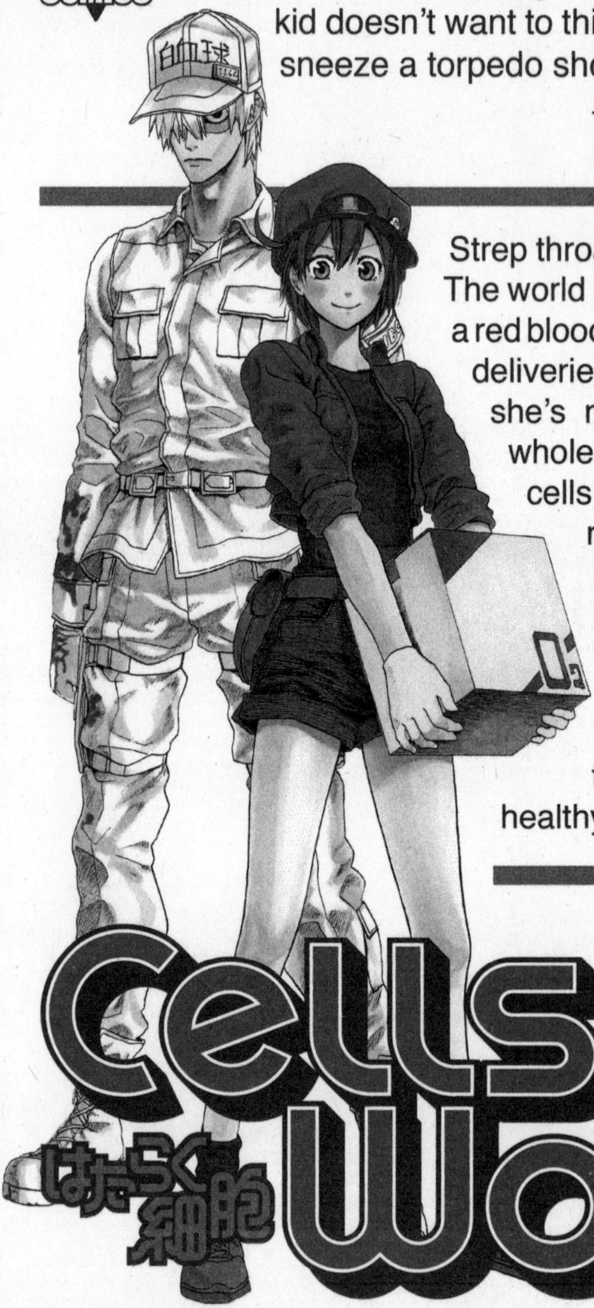

Strep throat! Hay fever! Influenza! The world is a dangerous place for a red blood cell just trying to get her deliveries finished. Fortunately, she's not alone…she's got a whole human body's worth of cells ready to help out! The mysterious white blood cells, the buff and brash killer T cells, even the cute little platelets— everyone's got to come together if they want to keep you healthy!

Cells at Work!

はたらく細胞

By Akane Shimizu

The Black Museum The Ghost and the Lady

By Kazuhiro Fujita

Deep in Scotland Yard in London sits an evidence room dedicated to the greatest mysteries of British history. In this "Black Museum" sits a misshapen hunk of lead—two bullets fused together—the key to a wartime encounter between Florence Nightingale, the mother of modern nursing, and a supernatural Man in Grey. This story is unknown to most scholars of history, but a special guest of the museum will tell the tale of The Ghost and the Lady...

Praise for Kazuhiro Fujita's *Ushio and Tora*

"A charming revival that combines a classic look with modern depth and pacing... **Essential viewing both for curmudgeons and new fans alike.**" — Anime News Network

"**GREAT!** The first episode of Ushio and Tora captures the essence of '90s anime." — IGN

HAPPINESS

—ハピネス—

By Shuzo Oshimi

From the creator of *The Flowers of Evil*

Nothing interesting is happening in Makoto Ozaki's first year of high school. His life is a series of quiet humiliations: low-grade bullies, unreliable friends, and the constant frustration of his adolescent lust. But one night, a pale, thin girl knocks him to the ground in an alley and offers him a choice. Now everything is different. Daylight is searingly bright. Food tastes awful. And worse than anything is the terrible, consuming thirst...

Praise for Shuzo Oshimi's *The Flowers of Evil*

"A shockingly readable story that vividly—one might even say queasily—evokes the fear and confusion of discovering one's own sexuality. Recommended." —The Manga Critic

"A page-turning tale of sordid middle school blackmail." —Otaku USA Magazine

"A stunning new horror manga." —Third Eye Comics

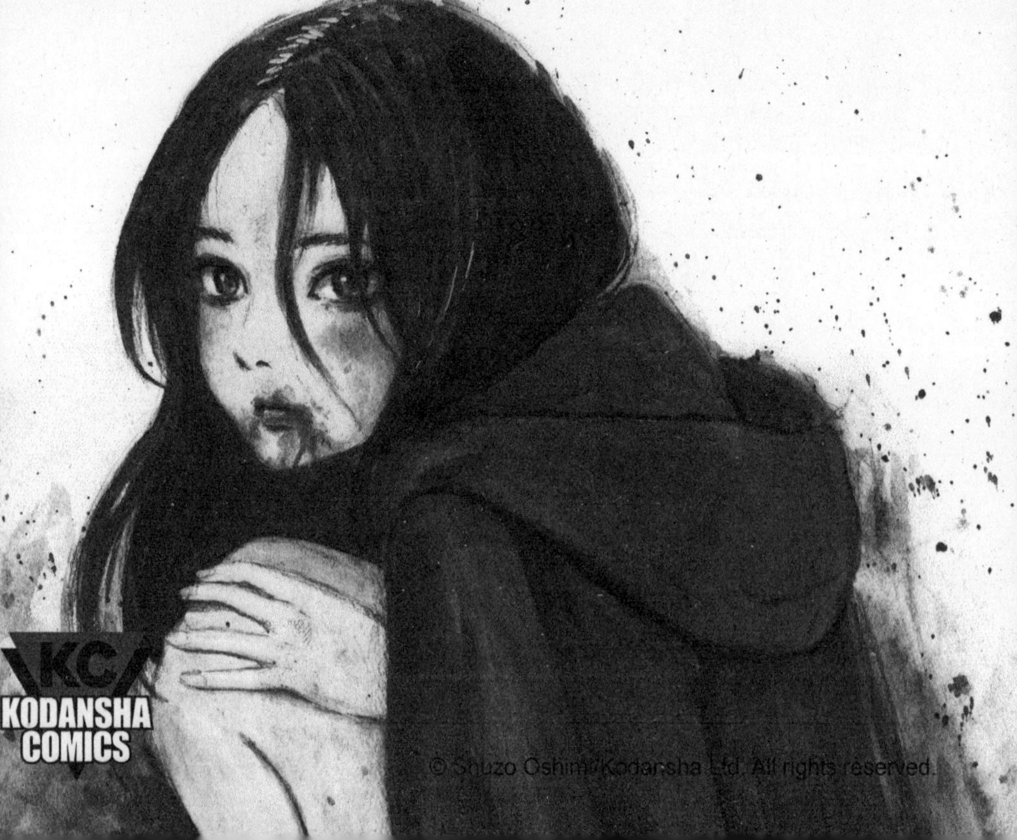

KODANSHA COMICS

KC KODANSHA COMICS

Japan's most powerful spirit medium delves into the ghost world's greatest mysteries!

Story by Kyo Shirodaira, famed author of mystery fiction and creator of *Spiral*, *Blast of Tempest*, and *The Record of a Fallen Vampire*.

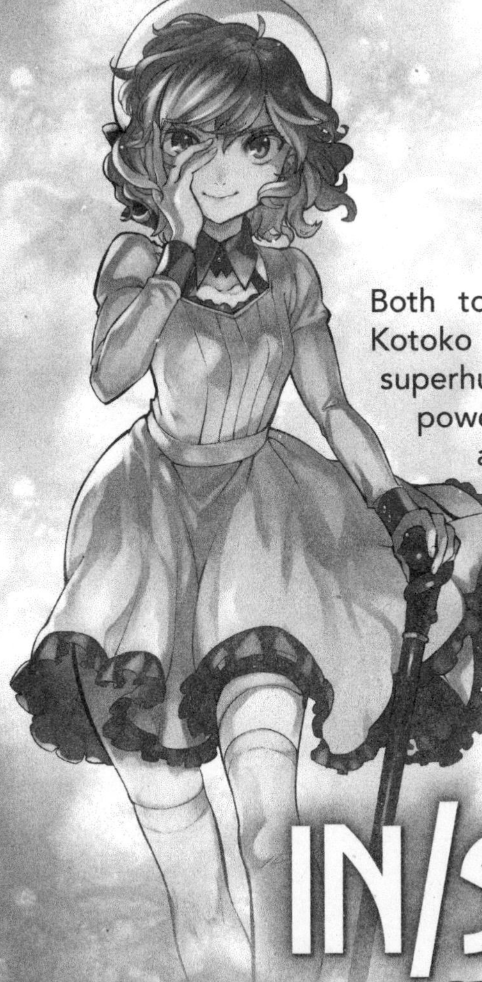

Both touched by spirits called yôkai, Kotoko and Kurô have gained unique superhuman powers. But to gain her powers Kotoko has given up an eye and a leg, and Kurô's personal life is in shambles. So when Kotoko suggests they team up to deal with renegades from the spirit world, Kurô doesn't have many other choices, but Kotoko might just have a few ulterior motives...

IN/SPECTRE

STORY BY KYO SHIRODAIRA
ART BY CHASHIBA KATASE

KODANSHA COMICS

New action series from Hiroyuki Takei, creator of the classic shonen franchise Shaman King!

In medieval Japan, a bell hanging on the collar is a sign that a cat has a master. Norachiyo's bell hangs from his katana sheath, but he is nonetheless a stray — a ronin. This one-eyed cat samurai travels across a dishonest world, cutting through pretense and deception with his blade.

NEKOGAHARA

STRAY CAT SAMURAI

By
Hiroyuki Takei

Having lost his wife, high school teacher Kōhei Inuzuka is doing his best to raise his young daughter Tsumugi as a single father. He's pretty bad at cooking and doesn't have a huge appetite to begin with, but chance brings his little family together with one of his students, the lonely Kotori. The three of them are anything but comfortable in the kitchen, but the healing power of home cooking might just work on their grieving hearts.

"This season's number-one feel-good anime!" —Anime News Network

"A beautifully-drawn story about comfort food and family and grief. Recommended." —Otaku USA Magazine

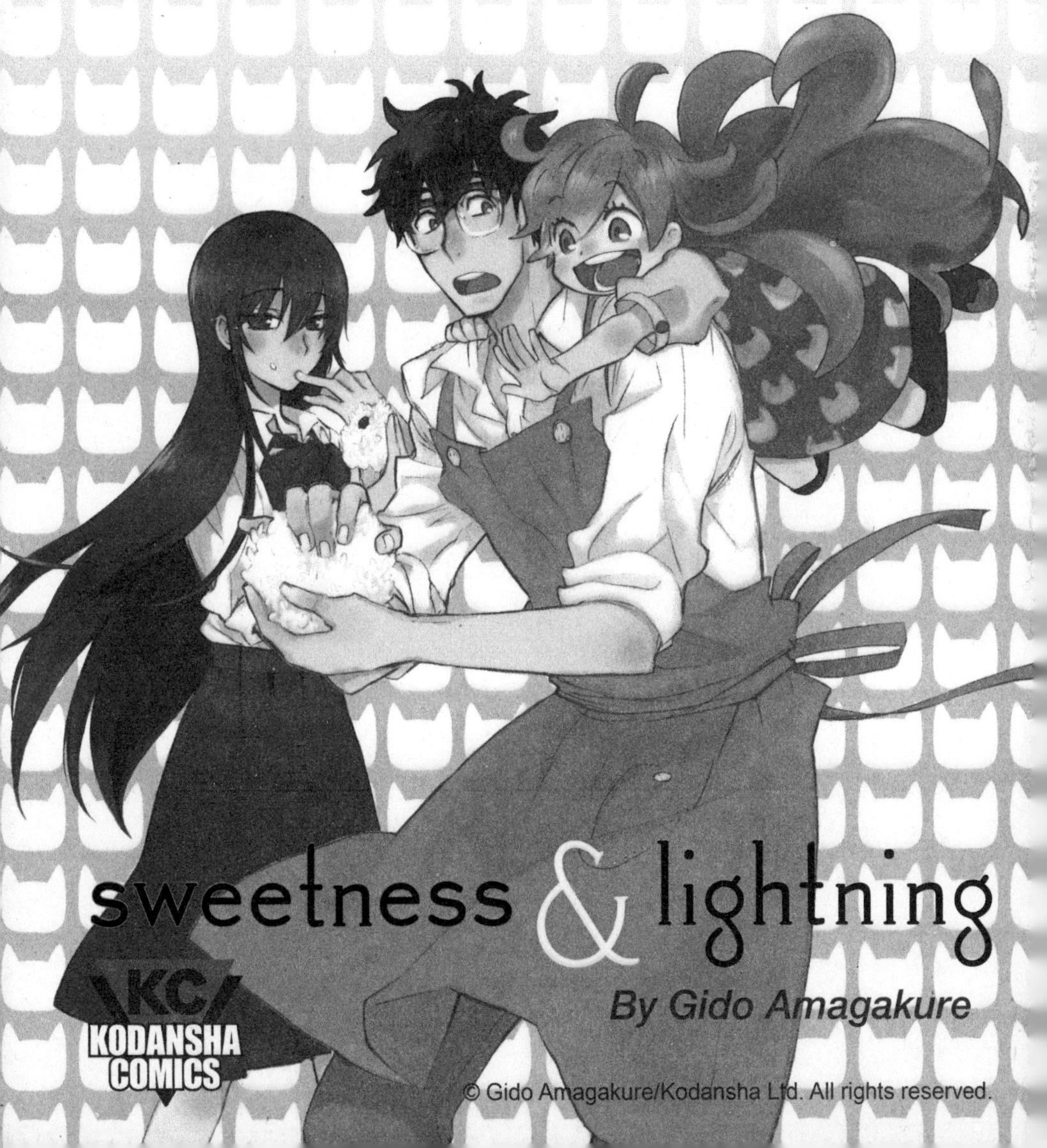

sweetness & lightning

By Gido Amagakure

KC KODANSHA COMICS

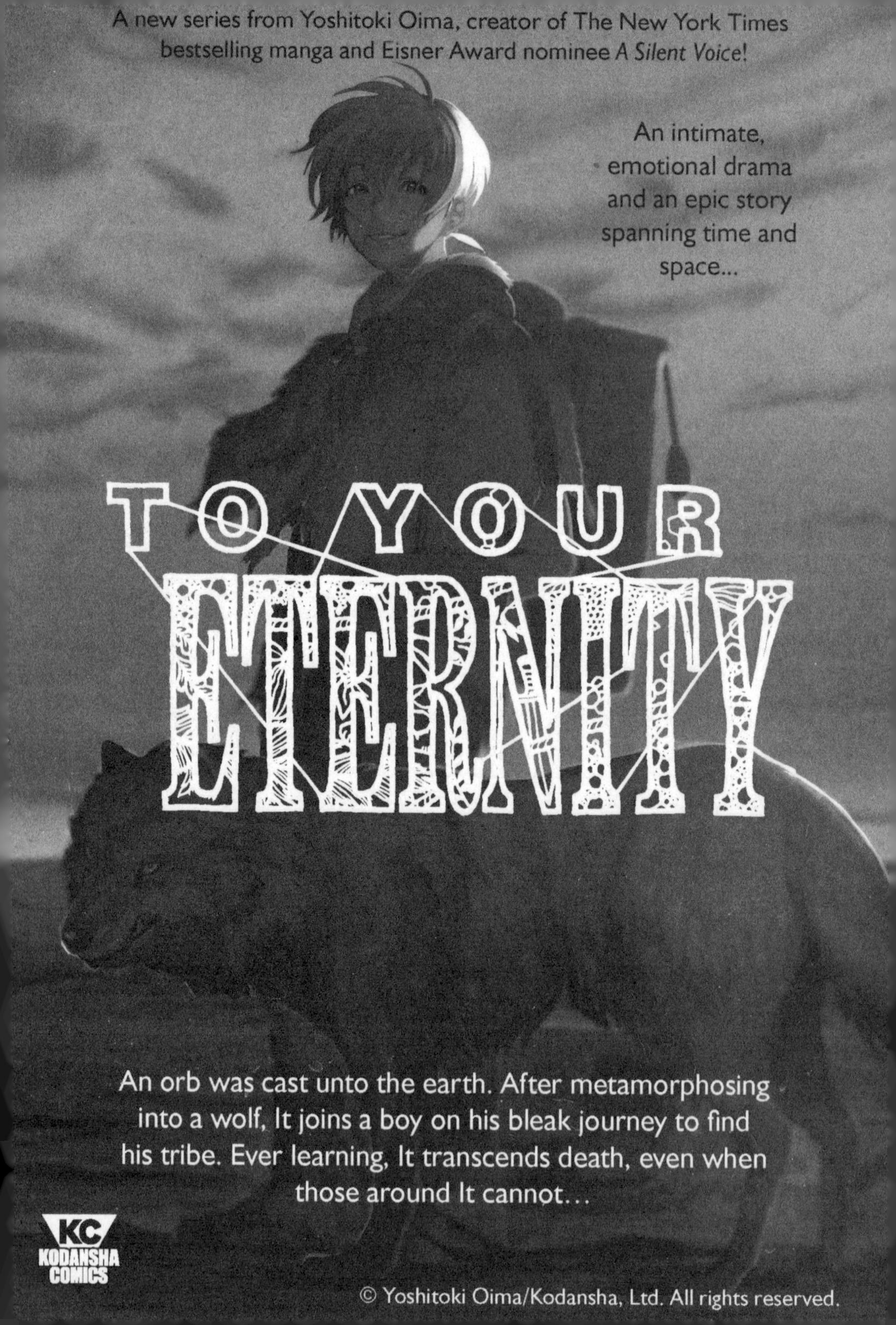
A new series from Yoshitoki Oima, creator of The New York Times bestselling manga and Eisner Award nominee *A Silent Voice*!
An intimate, emotional drama and an epic story spanning time and space...
TO YOUR ETERNITY
An orb was cast unto the earth. After metamorphosing into a wolf, It joins a boy on his bleak journey to find his tribe. Ever learning, It transcends death, even when those around It cannot...
KC KODANSHA COMICS
© Yoshitoki Oima/Kodansha, Ltd. All rights reserved.

"I'm pleasantly surprised to find modern shojo using cross-dressing as a dramatic device to deliver social commentary... Recommended."

-Otaku USA Magazine

The prince in his dark days

By Hico Yamanaka

A drunkard for a father, a household of poverty... For 17-year-old Atsuko, misfortune is all she knows and believes in. Until one day, a chance encounter with Itaru-the wealthy heir of a huge corporation-changes everything. The two look identical, uncannily so. When Itaru curiously goes missing Atsuko is roped into being his stand-in. There, in his shoes, Atsuko must parade like a prince in a palace. She encounters many new experiences, but at what cost…?

WAITING FOR SPRING

A sweet romantic story of a soft-spoken high school freshman and her quest to make friends. For fans of earnest, fun, and dramatic shojo like *Kimi ni Todoke* and *Say I Love You*.

KISS ME AT THE STROKE OF MIDNIGHT

An all-new Cinderella comedy perfect for fans of *My Little Monster* and *Say I Love You*!

LOVE AND LIES

Love is forbidden. When you turn 16, the government will assign you your marriage partner. This dystopian manga about teen love and defiance is a sexy, funny, and dramatic new hit! Anime now streaming on Anime Strike!

KC KODANSHA COMICS

YOUR NEW FAVORITE ROMANCE MANGA IS WAITING FOR YOU!

THAT WOLF-BOY IS MINE!

A beast-boy comedy and drama perfect for fans of *Fruits Basket*!

"A tantalizing, understated slice-of-life romance with an interesting supernatural twist."
- Taykobon

WAKE UP, SLEEPING BEAUTY

This heartrending romantic manga is not the fairy tale you remember! This time, Prince Charming is a teenage housekeeper, and Sleeping Beauty's curse threatens to pull them both into deep trouble.

Land of the Lustrous volume 9 is a work of fiction. Names, characters, places, and incidents are the products of the author's imagination or are used fictitiously. Any resemblance to actual events, locales, or persons, living or dead, is entirely coincidental.

A Kodansha Comics Trade Paperback Original.

Published in the United States by Kodansha Comics, an imprint of Kodansha USA Publishing, LLC, New York.

Publication rights for this English edition arranged through Kodansha Ltd., Tokyo.

First published in Japan in 2018 by Kodansha Ltd., Tokyo.

ISBN 978-1-63236-844-7

Printed in the United States of America.

www.kodanshacomics.com

9 8 7 6 5 4 3 2 1

Translator: Alethea Nibley & Athena Nibley
Lettering: Evan Hayden
Editing: Ajani Oloye